BLOOD SPORT

BLOOD SPORT

Alex Rodriguez, Biogenesis, and the
Quest to End Baseball's Steroid Era

TIM ELFRINK AND
GUS GARCIA-ROBERTS

DUTTON
— est. 1852 —

DUTTON
—• est. 1852 •—

Published by the Penguin Group
Penguin Group (USA) LLC
375 Hudson Street
New York, New York 10014

USA | Canada | UK | Ireland | Australia | New Zealand | India | South Africa | China
penguin.com
A Penguin Random House Company

LIBRARY OF CONGRESS CATALOGING-IN-PUBLICATION DATA
has been applied for.

ISBN 978-0-525-95463-7

Printed in the United States of America
10 9 8 7 6 5 4 3 2 1

Set in ITC Berkeley Oldstyle Std
Designed by Alissa Rose Theodor

To Adele and Jenny

CONTENTS

CAST OF CHARACTERS

BASEBALL PLAYERS

Suspended as a result of MLB's Biogenesis investigation

Alex Rodriguez

Shortstop for the Seattle Mariners and Texas Rangers, and third baseman for the New York Yankees. One of the greatest hitters of all time and the highest-grossing player in history.

Ryan Braun

Milwaukee Brewers outfielder and former University of Miami (UM) star

Nelson Cruz

Outfielder for the Texas Rangers through 2013

Jhonny Peralta

Shortstop for the Detroit Tigers through 2013

Everth Cabrera

San Diego Padres shortstop

Francisco Cervelli
New York Yankees catcher

Antonio Bastardo
Philadelphia Phillies relief pitcher

Jordany Valdespin
New York Mets second baseman

Jesus Montero
Seattle Mariners catcher and designated hitter

Fautino de los Santos
Relief pitcher who last played for the Oakland A's in 2012

Jordan Norberto
Minor league relief pitcher, most recently in the Oakland A's system

Cesar Carrillo
Former UM star and minor league pitcher in the Detroit Tigers system

Cesar Puello
Minor league outfielder in the New York Mets system

Sergio Escalona
Minor league pitcher in the Houston Astros system

Fernando Martinez
Minor league outfielder in the New York Yankees system

Suspended earlier for failing drug tests while on the Biogenesis regimen

Melky Cabrera

Outfielder for the New York Yankees, Atlanta Braves, Kansas City Royals, San Francisco Giants, and Toronto Blue Jays

Bartolo Colon

Veteran pitcher for eight teams including the New York Yankees and Oakland A's

Yasmani Grandal

San Diego Padres catcher, former UM star

Manny Ramirez

Outfielder for the Boston Red Sox and Los Angeles Dodgers

Ronny Paulino

Journeyman catcher who last played in MLB for the Baltimore Orioles in 2012

MEDICINE MEN

Tony Bosch

The unlicensed proprietor of Biogenesis, a Coral Gables anti-aging clinic

Dr. Pedro Bosch

Tony's father, a licensed doctor in Florida

Dr. Anthony Galea

A Toronto-based expert in sports medicine

THE BIOGENESIS CREW

Porter Fischer
Former marketing manager for Biogenesis

Yuri Sucart
Alex Rodriguez's cousin

Jorge "Oggi" Velazquez
Tony Bosch's former business partner in another anti-aging clinic

Anthony and Pete Carbone
Owners of several tanning salons in South Florida, including a South Miami location where Bosch and Velazquez had a clinic

Gary L. Jones
An ex-con tanning bed repairman

UNIVERSITY OF MIAMI

Lazaro "Lazer" Collazo
UM's pitching coach until 2003

Jimmy Goins
Strength and conditioning trainer for the baseball and track and field teams

Marcelo Albir
Former pitcher

Gaby Sanchez

Former UM slugger–turned–first baseman for the Miami Marlins and Pittsburgh Pirates

MLB EXECUTIVES

Allan "Bud" H. Selig

Commissioner since 1992, former Milwaukee Brewers owner

Robert D. Manfred Jr.

Chief operating officer and Selig's right-hand man

Daniel R. Halem

Executive vice president for labor relations

Daniel T. Mullin

Senior vice president of investigations

OTHER KEY FIGURES

Sam and Seth Levinson

Owners of ACES Inc., a Brooklyn-based sports agency

Jerome Hill

Florida Department of Health investigator

Jose "Pepe" Gomez

Rodriguez's longtime friend, "business agent," and right-hand man

STEROID ERA FIGURES

Jose Canseco

Former outfielder who published a memoir in 2005 admitting he'd used steroids throughout his career and naming multiple teammates as steroid users

George Mitchell

Senator who led an inquiry into baseball's steroid problems that resulted in the 2007 Mitchell Report, which named eighty-nine players tied to steroids and recommended mass reforms

Kirk Radomski

Former New York Mets clubhouse manager and steroid dealer who was a key source for the Mitchell Report

Greg Stejskal

Former FBI agent who led a landmark early steroid case

BLOOD SPORT

"Collateral Damage"

Porter Fischer wanted his money back. All $4,000 of it. He felt his volcanic temper bubbling, the hot rage raising the tendons in his muscle-rippled neck, but he steeled himself not to give in. After all, he wasn't being unreasonable.

Tony Bosch had promised, hadn't he? He'd said he'd pay Fischer back in $1,200 increments, returning all of Fischer's money plus a tidy profit. After weeks of absurd excuses and evasions, though, he'd seen only a fraction of it. As he barged into Bosch's cluttered back office inside Biogenesis, his anti-aging clinic on US 1, just a deep fly ball from the University of Miami's Alex Rodriguez Park, Fischer swallowed his fury.

Surely, they could talk like adults.

But as Fischer stared at Bosch's perfectly tanned face, he saw only mockery looking back. Tiny wrinkles bloomed around Bosch's lively brown eyes as the hint of a smile played at his mouth. He wouldn't be getting his money back this week, Bosch told Fischer.

"What are you going to do about it?" Bosch asked in a gravelly tone.

Fischer felt his heart jackhammering, and he knew he wouldn't fight the anger anymore. He could beat the hell out of the doctor right there, no question. Thanks to the two years of anabolic steroids and testosterone that Bosch had sold him, the middle-aged marketing specialist was ripped.

That's exactly why he'd invested in Biogenesis in the first place. If Bosch could turn a tubby fortysomething like Fischer into a Stallone stunt double, just think of the profits waiting to be made. Of course, that was before Fischer knew the details of the doctor's mysterious cash flow problem, his habit of leaving business partners in the lurch, or the cadre of high-profile clients who paid for Bosch's lothario lifestyle but ultimately led to the clinic's demise.

Fischer realized he'd probably head to jail if he kicked in Bosch's face. His mind raced. Suddenly, he remembered a meeting a few weeks back. Bosch had been railing against his staff for not bringing in enough new patients. What was it he'd said? "I don't need any of you guys. I can do all of this from the trunk of my car. All I need is these patient files," Fischer remembered him yelling, pointing to the boxes of records in his office.

Fischer knew exactly what to do.

"I'm leaving, but I'm telling you this right now," he growled, his white knuckles closed tight around Bosch's office door, "if I don't see my money soon, there's going to be collateral damage."

Eleven months later, in late September 2013, a strange crowd encamped like gypsies on one of midtown Manhattan's most moneyed blocks.

First came the notebook-clutching reporters, the camera crews, and ambush photographers. They were all assigned a perp walk—yell questions and snap photos as a person is led in and out of a building at his lowest moment—but instead of a courthouse, they were posted outside 245 Park Avenue.

It's a cold and innocuous building, with no signage betraying that Major League Baseball occupies multiple floors of the modernist skyscraper. On this day, unsmiling bruisers in dark suits guarded the glass-and-blond-wood foyer.

Then came the "protesters." They were twelve people—mostly men, all claiming to be from the north Manhattan neighborhood of Washington Heights—quietly holding miniature Dominican flags and signs decorated with the same neat handwriting.

BUD RESIGN, read one, a reference to MLB Commissioner Bud H. Selig, who had already announced his resignation effective at the end of the 2014 season. FAKE JUSTICE, read another.

Many bore the same message: BOSCH LIAR!

At the time, the US government was shut down from political infighting in Washington, slicing services to the bare bones and costing federal workers their paychecks. Yet these protesters were here to agitate for an athlete with a net worth of a quarter-billion dollars in a dispute with his employer. The rabble's ranks swelled into the hundreds. If you guessed that money was exchanged for their support, you were right.

A few New Yorkers stopped on their morning commutes to inquire about the growing commotion. The reporters were soon sick of fielding the question.

"A-Rod," they replied with exasperation.

"Oh," came the stock reply from the pedestrians before resuming their hustle to the Grand Central train station. "A-Rod."

To the tabloid-fed denizens of that city, in the previous ten months "A-Rod" came to signify more than the nickname of Alex Rodriguez, the third baseman for the New York Yankees and the highest-paid player in the game.

"A-Rod" meant the winding scandal swallowing Rodriguez's career whole, the million-dollar legal entourages and strategic media leaks, the secret grand jury proceedings in Florida involving a fake doctor, the bags of cash offered by MLB investigators in the back of darkened sport utility vehicles, and the documents stolen and resold after broad-daylight break-ins.

It meant Biogenesis.

Outside of MLB's Park Avenue headquarters, a jumbo black Escalade pulled up to the sidewalk, sending photographers and cameramen sprinting toward it.

Rodriguez stepped out, dressed like a Brooks Brothers model in a trim blue suit, dark hair closely cropped over a heavy-browed face tweezed and smoothed of the slightest wrinkles. He was flanked by four members of his powerhouse legal team, a well-dressed crew of criminal defenders and high-powered corporate litigators seasoned at fighting MLB over doping accusations. An attorney who once was a hockey enforcer used his beefy arms to cut through the crush of reporters.

Rodriguez made a beeline for the corralled protesters. He clutched their hands like a politician, thanking them in Spanish.

As he pivoted, strode the steps, and disappeared into the building, they broke into a chant. "A-Rod!" they yelled. "A-Rod! A-Rod! A-Rod!"

It was the warm Monday morning of September 30, 2013. The Yankees' lackluster season had ended the day earlier with a fourth-place finish, twelve games behind the hated Red Sox. It had been a paranoid and lonesome summer for their star slugger, who had waged public, private, and legal wars with the commissioner's office, the Yankees, and his own players union. He had been limited to forty-four games due to injury, told to "shut the fuck up" by his own general manager, and drilled with a fastball by a sanctimonious pitcher in Fenway Park. Through it all, he faced expulsion from the sport in which he had built his fortune.

For Rodriguez, the games now truly began.

Anthony Bosch used a side-street door to enter the MLB headquarters building, skirting the protestors waving posters with his name scrawled next to LIAR.

What had started as an argument over a few thousand dollars between this self-proclaimed doctor and an investor in Florida had boiled over into a cheating scandal of a magnitude not weathered by baseball since Chicago gangsters teamed up with White Sox players to fix the World Series nearly a century earlier.

The 1919 Black Sox conspiracy had resulted in lifetime bans for eight players and signaled, emphatically, that baseball would no longer tolerate dalliances with gamblers.

The Biogenesis scandal, as the fallout from Tony Bosch's clinic has been dubbed, has in many ways had equal import. A commissioner notorious for accommodating baseball's Steroid Era pivoted 180 degrees, doling out fifteen lengthy suspensions in the biggest mass discipline over performance-enhancing drugs in the history of American sports. At least a decade late, Selig was attempting to get his Kenesaw Mountain Landis on, eradicating performance-enhancing substances from a game overrun by them, in the same fashion that the legendary commissioner had exiled wise guys.

Standing in his way, though, was Alex Rodriguez, once corporate base-ball's Miami-bred Latino savior. A-Rod's tabloid-dominating claims that Selig was unfairly targeting him forced baseball fans into opposing camps, either believing that a group of players tried to scam the game or that the most powerful men in MLB orchestrated a conspiracy to take down the era's most famous player.

The full, untold story behind Biogenesis—as reported through Bosch's notebooks, which started it all, arbitration hearing testimony obtained by these authors, unreported state investigative records, thousands of pages of court records, and dozens of interviews with key players from superstar entourages to MLB offices—is far more complicated, more bitter, more trou-bling, and more downright bizarre than either of those narratives.

It's a story in which tanning salon operators and a convicted counter-feiter team up to outsmart Ivy League–educated attorneys and a self-proclaimed biochemist loses a vial of his superstar client's blood on the dance floor of a nightclub. A steroid dealer named Oggi is said to be threat-ening murder. Private eyes lead high-speed pursuits down Miami's busiest thoroughfare, baseball detectives sleep with a potential witness and possi-bly interfere with a law-enforcement investigation, thousands of fifty- and hundred-dollar bills are handed off in between tuna melts at seedy diners, and the Office of the Commissioner of Baseball agrees to put in a good word to prosecutors for a steroid dealer potentially facing charges for deal-ing to kids.

A multibillion-dollar gray market for human growth hormone thrives thanks to a governor whose company once perpetuated the nation's biggest

Medicare fraud. Teenagers, including a fifteen-year-old Dominican phenom, are pushed by parents, agents, and well-respected youth coaches into juicing in order to make it in baseball. Rodriguez, Ryan Braun, Nelson Cruz, and other wealthy stars buy drugs from the same storefront as a Spanish gangster and a Grammy-winning crooner. And one of the top university baseball programs in the nation ignores a glaring steroid problem.

For Selig and Major League Baseball, punishing the Biogenesis bad guys signaled baseball's clean break with drug cheats, a reckoning overdue since at least 2003, when a clinic in the Bay Area was exposed as the secret weapon behind the record-breaking home run numbers of Barry Bonds and other sluggers. But Biogenesis proves that since that early scandal, the Steroid Era never really ended. It evolved. And considering the huge potential financial payoff for cheating, the competitive pressure that drives ballplayers to seek a synthetic edge even as adolescents, and the drive by self-declared gurus such as Anthony Bosch to win an arms race against drug testers, that's an evolution that will be extremely difficult to stop.

B osch wasn't thinking about any of this on that morning in Manhattan. His main concern: making sure he looked good in the newspapers the next day. In New York as a star witness for the prosecution, testifying against his former top client, Bosch had tired of every media outlet in the country using the same dopey mug shot from a traffic offense.

So after sneaking past the protesters and reporters, he had his publicist send a new photo to the media. "Please discontinue using the mug shot," she pleaded.

The preferred photo showed Bosch strolling through the MLB headquarters, a place a South Florida grifter like him could never have reasonably expected to end up. He was dressed nattily in a suit and, for the professorial look, wearing his reading glasses.

And he was beaming.

CHAPTER ONE

A Cousin with a Rocket Launcher

The crisp ping of metal on rubber and hard cork echoed across the neatly trimmed fields just outside Birmingham, Alabama. A few dozen spectators in lawn chairs arched their necks in unison, tracking a softball arcing across the sky.

Tony Bosch was twenty-seven years old, with a preppy mop of black hair over thick eyebrows. He'd worked for years and spent thousands of dollars waiting for this moment.

When the final out of the game landed harmlessly in the outfielder's glove, every fielder sprinted toward a second-base celebratory pile-on.

It was 1990, and the Miami Meds were national softball champions.

Bosch hadn't played an inning of the tournament. But like an extremely low-rent George Steinbrenner striking deals for beer-bellied all-stars, he was the man who'd made this title happen. Ever since he'd grown up obsessed with baseball in Queens, New York, Bosch had struggled to find a way into the game. Too short and slow to stick as a player, he'd long since abandoned his dream of smacking game-winning homers like his childhood New York Mets heroes Tommie Agee and Cleon Jones.

But here, in the intensely competitive late '80s and early '90s Miami softball circuit, where coke dealers funded teams like glamour projects and major league stars including Jose and Ozzie Canseco showed up to bash slow-pitched leather grapefruits over the wall, Bosch had found his niche.

He'd turned his medical supply company—Miami Med Marketing, Inc.—into one of the biggest sponsors in the local league, drawing top-notch league players and even a few former college stars to wear nylon tributes to his beloved Mets.

On weeknights after work and weekend mornings before games, he'd obsess over statistics and watch video of his upcoming opponents. He'd fill notebooks with his neat, all-caps handwriting, plotting out who would pinch-hit, how he'd arrange his fielders for each batter, and what situational matchups he'd expect. On game day, he'd be on the bench commanding the field. Every once in a while, if the game was a blowout, he might even pencil in his own name and take an at-bat or two.

"For Tony, this was absolutely a passion. He put in just an incredible amount of time and money," says Roger De Armas, a lifelong friend and Tony's partner in Miami Meds, both the company and the softball team. "He was super excited to win it all."

Sure, it was far from Major League Baseball, but on that night in Alabama, softball brought Tony a joy as unalloyed and pure as he'd felt as a kid watching the 1969 Miracle Mets hustle their way to a World Series ring.

Anyone who knew Tony knew that he truly loved baseball. But moments like this, where the game returned the affection, were rare. In truth, Tony Bosch's relationship with the game more closely mirrored the doomed marriages and acrimonious business partnerships that stalked his life. The ill-fated flirtation ended with a historic scandal and attorneys brawling on Park Avenue.

Tony's family came from a nation with its own conflicted relationship with baseball. In Cuba, politics and sports were often intertwined, as was violence. That explosive strand ran through the Bosch family history.

His father, Pedro, was born on October 19, 1937, in Jatibonico, a hamlet of forty thousand people right in the center of the Cuban island. More than two hundred miles southeast of bustling, cosmopolitan Havana, with its world-famous casinos and brothels, and nearly as far from the cooling ocean currents of the Caribbean coast, Jatibonico was sun-baked and fly-ridden. It was the sort of unpaved provincial town a gifted student like Pedro fled as soon as he could.

He did so in September 1955. The noisy chaos of Havana would have been a shock for any seventeen-year-old from the sticks, but Pedro Bosch must have felt especially small when he arrived at the University of Havana and enrolled in the school of medicine. The first mention of his name placed him in the shadow of a revolutionary cousin who was already a towering figure at the med school.

Orlando Bosch was nine years older than Pedro, from an even smaller Cuban village eighty miles west of Jatibonico. Like his younger first cousin, he was too talented and restless for life in a country town.

During his own tenure at the university, Orlando had become chums with a loquacious, brilliantly charismatic classmate named Fidel Castro. Orlando's and Fidel's paths followed close trajectories: As the fiery Orlando fought his way to become president of the medical students, the captivating Fidel won the same leadership role in the law school.

They both loathed Cuba's corrupt, American-supported puppet regime, especially after a puffed-up military officer named Fulgencio Batista grabbed power in a 1952 coup. The palm-shaded university campus became ground zero for dissent, and Bosch and Castro were among the most active student leaders. The pair regularly plotted revolution in the school's decaying, Greek-inspired buildings.

Fidel turned Cuba upside down starting in late 1956, when he crash-landed a yacht filled with rebels to spark a bloody three-year revolution. But during their school years, Orlando Bosch was arguably the more feared of the two campus leaders. His fellow med students had nicknamed him *Piro*, short for *pyromaniac*, as a nod to his explosive temper. During one campus uprising, he famously punched a police lieutenant.

Pedro arrived at the school two years after Orlando graduated. The older cousin had briefly lived in the United States, studying pediatrics at an Ohio university, before returning to his native province to become the first doctor administering polio vaccine in the rural area. Pedro was an equally proficient student. He earned a spot at the Calixto Garcia Hospital in downtown Havana and worked his way from the ob-gyn department to general surgery.

During the revolution, Orlando was a leader of the 26th of July Movement, Fidel's revolutionary organization, in his native Santa Clara Province. Orlando met guerrilla forces in the rugged mountains around central Cuba, plotting attacks on Batista's garrisons and communicating with Fidel and his revolutionary leader, Che Guevara.

While Orlando was fighting through the jungle with Fidel and Che, Pedro learned medicine. As Fidel's rebels and Batista's soldiers massacred one another, Pedro Bosch tended to patients and studied with physicians at Calixto Garcia. As Che and Castro led the decisive final march into Havana in 1959, which finally ended with Batista being ousted from power, Bosch worked in the surgery department. At school, he met another young med student named Stella, whom he soon married.

But if the teenager from Jatibonico mirrored his famous cousin in smarts and medical proficiency, he lacked Orlando's explosive political gene. Pedro hadn't escaped dusty Jatibonico and learned medicine in order to practice it for a pittance in a Socialist paradise.

In 1961, soon after Castro cemented his new revolutionary Marxist government, Pedro and Stella fled the island to Miami. Pedro and his wife then moved to New York, settling into a small Cuban niche in Astoria, Queens. In 1963, Tony was born. As Pedro perfected his credentials, at one point moving alone to Spain to complete his training at a Madrid university, Stella remained behind with baby Tony.

In a New York neighborhood packed with Greeks, the Bosches joined a budding network of other Cuban immigrants who had escaped Fidel's reign. These countrymen included Roger De Armas's parents.

Roger's earliest memories in New York are of watching baseball with kindergarten-aged Tony Bosch, who loved playing catch in the street and talking about his hometown team.

"Tony always had his hands on a baseball," Roger remembers.

The New York Mets were a team only a six-year-old could truly love. They were nearly the same age as Tony Bosch, in fact, and their pedigree was that of the worst team in history, playing in garish orange-and-blue uniforms in a concrete stadium in New York City's blue-collar borough.

As the 1969 season kicked off, Bosch was just old enough to start seriously idolizing the boys of summer down the road. For most of the year, the Mets looked like they'd be adding another tally to their long losing streak. By August 13, the team was ten games behind the first-place Cubs.

Then miracles started happening by the filthy Flushing Bay. Led by fireballing young aces Tom Seaver and Nolan Ryan and unlikely offensive heroes like the workmanlike Ron Swoboda, the Mets reeled off thirty-four wins while losing only seventeen in the season's final two months. In the end, they powered past the Cubs and into the playoffs. Then, even more improbably, the Amazin's swept the Braves to win the National League and destroyed the Orioles 4–1 in the World Series. The Miracle Mets were world champs, and young Tony Bosch—listening in on the radio, catching glimpses on the TV—was hooked.

The next year, Pedro earned a residency in the ER at Miami's North Shore Medical Center, and soon thereafter, young Tony packed up his Seaver posters, his bat, and his glove, and moved with his parents to Coral Gables, the leafy, moneyed neighborhood that's home to the University of Miami.

While Pedro followed an ambitious career track, his notorious cousin had gone well off the rails. Orlando Bosch, like many formerly in Fidel Castro's camp, had quickly come to believe that "El Comandante" was just as bad or worse than the despotic president he'd overthrown.

Orlando had also moved to Miami, harboring his incongruous cocktail of medicine and violence. He was fired from his position as assistant director of a hospital after his bosses found out he'd been storing bombs there. In 1964, he'd been caught towing a homemade torpedo through downtown

Miami during rush hour. In 1966, rural sheriffs in Central Florida had stopped Orlando's rickety Cadillac convertible and found six one-hundred-pound aerial bombs in the trunk.

And in 1968, Orlando had pulled his car over to the shoulder of the MacArthur Causeway, the highway spanning Biscayne Bay between South Beach and downtown Miami alongside the Port of Miami. He calmly opened his trunk, pulled out a fifty-seven-millimeter bazooka, and took aim at a Communist Polish freighter docked across the water.

Passing motorists gaped as he pulled the trigger. The rocket whistled over Government Cut and sizzled past docked ships before bouncing off the freighter and falling harmlessly into the channel.

And in 1976, when thirteen-year-old Anthony Bosch was in middle school, Orlando was tied to a far more atrocious crime while out on parole from the bazooka attack.

Cubana de Aviación Flight 455 had taken off from Barbados's Seawell Airport bound for Jamaica on October 6, 1976. Among the seventy-three passengers were twenty-four members of Cuba's national fencing team, which had just won gold at a competition of Central American and Caribbean nations. Eleven minutes after takeoff, two dynamite bombs wired with timers ripped through the jet.

The plane plummeted eighteen thousand feet into the Caribbean. All passengers on board died. Twelve days later, Bosch was arrested with another notorious Cuban terrorist, Luis Posada Carriles, in Venezuela and charged as the leader of the operation. He was ultimately acquitted in that country due to a lack of admissible evidence. Later-declassified American covert records incriminated him in the attack, though he continued claiming his innocence until his death in 2011.

The bombing monopolized Miami newspaper ink for months, and teenage Tony was linked by his last name to the most infamous Cuban terrorist. "Of course everyone knew they were related," De Armas says. "[But] it's not like Orlando was dropping by family barbecues, and they sure didn't bring him up. Having a cousin who blows up airliners isn't the kind of thing that you talk about a lot in public."

Tony's own upbringing in Miami was a world away from Third World environs and militant activism. He was a baseball-obsessed doctor's son, and in 1979 he enrolled as a freshman at the exclusive Christopher Columbus High School. An all-boys Catholic institution just west of Coral Gables, Columbus boasted one of the best academic programs in Dade County. Tony's fellow alumni included CEOs, a county mayor, the official poet at Barack Obama's 2013 presidential inauguration—and several professional baseball players.

The late '70s were a boom time for baseball in the Magic City. For nearly two decades, refugees from hardball-crazy Cuba like the Bosch family had been finding political refuge in Little Havana and Hialeah. They joined growing communities in the city from Venezuela, the Dominican Republic, and every other Latin baseball powerhouse. The city was a simmering hotbed for young players.

In fact, as Tony showed up for his freshman year, one of the best—and most hated—baseball players of his generation enrolled at Miami Coral Park High School, just a mile north of Columbus. Like Bosch, Jose Canseco's parents had fled Castro's Cuba for Miami. And just like Bosch, presteroidal Canseco struggled for playing time in a talent pool of mammoth boys.

Miami's high school teams had never been more stacked. "I didn't even make the varsity team until my senior year of high school," Canseco wrote in his first memoir, *Juiced*. "How many future major leaguers can you say that about?"

A short way south, Tony Bosch didn't make any more of a splash at Columbus High. He'd started playing on youth teams at the Big Five Club, an *exilio* institution in west Miami founded by the members of Havana's five most prestigious country clubs. But Tony never really filled out. By the time he showed up at Columbus, his unathletic build was already beginning to betray him.

And the Columbus baseball program was filthy with talent, both playing and coaching. The varsity squad included future big leaguer Orestes Destrade and Seattle Mariners draftee David Hartnett. The JV squad's head coach that year was a fresh-faced twenty-four-year-old who had agreed to teach at Columbus while he looked for a job as a baseball broadcaster. His name was Jim Hendry, and the few years he spent working his way up the coaching ranks at Columbus propeled him on to the most remarkable baseball career of any alum, including a nine-year stint as the Chicago Cubs general manager and vice president.

Hendry now works in the New York Yankees' front office, a workplace in which Bosch's name later became toxic. But the former Columbus coach can't add much to the portrait of the steroid dealer as a young athlete. "I don't remember this guy being much of a player at all," Hendry says. "If he was, he would've stuck with me."

"He was not a significant player on our team," agrees teammate Mickey Maspons.

Nick Martin-Hidalgo, another member of that freshman squad, is even more blunt: "He was no good," he says. "He spent a lot of time on the bench."

Christopher Columbus president Jim Bernhardt calls Bosch "just a shadow in the park."

Look at the team's yearbook photo and it's easy to see why. Even among the fourteen- and fifteen-year-olds in blue polyester Columbus jerseys, he looks small. Dark hair hangs over his eyes as he peers out past the shoulder of a larger, already more muscular teammate.

Bosch got the message. He never played competitive baseball again after his freshman year. But that doesn't mean he stopped thinking about how to find his way back in.

Preppy and privileged, teenage Tony Bosch couldn't have seemed more distant from his bomb-building cousin. But maybe he did share some of the same kinds of genes with Orlando Bosch. After never gaining footing in the game of baseball, he aimed his own kind of bazooka at the establishment.

You can't get much more American than a New York Yankee who collects Cognac, shops Armani, travels in a Maybach, owns a Picasso, and declares *Wall Street* to be his favorite film.

But Alex Rodriguez's grandfather had worked for centavos behind the San Juan Municipal Slaughterhouse in Santo Domingo, stretching and stitching cowhides into shoes. And before leaving the Dominican Republic for New York, Alex's father, Victor, was an outspoken activist against the brutal president who had ruled the island.

In the northernmost Manhattan neighborhood of Washington Heights, where the family landed and Rodriguez was born in 1975, his childhood apartment was crazy like the inside of the 1 train: parents, siblings, a steady stream of cousins, towers of ladies' shoes in boxes, and the customers who flocked to the apartment to buy them. With a protective mom, Lourdes, Alex was rarely allowed to leave this hive of activity.

So he ran up and down the apartment's hallway, one of those confined spaces that an adult covers in three quick steps but that unrolled like a playing field to a kid filled with rambunctious energy.

That's how Ana Lopez remembers her younger cousin every time she visited in the first four years of Alex's life. Alex would be running from his officious older half sister, screaming and laughing down that hallway, as he tried to avoid taking a shower. Or he'd be playing hallway baseball, using any ball he could get his hands on and a stick, running back and forth, always yelling. And always buck naked.

To Lopez, who lived in the Dominican Republic but visited every summer on her way to American camp, the Rodriguezes were like the Washington Heights Brady Bunch. Both Victor and Lourdes had children from previous marriages. Lourdes's son Joe shared a bedroom with Alex, and her daughter, Susy, had her own princess-themed boudoir. (Victor's son from his previous marriage, Victor Jr., was largely estranged from his father. He went on to be a high-ranking US Army official who barely knew Alex Rodriguez.) And Lopez remembers another constant presence in the crowded apartment, a chubby teenager who was inseparable from Alex.

Yuri Sucart—with the first name pronounced by Spanish-speaking tongues as "Judy"—was the son of one of Lourdes's brothers, Lopez says. A deadly car accident in the Dominican Republic had left Yuri orphaned as a baby. So extended family on both the island and in the United States took him in. Victor and Lourdes became Yuri's guardians for at least part of his childhood.

Thirteen years older than Alex Rodriguez, he was a big brother to the baby boy. "He's been with me since I was born," Rodriguez said much later, when his relationship with Sucart had turned notorious but he still kept him around—to a point.

Victor Rodriguez, Alex's father, made a living driving to outlet malls in New Jersey and Pennsylvania, filling his vehicle with Nine West and Anne Klein heels, and selling them out of his apartment to fellow Dominicans. Lourdes worked long hours on an assembly line at a Ford automotive plant in Mahwah, New Jersey. When that closed, Lourdes bounced to another Jersey town, getting work at the Ford plant in Edison.

Lourdes's brother, Augusto Bolivar Navarro, lived with his own family in Washington Heights. "Tio Bolivar," as family called him, was a Yankees fanatic. A gregarious, corpulent man, he spent his workdays in Manhattan's diamond district, prepping precious stones for display. At home, he angled his armchair in a corner of the living room and held court there so steadfastly that it was forever indented with a mold of Tio Bolivar's ass.

He hung a big photo of Alex as a kid in a baseball uniform on the wall. Visiting relatives teased him that the place looked like a memorabilia store.

When Tio Bolivar and Yuri crowded into the kitchen, those same relatives had another bit. "Get them out of the kitchen!" Lopez says family members yelled of the uncle and nephew. "They're going to eat everything!"

Bolivar was almost like a father to Alex and Yuri. When Victor ultimately left the family, Alex's uncle tried his best to fill that void. "It was a very close-knit family at that time," says Lopez.

It wasn't an easy life in Washington Heights. But there's a truth Alex Rodriguez's parents experienced, one known by many in Miami with Third World roots: Once you escape the grips of a despot, lesser struggles become almost sweet in comparison. And like Anthony Bosch, Rodriguez had the genes of a political agitator.

The general who had taken control of the Dominican Republic when Victor was an infant, Rafael Trujillo, was an effete, round-faced man whose head was crowned with a severe sheen of white hair. He was a plotter. He encouraged baseball in his country in order to keep the lower classes distracted, and the Dominican Republic would one day become the spigot that would flood the major leagues. He offered safe haven and a livelihood to Jews fleeing Europe during World War II, not for humanitarian reasons (he had just earlier ordered the massacre of more than twenty thousand Haitians) but because it was an opportunity to "whiten" his island.

But mostly, he slaughtered, imprisoned, and stole. In her unauthorized biography, *A-Rod*, Selena Roberts recounted the rebel leader mythology of Victor Rodriguez, an amateur baseball player. There were murky tales of Rodriguez's insurgency leading him to be dragged from a bar by Military Intelligence Service goons and beaten with brass knuckles.

It is clear that Rodriguez was outspoken *after* the coup that ended Trujillo's reign, a torrent of bullets killing the general in his blue Chevy Bel Air outside of Santo Domingo in 1961. Along with doctors, professors, and other Dominican activists, Rodriguez co-edited an anti-Trujillo newspaper called the *Tribuna Libre*. The newspaper called for the release of political prisoners and the erection of a monument to a countryman killed by Trujillo's regime, and it waxed passionate about the "patriotic frenzy that one day will inspire a cry welling hopelessly from our breast: LIBERTY!"

But for all his boldness, Victor was flighty. He sifted through business enterprises and cities like a blackjack player trying his luck at different tables. Ultimately, he decided that financial stability was worth breaking his son's heart.

When Alex was four, Victor decided that they would be better off in the Dominican Republic. The family moved back to Santo Domingo, living in Victor's sister's home, and began to struggle financially. Two years later, they bounced to Miami. Victor tried to convince Lourdes to move the family back to New York. He wanted the "fast-paced" life in the city, Alex later said, and Lourdes wanted to stay put.

So in 1985, when Alex was six, Victor packed a bag and left. "I thought he was coming back. I thought he had gone to the store or something," Alex Rodriguez told the *Seattle Times* thirteen years later, in a rare introspective interview. "I tried to tell myself that it didn't matter, that I didn't care. But times I was alone, I often cried. Where was my father? To this day, I still can't get close to people."

"He went back to New York to find a way to make a living," says Alex's cousin Ana Lopez. "But Tia Lourdes thought they had a future in Florida. I don't think he intended to be separated from them, because he adored those kids."

Alex Rodriguez didn't hear from Victor until the day he was picked first overall in the Major League Baseball draft, and his father called to congratulate him. Lourdes was pissed, Rodriguez later said: "My special day, Mom thought, and my father had no right to be a part of it."

After his baseball dreams died in high school, Tony Bosch always figured he'd find his destiny in medical school. Practicing medicine ran in the blood. Both his parents, as well as several cousins including Orlando, had donned a doctor's white coat. In 1977, his dad, Pedro, had opened his own general practice, the Coral Way Medical Center.

The center was a true family business. Tony's mom, Stella, was the financial director. Tony and his younger brother, Ashley, spent hours every week at the clinic.

"Tony always had a love for medicine," says Hernan Dominguez, a childhood friend and later a business partner, whose father was also a doctor.

Unfortunately, Tony Bosch was no more dedicated to his grades than he was to improving his baseball game. When he graduated in 1982, there was no hope of a premed program taking him in. He bounced in and out of undergrad programs at two private schools in North Carolina before coming back home to start a two-year respiratory medicine degree at Miami Dade College, a community school in downtown Miami.

While studying, he met Tiki Rodriguez, an easygoing Miami native who was charmed by Tony. They dated for a few years, and in August 1984, they married. De Armas walked as one of Bosch's best men. The next day, Bosch returned the favor by walking in De Armas's wedding. The two newly married couples joined each other for a honeymoon in Acapulco.

Tony Bosch was radiant, and not just because he was a newlywed. He was about to take the next step toward joining the family trade.

Working as a low-paid respiratory therapist didn't fit that bill. Bosch had enrolled at the Universidad Central Del Este in the Dominican Republic, one of the Caribbean's biggest medical schools. It wasn't recognized in the United States, but the degree would open doors toward getting into an American program, something Tony could never have earned with his middling grades. So after returning from their Mexican honeymoon, Bosch and Tiki packed up and moved to San Pedro de Macorís, the university town on the south coast of the Dominican Republic.

Once again, Tony couldn't cut it. To him, home was a handsome, two-story house on a tree-shaded lane in a wealthy Miami enclave. Now twenty-three years old, he suddenly found himself living in a poverty-stricken city in the heart of the Third World, where electricity and water were spotty, with a new wife to support and Spanish-language medical classes all day.

Bosch tried for about two years but eventually bailed out and moved back to Miami. "He moved down there with his wife and it was just too much responsibility," Dominguez says. "He had to drop out."

So he devised an easier way to break into medical business: salesman-ship. Bosch reconnected with De Armas, who'd recently moved back to Miami. The two old friends set up a business reselling medical supplies.

It wasn't a glamorous gig, but, to De Armas's surprise, the friends were good at it. Pedro's connections in the medical world and among Little Havana's tightly knit Cuban community gave them a natural in, and for the first time, Roger saw his childhood friend's true gift.

Tony Bosch couldn't hit or field and was nobody's idea of an athlete. He was smart, but not nearly driven enough to cut it in medical school. He didn't have his uncle Orlando's fiery passion or his dad's steely self-determination.

But damned if Tony couldn't sell anything.

"Great marketers are basically great at bullshit, and no one was better at bullshitting than Tony," De Armas says. "Tony could sell you a waterfront condo in the Everglades and you'd thank him on the way out."

While De Armas held down the office and organized orders, Tony visited doctors' offices around Dade County, selling them on new equipment, basic supplies, or anything else he could convince them to pay him for. With his coy smile and dark mess of hair, Tony was even more popular with the young women who worked at the front desks.

Miami Med Management Consultants made respectable profits. Bosch and his wife bought a small house in the Gables, and in 1987, they had a daughter.

Tony also found his way back out onto the diamond. He'd played recreational softball ever since graduating from high school. Now that he had a profitable company, which he shared with the equally baseball-loving De Armas, Bosch arrived at the idea of sponsoring a team.

Though the regional fad has been largely forgotten, in the late 1980s, softball in Miami was hitting a peak moment in the zeitgeist. Every weekend, on floodlit fields in Tropical Park or on baseball diamonds across Hialeah, thousands gathered to wallop slow-pitched balls and to swig beers after games. There's no doubt that the heart of the softball scene was recreational and booze-soaked, but there was also a hard-edged competitive spirit growing.

In part, it was fed by the same incredibly deep talent pool that had made high school ball such a challenge for kids like Tony Bosch. The gifted players who had made those teams, and even the guys who went on to star in college or play in the minors, all flooded softball leagues to recapture their glory days.

Miami's booming underworld of drug lords also saw an investment opportunity in the amateur teams. The city's immigrant influx had changed it in more ways than just its baseball pedigree. In 1980, Fidel Castro had hoodwinked President Jimmy Carter into allowing more than 125,000 Cubans to immigrate to Miami. What Carter didn't know was that a large number were violent criminals and mental patients culled from the island's asylums and prisons. The Mariel Boatlift, as the fiasco became known, remade Miami as thousands of hardened criminals slaughtered one another in South Beach and made Biscayne Bay the heart of America's cocaine trade.

Willy Falcon and Sal Magluta—a pair later betrayed by their own meticulous bookkeeping, which revealed the scope of their operation— imported roughly seventy-five tons of cocaine, worth about $1 billion, into Miami before they were caught. And they also built an ass-kicking softball team, called the Seahawks. Falcon and Magluta paid one nineteen-year-old Canadian pitcher $50,000, and gave him a bright red Porsche, to move to Florida to be the team's ringer.

"Some of the biggest sponsors back then are in prison now," says Jesus Morales, a longtime player, organizer, and unofficial historian of Miami's softball scene. "There were guys who would spend $200,000 or $250,000 sponsoring a softball team."

Bosch didn't have the liquid assets of a cocaine kingpin, but he and De Armas sank a few thousand dollars into uniforms, and the Miami Meds were born. Every year, they added a few more competitive players and stepped up a rung on the competitive ladder. By 1990, the team was so stacked that Bosch and De Armas only penciled themselves into the lineup if there was a blowout.

The best player on that year's squad was Paul Biocic, a speedy, powerful hitter who'd played college ball in Chicago before moving to Miami for work. "He truly loved what he was doing with the team," Biocic recalls of Bosch. "He didn't play hardly at all, but anything we needed done practice-wise, he was there: throwing batting practice, shagging flies, just helping out."

With the stacked roster, the team pulled off a Miracle Mets–esque run through the playoffs, rolling to a state title in Clearwater to earn a bid to Alabama. There, they blasted through a ninety-one-team field to earn a title game tilt with another Miami-area team.

With Biocic starring, they won and hoisted a national title. It was just softball, but it was a big deal. The victory earned a write-up in the *Miami Herald*'s sports section, and Tony Bosch exulted in the victory, hosting a drunken celebration at his house when the team returned to town. "He was ecstatic," De Armas says.

The story of how prepubescent Alex Rodriguez, the boy without a father, ended up playing organized ball is apocryphal, shifting in every newspaper profile, young adult tome, and unauthorized biography in which some version is retold. It's Major League Baseball's Malcolm-X-picking-up-the-Koran-in-prison moment. The elements are usually similar: sweltering Miami day. Eight-year-old Alex hanging alone on some monkey bars. A Little League team gathers to practice—or, alternatively, to play a game. They're one kid short.

A big, bearded coach lands his eyes on the jungle gym runt. "Hey, kid, do you want to play?"

The heart of the story is true. The coach was J. D. Arteaga, who is said to have been the first to notice that Alex—playing that day against kids two years older than him—was of a special talent and composure.

Arteaga's son, also named JD, became Rodriguez's best friend. The Arteagas brought him to the Hank Kline Boys & Girls Club and introduced him to Eduardo Marcelino Rodriguez, the trim, intense coach forever prowling the facility. If your elbow sagged while batting, Eddie Rodriguez was the sort who would come running out of the dugout—screaming a blue streak—and slap your arm back to proper stance. Alex craved such tough love.

Probing for acceptance and guidance from older male mentors was a quest in which Rodriguez partook well into adulthood, with varying degrees of success. Scott Boras, Jose Canseco, and Joe Torre all found themselves taking under their wing this insecure kid named Alex with the net worth of a CEO and the sweet stroke of Joe DiMaggio. "He was constantly looking for people he could trust," says childhood friend Tom Bernhardt.

Eddie was one of those first dad stand-ins, as Alex sometimes pulled out a sleeper couch to spend the night at the facility. "His mom worked two jobs," says Bernhardt of Alex, "so the Boys Club was basically his home."

It was also sometimes home for Eddie. Nicknamed "El Gallo" or "Macho Eddie," he had first been hired by the facility at age sixteen. During a divorce, Eddie Rodriguez, who then made $28,000 a year, also lived on a fold-out couch at the Boys & Girls Club. And in 1993, the *Miami Herald* reported that he was arrested and suspended for allegedly accepting a $400 bribe to fabricate paperwork getting a traffic offender out of community service at the club. (That record has been expunged and Rodriguez refused to discuss the case with the authors.)

But as the reigning shah of Miami-area Boys & Girls Clubs, Eddie was the keeper of regional elite youth baseball talent. Danny Tartabull, Rafael Palmeiro, and Jose Canseco, all of whom became baseball superstars, played ball at the local clubs when they were young.

Eddie Rodriguez, a Cuban-born former minor league ballplayer who wore skintight black shirts and big crucifix necklaces, mentored Alex throughout his childhood and into his professional career—turning against his protégé only when A-Rod was nearly middle-aged and his constant scandals pissed Eddie off for the last time.

A peculiar baseball-obsessed family sprouted at the Boys & Girls Club. The de facto hitting instructor was a wizened security guard the kids called "The Old Man." Septugenarian Rene Janero had played ball in Cuba and now lived on the club grounds. He didn't speak a lick of English, but he was a master of the fluid swing.

Alex Rodriguez then lived in a Miami suburb called West Kendall with his mom, Susy, Joe, and, at times, Yuri Sucart. Rodriguez, twelve years younger than Anthony Bosch, lived six miles down the traffic-clogged artery of US 1, also known as West Dixie Highway, from Coral Gables, where Bosch grew up.

That short drive signified a world of change between Bosch's upbringing and that of Rodriguez. High-end department stores became strip malls. Teenagers drove battered Mitsubishis instead of new BMWs. Red-tiled, white-stucco villas were replaced by the sort of shabby suburban family houses you'll see anywhere in America, albeit with palm trees in the yard.

This was the divide Rodriguez struggled to reconcile throughout his teenage years, even into adulthood. At the time, baseball earned him entry to exclusive prep schools. While his classmates' parents were doctors and attorneys, Lourdes's two jobs included shifts at a place called El Pollo Supremo.

He was a latchkey kid from Washington Heights and the Dominican Republic, trying to break into the rarefied environs belonging to the Bosch children of the world. "Alex probably felt inferior," says Tom Bernhardt, himself the son of a successful insurance agent. "On the outside he was cocky, but on the inside he was scared. He didn't know who to talk to. He was around all these affluent people. He must have thought, *I don't have the background that all these kids have, so how am I going to make it?* And the only answer was sports."

Rodriguez has said that he never knew how his private high school education was paid for. The answer, at least for one of the schools, was Tom's father, Jim Bernhardt. Jim, president of both the regional Boys &

Girls Club and Christopher Columbus High, admired the driven, lanky fourteen-year-old, whom he calls a "good listener." "I knew he couldn't go to a private school," says Bernhardt. "I paid his tuition. I wish that wouldn't be publicized, because he doesn't even know that today."

Seven years after Anthony Bosch graduated Columbus High, leaving barely a mark on the collective memory of the school's baseball community, Alex Rodriguez enrolled at the top Catholic school near Coral Gables.

And the funny thing is, he didn't fare much better on the baseball team than Bosch had.

His slick fielding had attracted attention at Gulliver Middle School. And under Eddie Rodriguez's tutelage, he had held his own in travel team lineups full of kids several years older than him and already displaying disturbing amounts of facial hair. So as has been the case ever since, Alex Rodriguez's arrival was preceded by hype. "We knew who he was," says Kelvin Cabrera, who was in the same freshman class at Columbus as Rodriguez. "The word was, 'Oh, there's this kid that's just ridiculous. He's going to be really, really good. This is *the guy.*'"

But when he got there, and tried out for a team that already included future major leaguer Mike Lowell, Rodriguez sure didn't look like much. Placed up against high schoolers, he was tiny. "He was this skinny, scrawny kid," says Luis "Wicho" Hernandez, a senior during Rodriguez's freshman year and a starting second baseman on the team. "He hadn't filled out yet."

Says another teammate: "He was so skinny he could hide behind a palm tree at Columbus."

In fact, it appeared momentarily as if Rodriguez might have a brighter future in basketball than baseball. "He was a very cerebral player," says Brother Butch Staiano, the Columbus varsity basketball coach. Rodriguez made quick mastery of drawn-up plays. A rash of guard injuries led Staiano to put him on the varsity squad in his freshman year.

His first game, he made several baskets with only one turnover in a close loss to vaunted Miami High, by far the best team in the county. Soon the beanpole in the navy-blue jersey was leading his team off the bench. "He was one of only three kids that I ever played on varsity as a freshman," says Staiano. "I thought he had a shot at being a Division-I basketball player."

But Rodriguez, who idolized Baltimore Orioles shortstop Cal Ripken Jr., had his heart set on hardball. Blocking him at that position on the baseball varsity squad was another freshman, named Ryan Rodriguez. Unlike Alex, his nemesis had peaked early, filling out a six-foot, 170-pound frame by age twelve. The varsity baseball coach, Brother Herb Baker, a member of the Marist Brothers, a teaching order in the Roman Catholic church, was testy and hype-averse. He chose the solid, unremarkable Ryan over Alex, who often appeared to fancy himself already a big leaguer in his flashy fielding and the way he swaggered with bat in hand.

"He told Alex that as long as Ryan Rodriguez was on the team," Hernandez says of Baker, "Ryan would be the starting shortstop."

Says Tom Bernhardt, who went to Christopher Columbus with Rodriguez, of Baker: "He has a temper, and he says things he probably wishes he wouldn't say." Alex Rodriguez was relegated to junior varsity.

The consensus was that Rodriguez was too small to be a potential major league ballplayer. During a shit-shooting session in Eddie Rodriguez's office, the gruff coach declared that Rodriguez would be his third choice to have a big league future—behind J. D. Arteaga and Tom Bernhardt. "Well, you're not strong enough," Eddie reasoned bluntly when Alex asked why the coach discounted his chances. "If you get a lot stronger, maybe you'll have an opportunity to get there." They were words Alex apparently took to heart.

By all accounts, Alex wasn't wounded by the twin snubs of Herb Baker and Eddie Rodriguez. When his dad left, it appeared to have inoculated him against further daggers. Instead, he was motivated. "A certain part of Alex sees himself as the underdog," says Hernandez. "So I don't think he was hurt. I think his reaction was 'Oh yeah? I'll show you.'"

Rodriguez called Baker's bluff. Before his sophomore year, he followed J. D. Arteaga ten miles north, to Westminster Christian. His mom eked out his tuition through grants. If Columbus High had been the waitress's son's introduction to the haves, the tiny, elite Westminster was Rodriguez being steeped in the 1 percent. And the place was a baseball machine, boasting several players who went on to major league careers. The squad was led by Rich Hofman, the winning-obsessed coach whose team's success always blew away what would be expected of a school with such a small student body.

By his junior season, Alex grew his physique to match such a juggernaut squad. "It's the last time the world saw Alex Rodriguez," says one former Christopher Columbus teammate, "and not A-Rod."

CHAPTER TWO

Mystery Elixirs, Speed, and Steroids

Pittsburgh's Recreation Park simmered with humidity as James "Pud" Galvin strolled to the mound to face the Boston Beaneaters. It was August 13, 1889, and the Beaneaters had tormented Galvin's Alleghenys all season. The two teams had played eleven times and Boston had won every single contest.

Galvin was one of the most accomplished players alive, but at thirty-two years old, the thousands of innings he'd wrung out of his roly-poly frame were starting to take a toll. He was on his way to topping three hundred innings for the year as usual, but he was giving up more runs than any other time in his career. Like most of the league, the Beaneaters weren't quaking anymore at his pinpoint accuracy and crafty changeups.

Tonight, though, as Galvin rocketed warm-up heaters at his catcher, he knew he had a secret weapon.

With a square, chubby face and waxed black mustache, Galvin looked more like a jolly neighborhood butcher than a hurler. Fans around the country learned Galvin's name in 1876, when he recorded the first-known perfect game against a professional squad out of Detroit. The feat came just a few hours after he pitched a no-hitter against another Michigan club.

Like any great ballplayer, Galvin accumulated as many nicknames as plaudits. They called him "Pud" for the way his fastball turned hitters to pudding (or maybe for his pudgy body), "Gentle Jeems" for his laid-back attitude on the mound, and "Little Steam Engine" for the drive and power packed into his stout frame.

Galvin had once won an astounding ninety-two games in two seasons for the Buffalo Bisons, while perfecting a pick-off move so good it caught opponents with "trousers at half mast," according to a newspaper account of him picking off three base runners in one inning.

But in a league where few pitchers made it past thirty years old, Galvin was elderly. He had been mediocre and worse in the last two seasons. The dog days of August had left the Little Steam Engine huffing and puffing down the tracks.

That's why, the day before the contest with the Beaneaters, Galvin had agreed to a curious proposition from the physicians at the nearby Western Pennsylvania Medical College. The doctors hoped to use the aging pitcher as a test subject for a fad blazing across the nation.

The trend had exploded about a month and a half earlier across the Atlantic, when famed French physician Dr. Charles-Édouard Brown-Séquard addressed his contemporaries at Paris's Société de Biologie with a report that soon dashed across wire services worldwide. The doctor calmly told a gruesome tale of chopping testicles off live dogs and guinea pigs, grinding the organs into a paste, refining it into liquid, and then shooting the vile concoction under his own skin. The result? The seventy-two-year-old visionary felt at least a decade younger with no ill effects.

Doctors were skeptical, but Brown-Séquard was not a snake oil salesman—in fact, the Frenchman was among Europe's best-known scientists. Stories about his new discovery soon appeared in every newspaper around the United States. Many described the electrifying results local physicians had found by copying his technique.

Around the country, stories described "broken-down" war veterans shot up with the testicle extracts and suddenly performing feats of strength. "A man read a newspaper in twilight without spectacles, which he had not done for ten years," reported a wire story out of Indianapolis, where dozens had begged for shots from their doctors. "Among the decrepit old men of the city, the elixir has become the rage."

More than a century before Bosch and his ilk promised vitality and youth in injections and chewables, America was in the throes of the original "anti-aging" craze. And ballplayers soon got involved.

Galvin wasn't quite a decrepit old man, but he was battered enough to try anything. So the day before facing the Beaneaters, he'd traveled to the medical college and taken a shot of Brown-Séquard's elixir—probably made from sheep testicles—under the skin on his stomach.

Pud could hardly have made a better advertisement for Brown-Séquard's backers. With sheep testosterone coursing through his system, the rejuvenated hurler held the mighty Beaneaters to just five singles in nine innings. The career .201 hitter even smacked a run-scoring double and an RBI triple on the other side of the plate while leading the Alleghenys to a 9-0 thumping of Boston.

"If there still be doubting Thomases who conceded no virtue in the elixir, they are respectfully referred to Galvin's record in yesterday's Boston-Pittsburgh game," a *Washington Post* writer crowed in the next morning's edition. "It is the best proof yet furnished of the value of the discovery."

Calling Pud Galvin baseball's first juicer would be a stretch. Not long after the summer of Brown-Séquard mania faded to autumn, the "doubting Thomases" had shown that his testicle cocktails were medical nonsense. If anything had actually rejuvenated the aging Pud Galvin on the mound on that steamy summer day against the Boston Beaneaters, it was a raging case of the placebo effect.

But Galvin's tale does illustrate a deeper truth about our national pastime. Dating back to the earliest days of hurlers with fancy mustaches and nicknames like "Gentleman Jeems," a win-at-all-costs undercurrent has always thrived in baseball's shadows, driving players to ingest substances with no thought as to possible side effects.

Baseball history is as replete with cheaters as heroes, and the two are often hard to tell apart. Pitchers who greased balls with Vaseline and slashed them with craftily hidden razors share space in Cooperstown with Ruth and

Mantle, and when the cheaters got caught, fans have often been more likely to congratulate them for their cunning than to demand asterisks beside their names.

"Galvin's story, to me, reconfirmed that the game is fifty percent psychological and fifty percent physical," says Roger Abrams, a longtime baseball labor arbitrator who discovered newspaper clips about Galvin's injections. "It's not how you play the game but whether you win, and that's always been the case."

Galvin's experiments are also an early moment in the long history of drugs coursing through hardball's veins. Ballplayers' chemical dependencies have reflected the trends of ordinary Americans, from the amphetamine boom to the rise of cocaine to the bodybuilding-fueled birth of steroid culture and "anti-aging" medicine. Throughout every era, a dysfunctional relationship among baseball's owners, commissioners, and players union helped guarantee a permissive, consequence-free atmosphere that let each drug boom flourish until scandals—from coke busts to steroid rings—marred the game.

"Baseball players will take anything," pitcher Jim Bouton famously wrote. "If you had a pill that would guarantee a pitcher twenty wins but might take five years off his life, he'd take it."

Amphetamines may not have offered ballplayers quite that Mephistophelean a bargain, but they were the first performance-enhancing drug to find a widespread foothold in American sports.

For Pud Galvin and the whole next generation of players, it didn't matter how badly they wanted to enhance their performance through science because the science simply didn't exist. Brown-Séquard's wasn't the only crap elixir catching the American imagination at the turn of the twentieth century. The FDA didn't demand truth-in-advertising for drugs until 1906, and through Prohibition many top-selling "medicines" were simply alcohol-based potions that didn't do much more than get users drunk. Even if Babe Ruth or the other Bronx Bombers had wanted to juice their swings, there was nothing on the market to build their bodies—illegally or not. (Though Ruth *was* an enthusiastic drunk at a time when alcohol was just as illegal as steroids are today.)

Back in 1901, the first synthesized hormonal drug, Adrenalin, came on the market, and its commercial success inspired two decades of experimentation by chemists to find other useful hormones. The next big splash came in 1921 with insulin, which sparked even more research.

Eight years later, a young chemist named Gordon Alles, who spent his days making mixtures of pollen and cat hair for a Los Angeles allergist, used his free time to experiment with a compound called beta-phenylisopropylamine. He'd hoped it might help asthma patients, but when he started injecting it himself he noticed some curious side effects: his blood pressure rose, his mind became more focused and overactive, and he was suffused with a "feeling of well-being." Alles had invented synthetic amphetamines. (A few years later, Alles tweaked a few oxygen molecules and accidentally invented Ecstasy—that self-experiment proved even more eventful, including hallucinations of smoke filling the room.)

Alles's patents eventually became Benzedrine asthma inhalers, which beatniks discovered could be cracked open to get to the amphetamine-coated strips inside. Popping "bennies" was soon the rage, and even before then, the Nazis pioneered the drug's performance-enhancing use by giving huge quantities to troops, creating fearless—and sometimes hallucinating—paratroopers and dive-bombers. The Allies soon followed suit and by war's end, American troops were eating Benzedrine and Dexedrine, its successor, like candy.

Among those soldiers were thousands of major leaguers. When they returned to the diamonds at the war's end, they realized that the same pills that had helped them stay focused through the brutal campaign could do the same during their 154-game slogs.

Other professional sports had already proven speed could help. Cyclists had been using amphetamines since the late '30s to survive grueling continental races, and one British doctor at the 1948 Olympics described riders doping themselves "like racehorses" with Benzedrine.

Though amphetamines were banned in college and high school athletics by the late '50s, American pro leagues didn't just allow them, they embraced them. Houston Ridge, a defensive lineman, later sued the NFL and described a San Diego Chargers locker room in the early '60s where players were force-fed steroids and amphetamines to the point that he played through broken bones without realizing it. A 1972 doctoral thesis found that nearly all football pros took amphetamines, with an average dose almost seven times stronger than the recommended prescription.

In baseball, pitcher Jim Brosnan was among the first to talk about his greenies habit. In *The Long Season*, his bestselling account of his 1959 tour with the Cardinals and Reds, he recalls interrogating a team doctor who ran out of his favorite brand. "Where's my Dexamyl, Doc?" Brosnan asked. "How'm I going to get through the day?"

By the time Hall of Famer Johnny Bench made the big leagues eight years later, he found his team's physician was always fully stocked. "The trainers had them and nobody thought twice about passing them out," Bench wrote in his own autobiography.

Bench once watched a teammate pop greenies until "his eyes would get all googly and he wouldn't answer a question, just stay as high as could be and pitch his head off."

"Pills were misused and not just by pitchers, and for that I blame the trainers who dispensed them as much as the players who took them," Bench wrote. "In the pros, you look for any leg up and a lot of guys, especially pitchers facing a tough start, thought daps and dexys were that edge."

Marvin Miller, the longtime head of the Players Association, recalled some clubs where players didn't even have to go to the trainer for a boost. "In most locker rooms, most clubhouses, amphetamines—red ones, green ones, et cetera—were lying out there in the open, in a bowl, as if they were jelly beans," he told reporters.

The draw was simple. On a physical level, amphetamines gave a quick jolt of energy; mentally, they helped imbue a sense of power and strength. Of course, that combination could be a double-edged sword, and by the mid-1960s, the medical literature was becoming clear that speed was also highly addictive and could lead to hallucinations and paranoia.

"Some of the guys have to take one just to get their hearts to start beating," Jim Bouton wrote in *Ball Four, Plus Ball Five*. "I've taken greenies, but I think [teammate] Darrell Brandon is right when he says that the trouble with them is that they make you feel so great that you think you're really smoking the ball even when you're not. They give you a false sense of security."

The same year Bouton's book rattled MLB with its unsentimental portrait of life on the mound, baseball's love affair with speed hit a road bump. In 1970, Congress passed the Comprehensive Drug Abuse Prevention and Control Act, the landmark bill that created five "schedules" for drugs based on their addictiveness and risks; amphetamines ended up Schedule II, the second-most–tightly controlled category.

Faced with a federal crackdown and then with the newly created Drug Enforcement Administration, teams couldn't openly pass around greenies as if they were Tic Tacs. But like every other front in the new War on Drugs, stricter laws didn't erase appetites inside baseball's clubhouses. Instead, players turned to their team physicians to procure their speed.

With both the commissioner's office and the Players Association mute on drug use, the league was primed for embarrassment on a national scale. It wasn't the last time.

I n mid-November 1980, the Philadelphia Phillies organization was still riding an all-natural high.

The Phils were one of the oldest franchises in baseball, dating their team back to 1883 when Pud Galvin was still in his prime. But the Phillies— once bought by a lumber baron who was banned for life midseason when he got caught gambling on the game—had spent nearly a century racking up dubious achievements: the most recorded losses of any team in American professional sports, for one, and also the only franchise among the original sixteen to have never won a World Series.

Whatever curse lay over the Phillies—which the baseball gods hadn't even blessed with a cute story like the Cubs' billy goat episode—was shattered by a 1980 roster lousy with talent. At third base, Mike Schmidt roared to an MVP year with forty-eight home runs and 121 RBIs, while Steve Carlton won the Cy Young with a 24-9, 2.34 ERA season. The Phils even rode the thirty-nine-year-old Pete Rose for 185 hits.

And on October 21, 1980, in Game Six of the World Series, the Phils dispatched the Kansas City Royals 4–1 in front of sixty-five thousand delirious fans. The Phillies, finally, were champions.

Amid all the revelry, no one on the team paid much mind four weeks later when a physician named Dr. Patrick Mazza was arrested in Reading, a town an hour north of Philly. On November 21, the local district attorney announced the charges against Mazza, the team doctor for the Phillies' local minor league affiliate. Between 1978 and 1980, prosecutors said, Mazza had illegally prescribed the amphetamines Dexamyl, Eskatrol, Dexedrine, and Preludin at least twenty-three times.

Curiously, Mazza had gotten those drugs by filing false prescriptions in the names of Phillies stars and their wives, including Rose, Carlton, Larry Christenson, Randy Lerch, Larry Bowa, Tim McCarver, and Greg Luzinski. "It was possible that by using the names of well-known people, there would be little question by the druggists in the issuances of the prescriptions," the local prosecutor speculated afterward.

The truth turned out to be far more straightforward. The players all denied asking for the drugs, but prosecutors quickly realized they'd been duped. "They were made at the request of the ballplayers," Mazza told the court, adding that Bowa said he needed "something to pick him up," Rose "was having trouble with his weight," and "Steve, being a moody person and a loner, needed something to pep him up."

(Mazza's case was later dismissed. The authors of this book attempted to interview weight-loss patient Rose about this episode. Through a spokesperson, the all-time hit king Rose—banned for life from baseball for gambling on the sport—cited a "standing rule" demanding $500 per interview. The authors declined.)

The Phillies' arrangement was hardly unusual. All over MLB, players looked to discreet physicians to get the meds they wanted. When Bouton played for the Seattle Pilots in 1969, he wrote that greenies "are against club policy. So we get them from players on other teams who have friends who are doctors or friends who know where to get greenies. One of our lads is going to have a bunch of greenies mailed to him by some of the guys on the Red Sox."

And an investigation by *Sports Illustrated*'s Bil Gilbert found the 1968 World Series so chock-full of pharmacological help he called it "a matchup between Detroit and St. Louis druggists," with amphetamines, barbiturates, antidepressants, and muscle relaxers all in heavy rotation.

Whether Mazza's treatments were standard fare or not, District Attorney LeRoy Zimmerman was apoplectic. "Unfortunately and regrettably," he told the press, "there is nothing in the law in Pennsylvania to make what the Phillies did a crime. Although it may be unethical, improper, a lack of candor, a lack of cooperativeness and deplorable, there is no criminal violation of the perjury statute."

Mazza's attorney, Emmanuel Dimitriou, was less verbose: "What you have here are a bunch of ballplayers who are world champions, but who are also champions of lying."

The case marked the first time in MLB history that a true performance-enhancing drug scandal had hit the newspapers, but there was hardly fiery outrage from fans. Greenies were baseball's first PED, but unlike the chemicals to come, fans didn't see them skewing the statistics that are such a holy link between the eras of America's oldest sport.

"The customers honestly don't give a damn," says Dr. Charles Yesalis, a Penn State professor who studies PEDs in professional sports, speaking about baseball's drug scandals in general. "Have you ever seen big protests outside stadia? . . . During or after scandals, do TV ratings or attendance really drop?"

Still, the case should have been a warning sign. For the first time, baseball's lax internal policing had run up against a criminal trial and some of its biggest stars had been exposed. With a lack of outcry, though, the Phillies' near-miss sparked no drug testing or stricter league-wide policies.

T hree years after baseball's speed habit made front-page news, another drug trend much more seriously scarred hardball's reputation.

Like the Mazza affair, the case that later became known as the Pittsburgh drug trials started with a character only tangentially tied to the pro baseball club. Former pitching prospect Kevin Koch was only twenty-five but was a long way from his playing days. He was notable for a different reason: Since 1979, he'd been the man inside the Pirate Parrot, Pittsburgh's lime-green mascot.

Between bouts of prancing around on the dugout roof, Koch had made friends with players, including superstar outfielder Dave Parker, with whom he'd bonded over a shared love of cocaine. Koch began supplying Parker and his teammates, and soon brought in a loose circle of friends who all helped keep the big leaguers well supplied with coke. They did it less for profit than for the chance to hang out with big leaguers; none were professional drug dealers.

By 1984, it was far from secret that coke had been popularized in the major leagues in a big way. The previous fall, a sting had zeroed in on nearly a dozen Kansas City Royals players suspected of buying cocaine; in October, All-Star pitcher Vida Blue, outfielder Willie Wilson, first baseman Willie Aikens, and outfielder Jerry Martin all pleaded guilty to misdemeanor possession and were sentenced to ninety days in the pen.

Then-commissioner Bowie Kuhn was worried enough that he visited the players' dealer in prison to pump him for intel on how many others were hooked.

The answer was many. Star first baseman Keith Hernandez later estimated that 40 percent of big leaguers used coke. The early '80s were a
perfect collision of a blossoming drug culture for baseball; as cocaine flowed
in through Miami's new class of Cuban-born gangsters, a generation of
young players flush with cash and vulnerable to addiction spread the gospel
of cocaine from one clubhouse to another.

"My opinion is that it became an epidemic during the work stoppage
in 1981, when you had a lot of young guys with too much time on their
hands and some apprehension about their future," says Sam Reich, the Pittsburgh defense attorney who represented many of the players involved.

The Pittsburgh scandal started with a deeply troubled southpaw reliever named Rod Scurry, the Pirates' former top draft pick who'd recorded
a 1.74 ERA in 1982. Scurry's performance fell off a cliff in 1983, though, his
ERA jumping almost four points and his habit growing until he was doing
bumps in the pen. On April 7, 1984, after a terrible spring training outing,
Scurry binged in his hotel room and, hallucinating that snakes were swarm-
ing him, trashed the place.

The incident forced the Pirates to send Scurry to rehab, but it also
caught the eye of federal agents who'd been sniffing around drug use by
big leaguers. They soon convinced Scurry to cooperate, and he led them
to Koch and his friends, most prominently a caterer and coke dealer
named Charlie Strong. (Koch, the Pirates mascot, later went undercover
for the feds, trading in his fuzzy parrot costume for a wire taped to his
belly.)

In early 1985—in a prelude to the BALCO steroid investigation to
follow two decades later—a grand jury was marshaled in Pittsburgh and a
stream of big leaguers amid tight secrecy marched into the courthouse to
talk under oath about MLB's cocaine habit. Reporters soon caught on, and
a fevered speculation broke out that some of Pittsburgh's biggest sports stars
were about to be indicted.

The public ate up the headlines as the story exploded out of Pennsylvania onto front pages nationwide. Amid the white flight and Reagan's in-

tensifying War on Drugs, the story confirmed many Americans' worst fears: The national pastime had been infiltrated by cocaine.

When the hammer finally dropped on May 30, Strong and six others were indicted, but unlike in the Kansas City case, no big leaguers were charged. This time, prosecutors went after the dealers, not the users. But if baseball's new commissioner, Peter Ueberroth, breathed easier at the news, he wasn't much relieved by the time the trial started a few months later.

Led by Strong's flamboyant attorney, Adam Renfroe, the cooperating players—who'd been given immunity—were grilled on the stand about their drug habits. National front-page stories detailed MLB's raging coke problem. Hernandez admitted he'd used cocaine for about three years. Parker copped to introducing a dealer to the Pirates clubhouse and to arranging buys for his teammates. And All-Star Tim Raines even admitted that he'd kept a bottle of cocaine in his back pocket, wrapped in a batting glove, during games. To avoid breaking the vials during slides, he told the court, "I'd go in headfirst."

For all the headlines and moral outrage, cocaine wasn't a performance-enhancing drug. In fact, coke addiction derailed many players, including Scurry, who washed out of the league in 1986 and died from his addiction six years later. But the drug trials—which ended with guilty verdicts for Strong and his codefendants—were an important point in MLB history.

The case forced players to talk openly about how, more than a decade after the drugs were outlawed, amphetamines were still rampant in MLB. Dale Berra testified under oath that players openly popped greenies and that All-Star Willie Stargell had procured the drugs for his teammates, a charge Stargell emphatically denied.

More important, the case exposed how the dysfunctional relationship between the commissioner's office and the players union prevented any real attempts at drug reform. That same imbalance, in just a few years, ensured that another drug epidemic—this one with very real effects on players' performances—also raged, unaddressed, through baseball's clubhouses.

"The problem is serious," Bowie Kuhn had warned in early 1984. In June, three months before he retired, Kuhn and the union agreed to a new testing program; if a panel agreed there was "just cause," they could order a player tested. But the provision was aimed exclusively at cocaine abuse, with no steroid or amphetamine testing, and it didn't work: Almost no one was found to have "just cause."

So Ueberroth, after taking power, tried to institute a more serious policy after the Pittsburgh case. In September 1985, he sent a letter directly to every player asking them to submit to voluntary testing, pleading that "there's a cloud hanging over baseball and it's a cloud called drugs."

Union chief Donald Fehr—not for the last time—pushed back hard, calling the proposal "very possibly, if not probably" against labor law and advising players to dump Ueberroth's letter in the trash. (Fehr had good reason to distrust the owners Ueberroth represented; that same off-season, they began secretly working to undermine free agency by colluding to underpay players.)

In the end, Ueberroth suspended eleven over the Pittsburgh scandal but allowed most to return early in exchange for donating money to a drug rehab program. Just as with the Phillies' amphetamine case, the mistrust between owners and players had ensured another missed chance to confront rampant drug use. The union's refusal to allow testing while owners picked financial battles instead was a prelude of standoffs to come.

The first commercial synthetic steroid, Dianabol, hit American markets in the late '50s. It was the brainchild of a Maryland physician named Dr. John "Montana Jack" Ziegler, a towering, six-foot-four man who'd been severely injured fighting in the Pacific Theater. His interest in muscle-building drugs had been piqued in 1954 when he accompanied the US weight-lifting squad to Europe and a Russian team doctor confided, after knocking down a few drinks, that his boys were doped up with synthetic testosterone.

Zielger was a country doctor, but he had a side gig doing research for

Ciba, a pharmaceutical company. He also lifted weights at York Barbell Company with Bob Hoffman, one of the first famous strongmen in America, and when he returned from Europe he began tinkering with testosterone formulas at Ciba and then testing them on his weight-lifting pals.

Ciba bought his first formula, methandrostenolone, and released it in 1959 as a pink pill called Dianabol, which was experimentally marketed toward easing various symptoms in the elderly and burn victims. But off-label, with Ziegler's guidance, weight lifters started popping Dianabol and pumping iron. Along with Ziegler's next creation—an injectable steroid called Winstrol released in 1963—American athletics were changed forever.

Ziegler came to deeply regret his role as the forefather of doping, refusing to continue helping bodybuilders when he realized that they were taking massive quantities of his drugs against his advice. "I wish to God now I'd never done it," Ziegler later said. "I'd like to go back and take that whole chapter out of my life." He died of heart disease, which he attributed in part to his own steroid use, at the age of sixty-three.

By the mid-'60s, Ziegler's inventions had revolutionized weight lifting and made significant inroads into professional football, where bulky muscle seemed to have the most immediate benefit. In his lawsuit, former defensive lineman Houston Ridge described how the 1963 San Diego Chargers forced players to take Diabanol twice a day during training camp, fining players $50 for not 'roiding with breakfast. (Ridge settled with the team for $265,000.)

But most baseball players didn't see the allure of steroids. Baseball was a sport obsessed with tradition, and nearly everyone was sure a ripped physique would ruin hitters' swings and pitchers' mechanics. Babe Ruth, after all, was hardly cut like a Greek god.

Tom House saw that attitude firsthand in 1969. The cerebral lefty was two years out of USC and struggling to make an impact in triple A, so he asked his coach if he could start a weight-training program. "If I see you lifting, one of two things will happen: I'm going to kick your rear end, or you are going to the minor leagues," House recalled his skipper saying.

House wasn't just one of the first to push back against that prevailing wisdom. He was also among the few players of his era to experiment with steroids. After ignoring his coach's warning, he started weight training in Santa Monica, then the heart of steroid culture. A weight-lifting partner turned him on to Dianabol, and House ended up adding thirty pounds of muscle. "I pretty much popped everything," he said. "We were doing steroids they wouldn't give to horses."

House pitched for a decade for the Braves, the Red Sox, and the Mariners and is best remembered for catching Hank Aaron's 715th homer in the Atlanta bullpen. He doesn't credit steroids with getting him there, though. "I got bigger, but my fastball didn't get any better," he told ESPN. "The weight was too much for my frame and my right knee went out on me."

With those injury concerns and strong pressure not to get too bulky, few other players toyed with Dianabol or Winstrol. (Though they tried just about anything else. "I've tried a lot of other things through the years," Jim Bouton wrote. "Like Butazolidin, which is what they give to horses. And DMSO—dimethylsulfoxide. . . . You rub it on with a plastic glove and as soon as it gets on your arm you can taste it in your mouth. It's not available anymore, though. Word is it can blind you. I've also taken shots— Novocaine, cortisone and Xylocaine.")

By nearly all accounts, steroids hadn't made serious inroads in MLB until after the Pittsburgh drug trials shined a light on the game's coke habit. And just like so much of that nose candy, the path that anabolic steroids took to reach big league clubhouses leads right back to Miami.

Not big or talented enough to play varsity ball for Coral Park High School until his senior year, teenage Jose Canseco was drafted on the cheap by the Oakland Athletics. The team threw a $10,000 bonus at him partly because the scout who signed him was the father of a Coral Park classmate.

In his first years of minor league ball, that pittance was looking like a ripoff. Canseco's first memoir, *Juiced,* paints a languid portrait of the slugger before he found the substances that gave him a career, lifelong notoriety, and the title for his book.

Canseco was a relatively puny 180 pounds of melancholy mass, neurotic about the fact that there were no Cubans in the big leagues and bizarrely apathetic. "Who was I to think that I was going to make it to Major League Baseball?" Canseco wondered. "I was kind of sleepwalking through games at that point."

It was an old Coral Park High buddy who gave him his first injection of liquid confidence. His mother had just died, Canseco said, energizing him to fulfill his vow to be "the best athlete in the world." In *Juiced*, Canseco identified the Coral Park steroid connection only as "Al." In an interview for this book, Canseco says that Al was a high school baseball player who was clearly juicing early in his amateur career. "I'd known him since he was thirteen or fourteen, and he was a big, strong guy even then," says Canseco. "I knew he was using some kind of chemicals."

So when Canseco was sick of being a middling minor leaguer, he knew to call Al. They discussed steroids over pizza and then filed into Al's room. Penned Canseco: "You actually feel the needle penetrating your buttock muscle that first time."

The way Canseco tells it—and despite all his faults, his most outrageous statements concerning steroids have proven to be true—that was a historic needle prick. Canseco takes credit for the steroid problem that overcame Major League Baseball. By that lineage, the national pastime's performance-enhancing substance problem can be traced back to a single Miami high school juicer named Al.

Canseco first started using steroids after the 1984 season, just as the Pittsburgh drug trials were about to expose cocaine's endemic use in MLB locker rooms. He started with synthetic testosterone and Deca Derbol, an anabolic steroid, and spent every day in the weight room. By the time he showed up for spring training in 1985, he had transformed into a ripped and confident 205-pound power hitter.

He spent the next season proving that baseball's conventional wisdom about steroids—that they made users too musclebound to play well—was one old wives' tale seriously lacking in fact. Canseco hit forty-one home runs on three professional levels, his scorching bat forcing the A's to take notice and promote him by September. "I can tell you now: Steroids were the key to it all," wrote Canseco.

By the time Canseco got to the majors, contracts were booming thanks to the onset of free agency. The average salary had almost tripled in five years, to $372,000, and routine eight-figure deals were on the horizon. Canseco says that players were finally beginning to see their bodies as a lucrative investment. "People changed the way they looked at baseball," Canseco says in an interview. "Instead of this unhealthy way players were living, they started lifting weights for the first time."

And they all wanted what Jose Canseco was having. In 1986, he won Rookie of the Year, hitting thirty-three homers to go with 113 RBIs. In the next six seasons, he made five All-Star teams and won an MVP.

In 1987, a rookie named Mark McGwire joined Canseco on the A's and knocked out forty-nine home runs—without any "chemical enhancement," according to Canseco. But Canseco says McGwire soon became an avid student of his regimen, and by the next season, the "Bash Brothers" combined for seventy-four home runs, leading the team to the World Series.

All the while, Canseco claimed in his book's most lasting image, they were in the clubhouse bathroom, shooting each other in the ass with steroids before games. Wrote Canseco: "The media dubbed us the Bash Brothers, but we were really the 'Roids Boys.'"

It was a pattern Canseco would follow throughout his journeyman career, spreading the epidemic to new teams with each trade.

On the Texas Rangers, Canseco claims he shared his chemical wisdom and steroid regimens with superstars Rafael Palmeiro, Ivan "Pudge" Rodriguez, and Juan Gonzalez. (All three deny they took steroids from Canseco, though Gonzalez is named in the Mitchell Report and Palmeiro later failed a drug test for steroids.) During a second tour with Oakland, Canseco says he and McGwire took the talented young Jason Giambi into the bathroom and helped turn him into a barely recognizable monster of a home run hitter.

By the early 1990s, Canseco's secret was extremely badly kept. Players around the league called steroids a "Jose Canseco Milkshake," and the star slugger's dad had threatened to beat up a *Washington Post* columnist for openly speculating about Canseco's substance use. When he'd get in a fight with a teammate, they'd scream, "You steroid-shooting motherfucker!"

With Canseco as the "Typhoid Mary" of steroids, the major leagues were about to embark on a record-destroying power surge so openly fraudulent that it demanded Congressional intervention.

CHAPTER THREE

License to Dope

The footage is shaky and shadowy, sound-tracked by players' moms screaming their lungs out from tin bleachers, but Alex Rodriguez already cuts a big league figure. As he steps to home plate, decked out in the dark green high school uniform of Westminster Christian, he makes mud with his spit and then troughs it with his cleats before adopting a swaggering, even-legged stance. When he takes his position at short, he appears a grown man on a child-size field, chattering instructions as he punches his fist into his glove.

All kids on baseball diamonds adopt the tics and mannerisms of pro ballplayers. What separated Rodriguez was that everybody at the park knew he would be one very soon.

It was May 11, 1993, and a grainy VHS tape shot by a fan that day shows the teenage A-Rod in West Palm Beach, taking on the underdog home team Cardinal Newman High in a playoff game. The Major League Baseball draft was only a few weeks away, and on the day before this game, the round-faced Seattle Mariners scout who had become Rodriguez's shadow put pen to paper in a report likely cementing the draft's first pick.

"Better at seventeen now than all the superstars in baseball were when they were seniors in HS," Roger Jongewaard wrote of Rodriguez, adding that watching him play imparted a "special feeling" and that the high schooler was "similar to [Derek] Jeter only bigger and better," the first of many times that Rodriguez was compared—often with less favorable results—with the eventual Yankees captain.

Rodriguez had committed to University of Miami, but the Coral Gables institution was well aware that he wouldn't enroll there if he signed with an MLB team. Rodriguez wasn't the only future baseball pro in Westminster's lineup that afternoon. Doug Mientkiewicz, Mickey Lopez, and Dan Perkins all joined him in the bigs, and four other Westminster teammates played in the minor leagues.

The kids on Cardinal Newman, meanwhile, grew up to peddle life insurance, practice corporate law, and sell medical equipment. But they popped in dusty recordings of this game—Alex Rodriguez's last in high school, as it turned out—whenever in need of a morale boost.

They love the part where Rodriguez clobbers a seventh-inning pitch 450 feet over the left-field fence, but the Cardinal Newman coach is able to convince the $25-a-game umpires that the ball had bounced before leaving the field. The umps ruled it a ground-rule double instead, Rodriguez slamming his helmet to the field in anger. "It got out so fast that I don't think the umpires saw it," former coach Jack Kokinda says now, proving that some dishonesty is fair game in baseball, "and I didn't have anything to lose."

But the game's ultimate highlight came in the bottom of the ninth, with a man on second and the score tied at four runs apiece. A future software developer hits a slow roller to the man-size teenage shortstop. Rodriguez, who has already committed two errors in the game, rears back wildly as he fields the ball and launches the throw high over the second baseman's head. The ball bounces off leather and into the outfield. A Cardinal Newman base runner races home from second and stomps on the plate with the game's winning run.

The video ends after the cameraperson, sitting in the stands, pans from the ebullient, arm-waving Cardinal Newman mob descending on home plate to Alex Rodriguez, now slumped in the grass near the lip of the infield. A teammate bends over him, trying in vain to console the million-dollar baby. "The best player in the country plays his worst game," Westminster coach Richard Hofman eulogized afterward in a *Miami Herald* interview. "He's human."

C all some of Alex Rodriguez's former high school teammates and ask them about young A-Rod, and what you'll hear in response is silence, dial tones, and statements like this:

"Alex has a lot of connections. I'm out of baseball, but I still want to make a living."

"Man, I like sleeping with both eyes closed. I don't want to sleep with one eye open."

The A-Rod cone of silence is not a recent development. Author Wayne Stewart encountered it back in the halcyon days of 2006, when reporting an inspirational text for young readers, *Alex Rodriguez: A Biography*. "It's almost like *omerta*, the mafia code," says Stewart, who has since come to believe his former subject "might be a sociopath." (Stewart isn't the only author to have found penetrating the psyche of Alex Rodriguez to be a difficult experience. After signing a deal in 2006 to write a biography of Rodriguez, revered author Richard Ben Cramer struggled for years to string together even a few thousand words on his subject, who he told friends was a "completely vacuous person." Cramer died in 2013 with the project abandoned, and his estate is being sued for the doomed A-Rod book advance.)

It's not baseless paranoia that makes Rodriguez's high school teammates cautious. Rodriguez is wealthy and litigious. And his former teammates know in which direction any conversation on Rodriguez's high school years will inevitably stray—steroids.

It was sixteen years after Rodriguez's graduation from Westminster when accusations that Rodriguez did steroids in high school were publicly aired in the unauthorized biography *A-Rod*, written by Selena Roberts. But even as he was still in that dark green high school uniform, the whispers about Rodriguez's miraculous bloom from junior varsity shrimp to hulking number one draft pick had become an incessant buzz.

"Absolutely there was speculation" about whether teenage Rodriguez was juicing, says Cardinal Newman shortstop Steve Kokinda, whose father, Jack, coached the team. "The guy was enormous . . . Twenty years ago, there weren't any guys like that in high school. He looked like a pro guy and we all looked like high school kids."

After transferring to Westminster, Rodriguez was mediocre at the plate in his sophomore season. "He was pretty scrawny," says Richard Hofman, the Westminster coach. As a young major leaguer, Rodriguez said that he'd like to be a civics teacher or a basketball coach. Between being benched at Columbus, Eddie Rodriguez's frank assessment of his big league chances, and a weak showing in that first year at Westminster, by the end of his sophomore season, summers off and a whistle on a lanyard were looking more likely than a career in professional baseball.

But when he reported to school for his junior year, he had transformed himself in the weight room, according to Coach Hofman. He had packed on twenty-five pounds of muscle. By his senior season, he had gained ten more pounds, and at six-foot-three and nearly two hundred pounds, he had become the tightly coiled combination of power and speed that had one college scout saying, "If you were to sit down in front of a computer and say, 'How would I construct the perfect shortstop?' you'd put all the data in and then you would see Alex Rodriguez."

His batting statistics boomed with the growth spurt. In his senior year, Rodriguez batted an otherworldly .505, almost doubling his sophomore mark of .270. In a high schooler's brief season, he popped nine homers and stole thirty-five bases in thirty-five tries. Rodriguez was also Westminster's starting quarterback, and later said it was pressure from football—not baseball—that drove him to bulk up in order to be able to bench press three hundred pounds.

Jealousy and innuendo about steroids trailed Westminster in its baseball games around the state, especially amid speculation that Rodriguez would rake in a million dollars or more in a signing bonus.

When Westminster demolished Florida Bible Christian School on its way to a state berth in 1992, Rodriguez's junior season, the school had its own ties to performance-enhancing substances. But its dugout had nothing but suspicion and disdain for Rodriguez. "Everybody knew who he was," says Florida Bible pitcher Anthony Cancio Bello of Rodriguez. "He was a showboat even back then. It felt like a man playing against kids. We were all thinking: *There's something wrong here.*"

Florida Bible outfielder Roddy Barnes wasn't as much suspicious as inspired. "He was a shrimp his sophomore year," says Barnes. "His junior year you saw the major changes. From one year to the next you saw his body composition change, and he went from an average player to an elite player. He became the perfect sculpture. He was a five-tool player; he knew the only thing holding him back was his stature, and he fixed that."

Barnes says that Rodriguez was one of those players whose sudden transformation made him consider procuring human growth hormone—which even in the early '90s Barnes says was popular among ballplayers his age. "Otherwise you watch these kids get these big contracts, and you kick yourself in the ass, like: 'Damn, I should have used HGH,'" says Barnes. (Now a fire captain, he stopped short of saying whether he did use HGH as a young ballplayer: "You can't ask, because I work for the fire service.")

In *A-Rod*, Roberts made the case that her subject's high school growth spurt was due to steroid use. She implicated a man named Steve Caruso, an amateur baseball coach, softball player, and greyhound racer who got loads of canine steroids on the cheap. Roberts cited "baseball sources in Miami" who claimed that Caruso generously doled out steroids to young ballplayers, including Rodriguez.

Roberts quoted an associate of Caruso's named Steve Ludt recalling that the young ballplayer and the steroid source were so close that he overheard a phone conversation in which Rodriguez invited Caruso to Seattle for his first game there.

Roberts also cited anonymous sources who said that Rodriguez juiced in high school with the knowledge of Coach Hofman. The coach, in an interview for this book, called Roberts's reporting "fraudulent" and said Roberts was "an obscure writer trying to make a name for herself by trumping up claims and all this dirt . . . I have no knowledge, recollection, or even suspicions at that time with any of my athletes, to be honest with you. Dead point, dead issue, beating a dead horse." (Roberts was criticized by at least one of her own colleagues for her reliance on anonymous sourcing, with *New York Times* columnist Murray Chass calling the book an "abomination.") A-Rod's own path to muscular domination may remain murky, but what's undeniable is that at the time he was crushing his way to a record signing bonus, steroids in South Florida high schools were as commonplace as third-period calculus.

Florida officials knew, or should have known, since at least the late 1980s that steroids and other performance-enhancing drugs were a problem for high schoolers. In 1986, South Plantation High's student newspaper, *Sword and Shield*, reported that 65 percent of students polled knew another kid on steroids. The teenage journalists' research was, remarkably, the only study on the subject. But there were plenty of other warnings: A couple of years later, Frank Pelegri, a wrestling coach at Southwest High School—home to Dade County's top grappling team—was fired after being accused of distributing steroids to the wrestlers.

Almost immediately, Pelegri—who admitted only that wrestlers had done steroids with his knowledge—found a new job. He was hired by athletic director Hofman to coach Westminster's wrestling team, and is currently the coach at South Florida's Monsignor Edward Pace High.

Then there was, in the early 1990s, a spate of high school weight lifters attacking one another at meets. School officials discovered the impetus for the rage. "We had several instances where kids on steroids went absolutely crazy," says Don Reynolds, who spent seven years as a district director and vice president of the Florida High School Athletic Association (FHSAA), the state governing body.

Reynolds and other FHSAA officials discovered that students were commonly having steroids delivered by mail through companies that advertised in the backs of weight-lifting magazines. "Steroid use in the state of Florida was rampant," says Don Reynolds. "I bet you there wasn't a school in Florida that didn't have some of that going on."

Though Reynolds and the FHSAA pushed for Florida to become the first state to drug-test student athletes, that plan was met with predictable opposition. "I think it's a bunch of crap, personally," grumbled an Immokalee football coach. The American Civil Liberties Union wasn't pleased with the idea of teenagers being coerced to pee in cups. And even Reynolds admits that the cost of testing a significant sample of students would have been prohibitive.

"There was so much opposition to it," says Reynolds, and enforcing a piss test—as Olympic and Major League Baseball officials could tell him—has never been a simple matter. He knew from experience that the parents of student athletes tended to battle every punishment. The testing idea died.

Florida-based Dr. William Nathaniel Taylor Jr., then one of the country's leading pioneers in steroid and HGH research, said that after writing a book on the science of steroids he was besieged by calls from parents who "wanted to make their son or daughter a blue chipper in athletics" and were looking for PED connections or prescriptions.

The pressure on kids to succeed in sports was overwhelming, and the laws against HGH in particular were toothless. In that regard, little has changed since the 1980s and '90s. Despite all the suspicion and scrutiny cast on a teenage Alex Rodriguez, there likely never will be proof that he did steroids in high school. (There's more than enough to go around in his later years, though.) But perhaps the most notable aspect of Rodriguez's Westminster years—and most relevant to Tony Bosch's empire to come— isn't that he may have doped back then, but that he wouldn't have been much of an abnormality if he had. He wasn't the first or last high school athlete to face extreme athletic pressure in a state where adults looked the other way from teenage steroid use.

Back in 1985, Taylor described to a newspaper reporter what thirty years later might be described as the Bosch business model. "If I wanted to be not as ethical," Taylor mused, "I could open up a sports medicine clinic on US 41 and inject every kid with steroids. I'd become a millionaire by the end of the year."

O n May 13, 1993, two days after Alex Rodriguez botched his last game as a high schooler, it was a gorgeous spring Friday afternoon a thousand miles up the East Coast. For the first time all year, people had broken out their short sleeves in Washington Heights, Rodriguez's crime-scarred neighborhood of birth.

To New York Police Department detective Hugh Sinclair, it was a lovely day for a drug bust. Undercover in the filthy clothing of an addict with his pockets stuffed with NYPD drug-buy money, Sinclair strolled down a block crowded with multiple drug operations and picked his targets.

Two coke dealers were posted outside a building lobby: a kid in a Timberland jacket and matching hat and his apparent "boss man," a pudgy Hispanic man with a mustache. After some haggling—Sinclair insisted he didn't want to pay "white-boy prices"—the detective gave them $35 and in return the cop pocketed two tinfoil packets of cocaine.

Sinclair and his partners staged hundreds of these busts, many for higher stakes. But this piddling drug sting had lasting effects in Alex Rodriguez's steroid saga.

Police vehicles skidded around the corner. Eighteen-year-old Lincoln Daniel Persaud, ostentatious in his Timberland outfit, was arrested immediately. After a search, a uniformed officer stepped forward with a suspect matching Boss Man's description.

The orphaned teenager who had grown up with Rodriguez in a cramped apartment a few blocks away, and then in the DR and in Miami, was now a squat, pudgy man with a wispy mustache and a thicket of hair landing somewhere between a Jheri curl and a mullet.

Thrown in the back of a police van, Boss Man screamed in Spanish that there had been a mistake, that they had the wrong guy.

*   *   *

"Sucart, Yuri. S-U-C-A-R-T. Bronx County."

He wore a starched shirt and a tie, and an interpreter translated from Spanish as he testified in his own defense at trial eighteen months after the arrest.

While Rodriguez gained national acclaim as a high school ballplayer, Yuri Sucart had been quietly building his own anonymous adult life. He had attended Santo Domingo's Universidad Mundial, and until 1986 worked as an assistant engineer for the Dominican water utility. For two years after that, he had been a blacksmith in Miami before moving to New York City.

He had married a beautician named Carmen. Along with her son from a previous marriage, they rented a small apartment in the Bronx. Carmen was pregnant with their first kid together. Despite not having a taxi medallion or even a valid driver's license, Sucart was a gypsy cab driver, shuttling passengers in his 1986 Chevy Caprice Classic. Between that and the few bucks they made exporting beauty supply products to the Dominican, where Carmen owned a salon, Sucart said they earned $300 a week.

It wasn't the lifestyle of a boss man. And as he leaned into the microphone, Sucart maintained his innocence, claiming that he had only been using a phone bank and hanging out at a nearby bodega when the cops swept him up. "What the police are saying is not true," he repeated several times.

The case did appear troubled. Sucart had no drugs and $21 on him when he was arrested, none of the bills NYPD-issued. Though Persaud implicated Sucart when he pleaded guilty to his own part of the drug sale, receiving probation, he then recanted on the witness stand. He said he had never met Sucart, and in fact had warned an officer at the arrest scene that he was not the right guy.

Asked why he had initially lied, Persaud said it was on his attorney's advice: "I was nervous then, and today I am nervous."

But the prosecutor made the case that Persaud was recanting out of fear, having recently burst into his office referring to Sucart as a "heavy player" and declaring that he would rather risk a perjury charge than "be found dead after testifying against Yuri." And Detective Sinclair testified that he was "one-hundred-percent sure" Sucart was the other dealer.

Eleven jurors believed Sucart. But one thought he was guilty. With the hung jury resulting in a mistrial, Sucart—previously free on bond—was dispatched to Rikers Island, New York City's notoriously crowded and violent jail, to await the next trial.

By March 1996, Sucart had spent several months in jail and been in legal limbo for nearly three years. He and Carmen now had two kids of their own, plus Carmen's son Alex, all of whom had moved back to the DR while Sucart was incarcerated.

And since Sucart's arrest, Alex Rodriguez had gone from high schooler to major leaguer. Sucart's little cousin had a seven-digit bank balance and 196 at-bats for the Seattle Mariners. It was spring training before the 1996 season in which Rodriguez was penciled in as the starting shortstop. If Sucart could shake himself of this legal saga, he had a standing offer to be Rodriguez's driver, his gofer, his laundry boy, his chef.

Sucart finally cried *tio*, pleading guilty to felony criminal sale of a controlled substance. Officially a convicted felon, he was sentenced to time already served, paid a $150 fine, and avoided deportation.

If he was actually guilty, Sucart was one bad boss man indeed. Twenty years later, his underling is still covering for him. Persaud, who still lives in Washington Heights, maintains that Sucart was only guilty of looking a lot like his real boss man, who has since died. "There was one guy that found it all real funny: my boss," says Persaud. "When I told him, 'You didn't get arrested because some other fat guy got arrested,' he was laughing . . . RIP."

B y 1996, primed for a major league breakout, Rodriguez had gotten his first taste of the financial fortune to come and made his first few enemies in the process.

As had been expected, Rodriguez was drafted first overall by the Seattle Mariners. Because most draftees have little leverage, signing with the MLB team that drafted them is usually a relatively simple process.

But Rodriguez's agent was Scott Boras, the Jack LaLanne of juicing every last drop of liquidity from major league team owners. Boras wielded Rodriguez's commitment to UM as a threat. If he didn't get the contract they wanted, the Mariners would lose their number one pick to dorm rooms, textbooks, and a Miami Hurricanes college baseball jersey.

Within months of Rodriguez's last game at Westminster, Boras guided the barely eighteen-year-old as he played financial hardball like a jaded veteran. Even before graduating high school, Rodriguez—telling a beat reporter that he wanted to play for the hometown Florida Marlins—asked the Mariners not to draft him. He had then refused to play for Team USA because it would theoretically cost him $500,000 in future baseball card endorsements. And with a deadline looming for Rodriguez to sign with the club or live up to his bluff and report to UM, Boras refused to budge from a signing bonus and contract demand that was outlandish at the time: $2.5 million.

It took Rodriguez temporarily dropping Boras—and recruiting local politician and family friend Joe Arriola—to keep a future with the Mariners from disintegrating. Arriola salvaged a contract worth roughly $1.3 million. Boras was furious.

Rodriguez's use of UM as leverage—without any intention of enrolling there—was brazenly transparent. Not that school brass minded. Though he never took a class at UM, Rodriguez harbored a relationship with the university for more than two decades. It became a mutually sycophantic marriage—and an extremely lucrative one for UM—that later caused headaches for the school.

After his release from Rikers, Sucart joined Rodriguez in Seattle. His occupation was personal assistant to the star. Other times, he was referred to as a personal trainer. In reality, says Seattle associate of Yuri Sucart's Wilhelm Ansdale Henricus, "He was pretty much a glorified butler. He was a go-to guy."

Rodriguez's high school coach Hofman traveled with his wife to Seattle on Rodriguez's invitation to witness his former star player's new big league lifestyle firsthand. He saw how Yuri played a docile Alfred to Rodriguez's Bruce Wayne. "He's a hardworking guy. He did everything for him, in terms of taking care of the mundane tasks that stars don't do," Hofman says of Sucart. "Yuri was somebody who takes care of all your business, drives you there, picks up your laundry, and takes care of things when you don't have time yourself."

The cousins lived together in a condo in downtown Seattle, right on the Puget Sound. A *Sporting News* reporter wrote that it was furnished in "upper-end early yuppie." The apartment looked like something Gordon Gekko, *Wall Street*'s antihero, might have lived in after banking his first million: leather couch, big stereo, big-screen television, golf clubs leaning against the wall, a batting trophy propped up against a window, a cigar humidor on the floor, an unrolled putting green with a sideways beer glass for a hole.

These digs—this life—were a far cry from the last addresses for both the cousins: a jail on Rikers Island for Sucart and a sibling-crowded suburban Miami home for Rodriguez. A profile from the era included a depiction of Rodriguez nearly hyperventilating after an encounter with sick kids at the Seattle Children's Hospital. "I feel very uncomfortable doing that," Rodriguez said afterward. "I usually let somebody from my foundation, Grand Slam for Kids, handle that sort of thing."

Rodriguez's girlfriend—and soon-to-be wife—Cynthia Scurtis was a fellow fitness enthusiast who he had met at a Miami gym. She remained in Florida, and Sucart's wife and kids also stayed home. In Seattle, Sucart reinvented himself.

He met a group of flashy businessmen at the Kingdome during a Mariners game. They became fast friends, throwing cash around in Belltown, Seattle's trendiest neighborhood. They were regulars at Assaggio, a posh Italian restaurant, and Axis, where they sucked down martinis and chorizo oysters. "Yuri and them would go out dining and drinking every night of the week," says Henricus, a member of the group of friends. Rodriguez joined them once a week or so for dinner, drinks, and a cigar.

Sucart attempted to parlay this friendship with investors into a business opportunity. Along with four of the buddies—Tim Attleson, Mario Pieris, Theodore George Bryant, and Nate Kreiter—Sucart founded Senok Management Group LLC, an "agency for professional athlete representation," according to state filings.

The goal was to use Sucart's connections in the Dominican Republic—and, inevitably, A-Rod's link—as a lure to bring ballplayers to the United States.

The operation quietly flopped with few clients. Henricus says he had stayed away from any enterprise with Sucart as the figurehead. "He seemed to be a jovial, good-natured cuddly bear kind of person," says Henricus. "He didn't seem—in all respect—really intelligent or smart to me. He seemed just to be a follower."

Rodriguez's cousin—round-bellied, easygoing, and always in the background—became ubiquitous in major league clubhouses where Rodriguez traveled. Sucart flew to cities a day ahead of his cousin, setting up hotels, since Rodriguez rarely stayed with the team, and toting baseball equipment. Although Rodriguez says he never did steroids during his Seattle tenure, later in the star's career there is no denying that another of Sucart's primary duties was facilitating Rodriguez's doping.

Rodriguez's seasons in Seattle justified those slobbering scouts who had stalked him in high school. In 1996, his first full season with the Mariners, Rodriguez hit thirty-six home runs, drove in 123 runs, and—at just barely twenty-one years old—won the American League batting title with a .358 average. Though he had started the season batting ninth, by the end of the year he was anchoring a dynamic lineup also featuring Ken Griffey Jr., the longtime Mariners superstar outfielder.

Rodriguez's welcome to the bigs was also near the apex of the first Steroid Era. In 1996, a whopping sixteen sluggers hit forty home runs, and Mark McGwire led them all with fifty-two, a warm-up act for the next two seasons. Even then, the first overture toward PED testing in the major leagues was still seven years away.

On the topic of notorious steroid users: In the winters, the former Miami kid Jose Canseco took Rodriguez, eleven years his junior, under his wing. In the latter half of the 1990s, when Canseco says he first started hanging out with Rodriguez, he was bouncing between teams as an aging hired gun with a well-known reputation for juicing and trouble. He had been arrested many times, including for ramming his wife's BMW with his Porsche, and he soon tested positive in jail for steroids.

And Canseco claimed to have dated Madonna a couple of years earlier, just as Rodriguez reportedly went on to do.

In a strange way, in Canseco's companionship Rodriguez was looking—quite literally—for trouble. Despite steroid rumors that had followed him since high school, Rodriguez's public image was that of the corporate golden boy. It was a reputation that he later admitted rankled him and that he spent the next couple of decades thoroughly pulverizing. "He's Mr. Clean," Seattle teammate David Segui, himself later revealed in the Mitchell Report as one of the league's more notorious dopers, said of Rodriguez at the time. "He doesn't like to hear that, but he is. He likes everybody in here to think he's some kind of thug from Miami, but he's as milk-and-cookies as it gets."

Canseco gave him a guided tour of the dark side. They drove in Canseco's Porsche to his twenty-two-thousand-square-foot mansion in Fort Lauderdale, surrounded by acres of poplar trees.

They worked out in Canseco's home gym. "I saw a lot of me in him," Canseco says now. "I told him, 'Alex, you're going to be the next forty/forty guy.' I knew he was going to become the best baseball player in the world. I even told his mom that. Alex didn't believe me."

But Rodriguez certainly took the prophecy—that he could join the club of players who'd hit forty homers and stolen forty bases, a feat then accomplished only by Canseco and Barry Bonds—to heart. He bought a yellow Lab puppy with the kennel club name of "A-Rod's 40-40 of Devonshire."

The relationship between the Miami-bred stars quickly soured. The first time Rodriguez saw Canseco's wife, Jessica, the former Bash Brother says, the twentysomething kid remarked: "That was the most beautiful woman I've ever seen."

"I realized he wasn't a guy to be trusted after that," says Canseco.

In his second book, *Vindicated*—in which one chapter ends with a note to A-Rod: "I hate your fucking guts"—Canseco claims that Rodriguez attempted to have an affair with Jessica, whom he had since divorced.

Canseco made allegations more pertinent than infidelity in *Vindicated*. He claimed that "in the latter half of the 1990s," Rodriguez asked Canseco for a steroid connect. After Rodriguez's monster rookie season, he had established the sky-high expectations that both drove his superstar status and burdened his psyche for years. In 1997, his production dipped. He still batted .300 with twenty-three home runs, eighty-four runs batted in, and one hundred runs scored. He started the All-Star Game at shortstop, a particularly special milestone because of who had hogged that honor for the previous thirteen years: his boyhood idol Cal Ripken Jr.

Rodriguez compared the thrill of taking batting practice with Ripken to that of "a teenage girl going out to dinner with Madonna"—adulation of the Material Girl being the common thread running through Rodriguez's career. It was the high point of what would have been a fantastic year for any other twenty-two-year-old, but for the best young player alive in the midst of the steroid era, the season was a letdown.

In his book, Canseco wrote that he introduced Rodriguez to a Miami physical trainer nicknamed "Max," who was also a steroids provider. If Rodriguez hadn't already been doping, Canseco says in no uncertain terms that he started then.

"I saw the changes in his body in a short time," Canseco wrote. "Hell, if you ask me, I did everything but inject the guy myself."

Joseph Dion, a trainer in Pinecrest, Florida, was ultimately identified by *Sports Illustrated* as "Max." In an interview with one of the authors of this book, Dion confirmed that he trained Rodriguez but vehemently denied having anything to do with steroids. "I hear he wrote a whole bunch of lies," Dion said of Canseco. "My life is so clean I don't even take vitamins."

After the accusation, Dion said, much of his professional client base dried up. He still trained anonymous wealthy folk and their kids, including soccer and baseball players from the Miami-area Gulliver private school.

For his own part, Rodriguez told reporters that he had worked out with Dion but denied the steroid accusations and said that he had actually been introduced to the trainer by his old Boys & Girls Club mentor, Eddie Rodriguez.

Whether or not it was with the chemical assistance of "Max," Rodriguez justified both his dog's name and Canseco's psychic abilities the next year, slamming forty-two home runs and swiping forty-six bases. He hit forty home runs the next two seasons as well. By the end of the 2000 season—with a $10 million Mariners contract expiring—Rodriguez was at peak marketability. Griffey Jr. had departed via free agency the year before. In 2000, Rodriguez had picked up the slack, leading the team to ninety-one wins and the American League Championship Series, which the Mariners lost in six games to the New York Yankees. Rodriguez's agent, Boras, believed he had grown too big for small-market, mild-mannered Seattle.

He was inarguably the best-hitting shortstop in history. And according to a seventy-three-page gold-embossed book that Boras distributed to major league suitors, pitting his stats against the all-time elites of the game, Rodriguez was essentially Babe Ruth with defined pectoral muscles.

Winning possession of this human heirloom, then, was Tom Hicks, the owner of the cash-rich Texas Rangers, who was eager to make a splash with a monster signing. He certainly did that, signing Rodriguez to a ten-year, $252-million contract, exactly twice as lucrative as NBA superstar Kevin Garnett's contract with the Minnesota Timberwolves, which had previously been the biggest deal in pro sports.

In Dallas—a city that likes oversize things—Rodriguez became more of a pure slugger. As the sports world eventually learned, it was a metamorphosis aided by Rodriguez's use of anabolic steroids. Years later, that Rangers squad was seen as Team Zero in baseball's raging PEDs epidemic. Rodriguez's teammates included Ivan Rodriguez, whom Jose Canseco linked to steroids; Juan Gonzalez, who was named in the Mitchell Report; and old Boys & Girls Club chum Rafael Palmeiro, who later failed a steroid test.

Rodriguez was no longer the speedster he had been in Seattle, his stolen-base numbers dropping as far as the single digits. But he broke the fifty-homer mark in 2001, his first season with the Rangers, and in 2002 led the American League with fifty-seven homers. Only seven players had ever hit more in a single season, with three of them—Bonds, McGwire, and Sammy Sosa—representing the holy trinity of the Steroid Era.

In 2003, Rodriguez led the league in homers for the third consecutive time, hitting forty-seven. He also led the league in runs and slugging percentage and won a Gold Glove Award as the league's best-fielding shortstop. He also won his first MVP award that season. At twenty-seven years old, he became the youngest player in history to hit three hundred home runs, gestating in earnest the speculation that he would one day be on the hunt for the all-time home run crown.

As far as individual accomplishments go, that season was the pinnacle of Rodriguez's career. It was also, unknown to most everybody outside of top Players Association offices, the genesis of his later public outing as a steroid user.

For Rodriguez's entire career up this point, MLB had no drug-testing policy in place. The first time the league ran essentially a blind urine poll to determine how widespread doping was, Rodriguez was one of the infamous 104 players who, as it was later revealed by *Sports Illustrated*, failed.

The plan for that initial sampling was that it would be anonymous and no player would be punished for failing: The testing was only to gauge whether more than 5 percent of MLB players would test positive, which they did, triggering an actual drug program for the league.

Rodriguez failed the test in 2003 despite the fact that players knew the sampling was coming. Rodriguez tested positive for Primobolan, a steroid, and testosterone. The test was kept secret, and it was six years until Rodriguez himself told of the key role his cousin Yuri Sucart played in his daily routine besides pairing his socks.

The revelations to come were a result of the union failing to destroy the tests as advertised, and law-enforcement raids of drug-testing labs in 2004. But the fallout came later in Rodriguez's career, and later in this book.

In 2003, in the eyes of baseball fans, Rodriguez was somewhat soulless— a grating corporate shill following the biggest dollars to any team—but he wasn't yet a cheater. That was a reputation he didn't have until he landed on the world's biggest media stage.

Despite Rodriguez's gaudy personal performance, the Rangers floundered in last place. Along with Rodriguez, Hicks had also thrown $65 million at Korean pitcher Chan Ho Park, who had enjoyed a few good seasons with the Los Angeles Dodgers. Park was regularly battered in slugger-friendly Ballpark in Arlington, and after he succumbed to multiple injuries, his and Rodriguez's deals were ultimately be considered two of the worst free-agent signings in baseball history.

Rodriguez played all but one game in three seasons with Texas, but it wasn't enough to muscle the Rangers to the playoffs even once. He may have been the LeBron James of his sport—skipping college and jumping straight to nine-figure playing and Nike contracts—but unlike in basketball, it takes more than one transcendent superstar to carry a baseball team.

The $252-million-dollar deal is often pointed to as the moment when Rodriguez soured. He was under pressure to justify an unfathomable contract. Rodriguez became AROD Corporation, the California-based entity that paid Sucart's salary. In December 2003, Rodriguez and partners founded his Florida real estate development company, Newport Property Ventures Ltd. No longer just a baseball player, Rodriguez was a budding CEO. And some of the decisions he made in the years to come—including his treatment of Sucart—appeared cold-blooded.

After the 2003 season, the Rangers and Rodriguez finally threw in the towel on their fruitless marriage. Texas nearly dealt him to the Boston Red Sox for Manny Ramirez, the Washington Heights–raised slugger with a $20 million–plus salary and an unmatched reputation for mystifying antics. The Red Sox were reeling from a devastating loss in the American League Championship Series, after Yankees third baseman Aaron Boone clobbered a Game Seven eleventh-inning walkoff home run to steal Boston's ticket to the World Series. Boston hadn't won a championship since 1918, the year before the team traded Babe Ruth to the Yankees, and the Red Sox front office was convinced they needed a revolutionary move. Relocating the best young shortstop in history to Fenway Park fit the bill.

In complicated negotiations among the Rangers, the Red Sox, and himself, Rodriguez and his agent, Boras, agreed to defer or reduce some of his guaranteed salary in order to make the deal happen. (This was not altruism. His deal would've been shortened, resulting in another shot at a monster contract, and dropping Rodriguez into sports' most famous rivalry almost certainly would have increased his marketability.)

But the Players Association, disagreeable to the precedent of the game's highest-paid player leaving cash on the table, blocked the trade. It was the first of several times Rodriguez felt stunted or betrayed by the union.

When Aaron Boone tore a knee ligament before the 2004 season, the AROD logo—trademarked in Seattle in 1996—must have shone in the Gotham sky. In infallible team captain, Derek Jeter, of course, the Yankees already had a shortstop, Rodriguez's lifelong fielding position.

But George Steinbrenner was still the boss of the Yanks. The demanding, ill-tempered owner was always unmuzzled and often spoke by throwing around gobs of baseball television profit.

One of the only teams in baseball capable of a nine-figure impulse buy, Steinbrenner's Yankees traded budding superstar Alfonso Soriano to Texas for Rodriguez. Jeter stayed at short, and Rodriguez became a full-time third baseman.

For Red Sox Nation, losing A-Rod to the hated Yankees thanks to the greed—and *conspiracy?*—of a millionaires' union felt like a horrible acid flashback to 1919. "The Curse of A-Rod" was marketed by a Boston attorney in 2004, for adornment on everything from rainwear to cloth baby bibs.

But what has transpired since—Rodriguez damning the Yankees with endless steroid controversy, an insurmountable salary, and, most important, weak postseason performances and a lack of fence-clearing dingers, while the Red Sox have broken their own curse and won three championships— should have Bostonians counting their blessings.

As had been the case in Texas, Rodriguez's first four years in the Bronx were marked by incredible solo statistics and disappointing team results. He won the second and third MVP awards of his career in 2005 and 2007.

That latter year was particularly a statistical juggernaut, one in which he hit fifty-four home runs—including his five hundredth, making him, at just barely thirty-two years old, the youngest ever to that mark—with 156 RBIs and 143 runs.

But what hasn't been reported until now is that Rodriguez's 2007 MVP season was also tainted with PEDs—albeit this time legally under the rules of Major League Baseball.

From his junior year of high school on, there had been suspicions—and ultimately in the case of his 2003 MVP season, proof—that Alex Rodriguez was using PEDs. But a transcript obtained by the authors of this book, revealing for the first time testimony from Rodriguez's confidential suspension appeal in fall 2013, suggests that he was using a powerful anabolic steroid when he was crowned the league's best hitter for the third time, in 2007.

Under the agreement between the league and the union, players can apply for what's called a "therapeutic use exemption" in order to use certain medical substances banned by MLB. A doctor appointed by both sides— called the independent program administrator (IPA)—reviews all applications, and if an exemption is granted, the player cannot be punished for using that substance. The exemption is good for one season.

Before the 2007 season, Rodriguez asked for permission to use testosterone, a substance long banned by baseball. The IPA was then Dr. Bryan W. Smith, a North Carolina physician. On February 16, 2007, two days before Rodriguez reported to spring training, Smith granted the exemption, allowing him to use testosterone without consequence all season long.

The exemption was revealed to these authors in a transcript of Rodriguez's grievance hearing more than six years later. MLB entered several exemptions applied for by Rodriguez in his Yankees tenure into evidence. During his testimony, MLB executive Rob Manfred called testosterone "the mother of all anabolics" and said that exemptions for the substance are "very rare," partly because "some people who have been involved in this field feel that with a young male, healthy young male, the most likely cause of low testosterone requiring this type of therapy would be prior steroid use."

In fact, the World Anti-Doping Agency's own therapeutic-use standards require stringent tests to prove low hormone levels aren't due to past PED use. That agency also requires a committee of three doctors to sign off on exemptions rather than baseball's single IPA.

Statistics requested two years later by Congressman John Tierney, in the wake of a government probe into baseball's PED problem, reveal just how rare testosterone exemptions are. In 2007, of 1,354 players subject to testing, 111 players were granted a therapeutic-use exemption. Only two players, apparently including Rodriguez, received an exemption for "androgen deficiency medications," the category of medicine that would include a testosterone prescription. (The other exemptions that year involved baldness, hypertension, and—predominantly—attention deficit disorder. The alarmingly high number of exemptions for the latter was Congressman Tierney's main concern. "I think it begs a question: Are people using this as a loophole or an end run around the law?" said Tierney then. "Are they taking these because they are perceived as a performance-enhancing drug, or do they have a legitimate medicinal purpose?")

While being secretly allowed to take testosterone, Rodriguez's 2007 regular season was one of the best of his career. He did not again top his slugging percentage of .645. But despite using "the mother of all anabolics," that kid who threw away his last game at Westminster seemed to persist in Rodriguez. His monster production tended to dissolve in the postseason, the only stage that truly matters in the Bronx.

Starting in 2005, he hit for an anemic average with little pop in October as the Yankees floundered through the first of three straight divisional series defeats. In 2006, during which he managed only one hit in fourteen postseason at-bats, manager Joe Torre had appeared to confirm his neurotic star's ineptitude by dropping him to an insulting eighth in the batting order. And in 2007, the MVP was suddenly mediocre again, batting .267 with one homer and six strikeouts in fifteen at-bats as the Yankees were quickly dispatched by the Cleveland Indians.

But Rodriguez still managed to, as the New York Times put it, "hijack" that year's postseason.

Under the New York City klieg lights, Rodriguez had been a gaffe and scandal machine. While running the bases, he had yelled, "Mine!" at a Blue Jays fielder, causing him to drop a fly ball, and had illegally karate-chopped Red Sox pitcher Bronson Arroyo's glove to avoid getting tagged out. ("I'll even cheat to win," Rodriguez once said, one of those statements regrettable in hindsight.) He was a married lothario, harassed by rival fans with cutout masks of Madonna after he was romantically linked to her, and labeled "Stray-Rod" by the New York Post when he was photographed leaving a Toronto strip club with a "mystery blonde."

He topped all of that befuddling and loathsome behavior when, during the eighth inning of the fourth game of the 2007 World Series, with the Red Sox about to sweep the Colorado Rockies for their second championship since being unable to snag A-Rod, Fox announcer Joe Buck suddenly broke away from the action. "There's big news brewing," Buck declared.

Rodriguez's elaborate playing contract included the clause that he could opt out of the final years of the deal following the 2007 season. For years, he had promised that he would not exercise that clause, and the Yankees had vowed they would not negotiate a new contract with him if he did. But in the height of a World Series spectacle that had nothing to do with Rodriguez, his agent, Scott Boras, fired off e-mails to reporters announcing that they would be opting out.

Rodriguez later famously posed for a magazine photo spread in which he kissed himself in the mirror. Here was the broadcast television equivalent. "For five minutes in the top of the eighth in Game Four, Fox's broadcast stopped being about the Red Sox and the Rockies and became the 'World Series Presents A-Rod,'" wrote *New York Times* columnist Richard Sandomir. "If he were charged for those minutes as if they were commercials, he'd have paid $4 million."

While the Red Sox were still popping champagne bottles, Yankees cochairman Hank Steinbrenner, son of ailing owner, George, suggested that Rodriguez's maneuver had severed his relationship with the team. "If the guy really doesn't want to be a Yankee," said Hank, "then we don't want him."

A saga of last-minute resuscitation began, starting with a phone call from one of the most revered Yankees in history. "I told him he had to take responsibility and make it right," closer Mariano Rivera later said. "He had to call them."

Rodriguez's camp maintains that he had told Boras he wanted to stay a Yankee, but that the agent went rogue with the World Series–timed optout. So Rodriguez distanced himself from Boras—but didn't fire him—and cobbled together a strange emergency negotiation crew spearheaded by a financial manager he knew from Miami. With his wife in tow, Rodriguez's mea culpa tour brought him to the house of Hank Steinbrenner's brother, Hal, where he apologized to the Steinbrenners; Yankees general manager, Brian Cashman; and team president, Randy Levine—and shoved the blame onto Boras's lap.

It was a frenetic pattern Rodriguez first displayed as a high schooler who had ostracized the Seattle Mariners, and later again displayed as an aging slugger who had gone to the trenches against his team, league, and union. Time and again, he followed the lead of hard-charging representatives making millions off of him, until he reached the precipice of no return. That's when he would suddenly appear to wake up and attempt to salvage his relationships, invariably with the assistance of some longtime confidante. It was a tightwire act nearly impossible to sustain.

But the opt-out saga—in which Jay Z and Warren Buffett were among Rodriguez's advisors—epitomized not only A-Rod but the Yankees as well. The team had sworn it wouldn't renegotiate. But Rodriguez was a stadium draw and perennial MVP candidate who was primed to assault baseball's career home run record, and George Steinbrenner was still the most free-spending owner in the sport.

Just six weeks after Rodriguez went kamikaze on the World Series, the Yankees inked him to a new ten-year deal breaking his own previous financial record, guaranteeing him $275 million to stay in pinstripes until 2017. In addition, the Yankees added $6-million-a-pop clauses for each all-time home run leader he passed, starting with Willie Mays at 660 and ending with newly crowned record holder Barry Bonds at 762. With Mark McGwire, Sosa, and Bonds, the Yankees were aware of the stadium sellouts that came with a home run–record chase.

The 2007 MVP season had been a banner year for Rodriguez and a major rationale for the record-breaking contract he received immediately afterward. It was also a season, we now know, in which he was permitted to use testosterone. But he wasn't done with exemptions that allowed him to boost his testosterone levels with substances banned to other players.

Before the 2008 season, in a development unreported until now, Rodriguez again sought permission to use banned substances. In January 2008, he requested two exemptions, as revealed by the transcripts obtained by these authors. Rodriguez wanted to use clomiphene citrate, a drug designed to increase fertility in women. Men who suffer from hypogonadism—that is, a dearth of testosterone—use it to block estrogen in their bodies. And it's popular with bodybuilders at the tail ends of steroid cycles because it can also stimulate the body to make more testosterone.

Rodriguez also requested permission to use human chorionic gonadotropin, a growth hormone known as hCG, popularly used for weight loss and as part of a steroid cycle.

HCG was banned in baseball, and clomiphene citrate was first banned the season that Rodriguez applied to use it. The program administrator, Dr. Bryan W. Smith, approved Rodriguez's use of clomiphene citrate in 2008. His use of hCG was denied, but according to the transcript of Manfred's arbitration testimony, that denial was "more of a recordkeeping thing than anything else." Rodriguez's physician communicated with Dr. Smith, and "in their back-and-forth the physician informed Dr. Smith that the player was no longer using the substance in question," Manfred testified.

With the permission to use clomiphene citrate, Rodriguez was once again one of the rare players able to take medicine designed to increase testosterone levels. In 2008, only three players were granted exemptions for hypogonadism. In fact, from the 2006 season through 2013, only seventeen exemptions—or just more than two per year—were granted for the stated reasons that could require a medical testosterone boost: androgen deficiencies and hypogonadism.

By 2008, Rodriguez had spent at least a significant portion of his career—including, at a minimum, two of this three MVP seasons—using anabolic steroids and other performance-enhancing drugs. He had shown a special affinity for synthetic testosterone. Those seasons at the top of the sport had made him by far the richest man in MLB, a league that at this time was finally coming to terms with its steroid problem. Rodriguez had a guaranteed contract until the age of forty-two.

The only wise thing to do would be to safely ride out that contract, while continuing to apply for dubious exemptions but staying on the right side of baseball law.

But Rodriguez wasn't the type for lucrative laurel-resting.

*   *   *

As A-Rod's star rocketed higher and he became more notorious, his tubby cousin tagged along in the shadows from Seattle to Texas to New York. Roger Ball has known Alex Rodriguez's family since Rodriguez was a Westminster phenom. Ball's family lived in the same Kendall development. Ball is good friends with Yuri Sucart, whom he calls "Shrek" due to his resemblance to the good-natured animated ogre.

Even as his cousin and employer was traded to the city where it had gone down, Sucart didn't talk about that cocaine-dealing conviction to his buddy Ball. "I knew that he got into some issues up there [in New York], but he never went into detail," says Ball.

Years after the trade, when Rodriguez thrust Sucart into the eye of a national news storm, the formerly anonymous relative had his image on the cover of New York tabloids and be the focus of a three-thousand-word ESPN.com story.

Still, no reporter learned of his conviction.

But that old secret kept Sucart paralyzed. Because of it he could never be an American citizen and was at least once stopped on his way into Miami from the Dominican Republic. He was nearly deported, saved only by an emergency injunction based partly on filings showing his employment by Rodriguez.

Sucart tried to get out from under his cousin's thumb. In 2006, Rodriguez paid him $57,499.92 a year. Sucart parlayed these earnings into the makings of his own miniature real estate empire. He took out more than a million dollars in mortgages, buying several properties in Miami-Dade County. Some were single-family homes, others several-unit rental properties in one of the roughest neighborhoods in the Miami area.

Unfortunately, he went on this buying spree right before the South Florida housing bubble burst as violently as any market in the United States.

Whether or not Sucart really had been a Washington Heights heavy player a decade earlier, he was now a convicted felon with a flimsy immigration status and no other job prospects. He was naturally subservient and harbored an ingrained devotion to family.

It all added up to put Sucart in no position to deny his favorite cousin if asked to do something illegal.

For Alex Rodriguez, $252 million couldn't buy you a better PED connection at the same time that a new, nearly undetectable drug began making its way into professional sports.

CHAPTER FOUR

Gurus of Growth Hormone

From the rutted, puddle-strewn road between Ladyville and Belize City, there's not much to distinguish the Central America Health Sciences University (CAHSU) from the call center next door. They occupy neighboring red-and-white structures erected in a gravel plot hewn from tropical vegetation. Inside one, twentysomething Belizeans endure tedious days answering customer service calls from America's pissed-off smartphone users. In the other, twentysomethings mostly from India and China listen to lectures on anatomy and macrobiology.

The tiny medical school is backwater and provincial enough for a melancholy Graham Greene novel. Yet for Tony Bosch, the cramped classrooms on the edge of an impoverished Central American capital were a gateway to the medical fraternity he'd desperately wanted into his whole life.

Here, he could finally nab the degree that had eluded him two decades before in Santo Domingo. More important, the Caribbean college could thrust Bosch into the hottest medical trend in America—a gray market boom in HGH, steroids, and testosterone packaged under the futurist title of "anti-aging medicine." That expanding billion-dollar industry was born in this same Belizean academy, where an antisteroid zealot–turned–chemical evangelist named Robert Goldman and his business partner, Ronald Klatz, nabbed their own quickie MDs.

Until Tony Bosch came along, that pair were far and away CAHSU's most famous alumni. Not that his alma mater is all that excited to claim Bosch nowadays.

"Just look at that bomber who is a [Harvard] graduate," says CAHSU's CEO, Dr. Murali Rudraraju, referring to the Unabomber. "He was the best of the best as a student, but at the end of the day, you graduate from X or Y university with your degree and then you decide whether to do something good or bad."

It took Bosch a decade to find an unorthodox path to medical school amid the ruins of his life in the early '90s. The softball glory Bosch found in Alabama hadn't solved his deeper issues. His Miami Meds may have been tops in the nation, but his personal finances were nearing a Ponzi-like collapse.

Bosch was hopeless at managing money and keeping promises. De Armas had worked to keep his charismatic partner in check, but he often didn't succeed. Business lunches often turned into $500 drunken celebrations, with no medical orders placed at the end. Orders that did come in were laden with pledges that could never be kept.

"Tony was a great marketer, but he'd say anything to close a deal and then leave us to worry about the details," De Armas says. "And he's the worst administrator I ever met. If he had one dollar to work with, he'd spend two dollars every single time."

The friends had brought in an investor named Tonie Lanza, who'd sold her own medical supply business for a profit a few years earlier. "They were really aggressive young kids, and from the outside, it looked like they were working really hard to be successful," Lanza says.

She took out a second mortgage and sank $65,000 into the business. Lanza quickly realized that staking cash on Tony Bosch's promises was about as safe an investment as Enron stock circa 2001. Lanza blamed the failures on Bosch's partying. "They were not good business people," she says. "Their interest was not focused on running a successful business."

De Armas agrees that Bosch was already spending too much time and money at nightclubs, even with a young daughter and a newborn son at home. "He liked to schmooze, to drink and party, and he could get away with it because it was part of his gig as the marketer," he says.

By 1991, Miami Med was belly-up. A judge ordered them to pay a bank for Lanza's mortgage, and she lost everything. "I never got a dime back," she says. "It was a bad, bad experience."

Bosch was out of business. The softball team was disbanded. De Armas packed up and moved to Sarasota, looking for new work. A few months later, Tiki filed for divorce. She was tired of her hard-partying, forever-broke husband. Their Coral Gables home went into foreclosure, with more than $184,000 still in arrears on the mortgage.

Bosch was adrift. His career, his young family, his reputation as a slow-pitch tycoon—everything had been shredded to bits within months.

He found work as a respiratory therapist and cannonballed into the social scene in Brickell and Key Biscayne, two of Miami's toniest waterfront neighborhoods. The work was dull, but the barhopping was anything but. Bosch had always been a boozer, and as a newly single, attractive guy from a Cuban clan infamous for his cousin Orlando's exploits, his life took a turn for the bacchanalian. Attend a party in the young Latino scene in Coconut Grove or Coral Gables in the mid-'90s, and there was a good chance Tony was there with a Habana Libre on the rocks and different gorgeous woman on his arm.

"Tony likes socializing. He has a lot of friends, and he's let a lot of people into his world that I'd never agree with," says Hernan Dominguez, his longtime friend and business partner. "Anyone can saddle up to Tony because he's a very social and open person."

Amid the partying, Bosch never lost his entrepreneurial spirit. He rarely went more than a year without a manic burst of energy and self-belief propelling him into some new scheme. Starting in 1990, he founded his own therapy business and a curiously spelled financial group, the Organization of Yung Investors. The next year came a new partnership with Roger De Armas called the Florida Latin Association of Medical Equipment Suppliers, followed shortly by a community center and a distribution company.

None lasted more than a year or two. Tony as always had boundless ideas and zero discipline, and lawsuits trailed like sharks behind his financially bleeding enterprises. A landlord sued in 1994. Another man sued over a contract a few years later. In 1996, Tiki filed the first of what would become a litany of unpaid child-support claims against her ex-husband, alleging that he'd racked up more than $17,000 in unpaid bills for their kids. A judge ordered Bosch to send his ex-wife $496 a week, as banks circled over the desiccated remains of his credit.

Yet around 1997, a surprising calm began to settle on Bosch's gale-tossed lifestyle. Through a friend of a friend, he met a stunning blonde a decade his junior named Aliette Baro. She was different from the arm candy he'd usually take partying. By the end of the year, they married. Within a few years, they started a family with another daughter and a son.

Tony also seemed to finally find some business stability. Shortly after their marriage, Aliette—who was free from Tony's troubled lawsuit history—cofounded a firm with his brother, Ashley, called DMG Health Care. With Bosch's reams of contacts in the local medical world and his brother's more stable business management, they set up shop in a strip mall north of the airport.

Bosch was suddenly living life in a bull market. He and Aliette moved into one-story home with a brick-paved driveway just a few blocks away from the famed Biltmore Hotel in Coral Gables. On weekends, they met at his parents' nearby house.

De Armas was happy for him and visited Bosch to catch up whenever he was back in town. If Tony wasn't exactly the phenomenal success story they'd always imagined back in the good old days of Miami Med, he could be doing a lot worse.

But anyone who thought Tony Bosch would settle for a wife, kids, and a modestly successful business didn't know his inner dialogue. Like his infamous cousin Orlando, he'd always been a writer and a dreamer, spending free hours plotting business moves and sketching plans in his notebooks. His tastes always exceeded his means, and his dreams always eclipsed his reality.

Tony wanted to live to be one hundred, to write bestselling books, and above all, to be famous and wealthy. Even as he settled into life with his beautiful young wife and two kids, Bosch was thinking bigger.

One day in early 2003, De Armas stopped by Bosch's house to say hello, and Aliette greeted him outside.

"He's not here," she told Bosch's old friend. "He won't be here for a while. He's moved to Belize."

N o drug craze truly hits its peak until a doomsaying Cassandra lights up news broadcasts with predictions about hordes of youth crumbling under its influence. It happened with steroids in the early '80s. As the drugs blazed from West Coast bodybuilders to suburban high schools, Robert Goldman gave synthetic testosterone its very own *Reefer Madness*.

Titled *Death in the Locker Room*, Goldman's book, published in 1984, is peppered with lurid accounts of freakish physical abnormalities and photos of grotesquely ripped women built like linebackers. Goldman's alarmist prose went beyond the already well-hyped fears about 'roid rage and shrinking testicles and drifted into the dubious, like an assertion that doped-up bodybuilders could sexually transmit cancer to their lovers.

The approach worked as well as any good horror story. Goldman sold thousands of copies and briefly became the curly-headed, handsome face of antisteroid advocacy, publishing two follow-ups, *Death in the Locker Room: Steroids, Cocaine, & Sports* and *Death in the Locker Room II: Drugs & Sports*. For reporters looking for a juicy quote about the evils of steroids, Goldman was the man happy to predict an epidemic of corpses with huge pecs.

Within a decade, though, this anabolic critic abruptly transformed into the guru of growth hormone, bringing an underground industry into the spotlight and creating a profitable safe haven for thousands of drug-slinging businessmen like Tony Bosch.

Born and raised in Brooklyn, Goldman made his name by setting obscure strength records. He once ripped through 13,500 straight sit-ups and then nabbed a *Guinness* book nod for finishing 321 handstand push-ups while clad only in a luridly striped Speedo. He turned that minor fame into a job at fitness celebrity Jack LaLanne's New York gym. By the early '80s, he watched uneasily as steroids swept through the bodybuilding scene, and his antidrug activism solidified after meeting Dr. John Ziegler, who had invented the first anabolic drugs three decades earlier. By the time Goldman encountered him, Ziegler had forsworn his creation and was tormented by how he'd changed the sports world. "I became his protégé student, studying under him in the last years of his life," Goldman says in an online documentary about his own life. He dedicated his book to the regretful innovator.

Six years after *Death in the Locker Room*, though, a new drug completely altered Goldman's thinking about chemical enhancement. The spark for his 180-degree career shift came in 1990 in Wisconsin, where an aging researcher named Dr. Daniel Rudman devised a study to test out a relatively new synthetic product called human growth hormone.

Scientists had known for decades that pituitary gland hormones were important to the body's development. By the early '50s, scientists in California and at Yale isolated hormones from cows and pigs, and in 1956, a pair of Berkeley researchers isolated HGH from a human pituitary. Within four years, they demonstrated that the drug helped children with severe growth deficiencies. Because the drug came from human cadavers, though, it was quite expensive. Through the mid-'80s, fewer than eight thousand kids in the United States got HGH treatments.

Thanks to bodybuilding guides like the mail-order *Underground Steroid Handbook*, the hormone's legend spread from stunted kids to ripped musclemen. HGH was tough to get, but serious bodybuilders—who would do anything to seek out new hormones to test their effects in the weight room—had already learned that combined with steroids, it sped muscle growth and reduced healing times.

But in 1985, growth hormone was in danger of disappearing from the market altogether. A federal study found that the cadaver extracts were linked to at least four cases of Creutzfeldt-Jakob Disease, a fatal condition similar to mad cow disease that left victims with spongy holes in their brains. HGH was quickly banned in the United States and Europe. The outbreak ended up being a blessing in disguise for the hormone's backers, though; the ban spurred Genentech's first synthetic HGH to the market-place by the end of the year. It didn't take bodybuilders long to pick up on the benefits; Jose Canseco, for instance, says he started using growth hor-mones in the '90s (adding the scientifically dubious claim in *Juiced* that HGH inflated his penis size right along with his batting average).

It was Dr. Rudman's study that launched HGH out of gyms and into messianic territory—whether the doctor liked it or not. The trigger was his fateful 1990 report for the *New England Journal of Medicine* called "Effect of human growth hormone in men over 60 years old." Among those effects, he found, were thickened skin, more lean body mass, and less fat. In some respects, he wrote, the men seemed twenty years younger. Rudman knew his study was limited and tried to warn off overzealous interpretations. "This is not a fountain of youth," he wrote. "We need to emphasize that the aging process is very complicated."

It was a useless caveat. True believers latched onto the positive aspects of the report, certain that Rudman had unlocked the key to immortality. Goldman met some of them himself in the early '90s, he later told ESPN, including an old couple who'd shot each other up with HGH and lost twenty-five pounds and a cadre of seventy-year-old bodybuilders who'd carved years off their sagging pecs. A decade after sounding the warning sirens over steroids, Goldman found himself buying wholesale into the new drug revolution.

Along with his business partner, a Des Moines–trained osteopath named Ronald Klatz, Goldman called a dozen other doctors to Chicago in 1992. The pair's genius was to recognize early HGH's marketing potential. The dozen doctors founded an organization to promote their cause: the American Academy of Anti-Aging Medicine (or A4M). But both Klatz and Goldman, who'd gotten his own osteopathic degree in Chicago, lacked one key ingredient: MDs to bolster their evangelism. Where could two guys in their midthirties find an institution willing to give them the degrees they wanted?

They found their answer in Belize, at the Central American Health Sciences University. In 1996, CAHSU was housed in downtown Belize City, a humid cacophony of rusted jeeps slamming through potholes and street vendors hawking rasta beads to cruise ship tourists. The Caribbean is littered with high-admittance, low-cost medical schools, a trend that started in the '70s with colleges in Dominica, Grenada, and Montserrat and grew to more than sixty schools around the region. But CAHSU was a brand-new player in the game; Goldman and Klatz were members of its inaugural class.

The same year the pair landed in Belize, another landmark HGH study was published. The 1996 report in the *Annals of Internal Medicine* described a test set up to re-create Dr. Rudman's project, with the goal of replicating his results. The findings were devastating to HGH's anti-aging boosters. Although subjects had increased lean muscle and decreased fat, their strength, endurance, and mental abilities were unchanged and most suffered side effects like puffy ankles and sore joints. Many were in so much pain they asked to stop the trial. "We cannot recommend it," wrote the report's author, Dr. Maxine Papadakis. "It's not the fountain of youth."

That study didn't seem to change A4M's advocacy for HGH. Goldman and Klatz returned to Chicago in 1998, clutching new medical degrees they'd acquired in only two years in Belize. They told a *Chicago Tribune* reporter that they'd transferred credits and also finished "quite a number of months" of clinical rotations in Mexico. In 2000, the state of Illinois took umbrage to that claim, fining them $5,000 each and ordering them to drop their MDs and to use "D.O." to reflect their osteopathic training, since CAHSU is not recognized in the United States.

On paper, the pair made for a curious tandem to tout the miracle effects of human growth hormone. But their timing couldn't have been better. With Rudman's 1990 paper as the Quranic source document for their new movement (and scant mention of the follow-up study six years later), A4M staged popular annual conventions in Orlando and Vegas, charging doctors

$3,400 for certification as anti-aging specialists. Their slogan didn't beat around the bush: "Aging is not inevitable! The war on aging has begun!"

A4M's founders stress that their advocacy goes beyond just testosterone and hormone therapy and includes healthy eating and exercise. But it wasn't presentations about vegetables that were filling A4M's coffers with millions in dues. The crowds came to hear about new wonder drugs and to get tips on how to stay on the right side of the blurry gray line between highly profitable anti-aging clinic and illegal drug dealer.

The FDA has made its feelings clear on HGH. The feds have approved the drugs for just a handful of rare conditions, including growth deficiencies and short bowel syndrome, which by one measure less than forty-five thousand people in the whole nation suffer from. All other uses, including for performance enhancement among athletes, are banned. The simple fact, regulators say, is that few long-term studies have been done on just what HGH does to the human body. Some research suggests it contributes to heart disease and diabetes, while others link it to problems including carpal tunnel syndrome. Recent studies into testosterone, meanwhile, have demonstrated such a clear link between the drug and deadly heart attacks and strokes that the FDA ordered a full review in early 2014.

The feds' stance hasn't discouraged A4M's adherents. They found a simple loophole: adult hormone deficiency syndrome, a real syndrome in which adults lack normal levels of hormones like testosterone. Across the nation, "wellness" and "anti-aging" clinics sprouted up by the hundreds with the same basic operating model: diagnosing virtually anyone who walks in the door with a hormone deficiency and then selling them testosterone or HGH for up to $12,000 a month.

Critics say A4M has grossly inflated the disease to sell an expensive drug. "From my perspective, they've been trying to go around the regulations by claiming someone has this deficiency," says Dr. Peter Rost, a former Pfizer vice president who became a whistle-blower over the company's deceptive business practices, including for its bestselling HGH product, Genotropin.

Deceptive or not, it was an ingenious solution. Customers were happy to get their drugs. Doctors were happy with their new profit drivers. Drug companies were happy for a new niche market, with HGH pulling in $1.4 billion by 2011 and even outselling better-known antidepressants like Zoloft. The FDA, if not thrilled, could easily turn a blind eye. Unlike other gray-market meds like Oxycodone, HGH and testosterone didn't leave zombie-fied addicts robbing liquor stores and dropping dead in alleyways.

"Adult growth hormone deficiency syndrome is very rare," adds Dr. Thomas Perls, a researcher at Boston University who studies people who live past one hundred years old. "Yet there are huge profits being made by pharmaceutical companies. The growth of those profits makes absolutely no sense in terms of any growth in the increased prevalence of these conditions."

As in any drug culture, the new anti-aging boom did spawn its legion of oddball casualties. One enthusiastic early adopter was a handsome ex-cowboy from Arizona named Howard Turley. After reading Rudman's 1990 study, the fifty-nine-year-old found an illicit HGH supplier in Mexico and started shooting himself up daily. As he told Klatz for his 1997 book, *Stopping the Clock*, he found that the drug improved everything from his sex drive to his vision.

Like many of the sci-fi dreamers drawn to the promises of anti-aging, Turley wasn't content to stop with modest self-improvement. By the late '90s, he'd changed his name to "Lazarus Long," after an immortal character in a Robert Heinlein novel, and opened his own clinic in Cancun to peddle HGH. Then he cooked up a scheme for a nation called New Utopia, which he planned to erect on concrete pilings drilled into a shallow reef a few hundred miles offshore from the Cayman Islands. His manmade islands would "out-Cayman the Caymans" as a tax haven, he told a British reporter, and, with him ruling as Prince Long, would offer a regulation-free base for life extensionists.

Long's dreams ended when the SEC ordered him in 1999 to stop selling a $350 billion bond for his new nation, and daily HGH injections or not, his plans for Heinlein-esque immortality didn't work out either. He died in a Florida nursing home in 2012.

Still, plenty of more levelheaded businessmen recognized Klatz and Goldman's innovation for what it was: a fantastic profit driver. As one promotional magazine promised, a single anti-aging patient could "bring $4,000 to $20,000 in annual gross revenue."

As A4M grew, Florida became the fertile breeding ground for its age-conquering crusade. The state had always prided itself on a Wild West lack of regulation, particularly in its medical market. As a playground for wealthy retirees, it's full of customers willing to take a needle of HGH with their weekend Botox. By the end of the 2000s, more than 540 anti-aging and wellness clinics had sprouted up. The Sunshine State encumbered those businesses with virtually no rules. They weren't required to register with the Department of Health, and since most refused insurance money, the state's Agency for Health Care Administration wouldn't inspect them. Anyone could own one, and the clinics didn't even have to list a medical director.

As a painful round of federal investigations would soon reveal, that combination wasn't just a recipe for felons and questionable characters to make thousands selling untested drugs—it also created a perfect cover story for a shadow industry procuring PEDs for professional athletes.

B elize is just an hour and a half by air from Miami across the Gulf of Mexico, but its capital city feels light-years from the palm-lined boulevards of Coral Gables.

Anyone who enrolls at CAHSU expecting a tropical respite is in for a shock. Students, who pay between $4,000 to $6,000 for a degree, live in pastel-painted concrete hovels in a semipaved neighborhood called Los Lagos, where chickens run free between razor-wire fences. The school occupies two aging buildings guarded by chained-up dogs. Inside the low-ceilinged rooms, elementary school–style desks are crammed beneath ancient AC units blasting tepid air. In the anatomy lab, human dissections are possible only when police stumble across a corpse in the jungle and bring it in for an autopsy.

"They brought that Canadian fellow in here a couple weeks ago," says Dr. Rudraraju during a visit by an author of this book, referring to an Edmonton missionary whose throat had been slashed by unknown assailants at his nearby house on Christmas Day. "The students all got to watch that procedure in person."

For Tony Bosch, the conditions couldn't have been much more comfortable than his previous foray into medical school in the Dominican Republic. But this time, he stuck it out, for a year at least. In March 2003, Aliette and their two kids moved to the Central American capital and lived with him as he plugged through classes. Although the school won't discuss his time there, citing "student confidentiality," officials say he did complete his coursework. "We have very strict policies on attendance and exams here," Dr. Rudraraju says. "It's eighty percent minimum attendance or else you're out."

After about a year of basic courses, Bosch and his young family moved to El Paso in 2004. As in Miami, before his med school foray, Bosch looked poised to set up shop as a respectable businessman.

His mother, Stella, bought the family a $400,000 two-story house with a garage in the dry hills northeast of downtown, while Aliette's parents helped her open Cafe Mambo, a Cuban restaurant in a nearby strip mall. Tony picked the entrée recipes for the menu.

While his family sold *ropa vieja* and mojitos, Bosch continued his studies across the border at the Universidad Autonóma de Ciudad Juarez and took his first true crack at a medical business, incorporating a nutrition consultancy called Nutradoc. Advertising it as "the best weight loss system you will find online," the clinic provided clients with a rotating diet plan, leading to "a slimmer you in a matter of weeks." If the clinic was selling hCG, the weight-loss drug popular with steroid users, which Bosch frequently sold in Miami, it wasn't clearly advertised.

Bosch could have kept working on his foreign med school credits and tried to get entry into a US program. (CAHSU, at least, did recognize his work in Mexico; in 2007 the school issued him an MD degree that was not recognized in any US state.) But that wasn't his way.

"He wanted to be a doctor, but he wanted to do it in six months. He wanted to be a nutritional expert, but he wanted to make millions of dollars right away," says a member of his extended family familiar with Bosch's time in El Paso.

The signs were certainly there that Bosch hadn't suddenly become a responsible business owner. Even though the family had a free home to live in while his businesses got up and running, Bosch didn't exactly cut down on expenses. He bought a new GMC Yukon SUV and hired a maid at $200 per week. He enrolled his kids in a top-flight private Christian academy and even bought himself a membership at the posh Coronado Country Club, an enclave of tennis and golf tucked into the rugged mountains outside of town.

Where did the money come from? The Cuban restaurant wasn't successful, and Nutradoc didn't amount to much. In court filings, Aliette says her husband spent ten days every month on the road while they lived in El Paso—a curiously packed travel schedule for a local nutritionist. Bosch didn't make a name for himself with high-profile, major league clients for another three years, but it's possible he was already insinuating himself into the youth leagues and college ranks back in South Florida as soon as he landed back in the United States with an unrecognized medical degree.

Whatever cash he was making on the side, though, it wasn't enough to finance the lifestyle he'd built in West Texas. Just as it had two decades earlier—and would again—Tony's life tumbled apart in a flash.

Both Nutradoc and Cafe Mambo soon shuttered, and by the beginning of 2007, it was clear his second marriage was over. That March, he made Aliette an offer: If she'd accept a divorce without a legal fight and let him keep the kids, he'd give her $6,000 a month in alimony. She refused and took him to court. His landlord, meanwhile, sued over tens of thousands in unpaid rent at his office space, and Bosch ignored a speeding ticket until he ended up with a warrant. Before long, he added a restraining order to that list.

Aliette had rejected Tony's offer of cash for custody, but the warring couple did agree that he could take the kids back to Miami on April 5, 2007, to spend Easter with their grandparents, as long as Tony promised to return ten days later. But April 15 came and went and Aliette couldn't get her kids or her ex on the phone. Panicked, she started calling around and learned he'd gotten his daughter's grade-school transcripts and secretly enrolled her in a Miami school.

Aliette filed an emergency order trying to get her kids back, writing that she was "in fear for the children's well-being," and that she couldn't fly to Miami herself because she was "fearful of what [Bosch] might do." It was the first fusillade in a bitter divorce that rent Bosch apart in years to come and drove many of his more desperate decisions.

But for now, as he finally put his kids back on a plane to Texas under the threat of a judge's order, Bosch was already more focused on his new business prospects. Another marriage may have fallen apart, but back in Miami, Bosch was ready to join the revolution his fellow CAHSU alumni had spawned in his home state.

His first anti-aging enterprise, VIP Med, opened in September in a strip mall on Key Biscayne, a moneyed, white-collar island a few miles off downtown Miami, where Bosch had rented a condo near the ocean. Bosch was following the blueprint of an A4M establishment invented by Goldman and Katz, offering testosterone therapy and HGH to men and hCG weight-loss treatments to women. His records show that he later attended A4M conferences—even scribbling out a drug regimen for his most famous baseball client on a piece of official stationery from one such meeting of Goldman's group.

He cofounded VIP Med with a pair of dubiously qualified buddies: a guy who owned a pawnshop in the suburbs and a former paving company owner.

Bosch started mining what became a rich vein of clients—the wealthy,

Tony Bosch's handwritten regimen for Alex Rodriguez

mostly Latin crowd who lived nearby on the tiny island and socialized over drinks at the Ibis Lounge, the only bar in town. Bosch was still nothing if not a talented salesman. His pitch was easy: Need to lose a few pounds? Want some extra juice at the gym this week? Stop by on the way across the bridge to Miami!

"Whenever you ran into him, he'd talk about different types of supplements that were popular for weight loss, or what would help your workout be more effective," says Betty Tejada, a neighbor and family friend in Key Biscayne.

Bosch may not actually have been a doctor, but getting the medication he needed to play the game like an MD wasn't difficult. Most of the drugs that became his staple commodity are strictly regulated. To get testosterone, steroids, human growth hormone, or human chorionic gonadotropin (hCG, the drug popular both as a weight-loss tool for women and among steroid users because it helps restart the body's hormone production after a cycle), a licensed pharmacy must issue them using a script signed by a licensed doctor.

Among Tony's sources, medical records from his Biogenesis clinic suggest, was his father. Prescriptions were filled using the name and signature of Dr. Pedro Bosch—who remained an active and licensed doctor, well respected among Miami's Cuban community. Former Biogenesis employees say that Pedro was on the payroll. The elder Bosch has a clean state record, with no discipline from regulators and just a handful of malpractice suits that had generally found against the plaintiffs. He has steadfastly denied any connection to his son's later troubles.

But Pedro hadn't always steered clear of trouble. Two years after Tony opened VIP Med, he was charged by federal prosecutors in a civil case along with more than sixty other local physicians and pharmacy owners, all accused of a kickback scheme to defraud Medicare and Medicaid. The feds claimed Pedro and his cohorts had violated Stark Law, which prohibits doctors from getting payouts from labs where they send patients to bill the government; the rule is meant to discourage frivolous tests on the taxpayer dime. After three years in federal court, the case was closed with no charges or fines levied against the elder Bosch.

Besides his dad, Bosch had no trouble finding a cadre of other physicians ready to sign off on the drugs he needed. Through his years in the supply business, Bosch had plenty of less-than-by-the-book doctors on his roster. And another reason Florida has become the de facto home of the anti-aging movement is because so many retired doctors with valid prescription numbers live there. Many are happy to "rent" out their license for a set fee; a clinic owner like Bosch could easily plug them into a prescription form and get whatever he needed. Some services even broker such arrangements by dive-bombing doctors' offices with faxes offering them set fees if they'll "consult" for anti-aging clinics.

"That's aiding an unlicensed practice of medicine," says Dr. Kenneth Woliner, a Boca Raton physician and vocal critic of Florida's lack of regulation. "But this is widespread. This happens with a lot of these cash clinics," referring to operations like Bosch's that don't take insurance money.

Bosch also spent his first years in the business feverishly educating himself about the basics of dosing his patients with hormones and steroids. He turned to anyone who'd be willing to help him out, including a pair of disgraced local doctors.

One was his de facto medical advisor at VIP Med, a financially troubled physician named Dr. Jose Luis Rodriguez. Rodriguez fought through a federal bankruptcy in 2000 and an IRS lien in 2007 and gave up his own medical license the year before Bosch opened the clinic.

So did an even more troubled friend, a Spanish-born doctor named Carlos Diuana Nazir. Nazir had been charged in federal court in 2001 with selling unapproved, bogus impotence medications with seductive names like "Vigor" and "Power Gel." Nazir got two years in federal prison and a $1 million fine for his crimes. And after he got out, Bosch asked him for advice.

"He was training to learn how you dosify. How do you calculate doses in patients?" Nazir later said.

Whatever Bosch had learned in Belize, he was still a novice in his new guise of anti-aging guru. He wanted to know everything: "How do you not overdose somebody? What do you do when complications come in? How do you counteract?" Nazir said. "There are hormones for everything. The ones that counteract something that you don't want."

He learned to use synthetic testosterone, ordering it in differing concentrations from compounding pharmacies, which are licensed to combine and remix commercially available products into creams, lozenges, or injectibles; dozens have opened around South Florida to cater to anti-aging clinics. Sometimes he'd order concoctions with ratios more than fifteen times the testosterone that any legitimate patient would need. He bought vials of human growth hormone, and made himself familiar with the newest trend: peptides. The strings of amino acids such as GHRP-2/6 and CJC-1295— each of which are banned by Major League Baseball, the Olympics, and other pro sports—can trigger the body into making more of its own growth hormone. He also stocked up on hCG and learned plenty about good old-fashioned steroids themselves, from Deca-Durabolin to Winstrol to Anavar.

For now, Bosch was mostly selling the drugs to Key Biscayne's wealthy beachgoers with a promise of slimmer waists and bigger biceps. In his own way, he'd finally found a way into the family business. He bought himself a white lab coat and proudly embroidered DR. TONY BOSCH over the pocket. He framed his degree from CAHSU and hung it on the wall at VIP Med.

But Bosch had always been working toward finding a way into that other exclusive fraternity, where only the most talented men played their days away on emerald fields.

With his growing arsenal of illicit chemical knowledge, Bosch was poised to reignite that dream as well.

CHAPTER FIVE

Steroid Spring Cleaning

In October 2005, Kirk Radomski had a bad feeling. Call it a premonition. "You always know," says the former bodybuilder. "Listen, you grow up in the Bronx and you see things and hear things, and something just doesn't feel right."

Radomski, whose brash accent makes his regular reminders of the borough of his birth unnecessary, had for nearly a decade cornered the market on providing steroids to major league ballplayers. Athletes rang him at all hours of the day, seeking cycles. Sports agents knew he was the guy to call if their clients were having injury trouble or their statistics were sagging.

It was an accident, he says: The product of him working in the New York Mets clubhouse, having a scholarly knowledge of steroids, and not being the sort to turn away a friend seeking advice or even drugs. But to Radomski, who has a jaw like a sledgehammer and wears a military-style flattop, it had begun sinking in that he would be, in the eyes of the law, nothing more than a narcotics trafficker with particularly high-profile clients. And there was evidence all over his damn house.

So Radomski lit the fireplace inside his perfect suburban Long Island home. "I did spring cleaning," Radomski says, even though it was fall. He likes to say that his only partner in crime as a steroid dealer was the US Postal Service, since he almost always delivered drugs via the mail. So now he tossed package receipts, tracking labels, pieces of paper bearing phone numbers and addresses, notes from players—"everything I could find," he says—into the roaring fireplace and a paper shredder that he worked simultaneously.

The frenetic spring cleaning ended up saving the reputations of an untold percentage of Radomski's clients, he says. "There are a lot of players who are going to be in the Hall [of Fame] who I know were on the stuff," he says. But without the government having evidence that they bought anything from Radomski, "I didn't have a reason to throw these guys under the bus."

He adds: "I saved my ass, too."

There was one thing Radomski couldn't do anything about, though: checks from those players who were too lazy to pay in cash, already deposited and recorded by his bank. Though not all of his customers went that route, the exposure of just this portion of Radomski's major league clientele was enough to change the game forever.

On December 15, 2005, two months after the records purge, Radomski opened his front door to find a tall, completely bald federal agent who introduced himself as Jeff Novitzky. He used those words Radomski had half expected to hear for years—*money laundering, steroid distribution, conspiracy*—and unfolded a search warrant.

Sixteen years earlier, MLB's first big missed chance to tackle its blooming steroid problem started with a meeting between a legendary college football coach and an FBI agent.

When he took the helm of the University of Michigan Wolverines in 1969, Bo Schembechler revitalized the program with one of the great upsets in football history, knocking off defending national champion Ohio State to spark the famed "Ten-Year War" with the Buckeyes. For the next decade, Michigan and OSU traded Big Ten titles and Rose Bowl trips as Schembechler steamrolled to almost two hundred wins.

But twenty years later, Schembechler looked at the newest powerhouse in the conference—the Michigan State Spartans—and saw only chemical enhancement behind their run to glory.

The Spartans had bullied their way to the Big Ten title and a berth in the 1988 Rose Bowl behind a monstrous squad led by future pros Lorenzo White, Tim Moore, and a cartoonishly ripped, six-foot-six offensive lineman named Tony Mandarich, who later posed for the cover of *Sports Illustrated* under the headline THE INCREDIBLE BULK.

Schembechler had good reason to believe the squad's newfound success was powered by synthetic testosterone. Rumors had reached him that several Spartans had pissed dirty in a blind NCAA drug test at the Rose Bowl. Years later, Mandarich admitted that he'd used steroids at MSU and cheated a drug test before the game.

Fed up, Schembechler called in Greg Stejskal. For the past decade, he'd invited the towering, mustachioed Ann Arbor FBI field office supervisor to address his team about the dangers of cocaine and other recreational drugs. This time he called his G-man buddy to tell him that a number of his rivals, particularly Michigan State, were rife with steroids.

"But he also said what bothered him the most was that he did these summer camps," Stejskal says, "and lately the high schoolers were coming in and not asking whether they should do steroids, but when exactly they should start."

Stejskal had played college football at Nebraska, so he was personally offended by steroid-inflated stars like Mandarich taking over the sport. "I'll look into it," Stejskal promised.

Neither man sitting in Schembechler's wood-paneled office that morning knew their conversation would ignite the nation's first major crackdown on steroids, a case that eventually spanned three nations and nabbed seventy major dealers.

The small investigation that started in a Michigan college town ultimately presented MLB with its final, best shot to pump the brakes on the drug-fueled train steaming toward shattered records, bulked-up sluggers, and an inevitable reckoning with chemical enhancement. Not only did Stejskal's investigation show that steroids were flowing freely from gyms to locker rooms, he also offered MLB definitive proof that one of the game's biggest stars was juicing. The result was deafening silence.

As he launched into Schembechler's case, Stejskal had serendipitous timing on his side. A year earlier, President Ronald Reagan had signed a federal law banning all steroids for nonmedical purposes. But because the law focused narrowly on doctors overprescribing steroids, it did not allow for an FBI probe of users.

But in late 1989, a young US senator named Joe Biden—attempting to overcome a scandal during the last presidential campaign, when he'd been caught plagiarizing lines in a stump speech—saw getting tough on juicers as a way to get his mojo back. Canadian sprinter Ben Johnson had recently dominated headlines at the Seoul Olympics, having shattered a sprinting record before seeing his gold medal stripped when he failed a postrun urine sample for stanozolol, an anabolic steroid.

Without serious penalties for PED use in sports, Biden argued, kids would never take Reagan's new prohibition seriously. "Millions . . . still look to those people who are the stars on the athletic field as the role models in our schools," he said during one hearing. "If they are able to benefit from this use without any penalty, then it seems to me the message is overwhelming to the rest of America that drug abuse in any form is not that big a deal."

By the end of the year, the future vice president had shepherded through the landmark Anabolic Steroid Control Act, a bill that forever changed the landscape of American doping. Users faced a year in jail for possessing steroids and dealers looked at up to five years for selling them.

Yet despite the new legal ammunition from Washington, Stejskal could still only piece together the resources for a small operation. Along with his partner, Bill Randall, he went undercover at a few Detroit gyms that Michigan's strength coach had told them were notorious for steroids. They pretended to be Chicago businessmen looking for drugs while working out on the road. As the deadline for the six-month operation approached, the agents had trapped only a handful of small-time local dealers.

Then Washington called. "They told us the White House called the FBI because George H. W. Bush was asking what we were doing about steroids," Stejskal remembers. "They told us, 'You've got the only steroid case in the entire country.'"

Thanks to Bush's pressure, Stejskal and Randall received not only an extension but money for a full-on probe. Operation Equine, as it was dubbed, was a go. "We still thought this would basically be a regional thing, maybe a case that took us into Ohio," Stejskal says. "As it turns out, it went all over the country and into Canada and Mexico."

They worked the case like any other federal drug investigation: Steroid users led the undercover cops to neighborhood dealers, who then led them up the chain to the real players in the area—either unwittingly or while wearing a wire under threat of arrest. By 1992, the indictments started pouring out of grand juries.

In Canada, cops seized $20 million in illegal steroids while prosecutors charged thirty-seven men, including the son of the chief justice of Canada's Federal Court. In Cleveland, the feds nabbed the state's biggest dealer and his entire network. A repeat Mr. Ohio winner ended up in cuffs. In Detroit, the king of Michigan's anabolic steroid network ended up being a weight lifter with a too-good-to-be-true—but in fact, totally real—name: Joe DiMaggio.

I n 1992, the operation took its turn toward baseball. It all started with a young Southern California bodybuilder who liked to use cattle prods in his workouts.

American steroid culture was in a vibrant infancy in the mid-'80s, but Curtis Wenzlaff was already pushing its limits. Wenzlaff first tried steroids as a teenager at his local suburban California gym, quickly packing on forty pounds of muscle as he worked toward a college football scholarship. And the drugs were just the beginning.

Wenzlaff slept in a pitch-dark sensory deprivation chamber. He strapped a mask to his face and huffed pure oxygen while pounding iron.

And he tied himself to a leg machine and demanded that a spotter electro-
cute him with a cattle shocker to keep him going. The insane regimen—and
a hefty cycle of steroids—paid off with a scholarship to Cal State.

Soon after he graduated in 1987, a friend introduced him to Reggie
Jackson. The vociferous slugger had recently retired from a Hall of Fame
career and needed a new challenge. He became a regular at the weight lifter's gym, and Wenzlaff eventually moved into the baseball legend's sprawl-
ing Oakland mansion. (Both Jackson and Wenzlaff maintain the retired
slugger had no inkling of his steroid business.) Reggie began taking him to
Oakland Coliseum, guiding the trainer past security and into the locker
rooms. That's how Wenzlaff became one of the first in a long line of beefy
stowaways toting syringes into major league clubhouses.

Naturally, he hooked up with Jose Canseco. In 1988, Canseco reaped
the benefits of juicing, earning a spot in the history books with the first
40/40 season. Wenzlaff knew immediately from his physique that he was a
fellow adherent to the dark arts of the needle, but he found Canseco lacked
the sophisticated know-how native to West Coast bodybuilders. Wenzlaff
was experimenting with the wildest testosterone blends California's underground drug labs could cook up. "In terms of steroid knowledge," Wenzlaff
brags, "I was light-years ahead of him."

Wenzlaff played steroid guru to Canseco during off-season Miami
workouts, introducing him to a range of mixes like a new formula for the
discontinued steroid Parabolan. But Wenzlaff didn't just work with Canseco. By the start of the 1988 season, he was also selling to the younger
member of the Bash Brothers. Mark McGwire had followed up his stunning
rookie season's forty-nine home-run showing by swatting thirty-two as a
sophomore, but already he was looking toward Canseco's chemical en-
hancements.

Wenzlaff says he was the provider, keeping McGwire on regular cycles
of testosterone and anabolic steroids. McGwire ultimately admitted to his
steroid habit, after years of denial, but swore they only helped him "stay
healthy." Wenzlaff ridicules that argument, once telling a reporter of Mc-

Gwire's regimen: "If Paris Hilton was to take that array, she could run over Dick Butkus."

As the two A's sluggers exploded both in size and fame, Wenzlaff's under-the-table steroids business grew. He later claimed multiple major leaguers and Hollywood personalities among his clients, though he will only name Canseco and McGwire. In the summer of 1992, though, he brought on one customer too many, a friendly Chicago gym owner looking for steroids named Eddie Schmidt. At Wenzlaff's condo, Schmidt pointed at a photo prominently displayed on the wall and asked innocently, "Hey, who's that?"

"That's Jose Canseco," the dealer told him with a grin. "He's a friend of mine."

In September 1992, Wenzlaff met Schmidt at a Santa Monica motel for one last steroid sale. During the meeting, Schmidt called room service for some food. Wenzlaff answered the door, expecting a hotel employee with a cart full of snacks. Instead, he stared openmouthed at a tall federal agent brandishing his badge.

"You're under arrest," Greg Stejskal told him. Schmidt's real identity, of course, was Stejskal's FBI partner, Bill Randall. And Wenzlaff's Michigan friend who'd referred him was an informant working for the feds.

Wenzlaff knew he was going down hard. The only question was, who would he take with him?

B ud Selig worked hard to burnish his everyman Midwestern image. He drove a Chevy Caprice, worked from a blocky Milwaukee high-rise on Lake Michigan, and even ate the same lunch every weekday: a $1.50 hot dog and a Diet Coke from the custard stand around the corner from his office.

But Selig had seized the commissioner's seat through a good old-fashioned bloodless coup, and he'd done it because he believed fanatically in the job's two holy missions: making the owners heaps more money and protecting the hallowed traditions of the national pastime.

"The most important part of this job, clearly, is to protect the integrity of the sport," Selig said in a 2012 court deposition. "People live and die with baseball games. It's their life. The more you're in this sport, the more you understand that, how important it is to so many different people."

Truthfully, Selig had always understood that passion because a love of hardball had driven his own career. Selig was born in Milwaukee, Wisconsin's biggest city, and raised by a prominent Ford dealer. He dreamed of a life in academia, working as a historian and lecturing on the distant past. "I'm a great student of history," Selig said in the deposition. "I wanted to be a history professor."

Instead, at his father's urging, he went into the family business. But his passion was never used cars. Hank Aaron's long-ball heroics with the Milwaukee Braves had indelibly marked Selig as a young man at Milwaukee County Stadium. When the franchise fled to Atlanta in 1966, he regarded it as a great tragedy.

Selig made it his life's work to salve Milwaukee's wound. He sold his dealership, gathered investors, and launched failed attempts to buy the White Sox, as well as two expansion teams, which ended up in San Diego and Kansas City. In 1969, Selig finally got his wish when the Seattle Pilots folded after one year. Selig's group snatched the franchise for $10.8 million and brought baseball back to Wisconsin.

In the small market, Selig was a prudent owner and the Brewers were a middle-of-the-pack franchise, making it to one World Series, which they lost to the Cardinals in 1982. Behind the scenes, though, he was obsessed with the bottom line. Starting in 1985—just as the Pittsburgh drug trials were raging—Selig and his fellow owners began a scheme to drive down contracts by refusing to tender deals to free agents. Believing that rich clubs were bankrupting the small ones with massive contracts, Commissioner Ueberroth had spearheaded the move, which led to stars like Kirk Gibson and Tim Raines getting lowballed into re-signing at steep discounts. While the owners (including Selig) have never admitted to the plot, three independent arbitrators later found them guilty of collusion and ordered them to repay $280 million to players.

If Selig projected a quiet, pragmatic image in public, his behind-the-scenes move from the owner's box to the commissioner's seat came via bold mutiny. Fay Vincent, an entertainment lawyer and executive who had served as MLB's deputy commissioner, was promoted to baseball's top job in 1989. His was a President Garfield–esque stunted tenure, mostly because he tangled with Selig and the Milwaukee owner's budding ally in Robert Manfred.

Manfred, who has degrees from both Cornell and Harvard, later became Bud Selig's right hand and the de facto day-to-day head of the league. In 1990, he was brought in by the owners to try to end a strike that had already eaten up most of spring training and was threatening the start of the season as players and owners fought over free agency and arbitration rules. Midway through negotiations, he and union chief Donald Fehr agreed to take the weekend off from sparring. The way Manfred tells it, he was watching a college basketball game at Madison Square Garden when a staffer rushed in with the news: Vincent had secretly invited Fehr to his house to offer his own settlement behind Manfred's back—one much less favorable for owners. "Fay sowed the seeds of his own destruction," Manfred said.

In the eyes of Selig and Manfred, Vincent had come down on the wrong side of the perpetual power struggle between owners and the union. It was the defining struggle behind nearly every ongoing conflict in the sport, including its repeated failures to address the drug culture in the late '80s and early '90s. In September 1992, Selig headed a rebellion. With owners increasingly dismayed at Vincent's decision making and Selig among his most outspoken opponents, it wasn't difficult to organize a no-confidence vote, followed shortly by Vincent's resignation. The Milwaukee businessman took his place as interim commissioner and never relinquished the position, getting the job for good in 1998.

Selig believed baseball faced the most serious threats to its survival in a generation. That danger, however, had nothing to do with the home runs flying out of the Oakland Coliseum at a record clip as McGwire and Canseco injected each other's butt muscles with Wenzlaff's concoctions. Selig later maintained that he made it through the heart of the Steroid Era with nary a hint of what was going on. "I never even heard about it," he said in 2005, referring to steroids in the clubhouse. "I ran a team and nobody was closer to the players and I never heard any comment from them. It wasn't until 1998 or 1999 that I heard the discussion."

In his first years as acting commissioner, Selig was more focused on another problem: his belief that the owners had ceded too much power in their battles with the union. The result was that as many as a nineteen franchises were operating in the red, at least according to the owners' notoriously unreliable estimates. He knew firsthand that small-market teams like his Brewers could never compete on the field until the sport halted runaway salaries in New York and Boston.

With the union's agreement set to expire before the 1994 season, the owners and players prepared for a slugfest. Selig wanted an end to arbitration and to tighten free-agency rules—moves that would save owners from ever-inflating contracts; he even floated the idea of a salary cap. Players wanted blood from a man they thought represented all the owners who had colluded to rob them of $280 million. It was that crime that underpinned the decade of mistrust to come, helping to convince even those players who wanted to stop the inflow of steroids from allowing owners to institute a testing program.

"There is no question that collusion was the turning point of the relationship between the owners and the players," Fay Vincent later said. "It colors everything that is going on."

For all the animosity, steroid use simply wasn't part of the contract debate.

Even Ueberroth's brief battles with the union after the Pittsburgh drug trials over a testing program were a distant memory. In 1991, soon after Biden's Anabolic Steroid Control Act passed, Vincent had issued a terse two-page memo to every clubhouse headlined BASEBALL'S DRUG POLICY AND PREVENTION PROGRAM. Vincent warned that "there is no place for illegal drug use in baseball," noting that "this prohibition applies to all illegal drugs and controlled substances, including steroids." Players could face "expulsion" for ignoring the ban. But without drug tests, it was an empty rule. Most teams didn't even bother posting the memo in locker rooms.

On August 12, 1994, the last attempts at brokering a new labor deal broke down. The next day's games were canceled, and baseball wasn't resurrected until the following April. For the first time in the league's history, the World Series was erased by labor unrest. Selig viewed the shutdown as a necessary evil to get the game back on a profitable footing. But he seriously underestimated two effects of his historic work stoppage.

The first was public dismay. Canceling the World Series struck a chord among ordinary Americans who only saw millionaires squabbling with billionaires. The hapless Montreal Expos had the league's top record, Matt Williams had forty-three homers in August and was threatening Maris's single-season mark, and Tony Gwynn was batting near .400. All that potential history was dashed. Many fans swore they'd never buy another hot dog at the ballpark.

Selig arrived at his modest lakefront office building every Monday to find bundles of venomous letters on his desk. The commissioner thought he had to defeat the union to save the game, but he hadn't considered that his hard-line stance might do equal damage.

The second danger was more subtle. With baseball officially canceled, players scattered. A few stars signed contracts to play in Japan. Others went back to off-season leagues in the Caribbean or Venezuela. But the vast majority went home to local gyms to stay in shape.

By the mid-'90s, the steroid revolution that had gestated in Florida and California weight rooms had spread across the country. Baseball's decades-long bias against weight lifting was dead and buried. How could managers tell hitters with a straight face that bulky muscles would hurt their swings when Jose Canseco was mashing forty homers a year with Popeye biceps and Mark McGwire was protecting him with a neck carved from redwood?

Add the two facts together and the result was simple: Dozens of ball-players, freed from any oversight from their team's trainers and managers, hooked up with dealers at their local gyms during that '94 strike and started blasting iron and shooting steroids.

Although the truth was, MLB's Steroid Era had already begun in earnest before the 1994 strike. The time off just accelerated and spread the change. No longer were Jose Canseco and Mark McGwire lone, crazily muscular hitters aiming for the third deck. One example was Lenny Dykstra. He had earned his nickname, "Nails," with countless gritty plays: flying into walls, barreling through catchers, taking fastballs to the rib cage. Dykstra's game was built on energy, grit, and an OK bat with little pop. When he was traded from the Mets to Philly in '89, he hit only twenty-six home runs in four seasons.

But like so many other players, his stats suddenly inflated with his body. For Dykstra, the shift started in 1991, when he met a convicted cocaine dealer named Jeff Scott during spring training in Clearwater, Florida. The two hooked up at a bar when Dykstra joked about Scott's bulging physique. Soon enough, they were hitting strip clubs around Clearwater and then hitting the needle back at Scott's condo. By 1993, Dykstra reported to camp hilariously bulked up before proceeding to break the MLB record for at-bats in a season, leading the league in hits, and even blasting nineteen homers. When the strike hit the next season, Dykstra reported to Florida as usual. Instead of fielding grounders and working on his bunt, though, he spent months in Clearwater shooting Deca-Durabolin with Scott. He was far from alone.

The statistical signs were clear that Canseco's virus had become an epidemic. By the time the strike began, five players were on pace to finish with fifty homers: Williams, Barry Bonds, Frank Thomas, Jeff Bagwell, and Albert Belle. (A group, to be fair, that only included one man—Bonds—definitively tied to PED use.) In the years since 1961—that legendary summer when both Maris and Mantle had each launched more than fifty bombs—only three other players had ever topped that mark. Nineteen ninety-five brought even bigger numbers.

If that evidence didn't scream out to Selig that a chemically powered era was blossoming, baseball's leadership soon got a much more direct warning.

It happened inside the Boardroom, a smoky bar inside the FBI's training academy at Quantico that was usually haunted by agents blowing off steam after a day at the shooting range.

A few days after the strike began, Greg Stejskal was sipping a beer and watching a Monday Night Football game when a handful of MLB execs sidled up. They nodded at Stejskal, who had just finished giving the baseball suits one of his annual presentations about legal threats to professional sports. It was a talk that mostly focused on gambling rings.

Operation Equine had recently wrapped up as one of the most successful drug stings in history, nabbing more than seventy convictions of high-level steroid dealers. Sitting at the bar, Stejskal began chatting up Kevin Hallinan, an NYPD veteran who headed up baseball's security operations. They talked about prospects for the strike ending and the latest gambling cases the FBI had run into.

Then the MLB exec posed Stejskal a fateful question. "He asked what I knew about steroids," Stejskal says. "I said, 'You have some big issues in baseball. One of our guys gave us a lot of information about selling steroids to Canseco.'"

As baseball's top cop, Stejskal thought, surely Hallinan was the man to see how booming illegal steroid distribution could be a problem in MLB.

But Stejskal claims that Hallinan literally shrugged. "He said, 'We've heard rumors, but with all the problems with the strike, we can't get the players to agree to any testing. So we're not sure what to do about it,'" Stejskal recalls. (Hallinan later released a statement that he didn't recall meeting with Stejskal in Quantico or getting direct warnings about Canseco.)

Stejskal was then the nation's single leading expert on illegal steroid distribution. He had sources with firsthand knowledge about some of the game's biggest stars doping. "I told him we should follow up," Stejskal says.

But he says that Hallinan drained his beer and wandered out of the bar without pressing the issue. The federal agent never heard from baseball's security chief again.

A few months after players finally strapped on their cleats and resumed professional baseball in 1995, the steroid epidemic that had begun before the strike began spreading exponentially. The *Los Angeles Times* soon published one of the first reports hinting at how the drugs were fueling surging power numbers.

Padres GM Randy Smith guessed that up to 20 percent of the league was juicing, and All-Stars Tony Gwynn and Frank Thomas spoke on the record about their suspicions. "It's like the big secret we're not supposed to talk about," Gwynn said in the July 15 piece. "I'm standing there in the outfield when a guy comes up, and I'm thinking, 'Hey, I wonder if this guy is on steroids.'"

For decades, a forty home run season had been the benchmark of an extraordinary power hitter. As late as 1988 and 1989, only one player topped the mark each season. Suddenly, in '95 four players all topped forty bombs. The next season was Alex Rodriguez's rookie campaign, and his thirty-six home runs were only good enough to tie him for twenty-second in the major leagues as seventeen hitters notched forty homers. From 1997 through 2001, sixty-six hitters topped that mark. Recording at least forty jacks had suddenly become the standard for any decent-slugging outfielder or first baseman.

Two of those years saw eye-popping individual assaults on the record books. The summer of 1998 smashed its way into baseball history as the year that Mark McGwire—now a St. Louis Cardinal—and his rival on the Chicago Cubs, Sammy Sosa, riveted fans with a daily sprint toward Maris's record.

McGwire had been a steady power hitter since his days in Oakland, topping thirty homers every year except for two injury-shortened campaigns; but after getting traded to St. Louis in '97, he'd gone bananas, ripping twenty-four homers in just fifty-one games.

The Dominican outfielder Sosa, meanwhile, had broken into the league as a skinny speedster before suddenly erupting for regular thirty-homer campaigns starting in 1993; in '98, he had thirty-three home runs by the All-Star break.

As the two chased each other toward Maris's mark that year, no one embraced the rivalry more than Selig. When McGwire nailed a laser-beam shot—against Sosa's Cubs, of course—for the record-breaking homer number sixty-two, Selig watched alongside Cards legend Stan Musial.

While casual fans debated potential reasons for the power surge—was it poor expansion-team pitching or too-tight baseballs?—Bud Selig didn't overanalyze the phenomenon. Selig felt the electricity in the stadium when McGwire broke Maris's record. As the giant redhead circled the basepaths, Musial had leaned over and whispered: "This is the beginning of a renaissance." The commissioner knew the home run chase had been vital for the sport's bottom line.

The numbers didn't lie. After he canceled the Series in '94, fans stayed away in droves. Attendance in 1995 was down 20 percent. By '97, the year before McGwire's heroics, ticket sales were still down 10 percent. But as Mark and Sammy went for the record, millions came back. St. Louis topped three million fans in the seats. Tens of thousands showed up early on the road just to watch the sluggers rattling the upper decks in batting practice.

Baseball mattered again, Selig knew, because of those home runs. So even when McGwire's record year briefly brought PEDs into the conversation, Selig showed minimal interest. During the heart of the midsummer chase, an AP reporter had spotted a curious bottle in McGwire's locker labeled ANDROSTENEDIONE. His August story revealed that "Andro" was a steroid precursor already banned in the Olympics and the NFL.

Selig was so caught off guard he ran to his neighborhood Milwaukee pharmacy to see if Andro was on the shelves there. He promised a study into the health effects of such over-the-counter steroid precursors, but stuck up for McGwire. "I think what Mark McGwire has accomplished is so remarkable and he has handled it all so beautifully, we want to do everything we can to enjoy a great moment in baseball history," he told reporters.

Others went even further, attacking the AP for daring to touch the issue. Cards manager Tony LaRussa threatened to kick the wire service out of the clubhouse. *Boston Globe* columnist Dan Shaughnessy scolded the reporter that it was "no wonder the players loathe the media."

If Selig was sluggish to react to steroids, the players union was outright hostile to any move toward testing. Their mind-set had barely budged since the cocaine trials of the 1980s, with union president Donald Fehr and Gene Orza, his chief legal counsel, making it clear that Selig would face another strike if he pushed the issue. Orza believed steroids were no more dangerous than cigarettes and that any move to randomly test players would be "dictatorial."

But at the same time, new warnings about the dangers of steroids were piling up on Selig's desk. Two years after McGwire's record, a group of MLB team physicians met in Milwaukee to alert Selig that steroid abuse was causing an injury glut.

The commissioner missed the presentation. (He had slipped on an icy sidewalk and hurt his leg.) But Dr. John Cantwell, the Braves' team physician, says an "informal discussion" among the other doctors found agreement that serious injuries were on the rise and steroids were a likely culprit. A study had found that the number of players sidelined by injuries had climbed by more than 30 percent in the previous decade, and they were staying injured longer. As players huffed around the bases with forty extra pounds of muscle, hamstrings snapped like rubber bands and joints creaked like rusty gate hinges.

What really scared the medics was the rising potential for devastating steroid-related injuries. They all remembered a night in May 1999 when a young Tampa Bay pitcher named Tony Saunders went into his delivery, threw a wild pitch, and then fell to the ground shrieking in agony, his hand immobile and clawlike, as a stunned stadium stared in silence. His humerus bone had shattered from the elbow all the way to the shoulder. Jose Canseco, who played for the Rays that year, claimed in his book that Saunders's freak injury came after he'd overused steroids and HGH, a charge the pitcher denies.

Even pitchers who weren't on the juice had reason to worry. The year after Saunders's arm exploded, Red Sox reliever Bryce Florie was working a September matchup with the Yankees when slugger Ryan Thompson sent a laser up the middle. Before Florie could react, the ball demolished his orbital bone, cheek, and nose. Florie had no proof that Thompson was on steroids, but like all pitchers, he wondered how long it would be until someone died from a steroid-powered line drive.

"I've wondered whether that batter hit that ball harder than he was born to hit it, and whether that might have made a difference in milliseconds," Florie later wrote.

Cantwell and his colleagues wondered what would come first: union negotiations or the players' safety. "I had recently come from the Olympics, where penalties were very severe and testing was serious," says the Braves doctor. "I was very concerned that the players union was so strong they could prevent that from ever happening in baseball."

Faced with the mounting evidence, Selig in 2001 instituted a minor league drug-testing program. Because minor leaguers aren't unionized, Selig did not have to negotiate the new program with Fehr and Orza. It was a halting step forward—the program had no penalties for dopers—but it did help answer any lingering doubts Selig had about the prevalence of steroid use. In that first season, more than one in ten minor leaguers failed tests.

Three years after McGwire and Sosa's home run chase, neither Selig nor the public nor the brotherhood of baseball writers were quite as enthusiastic when Barry Bonds demolished the still-fresh record. Bonds had broken into the league as a blue-chip talent, the wiry, whip-fast son of All-Star

Bobby Bonds. The younger Bonds had always had pop to go with his speed, cranking forty-six homers in 1993, his first year in San Francisco.

But as Bonds watched McGwire earn the adulation of the country in 1998, something had cracked in his competitive psyche. He was still an elite player, but Bonds knew he'd never capture national headlines unless he inflated his physique, changed his game, and became an all-time masher. So between 1998 and his record-breaking 2001 campaign, Bonds added more than twenty-five pounds of pure muscle. The once-wiry outfielder developed a body that wouldn't look out of place stuffed into a WWF costume. His forehead bulged with new angles. And home runs screamed off his bat like bottle rockets.

On October 5, 2001, Bonds banged two home runs off the Dodgers to shatter McGwire's single-season record as he watched amid a delirious home crowd. He hit another the next night to set a new all-time mark: seventy-three.

Unlike Sosa and McGwire, Bonds was a notoriously sour character despised by many in the press and on opposing teams. The national vibe was muted, or even hostile, as Bonds demolished the record weeks after the 9/11 terrorist attacks. Even Selig must have perceived that fans were starting to view the absurd home run numbers as more troubling than exciting.

Less than a year later, the dominoes that cascaded into the crashing exposure of baseball's Steroid Era started tumbling.

A few weeks after Opening Day 2002, a former league MVP named Ken Caminiti became the first star to openly admit his career had been fueled by steroids. Known for his thick-browed glower and penchant for designer motorcycles, Caminiti had averaged just fourteen homers a year in his first seven full seasons. In 1996 he had suddenly erupted, belting forty out of the yard and hitting .326.

Caminiti also struggled with alcohol and heroin addictions but, as he told *Sports Illustrated*, he didn't regret riding steroids to that MVP award. "If a young player were to ask me what to do, I'm not going to tell him it's bad," the retired slugger told the magazine, while also admitting he'd abused the drugs so badly that his testicles had retreated into his body for almost four months in '96. "You have a chance to set your family up, to get your daughter into a better school. . . . So I can't say, 'Don't do it,' not when the guy next to you is as big as a house and he's going to take your job."

(Just two years later, the slugger, who had opened up to the magazine in part to confront his alcoholism, became the poster child for steroids' dark side when he lost his battle with addiction and died at forty-one from a heroin and cocaine overdose.)

Selig told *Sports Illustrated* he was "very worried" about the admission, which gave him the ammunition to push Fehr and the union to agree to a baby step toward testing: In 2003, every player would be anonymously screened once. If more than 5 percent failed, mandatory tests would start the next season.

Players wouldn't need a PhD to avoid a positive. Not only was HGH not being tested for, but everyone was alerted ahead of time to the plan. The *San Francisco Chronicle* also obtained a recording of Barry Bonds's trainer, Greg Anderson, warning the slugger of the precise dates he was likely to get screened, suggesting many players had ample warning before their tests.

Yet when the results came in, 104 players had failed out of 1,438, well above the 5 percent margin. Mandatory random drug testing was on in 2004, though for now, dopers would be kept anonymous and sent to counseling rather than face a ban. And that wasn't the only lasting result of those "anonymous" 2003 tests.

In a spasm of shortsightedness, the lab kept track of who each sample belonged to, and the players union failed to make sure those records were destroyed. In 2009, leaks to *Sports Illustrated* and the *New York Times* revealed four marquee names among the 104 dopers: Sammy Sosa, David Ortiz, Manny Ramirez, and Alex Rodriguez.

But even as baseball was conducting that anonymous first round of tests, the death blow was about to land to the freewheeling, steroid-shooting days that started with Jose Canseco and slowed with Ken Caminiti's admissions.

It started with an IRS agent digging through garbage.

*   *   *

Agent Jeff Novitzky—lanky, bald, and singularly focused—had in February 2003 begun the lonely work of investigating a San Francisco laboratory by parsing through its trash looking for financial documents and other evidence. The place was called Bay Area Laboratory Co-Operative. Novitzky was working off a tip that Anderson—Barry Bonds's trusted trainer—had been dealing steroids originating there.

The lab, better known by its abbreviation, BALCO, was the brainchild of a singular character named Victor Conte, a former funk bassist who'd reimagined himself as a cutting-edge nutritionist after buying a machine that could detect mineral deficiencies in blood. Conte had spent years insinuating himself into the competitive track and field circuits and trawling Internet bodybuilding forums. In public, he sold supplements and zinc pills. Behind the scenes he connected with cutting-edge steroid manufacturers and sold their discoveries to star athletes.

On December 3, 2003, Novitzky and dozens of federal agents raided BALCO and interrogated Conte. The case against the lab owner became a colossal embarrassment for Selig, Bonds, and scores of other top players.

A secret grand jury convened to consider charges against Conte. The proceedings quickly morphed into a sideshow of major leaguers parading into the courthouse to talk about their own drug habits and their ties to the steroid dealer. The testimony was supposed to be secret, but leaks galore later emerged.

With the story dominating sports pages and congressional pressure growing, the union finally caved to pressure, and baseball's first punitive PED policy was born. Just before the 2005 season started, the new Joint Drug Treatment and Prevention Program made results public for any failed test. And instead of counseling, dopers would face escalating penalties: ten games for a first failed test, thirty for a second, and sixty for the third.

But that progress didn't mean an end to MLB's embarrassment. In the months after the new policy started, bombshells started exploding in book-stores. The first landed that spring, when Jose Canseco published *Juiced*, his memoir of steroid abuse. Before the book was published, the establishment lavished scorn on the ex-slugger. Tony LaRussa speculated that Canseco had only written it because he was broke. One early reviewer noted that he was left with the "overwhelming impression that Mr. Canseco is delusional."

But a funny thing happened: The public read the book—in which Canseco named eight players as definite steroid users, including McG-wire—and mostly believed him. *Juiced* became a bestseller.

Canseco's confessions, combined with the ongoing Bonds saga, also spurred a tragicomic round of congressional hearings in March 2005, with House representatives grilling ballplayers over whether they'd used ste-roids. McGwire repeated, zen-like: "I'm not here to talk about the past," and Rafael Palmeiro pointed at the panel, wagged his finger, and insisted, "I have never used steroids." Five months later, he failed a test for stanozolol. Former hardball heroes were starting to resemble cigarette executives.

Just over a year later came *Game of Shadows* by *San Francisco Chronicle* reporters Mark Fainaru-Wada and Lance Williams. The book exposed Bonds's steroid-fueled transformation at the hands of Conte and MLB's utter incompetence in preventing bodybuilding drugs from changing the game. Like *Juiced*, the book became a bestseller, and, in the court of public opinion, demolished Bonds's claims that he'd assaulted the record books without chemical help.

Even with a legit—if belated—drug-testing policy in place, the hear-ings and the bestsellers forced the commissioner's hand (though Selig claims he's never actually perused the Canseco canon of literature). More impor-tant, with Congress threatening to set up an independent drug-testing or-ganization to air out MLB's dirty laundry, any lingering union resistance to anti-PED policies began to crumble.

"What baseball feared the most was that Congress would step in and legislate that they had to do drug testing. They desperately wanted to keep it in-house," says Richard McLaren, a Canadian attorney who later coauthored the Mitchell Report. "The idea of MLB being under the jurisdiction of an independent body was impossible for them."

So on March 30, 2006, Selig turned to Senator George Mitchell.

To say that Mitchell had worked through tricky conflicts before would be like saying Michael Jordan had hit a buzzer beater or two. Mitchell, who had turned down Bill Clinton's appointment to the Supreme Court, was the guy you called for the world's toughest circumstances. In 1998, he'd helped broker peace between Catholics and Protestants in Northern Ireland. Three years later, he brought Palestinians and Israelis together for a landmark compromise. He'd even survived three years as the Democratic Senate's majority leader while Republican George H. W. Bush held the White House.

But as 2006 edged toward summer, the seventy-two-year-old senator was starting to worry he'd been set up for epic failure. To start with, the union sent letters to every big leaguer warning that "any information provided could lead to discipline of you and/or others," and even worse, "Senator Mitchell cannot promise that information you disclose will not be given to a federal or state prosecutor." Although union chief Donald Fehr agreed to a brief interview with Mitchell, his chief operating officer, Gene Orza, wouldn't do the same. The union even forbade representatives of the Montreal lab in charge of drug testing from talking to Mitchell.

But there were plenty of other sources. The story of drugs in baseball is one of millionaire athletes and even wealthier team owners, but it is also one of two-bit ancillary characters: a cocaine-distributing mascot and an extreme weight lifter and—in the case of Kirk Radomski—a former Mets batboy from the Bronx.

Mitchell's investigation likely would have ended as a conspicuous flop if it wasn't for the ex-batboy.

I n December 2005, when Radomski opened the door of his Long Island home to Novitzky, armed with a search warrant, baseball's accidental steroid kingpin knew immediately that this was not a scandal that was going away without players being named.

In a reversal of most narcotics investigations, Novitzky was more concerned with gathering evidence on the customers than on the dealer. "We're not here to arrest you," Radomski recalls Novitzky saying. "We just need to talk to you."

To save his own hide, Radomski agreed to one of the more unique cooperation arrangements in history. Instead of building criminal cases against Radomski's customers and associates, he would be helping to expose them in a senator's effort to save baseball, with a promise that the agents would plead for leniency with the criminal courts afterward.

Unlike Victor Conte, Radomski wasn't a guy who'd set out to build an empire around PEDs. He was just a neighborhood kid from the Bronx who, in 1985, had gotten a part-time job in the Mets clubhouse because the team's equipment manager lived in a basement apartment around the corner.

When he got into bodybuilding—and regular steroid cycles—years later, players noticed his Schwarzenegger physique and started asking if he could get them a dose here and there.

When regular hookups like Mets outfielder David Segui moved to other teams, they passed along Radomski's name as a guy who could be trusted. Starting around 1995, Radomski found himself fielding orders from everyone from superstar pitchers like Kevin Brown to average hitters like Rondell White. He'd simply mail them the stuff through USPS and get cash or a check in return.

"I wasn't BALCO, which was an entire laboratory set up to create designer supplements for players," Radomski later wrote in his memoir, *Bases Loaded*. "I was one guy helping an occasional player on the side."

Radomski didn't consider pleading his innocence, and he soon accepted that he would have to betray his ballplayer friends. As part of his plea deal with the feds, Radomski agreed to bolster George Mitchell's inquiry. After running into a brick wall with the players union and the testing labs, Mitchell had scheduled a short initial meeting with the clubhouse attendant and greeted him with suspicion. When Radomski handed over a list of everyone he'd sold drugs to, the senator scoffed, "This is pretty hard to believe."

But when Radomski started to describe his dealings in undeniable detail, Mitchell canceled all his meetings for the day and spent almost nine hours with his new favorite witness. Though Radomski's "spring cleaning" that October had destroyed what would have been valuable evidence, the senator had the former dealer get thousands of archived checks from his bank, showing that he was paid by MLB players including Mo Vaughn, David Justice, Eric Gagne, and dozens of others. Reams of phone records backed up his accounts.

Radomski led law-enforcement investigators to Brian McNamee, a strength-training coach for the Toronto Blue Jays and the New York Yankees who called himself a doctor despite only having a PhD from a school he later admitted was a diploma mill. Facing prosecution as a "subdistributor" for Radomski, McNamee struck his own deal, agreeing to dish his own dirt on some of the biggest names to surface in in Mitchell's investigation.

McNamee told of Roger Clemens—who had put together one of the greatest pitching careers in major league history with the Boston Red Sox, Toronto Blue Jays, New York Yankees, and Houston Astros—joining base-ball steroid don Jose Canseco for lunch at the notorious slugger's home in Miami. More to the point, McNamee said under oath that he personally injected Clemens, Andy Pettitte—another Texan pitcher previously des-tined for the Hall of Fame—and Chuck Knoblauch, all of them Yankees teammates, with steroids and HGH. (Pettitte admitted to PED use and even implicated Clemens further. Clemens denied the accusations under oath and was tried—and ultimately acquitted—for perjury.)

Besides the Radomski/McNamee Venn diagram, Mitchell did have other sources that helped build his retrospective of the Steroid Era. Of par-ticular help was a far-reaching federal case, this one centered on Florida's booming anti-aging industry—the same industry where Tony Bosch was already setting up his own network.

An ambitious district attorney in Albany, New York, had decided to go after the online sites selling steroids and HGH, and his investigators zeroed in on an Orlando compounding lab called Signature Pharmacy and a ring of clinics that sold their drugs, most prominently a strip mall shop called Palm Beach Rejuvenation Center. They were all targeted in the cheekily named "Operation Which Doctor."

It didn't take investigators long to learn that the clinics were operating a 'roid-slinging racket, buoyed by a ring of doctors willing to sign their names to prescriptions for patients they'd never met. When agents raided Signature and a number of clinics, they carried out binders of patient records that later showed a host of professional athletes buying steroids and HGH, including Cardinals outfielder Rick Ankiel and Orioles outfielder Jay Gibbons.

Mitchell's report landed on December 13, 2007, and the 409-page document named eighty-nine players tied to steroid use—the vast majority backed up by records from Radomski. "For more than a decade, there has been widespread illegal use of anabolic steroids and other performance-enhancing substances by players in Major League Baseball," Mitchell's report begins.

The report documents in glaring detail how Selig and the players union—distracted by their perpetual tug-of-war over power and by the short-term popularity gains sparked by the ever-growing use of steroids—had let PEDs take over their sport.

It described the negative effects of the boom, from an increase in teenage steroid use to the devastating health effects. And it included a stark list of recommendations for Selig, including increased testing and penalties and the creation of a new baseball investigative team to go after drug cheats and their suppliers.

After reviewing Operation Which Doctor, Mitchell was also alarmed enough to warn that "businesses that describe themselves as anti-aging or rejuvenation centers sell steroids or human growth hormone" to anyone, and that such businesses—particularly in Florida—should be an ongoing concern to baseball. That proved a prophetic warning.

*   *   *

As the Mitchell Report landed on the front pages of nearly every daily newspaper in America, there were very few baseball heroes left un-scathed. Bonds and Clemens traded in their baseball uniforms for ill-fitting business suits as they fought twin perjury cases. Along with Pettitte, Palmeiro, McGwire, and a litany of other Steroid Era standouts, their Hall of Fame chances were likely shot.

But there was one remaining "seemingly clean" superstar, as Katie Couric put it. Three days after the Mitchell Report was released, *60 Minutes* profiled the Yankees superstar who a couple of months earlier had sealed his title as baseball's most irksome personality when he turned the World Series into an infomercial for his newly announced free agency.

For Alex Rodriguez, the appearance was part redemption tour, for that debacle and his poor playoff performance, and part victory lap. After all, the senator hadn't exposed Rodriguez as a user of performance-enhancing drugs—even though he had secretly tested positive for steroids four years earlier and, as first revealed by this book, also secured permission to use testosterone in 2007, the same year as the Mitchell Report.

As if to downplay the "Stray-Rod" headlines, Rodriguez's wife joined Couric's segment as well. (Less than a year later, she filed for divorce, alleg-ing infidelity and "other marital misconduct" before being silenced with a settlement that included a confidentiality agreement.) And Couric launched into a series of Mitchell-inspired questions that, in a couple of years, had body language analysts revisiting the segment to point out the telltale tics of dishonesty in his responses.

As millions watched on CBS, Rodriguez praised the commissioner he later fought tooth and nail. "I think Bud Selig and Major League Baseball have done a fine job of implementing some very strict rules," said Rodri-guez. "I mean, I got tested eight or nine times."

"For the record," Couric asked, "have you ever used steroids, human growth hormone, or any other performance-enhancing substance?"

Rodriguez responded: "No." And he then told Couric that he had never been tempted to use steroids either.

"You never felt like, 'This guy's doing it, maybe I should look into this, too'?" Couric pressed.

"I've never felt overmatched on the baseball field," Rodriguez said in a casual tone. "I've always been a very strong, dominant position, and I felt that if I did my work, since I've done since I was, you know, a rookie back in Seattle, I didn't have a problem competing at any level."

Rodriguez ducked his chin and puffed one cheek as if in brief rumination. "So . . . no."

CHAPTER SIX

"Dr. G, You Are the Best!"

O n February 17, 2009, Donald Hooton found his seat under a large wedding tent at George M. Steinbrenner Field, the New York Yankees' spring training facility in Tampa, Florida.

Behind him were what Hooton later described as "the New York sharks"—sports writers, photographers, and videographers representing seemingly every media outlet in that city, as well as national news agencies.

Seated glumly to his left were New York Yankees baseball players both venerable and minor. Derek Jeter, Andy Pettitte, Jorge Posada, Mariano Rivera, Phil Coke, and other teammates were dressed in designer T-shirts and baggy jeans, resembling media interns who had forgotten their notepads, squeezed into seats beside the reporters they usually tried to avoid like arthroscopic surgery.

At a banquet table in front of the scrum, Alex Rodriguez sat down between the Yankees' manager, Joe Girardi, and general manager, Brian Cashman. He wore a black dress shirt untucked over khakis.

Ten days earlier, *Sports Illustrated* had published a cover story reporting that Rodriguez had failed the purportedly anonymous drug test in 2003. As Hooton now watched, Rodriguez implicated his cousin for bringing him a mysterious Dominican substance. He blamed his lack of a college education. He paused for thirty-seven seconds to perform an action somewhat resembling crying.

And he pointed at Hooton. "And I hope that kids would not make the same mistake that I made," said Rodriguez, "and I hope to join Don Hooton, who has done some incredible things, who's sitting right over here."

Hooton's seventeen-year-old son, Taylor, had committed suicide in 2003. His depression was linked to steroids he took to be a better high school baseball player. Since then, Don Hooton had made his life's work publicizing the prevalence and dangers of kids using performance-enhancing substances. He had testified before Congress and met with Senator Mitchell. His quest had brought him to some remarkable places, none more "surreal," he says, than front and center at the inaugural A-Rod Steroid Remorse Junket.

All of the scandals, gaffes, and poor playoff performances were just a dress rehearsal for the news story that forever altered A-Rod's image.

Forget having his trade to the Red Sox blocked. Now Rodriguez actually had a legitimate reason to be pissed at the union. By not ensuring the anonymity or destruction of urine sample records in the 2003 test—which was meant only to reveal whether 5 percent of big leaguers were doping—federal agents raiding labs in California and Nevada had emerged with the samples of the 104 players who had tested dirty.

Though the list of dopers was under seal in federal court, sources had revealed to *Sports Illustrated* that Rodriguez had tested positive for testosterone and Primobolan, an expensive anabolic steroid not legally available in the United States. It was the first of three such stories to come in the next six months, with sources also revealing to the *New York Times* that Sammy Sosa, Manny Ramirez, and David Ortiz also failed that year's test. The revelations appeared to be coming from attorneys familiar with the list, and outspoken then–Chicago White Sox manager Ozzie Guillen hoped the whole thing would just be made public: "Can somebody in baseball—we're all begging, people—get that stupid list out and move on."

Immediately following the *Sports Illustrated* exposé and before this press conference, Rodriguez had admitted in a televised interview with ESPN's Peter Gammons that he had taken performance-enhancing drugs from 2001 to 2003. If he had confessed to that span of years, instead of just the season in which he was caught, in an attempt to appear more forthcoming, it was certainly a half measure. Rodriguez, after all, did not tell Gammons—or anybody—that he had requested permission to use testosterone and other banned substances in the two years prior to that interview, 2007 and 2008.

He blamed "tremendous pressure" from the record-breaking contract, his own youthful naïveté, and the permissive culture of the pre-Mitchell MLB. Or, as the baby-talking-under-pressure Rodriguez said, "it was such a loosey-goosey era."

Rodriguez had then claimed to be uncertain as to what he had taken that caused him to fail the urine test. "There's many things that you can take that are banned substances," he told Gammons. "I mean, there's things that have been removed from GNC today that would trigger a positive test. I'm not sure exactly what substance I used. But whatever it is, I feel terribly about it."

Following the half confession, Rangers owner Tom Hicks said he felt "personally betrayed." (Considering the number of implicated, admitted, or proven steroid users on that particular Texas team, the billionaire must feel perpetually abused.) Even Barack Obama weighed in, saying in his first presidential press conference that the Rodriguez news was "depressing" and adding, "it's unfortunate, because I think there are a lot of ballplayers who played it straight."

But Don Hooton saw an opportunity. He watched on television as Rodriguez said to Gammons that he had "the rest of my career to devote myself to children."

Hooton dug up a business card he had for Yankees president Randy Levine, whom he had met in his dealings with MLB. "If he's interested in working with kids," Hooton told Levine, "we've got a way to reach kids."

The Yankees and A-Rod's burgeoning squad of hired damage-control specialists jumped at the offer. Hooton was a VIP invitee at the spring training press conference. He didn't much care about Rodriguez's intentions as long as the superstar spoke to kids about the dangers of steroids. "There were a lot of people who told us, 'Alex and the team is just using you,'" says Hooton. "My response was, 'You're absolutely right, but we're using him, too.'"

Four years later, Rodriguez walked this same plank, but with little to no fellowship from fellow Yankees and team officials. And certainly not from Hooton. But this time around, the Yankees stood by their third baseman, who had hit eighty-nine home runs in the past two seasons. "We support Alex, and we will do everything we can to help him deal with this challenge and prepare for the upcoming season," the team declared in a statement.

Because after the first Steroid Era came the Apology Era. Only a year earlier, Yanks ace Pettitte, after being named in the Mitchell Report, had held a press conference in this same spring training facility to ask God, in an aw-shucks Texan drawl, for forgiveness for using growth hormone. When he pitched his last game several years later, the *New York Times* paid homage to his career with a lengthy tribute that made no mention of performance enhancers.

In the post-Mitchell hangover, baseball was handing out free passes. This was A-Rod's.

But Rodriguez—who only a year earlier had emphatically told Katie Couric on *60 Minutes* that he had never used performance-enhancing drugs—had a hard time getting his new story straight at the February 2009 press conference.

While in the Gammons interview only a week earlier he claimed he hadn't known he had failed a test, this time he acknowledged that in 2004 he had been informed of the possibility by MLBPA chief Gene Orza. He had told Gammons that Selena Roberts was a "stalker" who had broken into his Miami Beach house, but now he said that was a "misunderstanding of facts" and that he had apologized to her on the phone. And, most notably, Rodriguez no longer claimed that the mystery substance came from GNC.

The injectable drug was called "boli," he said. "Going back to 2001, my cousin started telling me about a substance that you could purchase over-the-counter in DR," Rodriguez said, reading from sheets of paper. "It was his understanding that it would give me a dramatic energy boost and [was] otherwise harmless. My cousin and I, one more ignorant than the other, decided it was a good idea to start taking it. My cousin would administer it to me, but neither of us knew how to use it properly, [proving] just how ignorant we both were."

Asked who transported the "boli" from the Dominican, Rodriguez replied: "Same person." He then refused to name his cousin. "I am here to stand front and center and take the blame because I am responsible for this."

But he had given the American sportswriting corps new prey to chase. And for them, figuring out to whom Rodriguez was referring was really just a matter of recollecting past assignments. When a features writer had Rodriguez as a subject, the cousin was the chubby, mustachioed chauffeur who drove the superstar to the interview. When a photographer shot Rodriguez for a magazine spread, he was the unobtrusive fellow in a tracksuit, hands patiently clasped as his cousin preened for the camera.

Within twenty-four hours of the Tampa press conference, ESPN had identified the cousin: Yuri Sucart. The name trended on Google. Bloggers posted aerial views of his family's Kendall home. An ESPN.com scribe got to work on a three-thousand-word chronicle of the life and times of Yuri Sucart, divulging everything from his favorite cigar store to his love of rice and beans with burnt bacon. He became daily fodder for the *New York Daily News* and the *New York Post*, tabloids in which he was referred to as A-Rod's "steroid mule."

Rodriguez didn't only sell out Sucart to the press. Rob Manfred, then MLB's executive vice president of labor relations, traveled to the spring training site to interview Rodriguez about the steroids revelation. It was the first instance in four consecutive years in which league officials traveled to Florida to discuss various PED controversies with Rodriguez. The embattled superstar sat with the executive, another MLB attorney, and a league investigator and revealed Sucart's role in traveling to the Dominican Republic for the "boli," which he gave to Rodriguez, according to Manfred's confidential arbitration testimony obtained by these authors. "I believe in the interview he also indicated that he helped in the administration of those drugs," Manfred added.

The league officials attempted to interview Sucart as well, but he refused to participate. The mysterious cousin also never issued as much as a prepared statement to the sportswriters hounding him. "As a result of the information Mr. Rodriguez had provided and based on his refusal to participate in an interview," as Manfred later testified, the league banned him from all MLB facilities. This was not a positive career development for a major league right-hand man.

Records reveal that for Sucart, the timing was particularly bad. His plan of buying a few properties around Miami and renting to tenants—a piddling version of his little cousin's Newport Property Ventures—had imploded with the real estate crash.

By the end of 2008, three of the Sucarts' properties, with mortgages of more than $1 million, were all in foreclosure. Yuri Sucart's real estate speculation caused him to lose his family's home and all properties but one shabby complex.

Sucart's friends blamed Rodriguez for using his cousin as a human shield, forever linking the previously anonymous Miamian to drugs in the process. "Yuri is a very honest guy, sincere and trustworthy," says friend Roger Ball. "He practically raised Alex at times. And he got 'F'-ed."

Immediately after finishing the press conference, Rodriguez made a beeline for Don Hooton and shook his hand as cameras clicked. In the weeks to come, the Taylor Hooton Foundation set up speaking engagements for Rodriguez.

Don Hooton and his remorseful superstar developed a regular routine at high schools, universities, and Boys & Girls Clubs in the Bronx, Tampa, Miami, and other cities up and down the East Coast. Hooton would speak for about forty-five minutes on the dangers of steroid use, and then Rodriguez would surprise the students by popping in and giving his own speech. "It was kind of like introducing Santa Claus," Hooton says of the students' typical reaction.

"God has given you all that you need," Hooton says Rodriguez told the kids. "You may not have enough to be a successful third baseman for the Yankees, but you have enough to be a doctor or a lawyer or a plumber. You have enough to succeed."

Then Rodriguez remarked that he wished the Taylor Hooton Foundation had been around when he was young, to steer him away from steroids.

Even in the first few weeks of that relationship with Hooton, as Rodriguez fought to regain his reputation as a clean player, he was already making the next connection that again publicly tied him to illicit substances.

In 2009, Rodriguez grappled with a hip injury but completed one of the most rewarding seasons of his career. He was finally able to silence the criticism that he choked under playoff pressure. And that quick recovery was thanks in part to undisclosed treatments from a Canadian physician he liked to call "Dr. G."

Dr. Anthony Galea's trouble with the law began, he says, with a phone call from the agent of a felonious football player in 2006. The call led Galea to a new career illicitly treating American pro athletes with cutting-edge—and in at least one case, banned—procedures, the elusive details of which became the target of an obsessive quest by MLB officials.

Running back Jamal Lewis had been one of the best players in University of Tennessee history. He was drafted by the Baltimore Ravens in the first round of the 2000 draft. He had run for 103 yards, including a touchdown, in the Ravens' Super Bowl victory over the New York Giants in his rookie season. In 2003, he was named that season's MVP of the National Football League.

But after being caught by tape-recorded conversations with an FBI informant, Lewis pleaded guilty to arranging for an associate to buy cocaine at a wholesale price. In 2005, he spent four months at a federal prison camp in Pensacola, Florida.

Lewis was back with the Ravens the next year, and his agent called Galea, who was well-known in Canada as a sports specialist and team doctor for the Canadian Football League's Toronto Argonauts. The agent told Galea of a "knee injury no one could fix" that had plagued Lewis since his college days, the doctor's attorneys later recounted in a court document—"a severe case of patella tendinitis."

Galea later professed that he "felt powerless" to turn down athletes like Lewis who were "begging him to see them in the US where they were unable to come to Toronto," even though he knew he was breaking the law.

That first trip was by the book, Galea maintains: He alerted border inspectors to his purpose, and his consultation with Lewis was supervised by a Ravens team doctor.

Formerly hobbled and freshly jail-sprung, Lewis responded as if touched by a "healer," which is often the word Galea's athletic patients use to describe him. He played all sixteen of his team's games and had more rushing attempts than any season in his career.

When NFL colleagues asked Lewis about his amazing recovery, he told them about the doctor north of the border. Galea's reputation spread through the league and into other American sports, until finally word of the Canadian miracle man reached two of the biggest names in sports: Alex Rodriguez and Tiger Woods.

In what could be considered a dry run for later, bigger trouble, customs officers stopped a man toting a medicine bag as he attempted to enter Australia for the 2000 Olympics in Sydney. Anthony Galea, who has arching, catlike facial features and wears his black hair spiky, explained that he was a member of Canada's medical team, according to a later account by the *Globe and Mail*.

The officers took a look in his bag and found ephedrine, an active ingredient in cold medicine, which is banned by the Olympic committee. And then they learned that Galea—who was staying with Canadian runners including top sprinter Donovan Bailey at a "safe house" outside of the Olympic Village—had, in fact, no official role with the national team.

Galea was allowed to enter the country without the banned drugs, and the incident was largely forgotten. But it elucidated the trouble with Galea, a medical maverick whose genius lay in fearless and successful adoption of procedures considered too bizarre or risky by mainstream physicians. Galea regularly shot himself with HGH, provided patients with a controversial calf's-blood extract that hadn't been approved in Canada or the United States, and pioneered a space-age blood-spinning procedure that made the World Anti-Doping Agency nervous.

In Dr. Galea's medicine bag, elite athletics and banned substances made their queasy intersection.

In fawning news articles before a seismic fall from grace and court filings after, Galea described his life in almost prophetic terms. The son of a beautician and a bookkeeper, Galea says he knew by age seventeen that he'd be a sports doctor. He told his neighbor of his plans, and she jokingly promised she'd work for him. "Years later, after completing his medical training [at Canada's McMaster University] Dr. Galea called her on her promise and she complied," Galea's attorneys wrote. "Donna still works as his office manager."

The director of a clinic called the Institute of Sports Medicine, and the official physician for the country's tennis and ski teams, Galea oversaw urine tests of Olympic athletes as a doping control officer. He warned of the proliferation of steroids, especially among boys. "We want males to look like Marky Mark, Jean-Claude Van Damme and Sylvester Stallone," Galea lamented in 1995. "So teenage boys do everything in their power to look like that."

Galea fathered a brood of picturesque, private-schooled kids. In 1999, at forty years old, he divorced the mother of his four children and married an eighteen-year-old tennis pro. "His behaviour change[d] dramatically," his former wife wrote in divorce filings. "He became disinterested in family life."

He had three more kids with his young new wife. His treatments became more daring, his actions eccentric.

Galea started tossing and turning in bed in his downtown Toronto condo. "Go to Jerusalem," a *Field of Dreams*–esque voice told Galea, who had been raised Catholic. He obeyed the voice and experienced a spiritual epiphany in an ancient olive grove. "It felt like someone had put an intravenous in my veins and poured in a combination of fire and love," Galea told an Israeli journalist, and he volunteered his care for the country's many wounded soldiers.

His treatments made him both famous and, ultimately, notorious. Galea took a liking to the medical patents of a Miami-area doctor named Allan R. Dunn, whose off-label use of human growth hormone consisted of scraping away scar tissue from inflamed joints and refilling the area with HGH. Dunn says he performs the procedure almost exclusively on elderly patients—the ubiquitous snowbirds of Florida—but he did use it to help former NFL player Abdul-Karim al-Jabbar recover from a career of hard hits.

Galea has frequently cited Dunn in medical lectures and court filings, constant shout-outs that irk the Florida doctor. "I wish he would stop doing that," says Dunn. "I would like to tell him to get lost. I don't want any part of him."

Galea put his own spin on Dunn's methods, adding a substance called Actovegin to the mix. The calf's-blood extract, said to quicken tissue recovery periods, has not been banned by the Olympics or major sports leagues, and the world's fastest man, Usain Bolt, has made trips to Germany to be administered the stuff. But its sale and import is not approved in Canada, and its use is illegal in the United States.

Galea found a way around both hurdles, as US authorities later learned.

With HGH and Actovegin, completing Galea's holy trinity of designer treatment procedures was his use of platelet-rich plasma injections. He gained fame among Canadian athletes for the technique, in which he placed a patient's own blood into a special spinning centrifuge before injecting it into an injury site, purportedly speeding recovery. The World Anti-Doping Agency banned the practice from athletes it governs, before legalizing it pending further evidence as to whether it enhances performance.

Galea gained his first significant MLB client in 2004, as revealed by a recent lawsuit. That year, Toronto slugger Carlos Delgado traveled to Galea's office for treatment, "with the knowledge of the Blue Jays," the since-retired player disclosed in a memorabilia-related dispute. Delgado doesn't reveal what the treatment was for, but that season he was inflicted by nagging knee injuries—Galea's specialty.

Galea's attorneys maintain that his treatments involve only injury recovery, never performance enhancement. "The use of HGH is involved in less than one percent of Dr. Galea's patients," reads one court filing in his defense.

Tiger Woods and Alex Rodriguez have a lot in common. They're both Florida-based kings of sport who have amassed incredible fortunes but spend an unenviable amount of time roasting in the media rotisserie.

They're not best buds by any means, says Woods's former swing coach, Hank Haney. Woods is closer to Jeter, Rodriguez's teammate and rival. But sometimes the best golfer and one of the best baseball players of all time get on the phone and discuss their mutual interest: amassing the top physical trainers in the world.

From late 2008 through 2009, when Woods was facing the worst injury of his career and Rodriguez was sidelined with a lingering hip problem, they sometimes talked about the cutting-edge techniques of the two Canadian physicians treating both of them at the same time: Anthony Galea and Mark Lindsay.

Lindsay was often professionally inseparable from Galea. Both are good-looking, prolific, married to younger athletes—in Lindsay's case, a skier—and both were often credited with nearly magical healing capabilities. They often traded referrals and ended up having the same patients.

They had both treated sprinter Donovan Bailey, and while Galea was dealing with Delgado's injuries, Lindsay had been in Florida rehabbing Mets speedster Jose Reyes's hamstring, which was also later treated by Galea.

Lindsay treated sprinter Tim Montgomery during the period in which he was immersed in BALCO's "Project World Record," in which Victor Conte's "supplements" were supposed to turn Montgomery into the fastest man in history. Conte told the *New York Daily News* that he met Lindsay through Bill Romanowski, the former NFL star and steroid user. "Mark is one of the best at active release techniques, and I referred a few athletes to him, including Tim Montgomery and Marion Jones," Conte told the newspaper, in the sort of glowing testimonial Lindsay likely preferred not to have broadcasted.

When he first hired Lindsay, Tiger Woods had just enjoyed a career-defining victory. On June 16, 2008, he had spent a day hobbling up hills and using his golf club like a cane in La Jolla, California, at the US Open. This was the year that other golfers were supposed to have a chance, thanks to an injury that—if you believe one of his closest coaches for six years—stemmed from Tiger Woods's military obsession.

Woods said he had damaged the anterior cruciate ligament in his left knee while running on a golf course. But in his own memoir and in an interview for this book, Haney maintains that after the death of his lieutenant colonel father, Woods had progressed from SEALs-themed video games to running in combat boots to making publicized visits with the elite soldiers to going on secret three-day Navy SEALs training excursions that had him parachuting out of planes ten times a day.

The world's most famous golfer talked seriously about getting a pass on age restrictions to join the world's most elite military unit. "You're all of a sudden not going to be Tiger Woods anymore, and you're going to be a Navy SEAL?" Haney says he asked the golfer incredulously. During a training mission at a Navy "kill house," Haney says, a soldier accidentally booted Woods in the knee, causing the injury.

Woods's agent, Mark Steinberg, has said that Haney's book is "full of guesses and false assumptions" and that "his stories about Tiger's injuries are simply not true."

Regardless of the backstory, Woods had undergone anthroscopic surgery just two months before the Open. He couldn't sleep. He couldn't practice his swing. He could barely walk, let alone play golf.

But this was pre–*National Enquirer* Tiger Woods, when all the world knew of him was a monkish devotion to his sport. He had consistently squelched competition for more than a decade. Unlikely as it was, it was hard not to see his comeback at the Open coming.

Rocco Mediate was one sixteen-foot putt from winning the tournament. He missed it. Woods made his own putt and won it all on the nineteenth hole. He was so hobbled after the victory that he couldn't walk up a hill to greet fans.

Woods then traveled to Utah for another knee surgery. Afterward, he cast around for a physical therapist who would help him return to golf in record time. "Tiger wanted to recover as fast as he could," says Haney. "He wanted somebody progressive." Lindsay was that physician. The details of Woods's treatment by Lindsay, and ultimately Anthony Galea, are disclosed in records from a later Florida Department of Health investigation, which have not been reported until now.

On September 16, Mark Lindsay traveled to Isleworth, the Florida golf community where Woods lived in a $2.4 million mansion. On a massage table between Woods' kitchen and his house's great room, Lindsay performed "manipulations and soft tissue therapy," according to an invoice, and charged $2,000 a session.

At Lindsay's referral, Galea joined Woods's recovery squad in January 2009. According to Haney, the Canadian doctor drove to the Orlando area from Tampa, site of Super Bowl XLIII, where Galea had treated Pittsburgh Steeler wide receiver Hines Ward for a sprained right knee.

Galea came armed with an ultrasound machine and his trusty centrifuge to spin Woods's blood, Haney says. Chris Hubman, Woods's chief financial officer, later described to investigators watching Galea set up his platelet-rich plasma injections.

They were an intense, and lucrative, rehab crew toiling full-time on Woods's knee—the Canadian physicians plus other trainers, who had the golfer going through two excruciating two-and-a-half-hour workouts per day. Periodically, Galea scanned Woods's knee with his ultrasound, and the myriad coaches and trainers gathered around to view the ACL gap closing like it was a fetus growing.

Woods paid Galea $3,500 a session, plus first-class expenses. The Canadians stayed at Arnold Palmer's Bay Hill Club & Lodge, a hotel on a nearby golf course. Lindsay's treatment lasted through October 2009, for a total of forty-nine trips to Florida. The total cost to the golfer for Lindsay's care was $118,979.87. Galea stopped earlier, in August 3, 2009, racking up a bill of $76,012.70 for fourteen visits to Woods's mansion.

By then, Woods was well into an emphatic return to golf. After eight months sidelined, he had returned in February 2009 and proceeded to win six tournaments that year. "There were some people who thought his career was over," says Haney. "For him to come back like that was remarkable. It was unbelievable."

But the wheels were about to fall off several wagons. Lindsay and Galea had both been breaking the law by even treating Woods in Florida, and would face possible felony charges. That November, the many extramarital affairs of Woods, father of two, were exposed, ending his marriage to Swedish model Elin Nordegren—and derailing his career. Authorities raided Galea's medical office after an underling was caught unlawfully bringing HGH over the border.

And ultimately, all eyes fell on Alex Rodriguez and his own secret treatment at the hands of the Canadian doctor.

Though all of Galea's dealings with American athletic patients were scrutinized in hindsight, his attorney says that the doctor gave Tiger Woods no banned substances. "All that treatment was PRP, or some other innocuous treatment," says Canadian attorney Brian Greenspan, referring to the blood-spinning program. "Never performance enhancement."

Haney says he never had any indication Galea even discussed growth hormone—which is banned by the PGA—with Woods. But, the swing coach points out, he also had no idea that Woods was cheating on his wife. "Who knows?" Haney says when asked if Galea might have given Woods HGH. "That seems to be a part of Galea's program, but who knows?"

Tiger Woods has steadfastly denied that Galea gave him HGH or any other banned substance. "I've never taken any illegal drug in my life," he has said.

In the month of spring training following Rodriguez's Sucart-blaming press conference, he was saddled with a tightness in his right thigh. It was a lingering, unresolved issue from the previous season, so in March 2009 the Yankees sent him to be examined by Dr. Marc Philippon, a thigh specialist in Vail, Colorado.

Dr. Philippon was a close associate with both Lindsay and Galea. In fact, later in 2009, Philippon wrote a letter to the Department of Homeland Security, supporting Galea's application for a visa to legally work in the United States and professing that the doctor "possesses and demonstrates a command of tissue regeneration that is unparalleled in the medical field."

After examining Rodriguez's thigh, Philippon diagnosed a torn labrum. He performed surgery and then recommended that the Yankees have Lindsay monitor his rehabilitation.

Both Philippon and the New York Yankees later claimed that they didn't find out until the next year that Rodriguez was also quietly treated by Dr. Anthony Galea.

It was common for his athlete clients to keep Galea's treatments from their employers, his attorneys wrote. "Agents for professional players began calling Dr. Galea to assess and treat the athletes' injury without disclosing the problem to the team," reads a federal court filing, "out of concern that the injury might affect the player's status or contract negotiations, especially in difficult cases where the customary treatments did not have a history of complete success."

As he claims with Woods and all of Galea's American pro sports patients, attorney Greenspan says that the doctor's treatment of Rodriguez consisted only of platelet-rich plasma injections and other allowed procedures.

But Major League Baseball officials—convinced that banned substances like HGH were involved—eventually resorted to desperate measures in their attempts to find out more about Galea's treatment of Rodriguez.

Expected to return in mid-May 2009, Rodriguez was instead back in pinstripes a week early. He slammed a three-run homer on the first pitch he saw.

Four months later, in September 2009, a woman named Mary Anne Catalano tried to pass the Peace Bridge port of entry into the United States. The bridge connects Ontario, Canada, to Buffalo, New York.

The bespectacled Catalano looks more like a librarian than a smuggler. She was driving a 2009 Nissan Rogue leased by Galea Investments Inc. Catalano was Galea's executive assistant.

Catalano told a border patrol officer that she was headed to the Buffalo airport. From there, she would fly to Washington, DC, to meet her boss, Galea, at a medical conference. She disclosed that she was traveling with medical equipment, which was needed for demonstration purposes.

The officer dug through her medical bag and found more than one hundred syringes, needles, the spinning centrifuge, and twenty-six ampules of medication and substances including one bottle each of Nutropin—a brand of HGH—and Actovegin, the calf's-blood substance not approved for use in the United States.

Special investigators from US Immigration and Customs Enforcement arrived at the bridge. Catalano briefly maintained her story. Then she asked the investigators if she could tell them the truth.

Catalano "told investigators that the reason for which [she] and Dr. Galea had come to the United States on that day and on numerous other occasions before then was for Dr. Galea to provide medical treatments to professional athletes in the United States," according to a federal indictment.

The reason she was meeting Galea in DC, she now admitted, was to give him the drugs needed to treat a professional athlete at a hotel there. That athlete's name is sealed in federal records, but the *New York Times* later reported he was a Washington Redskins football player. As was their routine, Galea gave Catalano a checklist of drugs to take over the Peace Bridge while the doctor flew from Toronto.

Catalano added that "Dr. Galea understood that treating these patients inside the United States was not lawful."

Galea had two primary treatments, she told investigators, according to court documents. One was the platelet-rich plasma injection. The second was an injection, into a muscle tear, of a drug cocktail including the growth hormone Nutropin. As with all growth hormones, the use of Nutropin is banned in major American sports.

In an interview for this book, Galea's Canadian attorney, Greenspan, denied Catalano's claim that the doctor treated pro athletes with HGH. "She was placed in a rather intimidating situation and questioned in a rather intimidating fashion," says Greenspan. "He's a healer, not a cheater."

But Catalano told investigators that she had unlawfully transported drugs over other borders for Galea. Because Actovegin couldn't be purchased in Canada or the United States, in 2007 Galea sent her to Germany to purchase a supply. The doctor instructed her not to declare the drug upon reentry to Canada. If she was ever stopped crossing a border, Galea had told her to use the medical conference cover story.

Galea had decided it was too risky for him to cross the border with drugs himself in February 2009, Catalano said. One month after starting his treatments of Tiger Woods, he was stopped by border inspectors who warned him he could not bring medical supplies into the United States. Galea told the officials "that he was a sports doctor giving a medical lecture in Florida and had medical equipment" for that purpose, according to customs records.

Catalano—who had worked for Galea since 1998, when she was fifteen—turned her work BlackBerry phone over to investigators, and when she next met with officials for ICE, FBI, and the Food and Drug Administration, she came armed with work calendars and a spreadsheet she created. "What's a nice girl like Mary Anne Catalano doing in a joint like this?" her attorney later cracked in court. (Galea has publicly stated that the HGH that Catalano had when she was arrested at the border was only for his own use. "I only brought enough for her to do two injections into me because I was away for two nights," Galea said in March 2010. "They made it look like I had 100 vials. I had one little vial and two doses were for me and you think that someone along the line would ask 'Well how much is there?'")

Using customs records, Catalano's materials, and interviews with clients, federal investigators re-created Galea's 2009 calendar. They began to put together the picture of a year in which the doctor crisscrossed the country with his illicit medical kit, traveling to Washington, DC; Orlandol; Tampa; Boston; San Francisco; San Diego; Cleveland; and New York City, according to federal records.

As the feds put together the case, Alex Rodriguez was enjoying a resurgent 2009. His season had started out rocky, to say the least. He had been hit by Selena Roberts's twin punches of the exposé concerning the failed 2003 test and an unauthorized biography that accused Rodriguez of doping in high school; gotten his broke cousin banned from MLB; and lost nearly the first quarter of the regular season to knee trouble.

But there's no salve like winning. Upon his return from injury in the second week of May, Rodriguez had no trouble finding his explosive power swing. During a homestand from May 16 to May 23, Rodriguez clobbered six home runs in eight games, including four games in a row. Two days after that stretch ended, he went 5-for-5 with four RBIs in an away game against the Texas Rangers. On the final game of the season, Rodriguez hit two home runs and racked up seven RBIs, landing him at exactly thirty home runs and one hundred RBIs despite playing only 124 games. It was a record twelfth straight time he hit both plateaus.

And for once, the thirty-four-year-old Rodriguez's bat didn't fail him in the postseason. His two home runs and six RBIs powered his team to a three-game sweep of the Minnesota Twins in the division series, where the Yankees had made three consecutive quick exits in postseasons previous. He homered in three straight games in a championship series victory against the Los Angeles Angels, including an eleventh-inning shot that saved Game Two for the Yankees. And he knocked in six runs in six games as the Yankees defeated the Phillies in the World Series, bringing a banner to the Bronx for the first time since 2000 and giving Rodriguez the first—and, thus far, only—championship ring of his career. With a .365 average, Rodriguez was given the Babe Ruth Award as the best postseason player.

The year that began with him crying in front of Peter Gammons ended with Rodriguez on a parade float in Manhattan's Financial District. "I wish we could come out and play again tomorrow for no reason," Rodriguez said of his teammates after that title win. "That's how much we love each other."

But it wouldn't be A-Rod and the Yanks if the romance didn't quickly get ugly.

On October 15, during the series against the Angels, Canadian cops had raided Galea's Institute of Sports Medicine. They had seized, along with a cache of Actovegin, an "NFL file folder" and a "professional players' journal."

The public was slowly learning details of the elite athletes caught up in the investigation. As the feds had in the BALCO case, investigators were piecing together the scope of Galea's treatments through interviews with his athlete clients. The information that those athletes divulged was protected through the federal sealing of records. The only danger they faced of prosecution and being exposed was if they lied.

Investigators gradually put together his American client list, and Galea ultimately admitted to treating approximately fifteen pro athletes in the country. The names of some of the athletes were mentioned in court or through law-enforcement leaks, including NFL players Jamal Lewis and Takeo Spikes, Jose Reyes and his then–Mets teammate Carlos Beltran, and Tiger Woods.

In December 2009, the Yankees front office was concerned by Galea's association with Mark Lindsay, who the team knew had treated Rodriguez. The team asked Rodriguez's reps if he had also been treated by Galea.

According to the team, despite the fact that he had been treated by Galea, their newly heroic third baseman said he had not.

Three months later—just as 2010 spring training rolled around for the defending World Champs, jostling A-Rod's annual controversy egg timer—the team learned that was not true. Rodriguez told reporters that federal investigators were to interview him about Galea. This time, the Yankees weren't going to blindly defend Rodriguez. "The Yankees never authorized Dr. Tony Galea to treat Alex Rodriguez, nor do we have any knowledge of any such treatment," the team said in a statement.

Like Galea's other American patients, Rodriguez was interviewed as part of the grand jury inquiry into the doctor. The interview took place in Tampa in the last days of 2010 spring training. That testimony, along with other records in the case divulging the details of Galea's treatments, has been sealed.

Galea was indicted in Buffalo federal court in May 2010 on charges of smuggling misbranded and unapproved drugs into the United States, conspiracy, fraud, and making false statements to officers of the Department of Homeland Security.

Without naming the athletes, the indictment recounted his treatment of two active NFL players. One said that Galea treated him once a week or more during the football season, injecting his knees, administering IV drips, and giving the player B_{12} shots to the arm. The other, who paid Galea around $50,000 over the span of two years, copped to "various treatments" but denied "that he knowingly received HGH and states that he carefully avoided using banned substances." The indictment also detailed Galea's regular delivery of $1,200 "kits" of HGH to a retired NFL player.

In July 2011, Galea pleaded guilty before trial to bringing misbranded drugs into the United States, a felony. In a presentencing letter, the doctor's attorney—while stating that Galea had "complete acceptance of responsibility and true remorse"—claimed that Galea was confused as to the legality of growth hormone in the United States, given the substance's "quirky regulatory history"; argued that the doctor had been in the process of applying for a legal American work visa; and said that his care for the athletes was not about money.

"In several instances he saved the careers of players or enabled them to achieve career milestones—such as Super Bowl success—which was [sic] otherwise unattainable," Galea's attorneys wrote.

In the filing, Galea described in vivid detail the virtues of his Canadian practice and his philanthropy, included a photo of the statue in his honor outside an Israeli hospital—by the pop artist Romero Britto, it depicts a brightly colored abstract clown with Galea's trademark black spiky hair—and submitted 123 gushing reference letters of support from doctors, team owners, and patients.

Apparently won over, Judge Richard J. Arcara sentenced Galea to time served, which was the night he spent in jail upon his arrest. Galea also paid a fine of $275,000. (According to prosecutors, he had billed more than $800,000 from American patients.)

In an interview for this book, Galea's Canadian attorney, Greenspan, combated the notion that Galea doped up American athletes. "The only thing he pleaded guilty to was bringing drugs into the United States without the proper labeling," says Greenspan, adding of the HGH Galea's assistant was caught trying to get across the border: "It was infinitesimal and for his personal use."

Greenspan says he is barred from disclosing Galea's treatment of Rodriguez due to patient-confidentiality rules. But "there's never been a finding" that Galea's treatments in the United States involved performance enhancement, the attorney says.

Judging from Judge Arcara's comments in court, that is only semantically correct. Without mentioning any names or even the sport of the athlete he was referring to, the judge confirmed that at the minimum one athlete received a banned substance from Galea. "We don't allege that Dr.

Galea intended to enhance the performance of his patients when they were athletes to make them bigger, faster and stronger," Arcara remarked during a sentencing hearing, "but he did know that at least one of the treatments that was given involved a substance that was banned by the sports leagues they played in."

The federal indictment wasn't the last bit of American discipline faced by Galea or his longtime colleague Lindsay. Because neither were licensed to practice medicine in Florida, both were breaking the law when they treated Woods or any other patients in the state. Practicing medicine without a license in Florida is a felony, punishable by up to a year in jail.

In December 2009, the Florida Department of Health opened a slow-moving probe into Galea's treatment of Woods after it was first reported in news articles. The case fell to a DOH investigator named Sidronio Casas. An unlicensed activity investigator with a law degree who earned $39,000 annually, Casas took a valiant stab at the assignment, knocking on the door to Tiger Woods's mansion and leaving his business card.

Woods refused to be interviewed by Casas, but through the golfer's attorney, the investigator was able to get Chris Hubman, chief financial officer of the golfer's personal corporation, to corroborate what he saw. "I believe Dr. Mark Lindsay referred Dr. Galea to Mr. Woods and Dr. Lindsay was present for some of the treatments as well," Hubman added in an e-mail, resulting in the DOH opening an additional investigation into Lindsay. Hubman provided the state with the nearly $200,000 in invoices from the two Canadians, a significant bill for just more than a year of periodic treatments.

MLB executive Rob Manfred and other league officials interviewed Rodriguez in 2010 about his treatment by Galea. And by January 2011, league investigators had launched what was a years-long effort to learn more about the Canadian doctor's treatment of Rodriguez. MLB investigator Victor Burgos called the state agency, according to an internal DOH memo, "wanting information [about Galea] and he had information to share." Attorney Nancy Snurkowski advised investigator Casas: "Please call collecting information, but not sharing." It appears that nothing substantive resulted from the call. Galea's treatment of Rodriguez is not mentioned by investigators in the case file.

When Casas sent evidence in the Galea case to a state law-enforcement body for possible prosecution, he was rebuffed, an investigator e-mailing him back that they were busy with pain-pill clinics at the time.

Far more befuddling was an internal response Casas received to his investigation.

In August 2011, with the investigation more than a year and a half old and Galea already convicted federally, DOH chief counsel Rickey Strong and senior attorney Snurkowski addressed a memo to two other members of the agency's legal department.

The memo laid out the evidence against Galea; the fact that even a Google search gave the agency probable cause that the doctor unlawfully practiced medicine in Florida; and the intense media interest in the case. "The issue at hand here is how do we want to proceed in this matter," reads the memo. "This investigation is over a year old, however, Nancy Snurkowski was instructed a year ago to 'stand down' because they did not want us interfering with their investigation. In addition, Nancy was instructed to 'stand down' because this investigation was also predicated during the time of Tiger's marital issues."

Near the beginning of the DOH's investigation in late 2009, Woods's personal life was exploding spectacularly with the news of multiple affairs. The DOH refuses to say how that factors into punishing somebody for practicing medicine unlawfully—although the clear implication is that the state agency wanted no part of any action that might make controversial headlines.

"I truly don't remember the content of what happened there," says Strong when asked to clarify the comment concerning Woods's marital issues. Snurkowski has since resigned from the agency. A DOH spokesperson said "all of the information we can provide on this case is documented in the case file."

Galea was sent a cease and desist letter from Florida, demanding that he no longer practice medicine without a license. The same sort of letter was sent to Mark Lindsay. There were no criminal charges, and despite them invoicing six figures from a single patient in a manner the state had deemed unlawful, there were no financial sanctions.

Anthony Bosch, masquerading as a doctor for years, would have been heartened by the Florida DOH's ineffectuality.

Galea is still a licensed doctor in Canada, and according to Greenspan, his practice is "busy as ever" and he continues to treat American athletes from all major sports leagues at his Toronto clinic. "I can assure you if we gave you a patient list, you'd know fifty of them," says Greenspan.

Galea even rereleased his book, *The Real Secret to Optimal Health*, in 2013, with a new cover blurb from a favored patient.

"Dr. G, you are the best!" wrote Alex Rodriguez.

CHAPTER SEVEN

Inside the Notebooks

On May 7, 2009, only one month after Alex Rodriguez held his own steroid press conference, Los Angeles Dodgers manager Joe Torre stepped up to a podium in Chavez Ravine and stared out at an army of cameras.

His hangdog features drooped as he confirmed the news: His star slugger, Manny Ramirez, had just earned a fifty-game suspension for failing a drug test.

"He was devastated," Torre told reporters. "The only advice I had for Manny is to not spend a whole lot of time thinking about something you can't change but to basically change the things you can."

Just two months earlier, Torre and Ramirez had sat together on stage in front of the same gaggle of local reporters and ESPN crews. Joined by Dodgers owner Frank McCourt and superagent Scott Boras, they'd gathered to announce that the thirty-seven-year-old slugger had signed a $45 million deal to keep him in LA for two more years.

Ramirez had long been baseball's most mysterious superstar, a dreadlocked cutup in baggy pants whose popular "Manny being Manny" image boiled a complex persona to a series of goofball moments: taking a leak inside the left-field wall mid-inning at Fenway Park, forgetting a paycheck in his boot in the Rangers locker room, and blasting the dirtiest hip-hop possible over Fenway's speakers during warm-ups.

That carefree perception had started to fray during his last years in Boston. His 2008 standoff with the Red Sox—which forced a trade to the

Dodgers that July, four years after the deal that would have bartered him for Rodriguez fell through—made him look calculating. Earlier that year, he'd shoved Jack McCormick, the team's beloved sixty-four-year-old traveling secretary, when he couldn't get tickets for an away game. Stories soon emerged of Manny neglecting family and friends back in the Washington Heights neighborhood where he'd grown up poor.

But on March 5, 2009, Manny had been back in prime goofball mode, ready to celebrate his new contract in his new sunny West Coast home. "I'm baaaaack," Manny mugged into the mic as McCourt slapped his legs and hooted with laughter.

No one was laughing now. Manny had started the new season on a tear, notching a .348 average with six homers, but now he'd be out through most of the summer. Worse, whatever was left of his naïve baseball savant act was gone forever. "Manny being Manny" had been killed by "Manny the doper."

Ramirez skipped the interview rounds, instead releasing just a short statement before disappearing to his home in South Florida: "Recently I saw a physician for a personal health issue. He gave me a medication, not a steroid, which he thought was OK to give me."

Manny's claims of ignorance took another hit within a matter of weeks, when the *New York Times* revealed that Ramirez and his former Red Sox teammate David Ortiz had been among the 104 players flagged for steroids in the 2003 round of testing that was supposed to remain anonymous but had also already burned Rodriguez.

This time around, an expensive new test had helped to out the slugger's cheating ways. At the Laboratoire de contrôle du dopage, the Montreal lab that runs baseball's drug tests, Manny's urine sample was flagged as suspicious; the lab then ran a pricey follow-up scan called carbon isotope testing, which can spot synthetic molecules that end up in the blood after using testosterone or steroids—even if a sample has passed a testosterone ratio test.

According to an MLB source with knowledge of his defense, Manny had presented a novel argument: that he'd failed because a licensed doctor had given him DHEA, a mild steroid that was not then banned by MLB and can trigger that test. It was a brilliant strategy because it's impossible to distinguish DHEA positives from steroid or testosterone—except it meant Ramirez had to turn over his medical records to prove it. Those files showed he'd also been given hCG, which is banned. So even though he wriggled out of the positive urine sample, Manny still ended up suspended.

Those medical files also introduced MLB officials to a Miami character whose role in his positive test was, at the time, only a blip on the league's radar.

"The first time I heard about Tony Bosch was in connection with our investigation of Manny Ramirez in 2009," Manfred later testified in Alex Rodriguez's confidential arbitration hearing. "The union produced to us medical records from Tony's father and there were references that came up in our investigation that, you know, there was this father who was a physician and a son that was involved in wellness clinics."

Manfred dispatched a team of investigators to look into the pair. In June, about a week before Manny was due to return to the lineup, news leaked that the DEA was also looking into Manny's provider. ESPN posted their names: a seventy-one-year-old Cuban-born doctor named Pedro Bosch, possibly aided by his son Tony.

Pedro loudly denied the report, calling it "outrageous and slanderous." He was emphatic: Manny Ramirez had never been his patient. Tony, though, was nowhere to be found.

The DEA wasn't the only agency that opened a probe into Manny's doping. A source in the Florida Department of Health says its state investigators opened a case on both Bosches. The source even furnished the authors of this book a case number. But the DEA never brought any charges, and Pedro Bosch's state license remained untainted. (A Florida DOH spokeswoman, given the case number connected to the 2009 investigation, says only that "due to confidentiality constraints . . . we can neither confirm nor deny the existence of a complaint.")

Tony did feel the heat, though. In one of his always-at-hand, undated notebooks, he wrote himself a numbered to-do list. Twelfth on the list, behind e-mails to write and meetings to remember, was this little reminder: "Deal with problems: Manny Ramirez, IRS, child support, smoking, finances, etc."

But from a back-alley marketing perspective, Bosch turned his high-profile outing as Ramirez's illicit physician into a plus. One longtime client, a University of Miami fraternity member and weight lifter who purchased steroids, HGH, testosterone, and other substances from Bosch, says the fake doctor often bragged about his adventures with Manny. Bosch recounted once refusing to leave Ramirez's apartment until the star paid his $24,000 meds bill. Bosch also said he rounded up attractive women for the star, according to the UM frat boy client, to whom the chatter was clearly boastful: "He was bragging about how he was Manny's boy."

When Bosch pitched his services to elite athletic clients, Ramirez's airhead reputation allowed him to push blame on to Manny for the failed PED test. Ramirez couldn't even last an inning in the Fenway outfield without having to dip into the Green Monster when nature called—of course he didn't have the mental wherewithal to follow Bosch's exacting instructions, which would have allowed him to pass a urine test.

And once the secret was out that Ramirez had been treated by Bosch at the time, the slugger's vastly improved statistics in 2008 acted as implied advertising for Bosch's services. After batting a relatively pedestrian .296 with twenty home runs in 2007, he had defied aging the next season, batting .332 with thirty-seven dingers at thirty-six years old.

One superstar took particular notice of Ramirez's improved stats.

B y 2010, Porter Fischer barely recognized himself. His gut hung low over his belt, his arms were shapeless, and his neck was ringed with blubber. He'd never been a fitness fanatic, but as a teen at Columbus High School in South Miami and a college student at Florida State, he'd stayed reasonably healthy.

But after a decade in the restaurant industry chasing orders and opening new Ruby Tuesday franchises in the Panhandle, he'd moved to Orlando in the mid-'90s and shifted careers into marketing. He slapped on a headset and stuffed himself into a cubicle. Suddenly, he was off his feet, spending all day at a computer coordinating giveaways at local bars. Somewhere between his weekly flights to corporate seminars, his three A.M. binge-eating, and his always-unhealthy appetite for beer, Fischer had woken up middle-aged and overweight.

"I got really fat," Fischer says. "I got up to two hundred twenty-eight pounds. My body fat was thirty-two percent or some shit. I went to a doctor, and he said, 'Your fucking cholesterol could kill a damn elephant.'"

Fischer's body wasn't the only part of his life that fell apart in Orlando. As it always seemed to, Fischer's problems had come thanks to an aversion to authority. The trouble this time started after Fischer had landed a gig in 2004 as a salesman for the Louisville, Kentucky–based National Tobacco, a firm that markets Zig-Zag rolling papers. He'd left his last job managing a theme park after a fiery argument with his boss.

This time around, a manager fired him in 2006 for allegedly selling extra Zig-Zag products on eBay. Police records make it clear that Zig-Zag suspected Fischer hadn't gone away quietly afterward.

E-mails from that boss's account started going out on the main listserv at 6:23 P.M. on November 26. The first had an attachment: a crude cartoon of a black man who had "OD'd" on watermelon and fried chicken, and a message, supposedly from the boss to his wife, that "if it were that easy, I'd start a melon patch tomorrow." Three more e-mails, each with a racist joke or image attached, hit company listservs in the next hour. The boss swore that someone had broken into his account.

National Tobacco soon filed a civil complaint in federal court, claiming an anonymous hacker had infiltrated its computers. Fischer was never named in the civil complaint, but the FBI got involved. On June 12, 2007, a team of agents surrounded a vacation cabin where Fischer was staying in central Florida. While the feds methodically searched the home, Marion

County sheriff's deputies allegedly found Fischer's weed stash in a coffee mug.

Fischer fought the marijuana charges, convincing a judge that there was no warrant to search for drugs, and he was acquitted. As for the feds, no charges ever came down; National Tobacco closed its civil complaint in 2010 without ever naming the anonymous hacker.

Fischer started over back in the same neighborhood where he'd grown up in South Miami. It wasn't an easy choice. Fischer traced most of his woes to his mom. The marriage between Ann Marie Porter and his helicopter pilot dad, Gary Fischer, was unhappy. Porter says she was "an authoritarian" who took her wrath out on him.

Fischer's parents divorced soon after he had graduated from Columbus, one year behind Tony Bosch, and headed for Florida State University. "If you want to know the source of my attitude, of 'Don't fuck with me,' that's exactly where it comes from," he says of his mother's punishments. "Now that I'm big and strong enough, I don't like to be pushed around."

Now, in early 2010, he was back to where it all began: his mother's house. Tortured history or not, the place was totally rent-free. The guesthouse was surrounded by a tall wooden fence, which separated it from his mother's home.

As Fischer mulled what to do with his life, he fell back on a favorite hobby—tanning. He became a regular at the nearby Boca Tanning Club, a franchise in a chain of twenty-four-hour jungle-themed operations where lotions started at $20 a bottle and Mike "The Situation" Sorrentino from *The Jersey Shore* was a spokesperson.

When he wasn't spraying himself nuanced hues of orange or flirting with the cute receptionists, Fischer hammed it up with the place's ownership and regulars. The tanning club was its own ecosystem, a pond stocked with a certain kind of suburban American cowboy—muscular, bronzed, and tattooed, always up for a nice quick moneymaking scheme, prone to violence, and carrying along murky pasts. The men he met there all came to play key roles in the twisting saga of Tony Bosch and Alex Rodriguez.

Pete and Anthony Carbone ran the place. Two brothers from Long Island, New York, they were only kids when they had watched their wealthy father fall off a boat and perish while sailing fifty miles away from Montauk in 1993. Friends from Northport High School, where Anthony transferred as a junior, say the younger Carbone came with a brawler's reputation and defended it well. "I don't remember him looking for a fight, but when they found him he would win," says one friend, who also remarked that the brothers were incisively smart. Teenage Anthony kept a stock ticker loaded on his computer and was a trader even in high school.

They had both played football and wrestled in high school. Elder brother Pete was musclebound, and Anthony had a lanky grappler's frame. Anthony, who was twenty-eight when he first met Fischer, later said he majored in criminal justice at Oneonta, a New York state school, and had chased that career south. "I wanted to be a cop when I came down to Florida," says Anthony now. "They didn't take me. I think I had too many speeding tickets."

So Anthony Carbone got into the low-overhead tanning business instead. Carbone calls himself an "area developer." Along with Pete, who reminded Fischer of a Sicilian wiseguy right out of *Goodfellas*, they ran a couple of salons and owned pieces of many others. "I want to retire at an early age and spend my days spearfishing and learning how to surf and be a better me," Anthony Carbone says. "Take up piano and find my creative side."

Then there was Gary Jones, a contractor who often came by to fix the tanning beds. Jones, at six-foot-one and 250 pounds, was built like a football linebacker, with a pudgy face and a mess of short, curly hair. Fischer gravitated toward him. Jones dispensed gravelly wisdom, and unlike the rest of the tanning salon crew, he wasn't young, cocky, and buff. Like Fischer, he was overweight and over the hill. Fischer pegged him as being in his fifties.

Sometimes Jones growled about being a bank robber decades earlier, and serving time in federal prison. But that could have belonged in the sizable bullshit category of tanning salon conversation, next to the image of Anthony Carbone tickling the ivories and painting watercolors.

A couple of years later, when he found himself a victim of an unbelievable plot possibly navigated by Jones, Fischer realized how little he knew about Jones, the sage ex-con whom he had so quickly befriended.

Jones had first sped into Florida in a late-model Corvette with his brother Robert riding shotgun and a vinyl duffel bag full of fake twenty-dollar bills.

It was January 1987, and the Joneses were in town for the Daytona 500. In the twelve days they spent in the area, they partied like redneck shahs, booking a motel room; patronizing establishments with names like Finky's and TC's Top Dog; buying race tickets and pit passes; and stocking up on souvenir mugs, T-shirts, and seat cushions—all with fake twenties. The change from each purchase was the real score. Secret Service agents in Jacksonville and Miami, tipped off by an informant, knew they were in the region to pass fake bills but couldn't nab Gary and his brother until they were back home in Waterbury, Connecticut.

In the small pond of two-bit Connecticut grifters, Gary Jones was—for this brief zenith—a whale. He and his gang dropped fourteen bogus twenties ringing in 1987 at a disco called Cat's Nightclub. He owned his own bar: T.P. Hustlers. Federal Teletypes tracked his whereabouts. Snitches sold info on him: the Tommy gun he owned, the secret compartment he was arranging to have installed in his Corvette. "Let's take a ride," Jones would tell an associate, and then they'd spend the day driving around Waterbury, passing twenties in convenience stores, fast-food joints, bail bonds outfits, bank deposits, and—of course—tanning salons.

One member of Jones's gang made a big show of his burgeoning pockets in front of a customer at the European Suntan Center. "Where did you get all that money?" asked the tanning patron. The man put the wad of twenties under his nose—"Look at it good; it's counterfeit money"—and offered to sell him some.

That man became one of those informants, confronted by the feds, whose intel led agents to trace $40,000 in fakes to Jones and friends. Sixty thousand dollars more in counterfeit twenties, prosecutors later theorized, had likely entered circulation undetected. "He fears for his life and the personal safety of members of his family," a prosecutor wrote of one codefendant, "in the event Gary Jones becomes aware of the fact that he is cooperating with the government."

Jones served two years of a six-year sentence at a prison in Otisville, New York, before his release in 1989. He followed Interstate 95 to Florida, that Oregon Trail for ex-cons and hustlers looking to circumvent the rule of weather and law. By the time Fischer met him, Jones had started his own tanning bed repair company: Tan-Tech Inc.

Jones bragged of crimes for which it's not clear if he was ever caught— smashing his truck through bank walls and escaping with two scores in one day. Though he says he "retired" from crime, his actions suggest that he was just waiting for an irresistible score to present itself. And Porter Fischer soon appeared the perfect mark.

S trange criminal occurrences went down at the Carbone brothers' salons—episodes that suggested Machiavellian schemes local police weren't interested in unraveling. If Fischer had known more about the clandestine goings-on tied to the Carbone brothers, he might have thought twice about casting his lot with them.

In the middle of one night in 2010, an overnight desk attendant at their Boca Raton outlet was attacked. "Where is the money?" two men asked the employee, named Adam Godley, as they threw him to the ground, kicked him, Maced him, and mussed his onion-shaped hairdo.

Boca Raton police officers reviewed the security footage at the club and told Anthony Carbone they'd be back to retrieve it as evidence the next morning. But when they returned, they were told the recording device and film had suddenly been stolen as well.

Cops had found that before the beatdown, one of the attackers had filled out a customer questionnaire. Using the man's information, they discovered that he was friends with Anthony Carbone. There were photos of them together on Facebook, and they had both been involved in a police incident in Northport, New York, where they were both from.

A source close to the tanning salon crew says that Carbone believed Godley had been stealing from the shop and arranged the beatdown as revenge. Carbone denies this, and he's never been officially accused of any crime involving the incident.

The alleged attacker was extradited to Florida on assault charges, but was freed after Godley disappeared. The Carbones threatened him "until he got so scared he had to leave the country," says Godley's mother.

The police closed the case. If the beatdown was arranged and the evidence destroyed, it certainly wasn't a master caper. But this is the tropics. You don't have to be Keyser Söze to get off scot-free.

Fischer particularly clung to Anthony's brother, Pete. The younger Carbone was everything Porter wanted to be: confident, slick, and comfortably married but still popular with the sculpted girls in the salon. Fischer attached himself to the salon owner and soon started bugging his new friend for work.

He'd managed restaurants for years, after all—why not bring him on to run the neighborhood salon? When Carbone rebuffed him, telling him "they couldn't afford him," Fischer sensed the true reason for the rejection. At forty-six, he was at least a decade older than Carbone or any of his employees. And worse, Fischer at last had to admit the truth: Inside Boca Tanning, he looked like the Midwestern couch potato tossed into a crowd of body-obsessed beach fiends.

The shame got him off his ass. He started biking every day along the alligator-choked canals bisecting the neighborhood's million-dollar mansions. He switched to Michelob Ultra.

And then, one day in December 2010, he walked into Boca Tanning to find a new operation had been set up inside.

In the back of the shop, a small room had been outfitted with a medical table and a few instruments, like a blood pressure machine. It was manned by a guy named Jorge Velazquez, a muscular five-foot-nine and 185-pound man with tightly cropped hair and a serious countenance. Pete Carbone had invited him to set up after meeting him at the liquor store Velazquez owned in Kendall. His nickname was "Oggi," short for his middle name, Augustine.

Like others in the crew, the New York–born Velazquez had a criminal record. According to cops, back in 1990 he had been an unsuccessful cat burglar, pilfering $6,000 worth of goods from a Miami-area home and getting busted when he tried to pawn the victim's class ring. (A judge withheld adjudication in exchange for probation.) His rap sheet of charges reads like a meathead Teletype: brawling, possession of cocaine and steroids, corruption of public moral decency, larceny, and assault.

The then-forty-year-old Velazquez was dating a student eighteen years his junior, in a relationship that was marred by violent outbursts, according to domestic violence reports later filed by the police. "The underlying fact is that he is an emotionally troubled individual," says that girlfriend's father, Carlos Alvarez Diez. "He is likely bipolar or has some other kind of behavioral disorder."

Velazquez had bought all in on the anti-aging craze, as evidenced by the vanity plates ANTI8GE and ANT1AGE, with which he adorned his Nissan sports car and Jeep SUV, vehicles that he tended to park in handicapped spaces.

As Oggi now explained to Fischer, his operation was called Boca Body. It offered hCG "weight-loss therapy." Fischer was intrigued.

At Velazquez's request, Fischer brought in a copy of a body-fat report he'd gotten from his doctor and handed it over to Oggi, who flipped through the pages like an expert, shaking his head softly at what he saw.

"Wow, these are high," Fischer remembers Oggi saying. "I don't know if we can do anything. But I'll show the doctor."

The "doctor" wasn't in that day, but when Fischer returned to Boca Tanning later that week, he first met Tony Bosch. "Dr. T" won him over immediately, especially when he offered the "Columbus discount" after realizing Porter had gone to the same high school.

Within a month, Fischer was on Bosch's full regimen: hCG for weight loss, plus a testosterone cocktail to tone his physique, topped off with the anabolic steroid Anavar to build pure muscle. He couldn't believe how well, or how quickly, it all worked.

It's not that Fischer didn't have any worries about what he was putting in his body. Most doctors, he had to admit, wouldn't give him stacks of needles and instructions to inject himself directly into the butt before workouts. In fact, he once asked Bosch about what, exactly, he was being sold.

"Oh, that's what Lance Armstrong takes," Fischer recalls him saying. At the time, Armstrong was already in the news for doping allegations, but he had not yet had his Tour de France titles stripped from him. Fischer figured the stuff was legit. "I mean, this guy had a coat that said 'Dr. Tony Bosch.' I thought he was a fucking doctor."

These days, Anthony Carbone denies any involvement with Bosch's operation. "I know Oggi was a partner in Boca Body," says Carbone. "It was not a business in [which] I was hands-on."

Carbone claims that he rarely met Bosch—the man wearing a white lab coat and occupying a sizable portion of his brother's tanning salon. "I heard he was lurking," Carbone says vaguely.

Whenever Fischer placed a new order, Bosch scribbled the details in a notebook. He'd do the same when he checked his voice mail, or seemingly out of nowhere Fischer would see him write in them, as if to just jot down a random musing. Fischer thought those notebooks—with black-and-white marbled covers, resembling something an eighth grader might use to take notes in chemistry class—were funny. A grown doctor, and here he was keeping a diary like a little boy.

When the shit hit the fan, those notebooks were the first thing Fischer thought of.

*   *   *

B osch had ended up in the back of a tanning salon because he'd had been chased out of Key Biscayne, his distaste for paying bills once again getting him in trouble. The dentist whose office he had used to set up his first Miami-area anti-aging operation accused him of stealing money and supplies, according to Jorge Jaen, a later business partner also burned by Bosch.

Always agile in outrunning creditors, Bosch found new digs for his transient business. Through his old friend and business partner, Hernan Dominguez, he staked out office space in Dominguez's father's medical office just behind Coral Gables Hospital. There, Bosch founded Orthomolecular Medical Association. It was an impressive name, referring to a type of alternative nutritional medicine. In reality, it was just another weight-loss and testosterone clinic.

By October 2010, he'd met Oggi, who had struck a deal for him to help set up Boca Body in the tanning salon. It was a natural fit. Tony had two kinds of ordinary customers: the flabby Porter Fischers of the world, looking to lose weight or build muscle; and the hard-core bodybuilders who made no pretenses about what they wanted—steroids, testosterone, and HGH. A salon like Boca Tanning was the rare place where both types congregated, from body-conscious middle-agers to weight lifters orange-spraying their carefully cultivated abs.

For those customers who would never think of themselves as "juicers," Tony Bosch's salesmanship carried the day. A look at one typical patient's file shows exactly how the unlicensed doctor played up nonexistent expertise and then offered a range of illegal drugs to men and women who wouldn't buy back-alley steroids in a Gold's Gym locker room.

First, Bosch asked his patients to fill out a "Health History Questionnaire." Bosch asked them how concerned they were with achieving twelve goals. Did they just want "to feel better overall"? Or was it their mission to "improve muscle conditioning"? He quizzed the prospective patients about their diet and exercise habits. A professional phlebotomist then took his blood, to be shipped off to a local lab. Finally, a staffer snapped digital pictures of the sheepish, shirtless patient trying to suck in his gut.

A few days later results arrived from the lab. No matter the answers to the questionnaire or the results of the blood test, Dr. Bosch's diagnosis was always the same. He'd tut-tut over the paperwork, shake his head quietly, and announce: *Your hormones and testosterone are out of balance. We need to begin hormone replacement and testosterone therapy.*

A thirty-two-year-old real estate developer named Al—whose medical file from the clinic the authors reviewed—is a prime example of what happened next. Al first met Bosch in October 2011, strolling into Tony's clinic looking for help with a pudgy gut. He was five-foot-ten, weighed 220 pounds, and wanted to cut forty pounds off his frame. Within weeks, Dr. Bosch had him on a cocktail of illegally prescribed drugs. Bosch put him on a weekly regimen of the women's fertility drug hCG, MIC (a combination of three amino acids), testosterone, and DHEA (a mild steroid). Later, he added human growth hormone to Al's weekly mix.

Bosch relied on word of mouth, wary of advertising his illicit services too openly. Betty Tejada, a longtime friend from Key Biscayne, recalled her neighbor talking up his drugs as a way to lose weight after childbirth. And Tony Lamberto, a sixty-three-year-old construction worker, has an infomercial-ready recollection of his experiences with Bosch's miracle drugs. He heard about Bosch after noticing his buddy Lalo at the gym had lost weight. "Oh my God, you're so skinny!" Lamberto says he asked his friend, "What's going on with you?"

Lalo's response: "I went to this guy Tony Bosch! I lost about forty pounds in one month."

So Lamberto—paying $80 a month for hCG—injected himself in the stomach once in the morning and once in the afternoon. He lost forty pounds, too. His wife saw Bosch, and she slimmed down, too. "My wife was fat, too," says Lamberto, "and we lost weight together!"

Not every prospective client was as beguiled by Bosch's official-looking lab results, white lab coat, and salesman's charm.

Bosch, constantly working his connections for new customers, met sixty-five-year-old Alan Telisman through his daughter, a Key Biscayne resident who had come to him for hCG weight loss. Bosch had Telisman, an already fit personal injury attorney, fill out the usual questionnaire in May 2012. Then he put together a heavy program of restricted drugs: 10 percent testosterone cream, MIC, and even Proviron, a bodybuilding androgen.

Telisman tried the program for about four months, visiting the clinic weekly and paying about $100 a visit, but decided he didn't like Bosch's operation. "I was under the impression he was a doctor until . . . [I] saw those diplomas from Belize hanging on the wall," Telisman says. "Then I checked when I got home and saw he was not licensed in Florida."

Bosch dated a sculptor at one point, as evidenced in a breakup missive he drafted in his notebooks—"I want to move on and find my happiness like you found yours"—and his client lists drew from that art scene, including some prominent names never before reported. Miguel Paredes, "who combines the exhilarating sense of New York graffiti art with the skill and perceptiveness of a truly exceptional artist," according to his website bio, was such an enthusiastic Bosch client that his bug-eyed creations adorned the clinic walls.

Elie "Booba" Yaffa made his name as a break dancer in Paris before rocketing to the upper tiers of a booming French-language hip-hop scene around the turn of the century. The muscular Senegalese Frenchman, who raps under the stage name "Booba," has sold more than ten million records— topping the French charts with 2006's "Ouest Side." He has 1.4 million followers on Twitter. Booba moved to Miami in 2012 and soon hooked up with Bosch, whose notebooks show dozens of meetings. Other clients say the tattooed musician was a regular sight at Biogenesis.

Jon Secada may not be as hip as Booba, but the Cuban-born singer has sold twice as many albums and is still revered in his hometown as the Grammy-winning star behind '90s hits such as "Angel" and "Just Another Day." Like Booba, he was a steady client, with dozens of entries in Bosch's records that show he was buying steroids, testosterone, and HGH for around $700 a month.

Unlike Alan Telisman, most Bosch clientele weren't discerning enough to actually check out his credentials. If they were, they likely would've been sprinting away from his clinic after just a thorough read of a disclaimer he handed out with his drugs.

First, Bosch warned that "hCG is not FDA approved for weight loss" and "there is no medical evidence to support the use of hCG for this purpose." Even more disturbingly, he noted that "although a link between HGH and cancer has not been established, Dr. Arturo Perez, Boca Body, and its agents cannot guarantee the possibility that such a link may exist," adding that "we do not recommend growth hormone treatment to anyone with a biologically active cancer."

But who was Dr. Arturo Perez? The physician died in 2011, as Florida online medical records would have shown any Bosch clients who checked.

The warning signs that Bosch wasn't what he seemed, in other words, were there for anyone who looked past the sales pitch. But the truth was, most people willing to buy drugs out of the back of a tanning salon were willing to suspend disbelief.

Anyway, a sizable swath of Bosch's clientele, partners, and associates— revealed in those notebooks he kept—weren't the kind to balk at purchasing some Schedule III drugs from an unlicensed doctor. Amid the real estate agents, bankers, and construction workers, Bosch was also the steroid connection for murderous drug lords and scheming fraudsters.

One of Bosch's most prolific clients and sometimes partner was Serge Emile Casimir. When Bosch dreamed up a new "business opportunity"— a monster "bio-identical hormone replacement therapy" center where he envisioned testosterone and HGH sales reaching $100,000 a month, for instance—he ran the idea by Casimir. The audacious plans didn't usually go anywhere, but Casimir was a confidante.

The bald, goateed Casimir was also a grifter, paying for a waterfront condo, new luxury cars, and a boat through a series of crimes including the world's oldest profession. He regularly crashed vehicles in an insurance scam, according to court records, and after he was fired from his day job as a car salesman, his boss there says he found out Casimir was a male prostitute. (Miami-area records show he was charged with prostitution in 1999 and 2000.) Casimir is currently awaiting trial in Mississippi for allegedly posing as an appliance dealer named Tommy Lest in order to bilk more than $25,000 from a businessman there.

Far higher up on the criminal food chain was Bosch's customer Orlando Birbragher, an iced-out, thoroughbred-riding Panamanian who once smuggled coke for Manuel Noriega. The puffy-faced, white fabrics–wearing Birbragher, busted by the DEA in 1994 for bringing contraband-stuffed appliances and stereo equipment into America for the Panamanian president's cocaine enterprise and selling machine guns to paramilitaries, flipped on the dictator and got off scot-free.

Ten years later, it turned out Birbragher—who spent more than a half-million dollars at a store called Starvin' Marvin Jewelry; owned a $186,000 Paso Fino horse name El Libro; lived in a $3 million mansion; skiffed a thirty-six-foot boat; and kept a Ferrari, Bentley, Porsche, and Range Rover in his garage—hadn't exactly gone straight. In fact, he was living Bosch's dream life, as the owner of BuyMeds.com, a website peddling pills through fraudulent prescriptions.

Sentenced to thirty-five months in prison for dealing controlled substances and money laundering, by the time Birbragher met Bosch he was free on probation, reporting to a judge that he had been a "model citizen."

Orlando and his wife, Alex Birbragher, made at least eight appointments with Bosch during this time. "Text address to send meds," Bosch wrote next to Orlando's name in one instance. Of course, under the terms of his probation, Birbragher was not allowed to "frequent places where controlled substances are illegally sold, used, distributed, or administered."

Continuing Bosch's tour of the Miami underworld, there was the time that his sale of PEDs unwittingly brought down a murderous international crime syndicate.

*   *   *

Alvaro Lopez Tardon was a dark-eyed, lean, and hyperactive Spaniard in his early thirties. Elaborate tattoos along his back snaked past the collars and cuffs of his designer shirts. Lopez Tardon was a devoted practitioner of Santeria, the Caribbean religion best known to outsiders for its ritual animal sacrifices.

It was through his new wife, Sharon, a beautiful American woman who had first become a patient in 2008, that Tardon met Bosch. Sharon asked that Bosch put her husband on the gold package, increasing his "youth, sexual intimacy, digestion, energy output, and weight management," as she later said.

Bosch had just what they needed. "We were given a package of eight bottles of HGH and a red substance," she later recalled, "that was to only be used by my husband."

On some days, Lopez Tardon, who lived in a waterfront condo in Miami's old-money enclave of Coconut Grove, drove a Bugatti Veyron. The car had a sticker price of well more than a million dollars. On others, he slummed it in a Lamborghini Murcielago or Ferrari F430.

Lopez Tardon told Bosch that he made his living as an automobile buyer for European clients. Bosch told Lopez Tardon that he was a doctor.

For three years, the husband and wife were regulars, picking up medication at one of Tony's facilities—first at Boca Body, and later at BioKem and Biogenesis—and keeping the medicine in their fridge. Sometimes Bosch personally delivered the stuff to their luxury flat overlooking Biscayne Bay, taking a few hundred dollars cash as payment.

With Bosch's wonder drugs, Lopez Tardon perfected his body. His abs were stacked and perfectly defined. He paid a professional photographer to stage glamour shots of his chiseled and inked-up physique while wearing only leather pants, his hair coiffed into a faux-hawk, mist gleaming on his chest.

But Bosch's medicine brought more than shimmering pecs. The side effects took control of Lopez Tardon, his wife later told investigators. "My husband became isolated, hostile and violent," she wrote. "He lost his sex drive and blamed me."

On March 1, 2011, Lopez Tardon barged into their apartment and demanded that Sharon sign paperwork that would let him extend his American visa. She refused. Alvaro, now more than two hundred pounds of pure muscle, snapped. Furniture flew, wineglasses shattered, and he slammed his own head against the television set until the screen spiderwebbed.

Then he grabbed a knife and chased after his terrified wife. Sharon screamed and ran into the laundry room, where her husband cornered her, held the knife to her throat, and punched her repeatedly in the stomach.

Sharon hit a panic button that had been preinstalled in the luxe condo, and police arrived to arrest Alvaro. Cops found diamonds, luxury watches, an inordinate number of cell phones, and more than $10,000 cash among Lopez Tardon's personal property, but let him go while awaiting trial on domestic violence charges.

But soon after the attack, a simmering Sharon decided to cooperate with the federal investigators looking to expose her husband's true line of work.

Two months later—on July 14, 2011—federal agents in Spain and Miami launched coordinated raids. In Miami, they burst into Alvaro Lopez Tardon's getaway penthouse on the thirty-eighth floor of a Brickell condo building. In Madrid, they raided the home of Alvaro's brother, Artemio Lopez Tardon, and found €100,000 stuffed in a laundry basket, another €400,000 secreted around the building, €5 million in an elevator shaft, and €19 million hidden beneath the floor near a ten-person Jacuzzi.

The Lopez Tardon brothers, federal prosecutors say, were actually the sadistic frontmen of the Los Miami Gang, Spain's biggest cocaine cartel.

In Miami, Alvaro had laundered more than $26 million in drug money, according to a federal indictment, by buying and reselling a huge fleet of luxury cars and waterfront condos. Back in Spain, he was wanted for at least five murders and scores of kidnappings and beatings tied to a war with a one-legged drug lord known as El Enano—"The Dwarf." The Dwarf had once beaten Artemio so badly that he went temporarily blind, and then shot him through both knees and left him for dead along a highway. (Alvaro Lopez Tardon has pled not guilty and, as of publication, is awaiting trial in Miami.)

Nearly a year after the federal indictment against her ex-husband, Sharon was interviewed by a Florida Department of Health investigator and described in writing the rage Bosch's medicine inspired in Alvaro Lopez Tardon.

The wife of a man living a murderous double life said Bosch had managed to trick her with his own charade—by convincing her, like so many other patients, that he was a licensed doctor.

Unlike Victor Conte, Bosch didn't build his business around concocting high-end drug cocktails for elite athletes. Not initially, at least.

If Bosch had kept to the "civilians" of Miami—the construction workers, real estate agents, and even the Spanish drug kingpins—he'd likely still be in business in a strip mall somewhere, just like hundreds of other anti-aging clinics in Florida, bringing in a six-figure annual revenue in plain sight of disinterested authorities.

But running a local anti-aging clinic was still far from his perception of himself as an important, brilliant man—a *Bosch*, dammit, the same as respected physician Pedro and off-the-rails guerrilla Orlando. Running a clinic and posing in a lab coat may have been closer to the wealthy and famous doctor he'd always wanted to be, but his notebooks make it clear that he still saw much bigger things in his future.

In one page, he outlined his vision for a chain of clinics in South Miami, Key Biscayne, Doral, and Aventura, all feeding profits into a management company, which would then park the money "offshore." The clinics, in turn, would support his own laboratory network, which could produce "private-label formulas" to sell to customers. Eventually, he wrote, the network would expand internationally to Panama, Colombia, and a destination spa in Belize.

His long-range goals—including his dream life span—were even more grandiose. Between dollar-sign doodles he mapped out his own goals: "real estate, limo, plane, research institute, yacht, 100 years old." And here's how he'd make it happen: "Create a brand for expansion, sell a percent for $15 million, invest $$ in a stem cell research therapy institute." Bosch's position in this brand would be "CEO / founder / chairman / lead physician / scientist / professor/author."

Forget peddling testosterone in a South Miami tanning salon. Anthony Bosch wanted to be the Oprah of anti-aging. To gain the capital to make his dreams come true, though, Bosch knew he would have to expand the base of the highest-paying clients he had, the guys who could make him famous: professional athletes looking for an illicit edge.

But first Bosch had to learn how to boost their bodies. His notebooks provide a guide to his chemical tinkering—a process vastly different from those of his predecessors in the PED game.

If BALCO was the blueprint for big league doping success, Conte had crafted a tough-to-follow act. While Conte himself was a self-taught nutritionist—lacking even Tony Bosch's basics from Belizean medical school—the former funk bassist did have the good sense to recognize his weakness.

So when Conte looked to move into the designer steroid game, he started by trawling online message boards haunted by hard-core bodybuilders. That's where he met Patrick Arnold, a brilliant weight lifter with a bachelor's in chemistry from the University of New Haven. Arnold was already a legend for popularizing Andro, the drug McGwire had been caught with during his home run chase; Arnold had synthesized it after finding it in old German patents.

Working with Conte, Arnold became the guru of secret steroids. He used a 1969 pharmacology textbook to find drugs that had never reached the market and thus weren't on any professional league's radars for testing. Three of his star creations—norbolethone, desoxymethyltestosterone (DMT), and tetrahydrogestrinone, better known as THG or "The Clear"—became

Conte's bestsellers to superstars such as Bonds and Marion Jones, the Olympian.

It was no easy job to re-create those drugs. Arnold had to try dozens of old formulas and then find bodybuilders to act as guinea pigs at the risk of destroying their livers. If one angry track coach hadn't stolen a syringe of "The Clear" and sent it to Don Catlin, the head of UCLA's anti-doping lab, the drug might have kept fooling testers for years.

Tony Bosch didn't come from that kind of chemistry know-how or from a bodybuilding background. There was no way he'd be synthesizing exotic East German concoctions.

What he did have, though, was ready access to the dozens of compounding pharmacies in South Florida that catered to the anti-aging industry. With just a prescription pad and the signature from a friendly doctor, Bosch had an arsenal of banned substances at his fingertips. Instead of inventing new designer steroids, he began experimenting with custom combinations of testosterone, peptides, and hormones inside creams and lozenges.

Bosch's method was to throw a GNC shelf full of supplements at the wall and then see what stuck. His signature product—a mix he later called "pink cream" that he sold to scores of big league players including Alex Rodriguez—lacks the elegant simplicity of a steroid like "The Clear."

The mix he settled on, according to his records, contains no fewer than eighteen ingredients: DHEA, a low-level steroid banned by the World Anti-Doping Agency but not at the time by MLB; the minerals zinc, potassium, and magnesium; a variety of amino acids—L-glutamine, 5-HTP, L-arginine, L-tyrosine, ornithine, and lysine—that are variously purported to improve blood flow, help muscles heal faster, and promote natural HGH production; taurine, the key ingredient in Red Bull; yohimbine, popular as an aphrodisiac; serotonin, the antidepressant; tryptophan, the sleep aid; Adenosine triphosphate (ATP), the key energy delivery system in muscles; ginseng, the energy-boosting herb; and, most important, a 3 percent concentration of pure synthetic testosterone.

Did that mishmash of amino acids and minerals—all of which, except the synthetic testosterone, were perfectly legal in MLB at the time—really help a batter looking to inflate his home run total? The reviews are mixed.

Travis Tygart, the chief executive officer of the US Anti-Doping Agency, says Bosch's full regimen for Alex Rodriguez—which included the pink cream, along with a battery of other chemicals—was quite complex. While it might lack the scientific punch of a Patrick Arnold creation or the international heft of a Lance Armstrong scheme—which USADA later proved included a web of doctors stealthily transporting blood across European borders—it was customized to evade MLB's specific tests.

"It was unbelievably individualized," Tygart says of Bosch's product. "It wasn't a mass effort organized by a team or a set of managers like in cycling. It was one quasi-doctor who put together a very sophisticated performance-enhancing package for his client."

Tygart points to Bosch's canny use of DHEA in the cream: the mild steroid might not do much to build strength, but it does provide a valuable "out" for dopers, as Manny Ramirez nearly proved.

Along with the "pink cream," Bosch's other key product was troches, or "gummies" as he called them. Troches are candy-like suspensions that drugs can be mixed into.

Bosch's genius, as he tinkered in a tanning salon with these creams and lozenges, wasn't in inventing some new, invisible stealth steroid. Instead, it was to convince his pro clients that the combination of his troches and creams—not to mention good old-fashioned human growth hormone, which baseball didn't test for until 2013—could keep their testosterone levels low enough that they could evade detection by testers while still giving them enough of a boost to elevate their game.

In the years after the Mitchell Report, MLB's main test was a check of the ratio of epitestosterone and testosterone, which should be 1:1. If a player soared above 4:1, they failed. The faux-doctor told his clients he'd found a sure way around it—by taking his pink cream at key times, and then boosting it with "microdoses" from his gummies, they could get the benefits of elevated testosterone without spiking their ratios.

There's disagreement among experts whether this is true. Patrick Arnold himself later mocked Bosch's claims, noting that "if you take testosterone sublingual before a game, you will pee positive afterward." Bosch simply wasn't "very sophisticated," Arnold said.

"This idea of microdosing to give yourself very small amounts throughout the day has been known for some time to thwart tests," says Dr. Charles Yesalis, a Penn State professor who studies PEDs. "But the notion these would help you in an instant in a game is ridiculous. These are training drugs, the steroids and growth hormones. The instantaneous, in-game effect would be meaningless, except as a placebo."

But Tygart says that combined with an off-season program, they can help. "That testosterone will give you more confidence," he says. "You're not going to suddenly grow muscle mass two hours before game time, but it will help you maintain and aid recovery in a significant way."

And perhaps most important, MLB's own experts later privately concluded that Bosch's regimen could evade their tests.

"I have had conversations with . . . our experts about the protocols and methods of administration that Mr. Bosch used," Rob Manfred later testified in Alex Rodriguez's confidential arbitration hearing. "And our experts do, in fact, believe that they, while maybe not perfect, could substantially reduce the likelihood of a player testing positive using those substances."

Those experts believed that Bosch's microdosing could probably keep his clients from failing the ratio test, Manfred testified, thus leaving only the carbon isotope test to nab them; and for that possibility, he'd included DHEA to cloud the results.

Either way, Bosch also knew that the placebo effect alone could sell his program to athletes grinding out 162 games a season. If he could help the hitters get bigger and stronger in the off-season, who cared if his in-game troches' effect was minimal—they gave players a self-belief they found just as important.

"These athletes are so competitive and so willing to do anything and everything to win," Tygart says.

Besides, Bosch did sell athletes what they wanted. There was no doubt-ing what testosterone and HGH could do, and he started including more exotic products, including peptides such as GHRP and CJC-1295, both of which stimulate the body to make its own HGH; both are banned by MLB, but are all but impossible to test for.

The brilliance of Bosch's developing scheme was twofold: The tradi-tional PEDs in his system would give athletes just the illegal edge they were looking for. And the "precise timing" and "microdosing" would keep them safe from the censors; if they failed, Bosch could always claim—as he had with Manny Ramirez and as he claimed multiple times in years to come—that they simply hadn't followed his instructions to a T.

It was a hell of a lot simpler than resurrecting strings of forgotten East German amino acids. And for a least a few years, it was a hell of a lot more profitable for Tony Bosch.

CHAPTER EIGHT

Bosch's Shadow Empire

The handshake that was both Tony Bosch's biggest break and the beginning of his downfall came very late on a sweltering night in Tampa.

It was July 30, 2010, and Bosch was flanked by Jorge "Oggi" Velazquez, the former cat burglar who had set up the meeting. To the ballplayer they both called "Cacique," they could have seemed a comical, perhaps disconcerting, couple as they walked into his hotel room: the short, hard-eyed former liquor store owner with a temper said to verge on bipolar, and the twitchy, ingratiating character everybody called "Dr. T."

This guy is the best at what he does, Velazquez promised, laying the salesmanship on thick. *He can provide you with everything you need.*

If the ballplayer had any misgivings, he missed his chance to cut bait with no harm done. Instead, Bosch later said, the first words out of Cacique's mouth were: "What did Manny Ramirez take in 2008 and 2009? What were you giving Manny Ramirez?"

The inquiry was rooted in both envy and concern. On Bosch's regimen, Ramirez had apparently rejuvenated his health and his swing, playing in all but nine regular season games, almost doubling his home run output from the previous season and knocking in 121 runs. Stuck in an extremely high-profile power slump, Cacique wanted that fountain of youth.

The flip side of that coin, of course, was that the only reason anybody knew Ramirez was taking anything at all was because he got caught. He'd pissed positive, and paperwork had given away Anthony Bosch.

But Ramirez was busted, Bosch now explained to Cacique, because he hadn't followed instructions. Ramirez had allowed somebody else to give him an intramuscular injection at the wrong time, causing the drugs to remain in his system when it came time for a league urine test. Getting caught, Bosch explained, was just Manny being Manny.

It was "nearly impossible" for his clients to test positive if they followed his instructions, Bosch promised. He would provide diagnostic

Another Bosch regimen for Rodriguez, using his nickname, "Cacique" blood testing, proper dosing, and exact times at which the drugs should be administered.

The ballplayer was sold. Bosch detailed the testosterone creams, growth hormone, and other substances he would be recommending, and they made plans to meet again.

Soon afterward, the nickname "Cacique" started appearing in Bosch's notebooks. Other times, Bosch simply dropped the lingo and write "AER" next to his new client's phone number, which started with Miami's area code of 305.

The initials stood, of course, for Alexander Emmanuel Rodriguez.

The meeting between Bosch and Rodriguez was one part luck, one part cosmic inevitability, and all parts Yuri Sucart.

In 2009 or early 2010, Sucart, who was friends with Velazquez, had a consultation with Bosch, according to a detailed arbitration decision made public during Rodriguez's later fight with the league. Sucart, who had carried around extra pounds since childhood, was nearing obesity in his late forties. As he had for construction workers and Spanish drug lords, Bosch put Sucart on a pounds-shedding regimen of supplements and hormones.

Sucart still doted on, and was employed by, his younger cousin. For Alex Rodriguez, the 2009 season, which had started in disgrace had ended in renaissance, in the form of the Yankees championship. Sure, Rodriguez had burned Sucart by outing him as his steroid source to investigators and reporters, costing his cousin access to MLB facilities, but he had also given him a salary bump. Sucart, who made under $60,000 in 2006, saw his pay raised to $100,000 over the five years following. Rodriguez even had the Yankees make an extra 2009 championship ring, worth thousands of dollars, for his newly banned-from-the-MLB cousin.

It was Sucart who used the nickname "Cacique" for Rodriguez, revealing the sycophantic extent of their relationship. Caciques were the indigenous chiefs on Hispanola, the island that later became Haiti and the Dominican Republic. They had utter power over their fiefdoms.

As Bosch treated Sucart, the chubby patient had often made reference to the man he called that name, or alternatively, "Primo." During his treatments, Sucart wore Yankees hats and shirts and that 2009 championship ring. He told Bosch that he worked for Rodriguez, and any Google search of Sucart—bringing up thousands of hits about the steroid scandal that had erupted just one spring earlier—would have informed the fake doctor that this was a relationship written in the stars.

Among the supplements Bosch gave Sucart were his signature "gummies" or fast-acting testosterone troches. Sucart told Bosch that he thought the troches packed an "unbelievable sense of energy recovery." He added that he had given one to "Primo" and that Rodriguez "loved it because of its explosive effect," according to the arbitration decision.

This long-distance flirtation between Bosch and Rodriguez lasted months until the superstar finally decided to take the plunge in late July 2010. Rodriguez was suffering a power outage that would worry only the world's most insecure slugger: He was stuck on 599 home runs.

After losing so much of 2009 to his hip injury, Rodriguez had stayed mostly healthy through the first four months of the 2010 season. He was no longer being treated by Anthony Galea, who was indicted in May 2010. Rodriguez's power numbers were unremarkable but steady: He had fourteen home runs by the All-Star break, and, batting behind the consistently mashing cleanup hitter Mark Teixeira, Rodriguez bolstered the Yankees' batting order as the team traded first place back and forth with the Tampa Bay Rays.

Rodriguez was named to the July 13 All-Star Game for the thirteenth time in his career. Despite the game being played in California at the Los Angeles Angels' stadium, the Yankees dominated the festivities. Their inimitable eighty-year-old owner, George Steinbrenner, who had retreated from the Bronx to Tampa in the last years of his life, had died that morning and was the subject of a pregame tribute. Eight Yankees made the All-Star team, and, as the World Series manager the year before, Joe Girardi now managed the American League team.

And it wouldn't be a Bronx-themed party without an A-Rod injury controversy. Girardi left Rodriguez on the bench all game as his team lost to the National League, leading to speculation that Rodriguez's right thumb was injured. The *New York Daily News* called it "thumb-gate."

But within a week of the regular season resuming, Rodriguez hit two more home runs, including number 599 on July 22. It came in a home game against the Kansas City Royals, the first of a four-game series. Five days before his thirty-fifth birthday, Rodriguez—who had already been the youngest player in history to hit five hundred home runs—was close to becoming the youngest to six hundred.

When he next came to the plate, the umpire threw the pitcher a specially marked ball for him to deal to Rodriguez. Umps continued to do so until he hit his next home run. This was MLB's method of authenticating Rodriguez's eventual milestone ball, a custom originating in the home run mania of the late '90s, when McGwire's seventieth home run ball was auctioned for $3 million.

But Rodriguez didn't swat another home run that game. And in fact, even as fans sold out Yankee Stadium every day hoping to witness history, Rodriguez was unable to clear a fence through the three games remaining in the homestand against Kansas City.

The Yankees left for a seven-game road trip on July 26, and Rodriguez lamented that he wouldn't hit number six hundred in front of the Bronx faithful. But he couldn't connect for four games in Cleveland, either.

For any other hitter, going two weeks without a home run would not even be noticed. But—in what seemed to be a career-long pattern for Rodriguez—what was at first celebratory was turning torturous. As sellout crowds followed him wherever he went, he complained that stadiums full of flashing cameras on each swing never let him forget the looming milestone. Those conspicuous, specially marked baseballs began to taunt him as the league went through more than one hundred of them.

Rodriguez's pursuit of milestones wasn't just about personal pride. His deal with the Yankees, after all, paid him $6 million for each of the top all-time home run leaders he passed, starting with Willie Mays at 660.

A column by ESPN New York scribe Andrew Marchand epitomized the incredible amount of pressure Rodriguez felt. "What Rodriguez's endless chase for his six hundredth home run is exposing is who he is and how he will be judged from this point," wrote Marchand. "A-Rod still is a very good regular-season player—maybe even great—but not elite anymore."

It seems likely that Rodriguez would have hooked up with Bosch eventually, his frustrating hunt for six hundred notwithstanding. After all, Rodriguez's job description brought with it a constant vise of pressure and scrutiny. Despite his enormous talent, Rodriguez spent his career seeking a synthetic edge, especially when struggling to meet mile-high expectations.

Rumors of PED use had chased him since he was the top high school ballplayer in the country, and steroids had fueled his monster seasons in Texas while he attempted to justify the biggest contract in sports history. In 2007 and 2008, he had been permitted to use testosterone and other banned substances as the much-maligned superstar anchor of the New York Yankees. After that he had been linked to Dr. Galea, the now-felonious physician whom a judge had confirmed had given banned substances to at least one American athlete, as Rodriguez pursued and attained that elusive championship ring.

Taken as a whole, Rodriguez's greatest baseball achievements were inseparable from his use of steroids and other PEDs. Now his body was corroding due to age and, possibly, years of steroid abuse. But all he needed was one more push to knock down those historic milestones and place him among the all-time greats.

Maybe the question wasn't: *How could he jeopardize everything to cheat?* Maybe at this point, it was: *How could he not?*

With six hundred looming, the call had come to Velazquez, who relayed it to Bosch: Rodriguez wanted to talk about potentially becoming a client. They met at a Tampa hotel following a loss against the Tampa Bay

Rays in which the hacking-for-the-upper-deck Rodriguez had floundered, going hitless in four at-bats.

Sucart, who despite MLB's ban had remained Rodriguez's ubiquitous shadow, joined his cousin, Velazquez, and Bosch at the hotel room as well.

In hindsight, Major League Baseball could have saved itself some grief if it had assigned a full-time tail to Sucart after Rodriguez first implicated him. Here was a baseball player who one season earlier had admitted to doping; the handler who had smuggled the stuff to him and injected him with it; a bodybuilder with a prior record including steroids possession and clear business ties to anti-aging clinics; and the doctor's son who in 2009 was linked to the banned substance taken by Manny Ramirez. As far as conspicuous summits go, this was the PED version of the meeting of the Five Families.

The four continued to meet often. Rodriguez played one more game in Tampa—still without hitting number six hundred—and returned with the team to New York. In the beginning of August, they all gathered again, this time at Rodriguez's $30,000-per-month two-bedroom divorcé digs at 15 Central Park West, the millionaires' lair also home to Denzel Washington and Sting.

Bosch explained that he insisted on drawing blood in order to design an appropriate protocol. The bogus doctor flew back to Miami with Alex Rodriguez's plasma. Bosch knew that vial contained the opportunity of his career. In Florida, he had the blood analyzed. Bosch consulted with a urologist, according to the arbitration document, possibly over the hefty amounts of testosterone he was about to start doling out to Rodriguez. And Bosch had lengthy conversations about Rodriguez's medical history with Sucart, the superstar's career-long tie to all things illicit.

Bosch dreamed up an elaborate and extremely detailed doping protocol that would take Rodriguez into December, built around testosterone, HGH, and growth hormone–producing peptides. The next time Bosch traveled to see Rodriguez in New York, his luggage was packed with preloaded syringes.

On August 4, his dry spell having chased him to Ohio, Florida, and back to the Bronx, Alex Rodriguez finally connected on a pitch that made a sold-out Yankee Stadium erupt with certainty. Number six hundred flew into Monument Park, the museum beyond center field honoring Yankees greats. As he rounded the bases, Rodriguez lifted his palms coyly. His teammates streamed out of the dugout to congratulate him, and he took a curtain call for the roaring crowd.

Fans knew only about the one positive steroid test back in 2003. That was still enough to forever mark Rodriguez as a cheater. But this was as close as he got to redemption and leadership in the eyes of the fans and his team: a championship ring and number six hundred out of the way.

Rodriguez wasn't on Bosch's regimen yet. But even as he circled the bases, and after the game when his colleagues celebrated him for succeeding without steroids—"That's a chapter of his life I think he's turned the page on," said hitting coach Kevin Long—he knew he'd found the man who would put him back on the juice.

For Rodriguez, one week past his thirty-fifth birthday, being "very good," ESPN's snarky appraisal, was not nearly enough. And he wasn't content being the steady five-slot hitter while Teixeira, five years his junior, played the marquee slugger. He was determined to knock down every one of those milestone bonuses in his contract. He wanted to be the lone member of the eight-hundred-home-run club, Bosch later said. To do that would take a nature-defying late-thirties power resurgence of the sort Barry Bonds had pioneered.

On August 14—seven days after his down-to-the-minute regimen with Bosch officially began—Rodriguez slammed three home runs in Kansas City. It was the fourth time he had hit three in a game. The last time he managed it, in 2005, he was still in his twenties.

After the locked-in game, Rodriguez admitted for the first time that his lagging power production had bothered him. "I haven't really hit for any power this year, so it's been frustrating," he said. "Being stuck at 599 was really a microcosm of what's happened all year. I've been able to drive in runs and hit some doubles here and there, but overall I've hit for no power."

But now, Tony Bosch had a believer.

*   *   *

As Sucart became more and more involved with Bosch, not only facilitating the man's relationship with Rodriguez but referring him to other patients, Bosch wrote a note to himself: "Start paying Yuri Sucart." The weight-loss patient had become a minority partner.

This was just another jot in the ledger that detailed Bosch's secret business model. To any casual observer, Bosch was running another strip-mall anti-aging clinic serving the Porter Fischers of Miami, regular Joes looking to lose a few pounds, pack on some muscle, or up their testosterone counts.

But from the first days he returned to Miami from Texas, Bosch had begun work on a far more profitable, secret enterprise: selling performance-enhancing drugs to athletes. His goal was a thriving roster of big leaguers crashing the record books on his perfectly tailored regimen—and paying him tens of thousands a month for the privilege. Getting to those pro stars wasn't a simple job, though. In the shadow economy of high-risk PED supply and demand, trustworthy word of mouth is paramount. Bosch zeroed in on three main avenues to cultivate his famous clientele: the youth coaches grooming the next generation of ballplayers; the University of Miami, where top prospects refined their game for the next level; and finally, the men such as Yuri Sucart, who lived on MLB's periphery and had ready access to the guys looking for Bosch's underground meds.

In the latter category, Bosch's records show his unsubtle technique: He made a beeline for anyone who had access to athletes, offering middlemen like Yuri a cut of the proceeds or discounts in return for their referrals.

When it came to his MLB clients—who weren't eager to fly to Miami and stroll into Bosch's testosterone clinic every time they needed new doses—Bosch relied on these cronies to ferry drugs and make sure he got paid.

Yuri Sucart wasn't the only MLB exile filling that role. One well-connected baseball hustler became Bosch's biggest connection to pro stars.

*   *   *

I n Washington Heights, the mostly Dominican New York neighborhood where Alex Rodriguez was born and Manny Ramirez was raised, Juan Carlos Nunez was the go-to conduit to the island. He owned a tiny store-front travel agency on 181st Street, which dealt almost exclusively in plane tickets to Santo Domingo.

Nunez became the wheeling-dealing problem solver for New York City's Dominicans. Want to get a generator to relatives back home suffering from the regular *apagones*, or power outages? Nunez and a business partner were ready to cash in: On Spanish-language channels, they aired a commercial with an *abuelita* screaming, "With all these blackouts, who can stand it? But what makes me really mad is I can't watch my soap operas!" Nunez promised to have a generator delivered and installed at any address in the DR within seventy-two hours.

Bald-headed and chubby, Nunez didn't have the physique of a ball-player. But his younger brothers, Tirzon and Jose, were both solid infielders by the time they were teenagers in the '90s. The brothers were a constant presence at the Youth Service League (YSL), a Brooklyn circuit known as a pressure cooker for New York's best hardball talent. Ramirez himself had made the ninety-minute-each-way subway trip to remote Brooklyn ball-fields to play for the YSL as a teenager.

As Tirzon and Jose played in tournaments as far away as North Carolina, their elder brother, Juan Carlos, dropped them off and picked them up in his BMW. "Juan pretty much raised them," says YSL director Mel Zitter. A consummate hustler, Juan soon figured out how to profit from his brothers' baseball connections. Future pros like Julio Lugo, who played in the YSL and then stayed active in the league upon adulthood, grew close with Nunez. New York Mets general manager Omar Minaya says he first met Nunez when he was an area scout studying YSL for talent. Nunez became famous among these Dominican friends in professional baseball for quickly arranging their travel back home. By 2005, he recruited some of those travel clients, including Minaya, David Ortiz, Pedro Martinez, and Octavio Dotel, for Dominican phone cards bearing their images.

But customers soon realized that the $2 cards, produced by Nunez's travel agency, had less time than advertised. Nunez found himself in an ugly war with the organizing body of the *bodegueros*, or store owners, to whom he had sold the bulk of the cards, a spat that included a lawsuit (which was later settled out of court) and the Bodega Association of the United States demonstrating outside MLB headquarters.

Major League Baseball took a fleeting interest in the calling-card war outside its windows. The Dominican players were barred from further endorsement of the cards. Years later, when an even more brazen scheme unraveled publicly, league officials wished that they had kept a trained eye on the Washington Heights travel agent.

One of the players Nunez met through his teenage brothers' baseball league was Lugo, a speedy second baseman who was born in the Dominican and attended a Brooklyn high school. YSL director Zitter believes that Lugo, who enjoyed a twelve-year career in the major leagues, connected Nunez with his Brooklyn-based agents, two brothers named Sam and Seth Levinson.

An attorney for the Levinsons, Jay Reisinger, says in an interview for this book that it was actually Omar Minaya who referred Nunez to the Levinsons, two of the most successful agents in baseball. "That's a lie," says Minaya, who says Lugo made the introduction and the brothers only called him for a reference concerning Nunez. "I told them that Nunez was clean. That's what I thought at the time."

While baseball fans tend to think that Senator George Mitchell aired all of baseball's dirty laundry with his report in late 2007, in fact there was a glaring omission. It hasn't just been clubhouse attendants, trainers, fixers, and cousins who have hooked up ballplayers with steroids over the years. Licensed player agents were also complicit with their clients' doping, attested under-oath steroid dealer Kirk Radomski, whose sworn statements and evidence concerning his claims have not been fully detailed publicly until now.

Radomski implicated one agency in particular as helping build his clubhouse enterprise: the Brooklyn-based ACES Inc., owned by the Levinsons. The brothers have built it into one of the most powerful and lucrative agencies in baseball, with contracts currently totaling an estimated $660 million.

The two diminutive siblings are from the cloistered borough of Staten Island. Seth, who is older, entered college at age sixteen, graduated from Pace University School of Law, became a lawyer in 1985, and immediately cofounded Athletes' Careers Enhanced and Secured Inc. Of the duo, Seth is the designated schmoozer and deal-maker. Sam, who is not an attorney, is the natural-born numbers-cruncher.

Radomski says he met the Levinsons when they were still sneaking around the bowels of Shea Stadium, trying to recruit players. "I was there when they had no clients, when they were little broke Jew boys," says Radomski, who is anything but politically correct. "They'd be in the tunnels, and the managers used to say: 'Get these guys out of here!'"

In those early days, baseball contracts were so relatively meager that some MLB players didn't bother to hire agents. There was little competition for clients. But as the owners' collusion scheme fell apart and baseball contracts boomed in the early '90s, the timing was perfect for the Levinsons.

ACES pioneered the incentive-laden contract, in which teams paid bonuses if their players won awards, were named to an All-Star team, or hit statistical thresholds. The payouts were relatively small, but the contract clauses gave the Levinsons the edge over other agents. It was with such legwork and perks that the Levinsons poached players like Todd Zeile, who jumped to ACES from superagent Scott Boras.

And Tiffany Hundley, the ex-wife of hard-hitting Mets catcher Todd Hundley, says that Seth Levinson parked himself next to her during home games. "Seth would just talk my ear off in the stands," says Tiffany, "and try to convince me to go with him." Ultimately, it worked: Tiffany set up a dinner with the Levinsons and her husband, where they flattered Todd by compar-ing his statistics with those of other catchers. He jumped to ACES. The total value of the Levinsons' contracts reached the hundreds of millions.

Radomski says that he visited the Levinsons' side-by-side houses in Staten Island and frequented ACES's Montague Street office to the point that security no longer made him sign in. The brothers gave the steroid dealer a gold card, which they also handed out to players, imprinted with the ACES logo and their cell phone numbers and other contact info.

Sam Levinson instructed Radomski to put clients on his "program," he says. (He ultimately affirmed his claims concerning the agency in a sworn affidavit under the penalty of perjury, at the request of MLB officials.) Though he wouldn't tell Sam the details of the program, the agent asked whether it was "safe," Radomski says, and appeared pleased with its results.

Hundley, who the Mitchell Report later confirmed was a Radomski customer, was the first ACES customer to buy steroids from the Bronx-born dealer. That first year—1996—he swatted forty-one home runs for the Mets. It was, at that time, a record number of homers in a season by a catcher, a bruising position. Radomski says that Hundley told him he had informed Sam Levinson that the dealer was providing him with Deca-Durabolin. "Whatever you're doing for Todd, keep it going," Radomski says Levinson told him.

On another day when Radomski was at the ACES office, Radomski later attested under oath, Sam handed him the phone. Then–Mets pitcher Mike Stanton wanted to know if Radomski could obtain HGH for him. (Stanton has denied that the Levinsons played a role in his doping.) As they discussed the drug and the dealer made plans to leave HGH in Stanton's locker, Radomski says, Seth left the office when he gleaned the topic of conversation. Sam stayed.

This was their alleged routine, perhaps a cover to protect Seth's bar license in the event of an implosion. "Seth was never involved," says Ra-domski. "It was always Sam, 'cause Seth's a lawyer. [As a lawyer] you got ethics, you got rules. Sam's not."

Radomski went to the ACES office "more than thirty times" to pick up payments for steroids given to players like Hundley and Rondell White, he says. The office manager, Anna, gave him a white envelope full of $50 and $100 bills banded in $1,000 increments, or she wrote a check. And in the case of catcher Paul Lo Duca when he was with the Los Angeles Dodgers and the Florida Marlins, Radomski was paid out of a joint Citibank account belonging to the player, Sam Levinson, and ACES Inc. The resulting two checks, for $3,200 each, were the strongest evidence of money going directly from ACES to Radomski.

But apparently Mitchell was uninterested in outing the Levinsons or any other agents. When he issued his report, there was no mention of any specific agents. And the senator actually went out of his way to shield the Levinsons. Copies of checks made out to Radomski were included as a public addendum to the Mitchell Report. But in the case of the Lo Duca checks, the name "Samuel W. Levinson % ACES Inc.," and the agency's address—188 Montague—were redacted. The authors of this book obtained copies of two such unredacted checks.

The Levinsons' attorney Reisinger says that his clients had nothing to do with those checks. As evidence, Reisinger sent a signed playing contract from Lo Duca that matches the signature on the checks paid to Radomski. "We categorically deny what Mr. Radomski says," attests Reisinger, who points out that Radomski did not make any claims against the Levinsons in his memoir. "It contradicts what he said in his book, and, quite frankly, what he told Senator Mitchell."

Reisinger downplays Radomski's claim that Senator Mitchell's investigators ignored legitimate evidence concerning ACES. "I personally participated in at least eight interviews on behalf of clients involved in the Mitchell Report. They did not lack for questions."

But Radomski apparently isn't the only former steroid operator who made claims to Mitchell about the Levinsons' role in at least one player's doping, according to federal court testimony. In 2012, during Roger Clemens's perjury trial for allegedly lying under oath about steroids, the former pitcher's attorney, Rusty Hardin, told the judge that Brian McNamee, the strength-training coach who played a role in Radomski's steroid operation, had also informed Mitchell that the Levinsons had procured steroids for Mike Stanton. "For instance, Mr. McNamee has always said that in the case of Mr. Stanton, that actually the steroids were delivered from Mr. Radomski to Mr. Stanton's agent, a lawyer in New York," said Hardin.

Hardin intended to have Seth Levinson testify in order to impeach McNamee's credibility, though that did not happen. "McNamee clearly has credibility issues," says Reisinger, who points out that in the perjury trial based largely on McNamee's witness statements, Clemens was acquitted.

N unez was hired in 2006, according to Reisinger, as an "independent contractor." Neither of the Levinson brothers speak Spanish, so Nunez was their human Rosetta Stone, managing the daily affairs of their Spanish-speaking clients. Along with Juan Carlos, the Levinsons also hired his brother Tirzon. According to the Players Association, Nunez was certified as a limited agent, with no contract negotiation abilities, in 2010. It appears that Nunez was also a recruiter for ACES: Zitter recalls him scouting YSL players for the agency.

Though the Levinsons have since attempted to distance themselves from Nunez, calling him only a "paid consultant," a baseball team executive disputes that. "They were always together," says the executive, who asked not to be named, of Juan Carlos and the Levinsons. "I'd see them together in stadiums and at the Winter Meetings."

Juan Carlos Nunez and his wife, Manuela, moved to Sunrise, a South Florida suburb, in 2009. Among the many ACES-signed players under Nunez's wing were two Dominican talents who, as they neared or passed baseball middle age, were falling short of their potential: Melky Cabrera and Nelson Cruz.

Cabrera had once been a top Yankees prospect, until his poor power numbers led him to being benched, traded, and ultimately released. Overweight and in danger of washing out of baseball early, that winter Cabrera turned to Rodriguez, his former teammate, for help. He moved to Miami and spent the off-season working out full-time with a trainer named Cesar Paublini, a former bodybuilder from Venezuela.

Three days a week, Cabrera and Rodriguez took cuts together in batting cages. A July 2012 *Daily News* story chronicled Cabrera's resulting "career renaissance," which the paper credited to his "astute decisions" to seek Rodriguez's guidance and Paublini's training. "He felt it was going to be better for his career to get in an environment that was conducive to him training six days a week," Rodriguez told the *Daily News*. "He wanted to get into a nutritional program and do all the right things to elevate his career."

It's not clear whether Rodriguez personally introduced his former teammate to Tony Bosch. But at the time, Rodriguez's own "nutritional program" was firmly controlled by Bosch. After his three-homer game in August, Rodriguez's surging power production had only made him more faithful to Bosch's troches, pink cream, and the rest of his custom protocol. A calf injury had forced him to the disabled list late that month, but he had returned quickly and had a September worthy of a younger A-Rod, slamming nine home runs with twenty-six RBIs in only twenty-two games.

Rodriguez had once again floundered in the playoffs as the Yankees lost to the Rangers in the American League Championship Series. Anthony Bosch could only do so much to help. He was a fake nutritional doctor, after all, not a fake psychiatrist. And sealing Bosch's sainthood in Rodriguez's eyes: On October 5, January 19, and February 19—after half a season and then an off-season on the Biogenesis regimen—Rodriguez had been randomly drug tested by the league. All three times, he'd pissed clean. Bosch later bragged on national television that it was his carefully timed low doses that had fooled the testers.

Whether Cabrera met Bosch through Rodriguez or another source, after that winter working out with A-Rod, his name shows up more than twenty times in Bosch's notebooks. The notations indicate Cabrera, who grew an Amish-style beard ringing his massive jaw, signed checks for $9,000 for "pink cream" and testosterone troches. Bosch often wrote his first name as "Melkys." Other times, he used his code name for him: "Mostro," perhaps a perversion of the Spanish word for *monster.*

If it was indeed Rodriguez who introduced Bosch to Cabrera—and by proxy Juan Carlos Nunez—then A-Rod actually planted the seed for the relationship that turned Biogenesis into a league-infecting scourge.

Soon Bosch began noting meetings with Nelson Cruz, whom he nick-named "Mohamad." The then–Texas Rangers outfielder was a model of frus-tration. He had the raw power to hit forty home runs in a season, but the brittle condition to never play a complete one. He had never managed to play 130 games, but he still hit thirty-three dingers in 2009.

According to Bosch's books, Cruz's standard bill for pink cream and troches came to $4,000, and Bosch at least once hand-delivered the stuff to Cruz in Texas.

Later notes reveal how elaborate the dealings were between Bosch and Nunez. In return for big, steady checks from millionaire players like Cabrera and Cruz, Bosch provided substances for no up-front charge to Nunez's young ballplayers who hadn't yet tasted a big league payday.

These included Mets prospects Cesar Puello, whom Bosch called "Mi Hijo" or "My Son," and Ricardo Cespedes, who was "DR." The latter player, scouted eagerly at a Dominican academy, hadn't even reached his sixteenth birthday and couldn't be signed to a professional contract. But Bosch's rec-ords suggest that he floated both players thousand-dollar doses in order to "accommodate your requests," as he later termed it to Nunez. (Major League Baseball never publicly tied Cespedes to Biogenesis. This is the first time his name has been revealed to be among Bosch's records. In interviews with MLB officials, according to a league source, Bosch denied supplying Ces-pedes with PEDs, and the young player denied receiving them.)

A Biogenesis workout cadre was forming in Miami, with Bosch keep-ing the players juiced and Paublini keeping them pumped. An undated photo that Paublini uploaded to Facebook shows the sweat-drenched trio of

Cabrera, Cruz, and Puello posing with the short and chiseled trainer in a gym. (Another Facebook photo shows Paublini training Cameron Diaz, Alex Rodriguez's ex-girlfriend.)

By early 2012, Nunez had become Tony Bosch's golden goose for major league customers. Biogenesis's roster soon overflowed with ACES clients. Bosch took stock of those clients early in the 2012 season. On a few pages where Bosch also jotted a casual reminder to return his brother's sweater and wrote "pick up Cialis from Manny," the fake doctor recorded his patients' early spring statistics. The names read like a roll call of current and former ACES Latin American stars: Melky Cabrera; Cruz; Puello; solid-hitting Detroit shortstop Jhonny Peralta; catchers Jesus Montero, Yasmani Grandal, and Francisco Cervelli; pitchers Fautino de los Santos, Sergio Escalona, Antonio Bastardo, and Jordan Norberto; outfielders Jordany Valde-spin and Fernando Martinez; and infielder Everth Cabrera.

It was nearly enough for Bosch to field his own baseball team, drawing from ten big league squads; the nations of the Dominican Republic, Venezuela, Cuba, and Nicaragua; and a single sports agency. The influx of ACES ballplayers caused business to boom so much that starting in April 2012, Bosch asked all of his major league clients to make out their PED-buying checks to a new company he'd incorporated, called RPO LLC. With its acronym standing for "Real Players Organization," the corporation was nothing more than a check-processing front for his top secret business.

For Nunez, the financial incentive to drive players to Bosch was clear. Beside the bonuses from players for improving their performance, the ACES clients—Melky Cabrera, Cruz, and Peralta in particular—racked up vastly improved numbers and signed contracts totaling hundreds of millions of dollars while on Bosch's regimen. To have his players doing so well certainly improved his standing with his bosses, Sam and Seth Levinson.

Whether the brothers knew what their underling was doing would soon become a burning concern for MLB.

CHAPTER NINE

"HS"

B y late 2011, Bosch's gypsy trail of low-rent offices had led him to 1390 South Dixie Highway in Coral Gables, directly across the street from the University of Miami's baseball field, the fittingly named Alex Rodriguez Park. It was from this office that he provided PEDs to more than a dozen major leaguers, including one of the greatest baseball players in UM history, and athletes from several other sports. Broken-down football legends bought illicit substances there, as did youth coaches and middle-aged dads looking to buy their sons drugs.

The address was a sterile complex that backed up on a canal clogged with tethered sailboats. Bosch rented a suite, and to his longtime patients who had followed him from dentists' offices to tanning salons, this felt like real respectability. Bosch eventually got a brand-new logo designed by Porter Fischer, and a new name after a falling-out with BioKem chief Carlos Acevedo: Biogenesis of America. "Instead of, like, some guy selling drugs out of the back of an office, it was *rejuvenation*," says a UM fraternity brother who had purchased steroids and testosterone from Bosch for years. "He was trying to look more legit."

And he had the bustling walk-in business of a town physician, even if he didn't have the medical license. The frat boy recalls that the waiting room was packed. And it wasn't just meatheads, he says: Biogenesis attracted people "of all shapes and sizes and colors," all of them waiting for their appointment with "Dr. Tony."

Casting his net next to UM made for some serendipitous clients. These included several ex-football stars made prematurely elderly by a career's worth of busted joints and rattled helmets.

Julio Cortes staggered into Biogenesis looking for help with brutally aching knees and a back prone to locking up. Three decades earlier, he was a hard-charging defensive end on the UM Hurricanes, part of the rowdy squad that won a national title in 1983. He went on to play three years of pro ball for the Seattle Seahawks and a few teams in Canada.

Now he was an investment agent and, like many of his former teammates, sometimes struggled to walk. He had another reason to give Bosch a shot: They'd attended Columbus High School together, and Cortes had even pummeled Bosch a few times when the undersize kid had briefly tried to make the football team. "Tony Bosch put me on a program that started with nutrients for the ligaments and the joints," and went on to include testosterone, Cortes says. "A month before I saw him, I was sitting on the ground and I couldn't get up. He put me on this program, and a month later I'm playing racquetball and feeling good."

Cortes says that unlike many of Bosch's clients, he was under no illusion that Bosch was a licensed doctor. But like a lot of Cuban Americans in Miami, he wasn't bothered by that detail. "Cuba has awesome doctors, but they come to Miami and they're not allowed to hold a pencil because they're technically not doctors here," he says.

Cortes was impressed at his chemical turnaround, so he started referring his buddies. A steady stream of ex-Hurricanes and former NFL players started creaking over to Bosch's shop for treatment. Among them: Bernie Kosar, a demigod in both Cleveland and Miami. The Hurricanes legend, who quarterbacked that 1983 national title, had gone first overall in the NFL Draft two years later, joining the Cleveland Browns in his native Ohio. After a twelve-season pro career, which he finished with the Miami Dolphins, Kosar has stumbled through a sometimes-incoherent retirement marred by batty behavior, bankruptcy, and drunk-driving arrests.

Bosch's records confirm that Kosar was a patient. Bosch contacted

Kosar, the notes indicate, and at least once sent him a shipment: "Delivery confirmation and payment, $600."

Compared to the highly addictive painkillers that NFL teams shovel at players, Cortes says Bosch's treatments were a healthier alternative. "We can either do this or get back on the oxy," Cortes says. "You read the papers about Kosar and he's a mess. He's slurring his words from the medication, from the oxy that the Browns gave him."

If he gave Cortes and Kosar testosterone, Bosch broke the law. But it's hard to see immediate harm in two ailing middle-aged men snagging testosterone if it helped heal their aches. After all, they had legitimate health problems and were certainly old enough to know what they were getting into.

But that wasn't true of everyone the UM frat boy noticed in Bosch's waiting rooms. Disturbingly, his customers were all ages, too. "Not only were adult patients waiting," says the UM student, "but fourteen-, fifteen-, and sixteen-year-old kids were there with their parents."

Another customer says the teenagers were a regular enough sight at the clinic that it dissuaded him from Bosch's services. "I remember seeing a dad bring his high school kid in there. He looked like he was fifteen or sixteen, maybe seventeen, and he had shorts on from his high school team," says the client, who asked not to be named because he went to Bosch for regular steroid cycles. "I'm [sic] twenty-four years old when I went there. . . . I did years of research into steroids, watched documentaries, and made my own educated adult decision. But a sixteen-year-old kid? That's not right."

Cortes noticed the young clientele, too. "There were guys from high school and college in there," he says. "I didn't like seeing that. I saw some college kids and young athletes in there all the time. They're coming in from right across the street. But it's not my business."

Those kids in the waiting room were a fraction of the underage clients who had become one of Bosch's biggest demographics.

* * *

I f you were an undersize high school athlete, Anthony Bosch knew your
pain. He had been that 120-pound lightweight craning his head over the
shoulder of a massive fellow high schooler on team photo day, his face hidden behind drooping bangs, practically invisible, remembered by coaches
and teammates years later only as some vague phantom loitering at the end
of the bench.

To Bosch, there was great unfairness in the notion that some kids went
on to play baseball for a living partly because they were big enough, and the
rest—because of a little genetic misfortune—claimed their Toyota Corolla,
their cubicle, and the dull commute that would drive them to their grave.
And there was even more injustice in size dooming a kid's athletic prospects
when the hairy teenage leviathan taking his college scholarship had himself
used PEDs to get so big.

Bosch had a philosophy concerning PED use in his favorite sport, a tao
that he later shared on national television. Synthetic cheating "was part of
baseball," Bosch told *60 Minutes*. He imagined himself as a batter, he explained, "and I know that the guy that's throwing the ninety-five-miles-per-hour
pitch is on sports performance–enhancing drugs. The guy who's gonna
catch the ball is on a program. The guy that I have to tag at third from a
throw from center field when he's sliding—he's on it. Fair play? Fair play—
if everybody's on it, wouldn't that be fair play?"

If this philosophy applied to big leaguers who were already set for life,
why shouldn't the same be true for teenage kids whose success on a baseball
field could pluck them from obscurity and poverty?

Such reasoning drove Bosch. So did the checks he received from parents and coaches. Looking at his notebooks, it appears he had no scruples
at all. One patient form among his records includes a note from Bosch asking that a student be excused from school from nine A.M. to two P.M. to come
to an appointment at Biogenesis. The boy's name and birthdate matches that
of a Miami-area baseball player. His date of birth is listed as November 10,
1998—making him fourteen at the time of the appointment.

If Bosch indeed believed there was nothing wrong with kids doping, he was far from alone. Florida, after all, had grappled with high school athletes juicing since at least the '80s, and a decade later steroid use among teenagers was prevalent enough for the opponents of a teenage Alex Rodriguez to swear he was on something. These days, parents openly coach one another in the bleachers about how to tell your doctor your son was stunted so that he would prescribe HGH.

As always, Bosch sought like-minded allies who acted as funnels to ever more customers. One of his most lucrative connections was an evangelical baseball coach who had been famous for building a baseball powerhouse where there was once only Broward County dirt.

A Hialeah kid, Tommy Martinez had played two seasons of bush league ball for the Cleveland Indians in the early '80s. In 1990, he convinced the principal of Florida Bible Christian School to let him launch a team. It was an unlikely proposition, considering that the school had no baseball diamond.

But Martinez had a vision. His massive fingers bore championship rings collected in high school and on the pro circuit in Italy. He was cut like a statue from a Roman ruin, and he wore his hair slicked back. "It almost look[ed] like he was cut out of a rock," says Roddy Barnes, who was a Florida Bible pitcher.

Barnes and the rest of the fledgling team got their workouts in by digging up dirt, mowing grass, and hopping over holes and debris as they ran laps in a de facto construction site. They built their own baseball diamond.

Martinez poached top players from all over Miami-Dade County through notes left on windshields and other dubious methods, and within six years, the Florida Bible boys were blowing out teams with scores like 41–1. A *Miami Herald* reporter posited that their performance was "more impossible than outstanding" and accused Martinez's players of cheating—but not by doping. Instead she suspected Martinez was fudging his players' hitting statistics, which he denied.

Martinez was prone to epic fits of rage. Barnes recalls him smashing through a closed door during one tantrum. And his favorite training exercises involved smoking line drives from close range at his teenage fielders. Pitcher Anthony Cancio Bello caught one of these bullets to the left eye. "Only now that I'm thinking back on it do I realize how dangerous that was," he says.

Florida Bible was district champion for seven straight years. In 1997, Martinez fell while erecting a net to keep home run balls from denting the school building; nearly paralyzed, he quit the school. Eight years later, he was head coach at Sagemont High, a prep school in Weston where he again brought his team to district berths. Between the two private schools, Martinez won seven Coach of the Year awards.

There's no indication that Martinez was providing his Florida Bible players with steroids. Barnes and Cancio Bello say he never approached them with illicit substances. But by his tenure at Sagemont, he had Bosch on his side. Bosch's notebooks show more than fifty purchases made by the coach or three of his players: his sons.

"Tommy will bring two new patients on Monday at 1:45 P.M.," read one early note. Martinez's own full name shows up nineteen times in Bosch's books, sometimes next to the phone number leading to his private baseball academy (Its slogan: "Pro Vision—Performance Training"). He paid in both cash and check. Bosch referred to Martinez's three boys by their first names, or other times simply as the "Martinezes." In all, the sons are listed at least fifty-four times. When one of them went on to play college ball, Bosch recorded that in a note.

In an interview for this book, Martinez denied that his sons had any association with Bosch. "My kids are still skinny and small," he says. Martinez claims he first went to Bosch when his weight exceeded three hundred pounds, his poor health ultimately causing him to resign from Sagemont. Bosch supplied him with hCG, growth hormones, B_{12} shots, and several other substances. Martinez offers an unusual rationale for why his sons' names make so many appearances in Bosch's books. He says that since the crippling accident at Florida Bible, he purchased oxycontin and other pills from "pain clinics," storefront operations that were ubiquitous in Florida until recently. In order not to have too long of a paper trail at both the pain clinics and in Biogenesis records, Martinez says, he used his sons' names when purchasing drugs from Bosch. "I have to be careful," Martinez says. "As far as pro ballplayers and all that, I didn't know that."

The records reveal that at least two of Martinez's private clients also patronized Bosch. Among the players Martinez trained at his ranch, which he outfitted with a batting cage, was one of the top high school players in South Florida. Brandon Sedell made at least fifteen appointments with Bosch, according to his notebooks. The catcher played for American Heritage High, one of the best baseball teams in the state, and in 2011 he won Player of the Year in Broward County. On November 6, 2010, in one typical note, Bosch wrote that Sedell—currently starting for Nova Southeastern University—paid him $500 in cash.

Martinez also trained Sebastian Diaz. The infielder, who played for University High School in Fort Lauderdale, is currently on the University of Miami Hurricanes. A Sebastian Diaz is listed thirty-three times in Bosch's books, in one instance next to the annotation "HS," for high school. But Diaz's attorney, David Kubulian, says his client doesn't know Bosch and never bought PEDs. "[He] denies vehemently ever visiting Mr. Bosch's clinic," Kubulian says.

Martinez also says he had nothing to do with Sedell's or Diaz's alleged association with the steroid clinic.

Another youth coach listed in Bosch's books, who had already been outed during the most famous PED investigation in baseball history, was Josias Manzanillo. "Pitching coach," Bosch wrote next to Manzanillo's name on a shortlist in his records that also included such regular clients as Sucart, Alex Rodriguez, and Tommy Martinez. As a relief pitcher, Manzanillo managed to play parts of eleven seasons on eight major league teams from 1991 through 2004, a career that was only remarkable for its dogged length and the number of unfortunate incidents in which he was involved.

Manzanillo earned mention in the Mitchell Report through two separate incidents. Radomski said that when the pitcher was on the Mets in 1994, Manzanillo asked the Mets staffer to inject him with steroids, and Radomski did so in the team clubhouse. Manzanillo's attorney told Senator Mitchell that the pitcher purchased only a cycle of steroids for $200 or $250 but then "chickened out or thought better of it" and didn't use the drugs. The Mitchell Report also notes that seven years later, a drug dealer who ferried pills from across the Mexican border was detained by security at the Anaheim Angels stadium. One of his baseball-player clients, the dealer confessed, was then–Pittsburgh Pirates pitcher Manzanillo.

The middling relief pitcher's other most memorable career moment had come on April 10, 1997, when a Manny Ramirez line drive exploded one of his testicles, resulting in surgery.

Manzanillo is cofounder of Manzy's Pitching Farm, a Broward County academy training kids of all ages. Though Bosch's records indicate that he at least targeted Manzanillo to become a client, the pitching coach says he has never even heard of Anthony Bosch. "I have no idea who you're talking about, to be honest," says Manzanillo. "I don't even know this guy."

Bosch's records also include a basketball coach with stunning NBA connections. Benigno "Benny" Fragela, a former Coral Gables High guard, has said that he played pickup basketball games with Miami Heat legend Alonzo Mourning and Chicago Bulls forward Carlos Boozer. Both became close friends and, ultimately, partners.

Since 2007, Boozer and Fragela have run a summer basketball camp at the Hank Kline Boys & Girls Club in Miami. Fragela is listed in state records as the cofounder of Boozer's Buddies, the Bulls star's Miami-based charity for children with sickle-cell anemia.

Through his own company, CBF Sports Management, Fragela has run Heat superstar Dwyane Wade's fantasy camp, his teammate Mario Chalmers's camps in Miami and Alaska, and recently New York Knicks power forward Kenyon Martin's basketball camp. His website still includes plans for a Nike launch event for LeBron James on Miami Beach's Lincoln Road in October 2013, though Fragela's attorney, Richard Barbara, says that Fragela did not ultimately run that event.

Considering that the events are funded through the players' charities, a secondhand link to Tony Bosch likely isn't the public relations they were seeking. Fragela's name appears at least twenty-three times in Bosch's notes, sometimes alongside annotations reading "basketball coach" or "HC"— head coach. The phone number listed next to his name leads to CBF Sports Management, his company. And the sums indicated to have been paid from Fragela to Bosch are significant: "paid 230 cash," "400," "pd $450."

Barbara, Fragela's attorney, says that the coach sought out Bosch for an Achilles injury. He was referred by a neighbor. Barbara would not say exactly what Fragela purchased from Bosch, but he vehemently maintains that Fragela never procured PEDs for the young basketball players in his charge. "This has nothing to do with what he does for a living," says Barbara.

Whether or not Martinez, Fragela, or Manzanillo were among them, coaches and parents supplied Bosch with young clients. He designed doping protocols for many high school athletes, according to his records. He often helpfully wrote "HS" next to their names. Those who have graduated now play college ball for teams called the Fighting Camels, the Jaspers, and the University of Miami Hurricanes. Even Yuri Sucart's son, a ballplayer for Westminster just like Alex Rodriguez, was also a frequent customer of Anthony Bosch, according to his records.

For Bosch, treating high school players was a volume game. Unfortunately, none of them had much cash, and the odds were low that even the best ones would end up playing professionally. But baseball players at a Division I university had a much higher chance of going pro—meaning bigger fees and high-caliber referrals for Bosch.

Bosch obsessed over building his UM client base. Multiple clients remember him getting downright schmaltzy in his attempts to impress patients with links to the school. One patient says he bragged about Manny

Ramirez and Melky Cabrera. Another says he wanted the patient to invite his UM ballplaying friends to meet him. "We gotta get dinner, you gotta come to the clinic and check it out," Bosch said.

Heavy-handed though his approach may have been, it worked. Eventually, he permeated the clubhouse across the street. He even sat in the stands and watched his clients play. Alfonso "Flaco" Otero, a longtime coach of UM baseball camps, says that he met Bosch during a baseball game at Alex Rodriguez Park, introduced by a friend who had been treated by the fake doctor. "He said [Bosch] was a person who helps big league ballplayers as far as their performance on the baseball field," Otero says. (He declined to name the friend.)

It hadn't been an accident that Bosch set up shop practically in the outfield of a incredibly successful university baseball program, where steroid use was an open secret long before he opened the Coral Gables clinic.

To Bosch, it must have been tempting to find a way into the UM team. This was the same guy who had sunk thousands into a real-life fantasy squad called the Miami Meds. Now he played a role in shaping some of the best young baseball players in the country. And this time, he made a profit.

Frankie Ratcliff's phone buzzed just before seven thirty P.M. on September 10, 2010. The text message was garbled but clear enough: "Got ur number frm my boy He said ur shit is good Can I get a half How Much?"

Ratcliff was best known on the University of Miami's palm-lined campus as an up-and-coming infielder on the storied Hurricanes baseball team. Three months earlier, the speedy Key West native had finished a promising freshman season at Alex Rodriguez Park, popping six homers to go with thirteen stolen bases and a .276 batting line.

But to a subset of kids in the Coral Gables dorms, Ratcliff was much more famous as a reliable connect for good weed.

Ratcliff didn't recognize the number vibrating his phone that Friday night, but that wasn't so unusual—pot dealers relied on word-of-mouth references on the giant campus. Ratcliff told his new customer he could sell him a half ounce, talking up its potency as they haggled for a price: "Shit is fire got purple in it," he bragged.

They settled on $220, and met on a bridge outside a residence hall. Just after Ratcliff handed over the goods, the new customer flashed a badge and arrested the young second baseman. A few miles south, police burst into his messy off-campus apartment with a drug-sniffing dog.

Inside a black Air Jordan shoe box in his bedroom, they found one hundred grams of weed in plastic Baggies and a scale. Then an officer yanked open the bottom drawer of Ratcliff's dresser. Two boxes sat inside. One had 100 twenty-nine-gauge insulin needles. The other contained nineteen blue-topped bottles of Hygetropin, a synthetic human growth hormone.

The arrest of a UM infielder for HGH possession made a local TV broadcast and got a few hundred words in the *Miami Herald*.

But unreported in that brief media attention, and until now, was the MLB reaction to the arrest. The league already had an eye trained on the campus. There were too many minor leaguers coming out of the school failing drug tests.

Now league investigators followed a trail that started with the Ratcliff arrest. An official worked with players and police and discovered that prominent UM players had been suspended, according to an MLB source familiar with the investigation, due to PEDs, but that such punishment was kept quiet by team administrators and coach Jim Morris. The league shared their concerns, which were not disclosed in the press, with the National Collegiate Athletic Association. "It showed that the University of Miami program is dirty as sin," says a former MLB official familiar with the league's investigation. It's not known whether the NCAA had any reaction. The University of Miami declined to comment for this book or to make Coach Morris available for an interview.

That MLB investigation didn't turn up that one of the players' off-campus sources was the fake doctor who set up shop across the street. But

Bosch's own records confirmed that. And it wasn't until UM alumni–turned–MLB stars started testing positive for PEDs that league officials learned how right they had been about the school's years-long PED problem. It started with a recently crowned MVP's positive test and a drawn-out saga of punishment and evasion, ultimately leading directly back to Bosch and Alex Rodriguez.

CHAPTER TEN

Infiltrating "The U"

They call it "The U." South Floridians are weaned on University of Miami athletics. The school is most famous for its lightning-rod football program, which raised hackles in the '80s as Jimmy Johnson's camo-clad crew rocked to 2 Live Crew and sparked the "Convicts vs. Catholics" rivalry with Notre Dame.

But UM's baseball teams are just as dominant. The school has worn a path to Omaha's College World Series since the early '70s and has won four national titles. Jim Morris has helmed the team since 1994 and wears two of those championship rings, from 1999 and 2001. One graduate in particular became among the best ballplayers of his generation—until he and several other fellow former UM Hurricanes drew national attention to the program for all the wrong reasons.

Tony Bosch's strongest link to the team came through his decades-long relationship with an incendiary pitching coach. Lazaro Collazo—who goes by "Lazer"—was a hard-throwing pitcher who anchored the relief squad on the UM team that won the 1985 College World Series.

He later returned as an assistant coach, and then the squad's pitching coach. Bald-headed and with the rock-solid bulk of a drill sergeant, he sports the sunglasses tan lines of a man who spends his life on a baseball field. While coaching at UM, he started a profitable side project, the Hardball Baseball League, a nomadic training league. Among his students: an adult Tony Bosch, always desperate to improve his personal game.

Though he was a well-respected pitching coach—taking future pros like Danny Graves and Jay Tessmer under his wing at UM—Collazo's erratic behavior tended to sabotage his career with Anthony Weiner–like frequency. In 2003, the NCAA found that the hardball academy had violated multiple rules, including Collazo using it to funnel talented high schoolers to the 'Canes and paying college players for their instruction.

The scandal nearly harpooned the baseball program. After seventeen years there, Collazo resigned. The players paid homage by hanging his number-forty-two jersey in the Hurricanes dugout.

His next gig, as head coach of Miami's Gulliver baseball team, imploded the next year in even more queasy fashion: He utilized a motivating tactic he was famous for, now with kids who were far too young. In the locker room after a loss, he whipped out his genitals in front of the high school team. He angrily wondered, according to a police report, if they "had a set of these or were equipped with a vagina." After resigning again—though lucky to avoid sexual abuse charges—he ultimately ended up working with his cousin, an uncertified baseball agent in Miami.

Still a ubiquitous figure in South Florida youth ball, Collazo maintained relationships with UM stars, and Bosch maintained a relationship with him. He appears more than a dozen times in Bosch's notebooks, which indicate that the steroid-peddler also treated Collazo's baseball-playing sons for $60 a week.

Bosch had an invaluable source for new customers in Collazo, who seemed to be known by every athlete from Miami to Havana—and not just baseball players. The records reveal that Collazo referred a "PT," meaning patient, named Antonio Gonzalez to Bosch. That's the name of a Miami attorney and manager to several Cuban boxers, including an up-and-coming lightweight star named Yuriorkis Gamboa. Soon enough, Bosch was prepping Gamboa for HBO-televised bouts in Las Vegas with a regimen of HGH, peptides, and testosterone, according to the records. Attorney Antonio S. Gonzalez denies introducing his client to Bosch, and Gamboa says he took only legal supplements.

Collazo was the same way about building his relationships in the tight world of Miami sports. He trained young kids who had raw ability and no money, just because he saw a glimmer of talent. That's why he had taken a prepubescent pitcher named Israel Chirino under his wing and become like a "father figure" to the kid, according to Kevin Santiago, who was Chirino's college roommate. And then when Chirino went to UM and got drafted by the White Sox, maybe Collazo hooked him up with Tony Bosch. That's how referrals work. That's what friends are for.

In one note dated September 2011, Bosch writes, "Lazer: Re: Meeting with Gaby Sanchez." The future major league first baseman, whose own PED problems in college have not been reported until now, was one of at least eleven UM players, coaches, and trainers whose names ultimately showed up in Bosch's notebooks.

The 2004 and 2005 Hurricanes baseball squads were two of the most talented teams in the school's storied hardball history. Those rosters included eight future major leaguers, including one—Ryan Braun—who went on to win a National League MVP award. Gaby Sanchez slammed homers, center fielder Jon Jay was a menace on the bases, and preternaturally talented relief pitcher Chris Perez threw ninety-mile-per-hour fastballs.

But beyond the bright lights at the stadium, some players also brought the program trouble. Five key players were suspended and expelled, including two stars who several sources say were banned for a full season for testing positive for PEDs. The teams never snagged the College World Series title for which they seemed destined.

In on-the-record interviews with the authors of this book, two players said that steroids were a known problem on the team; PED tests posed little deterrence; and that if Jim Morris and other coaches showed any concern, it was only that the issue might boil over and destroy the baseball program. Little had apparently changed five years later, when a UM player made similar claims to an MLB investigator.

In March 2004, the team had steamed to eighteen wins in twenty-two games when suddenly the team's veteran setup man, Shawn Valdes-Fauli, was dismissed and starter Brandon Camardese was suspended. UM is a private school, under no obligation to reveal the reasoning behind player discipline. Jim Morris was tight-lipped, and with no information one newspaper columnist congratulated the coach on his apparent sternness. "He could have indulged the player misbehavior for the sake of bringing a better overall team into the playoffs," wrote a *Miami Herald* scribe. "Instead, he did right. The coach taught."

Just over a month later came another suspension, this time of one of the best pitchers in Hurricanes history. Morris suspended closer George Huguet, and his otherworldly 0.39 ERA, for "violating team policy," fresh off setting a new team record for saves. Though Morris again wouldn't dish, Huguet's teammates knew he had drug issues—and not of the steroid variety. "He had 'Ricky Williams syndrome,'" says one ex–high school player who was friends with many on the UM team that year. Weed was his vice, he claims. Huguet never played another game for the 'Canes, and within a few years his life had spiraled far off course: Once destined for Major League Baseball, instead he—along with another former-athlete friend who sold AK-47s on Facebook—was busted selling cocaine to an undercover cop in Hialeah.

Amid the turmoil, the 2004 Hurricanes managed to make it to the second round of the World Series, buoyed by pitcher Cesar Carrillo's undefeated 12-0 record.

The summer following that season, Braun, Sanchez, and Carrillo all played for the collegiate Cape Cod League, on a team called the Brewster Whitecaps. Braun struggled all summer and ultimately left early, but what his Brewster teammates remember is the twenty-one-year-old kid bragging about his close relationship with thirty-year-old superstar Alex Rodriguez. "He said him and Alex worked out together in Miami some when Alex came into town," says Steve Tolleson, who went on to play for two major league teams. Another teammate remembers Braun ostentatiously talking to Rodriguez on the phone during a bus trip. And a third, outfielder Ryan Patterson, says most Brewster teammates found Braun's constant showboating about his famous friend to be annoying. "It bothered a few of the guys," says Patterson. "It was 'Alex has this car, and did this with me,' and the guys were like 'OK, can we play some baseball?'"

In 2005, the two suspensions that had the most obvious bearing on Biogenesis hit. A Christopher Columbus High graduate, pitcher Marcelo Albir was an heir to a mop fortune. His father, Carlos, owns the Miami-based ABCO Products. The elder Albir sits on bank boards and is a member of the Nicaraguan American Chamber of Commerce. Marcelo's brother, Carlos Jr., had already seized his corner office in the massive factory, where the walls are covered in highly stylized glossies of the string-topped cleaning implement.

But later police records indicate that Marcelo was no mild-mannered mop magnate. Arrest reports following his graduation from the school describe Albir pushing a Key West waitress as he railed about how much money he had spent at the bar, and another time yelling with friends at the bartender of a Miami-area hotel as they were getting kicked out for belligerence that they wished "they had their pistol with them because they would shoot him." (Neither arrest was ultimately prosecuted.)

Such antics were Albir's preferred stress relief even when he was at UM, according to an associate of the team who recalled him narrowly avoiding arrest at a South Beach club after it was explained that Albir was a Hurricane. Albir was close friends with teammate Sanchez, whose nickname among friends was "Hijo"—or "Son"—because he seemed perpetually attached to his father.

Albir and Sanchez were suspended in January 2005, again for those mysterious "university policy" violations. They did not play for the entire season. But the pair was, in fact, suspended after failing tests for PEDs, multiple sources with knowledge of the team confirm.

Outfielder Kevin Santiago says that he, Albir, and Sanchez were among seven players tested on a day in October 2004. Santiago remembers that it was the first time the school subjected students to a performance enhancing–drug test that wasn't during a College World Series. The students were instructed to give a urine sample in a bathroom adjacent to a trophy room. "I came in when Gaby was in there," says Santiago. "He was sitting in a stall and it looked like he was trying to buy time."

Some weeks later, the team first heard that Sanchez and Albir were suspended. Santiago says Morris held an all-team meeting. "'Certain guys have been suspended and I don't want to say what it was for,'" Santiago says Morris told the team. "'But I think you know what it was for.'

"The point of the meeting was, 'If you're using something, stop now, because we don't want the program to get into trouble,'" says Santiago.

Pitcher Raudel Alfonso says it was well-known that Sanchez and Albir had failed the PED test.

"Flaco" Otero was formerly a coach on the Westminster baseball squad and has run baseball camps at UM for more than twenty years. He's known Sanchez since he was twelve and confirms that the player was suspended for testing positive for PEDs. "That caught a lot of people by surprise," says Otero. "It was a mistake, and Gaby's moved on." When MLB investigated the program, the league also learned that the pair had failed a test for performance enhancers, according to two MLB officials.

And failing such a test at UM took some skill, says the Hialeah-born Alfonso. "Drug testing was a joke," says the former pitcher. "A plain-out joke."

He says that athletes were typically informed on a Sunday night that they would have to submit to a test early the next morning at the Hecht Center, the University of Miami's athletic administrative hive. He recalls UM football players speaking openly about using Whizzinators, the fake penis designed to fool drug testers. Another option was checking into the hospital with any ailment, which negated the test.

Third, if athletes didn't show up to the Hecht Center on time, they were told to go to an outside testing center. So the most common ploy was for ballplayers to give their driver's licenses to similar-looking teammates who they knew were clean, to urinate for them at an outside center.

The UM team's steroid reputation was so widespread it even reached players from other colleges. "Everybody knew that the guys from Miami somehow had a connection," says Ryan Patterson, who played for Louisiana State University and then in the Blue Jays and Marlins organizations. But besides the one speech following the suspensions of Albir and Sanchez, Morris and other coaches didn't seem too concerned about getting to the bottom of the problem. "They didn't care," says Raudel Alfonso. "They didn't give a shit."

And neither did major league scouts, apparently. The Hurricanes fell flat to end the 2005 season, losing against the Huskers in a game in Lincoln, Nebraska. But a whopping nine UM players were drafted by MLB teams that year. Four of the five players who went in the first ten rounds—Braun and Carrillo, both drafted in the first round; and Gaby Sanchez and Israel Chirino—were all named in Bosch's records, with Braun and Carrillo destined to be suspended in the Biogenesis case. Those names come as no surprise to teammates like Raudel Alfonso, who says they were all in the team clique surrounded by constant steroid rumors.

It's exactly those sorts of draft results that drive college players to juice. Though Alfonso says he didn't use steroids at UM, he gets why players did. The college baseball grind is "miserable," he says. You wake up at five A.M., work out and practice all week, play ball all weekend, and spend every day so sore you can't stand up in the shower. When you see another player able to stand up in the shower, you wonder if they're on PEDs, and you want some to feel that same comfort. "It was never 'I'll take steroids to throw harder or hit a few more home runs,'" says Alfonso. "It was all about recovery."

And they were everywhere. "It was maybe as easy as getting marijuana," posits Kevin Santiago, who also says he never used steroids but seriously considered it.

For his own part, Alfonso says if he wanted to procure steroids, he knows whom he would have asked first: Marcelo Albir. Another associate of the team, in an interview with an author of this book, said that when he did buy steroids himself that's exactly from whom he purchased them.

And Major League Baseball came to believe that Albir was the conduit to players like Braun for Tony Bosch as well, according to a league official with knowledge of the Biogenesis investigation.

Bosch didn't always make his rent check, but sometimes he could be prescient. One of the reasons he homed in on UM ballplayers was because they would potentially graduate to the bigs and open another avenue for Biogenesis into the major leagues. And that's exactly how it played out.

Years later, after Biogenesis exposés revealed to some extent Bosch's infiltration of UM player and coach ranks, the school still appeared more concerned with damage control than rooting out the problem. The university released a defensive statement pointing out that 3,380 student-athletes had been tested for PEDs since 2005 and that all had passed. But the school doesn't test for HGH. And "the university did not specify why it chose to release results that began in 2005," read an Associated Press article on the statement.

Of course, Sanchez and Albir had failed their tests the fall before.

In total, at least six players from those two UM seasons—Albir, Carrillo, Sanchez, Braun, Chirino, and third baseman Danny Valencia—were named in Bosch's records. Four were future major leaguers. Carrillo and Braun were later suspended over their ties to Bosch, while Albir was embroiled in expensive civil litigation. Sanchez, Valencia, and Chirino were either cleared of wrongdoing or never punished.

Though it's unclear when Bosch began treating them, the records make it obvious that the links to UM that Bosch maintained, particularly with Lazer Collazo, were key to his relationship with this stable of players.

Soon after noting that he planned to meet with the ex–pitching coach about the former UM star Sanchez, Bosch's records suggest he set up several meetings with the Marlins first baseman. By 2011, when it appears that the first meeting occurred, Sanchez was struggling desperately and would be shipped back to the minors. One of Bosch's notations next to Sanchez's name is simple: "$$$$." Sanchez was never suspended over his ties to Biogenesis, and baseball sources say they were unable to conclusively determine whether he was a Bosch client.

Once a prospect on par with Braun, Cesar Carrillo underwent Tommy John surgery in 2007 and never regained his pitching form. After several years of bush league ball, he made his big league debut for the Astros in 2009, but his first start came against the Milwaukee Brewers, a powerful lineup anchored by none other than Ryan Braun. Carrillo was shellacked, giving up eight runs, including a two-run homer to his ex-teammate. Two games later, he was sent back to the minors for good. The notebooks indicate that the pitcher turned to Tony Bosch to break back into the bigs. The Biogenesis chief had at least six meetings with Carrillo and noted that he had sold him HGH and testosterone.

Danny Valencia was a six-foot-two slugger who transferred to UM in 2005. He made it to the majors in 2010 with the Twins and racked up 330 at-bats and a .267 average while bouncing between Minnesota and the minors. Valencia is listed in one of Bosch's notebooks reviewed by the authors, under the heading "Baseball," along with a number of other pro clients including Braun and Alex Rodriguez. Like Sanchez, MLB officials later decided they did not have ample evidence that Valencia had been a Bosch client after the clinic owner claimed he had never treated him; it's possible he's listed as a prospective client that Bosch simply hoped to nab.

Israel Chirino—nicknamed "Chique"—never made it to the bigs, despite Collazo's and Bosch's best efforts. Drafted by the White Sox in 2004, his career sputtered to a halt in high-A ball in 2009. Like Carrillo, the records suggest that Chirino turned to Bosch for an unsuccessful comeback, with his name showing up in the notebooks at least four times.

As he treated these UM players–turned-pros, Bosch continued to acquire fresh clients with new classes at UM. In 2009, D. J. Swatscheno walked into his office. Once one of the top high school pitchers in Broward County, he asked Bosch's help in recovering from Tommy John surgery in his freshman year at UM. Swatscheno had the same drastic surgery as a sophomore, and then—after transferring to Florida International University—a remarkable third time in one college career. His name appears at least a dozen times in Bosch's books.

Swatcheno's teammate Yasmani Grandal was a prodigiously talented catcher from Miami Springs. By his senior season in 2010, the catcher was eating college pitching for breakfast: His year-end stats included a .401 batting average and fifteen homers. He was also one of Bosch's most loyal clients, as revealed by the notebooks. Bosch, who used the nickname "Springs" for the catcher, later hand-delivered drugs to him in spring training before his rookie year with the San Diego Padres.

Soon after Grandal's teammate Frankie Ratcliff was busted in 2010 with nineteen vials of HGH, Tony Bosch's reach into UM's current program grew even deeper. He began treating a well-respected veteran trainer: James "Jimmy" Goins, a balding, goateed man in his early thirties, had been working in UM's gyms since 2004. He was just the type of customer who made Bosch's eyes light up, and from his notebooks it's clear he had big plans for Goins. In one entry, he includes Goins's name under a scrawled heading about "Scores Sports Management," an agency that Bosch wanted to launch with former BioKem partner Carlos Acevedo.

On Saturday, February 11, 2011, Bosch recorded a meeting with Goins as a new patient. They met more than a dozen times afterward. A handwritten page dated the next month shows what Bosch was selling him: MIC, amino acids, Winstrol, testosterone, DHEA, and IGF-1, an insulin popular with bodybuilders to stimulate muscle growth.

Though Goins later denied distributing PEDs to students and sued *Miami New Times*, the *Miami Herald*, and other media outlets—a case later dismissed by a judge—Bosch's records suggest that he attempted to milk the trainer for his connections. On the same page of notes, he writes that he sold Goins a $75 Christmas gift certificate with a $100 bonus for referring new patients.

*   *   *

In the weeks after Ratcliff's arrest, MLB officials in South Florida did their best to unravel the doping tendrils snaking through the Hurricanes program. They didn't yet know of Bosch's growing influence on campus, but they had other reasons to worry that Ratcliff's arrest was a symptom of a deeper disease.

Their biggest concern, just a year after Alex Rodriguez's 2009 steroid admissions, was the star's overriding influence on campus. Though Rodriguez never attended the university, the $3.9 million he donated to the school the same year as the scandal had made him royalty in the baseball park bearing his name and everywhere else on campus. Like Kosar, he sat on the UM board of trustees.

Rodriguez had free rein in the locker room and used the team's weight rooms to train every off-season. He'd show up at Alex Rodriguez Park every morning around six A.M. to take ground balls or hit pitches from coach Mike Tosar, Collazo's other half at the helm of the Hardball Baseball Academy.

The most promising players gravitated toward him, and baseball officials, who'd grown ever more wary of the controversial superstar, worried about where that orbit would lead future big league stars. One prodigy, a key slugger on the 2008 'Canes named Yonder Alonso, was so tight with A-Rod he ended up moving into his mansion during the season and joining in his workouts, sources close to the program say.

MLB soon found a former UM baseball player to cooperate in the post-Ratcliff investigation. (That player, whose name the authors have agreed to keep anonymous, was interviewed for this book and confirmed the details of his testimony.) He told MLB that for several years a pitcher had supplied the squad through an uncle who was a convicted drug dealer. As the investigator looked into the former player's claims, that man was awaiting trial after being busted by the DEA for dealing Oxycodone through the mail. Authorities allowed an MLB official to speak to him, but he wasn't cooperative. The pitcher also gummed up.

The former player's account of PED permeation on the UM baseball squad was potentially explosive. Just like Raudel Alfonso, who had been on the team five years earlier, this player also believed that PED testing was flawed. He told the league that he believed head coach Morris helped players dodge NCAA drug testers, though he lacked any hard evidence. The method: Clean players like the ones cooperating with MLB were tested far more often than those who the coach knew were doping.

Less than two years after MLB's investigation into UM's steroid problem, Bosch's exposed clientele list showed that baseball officials were right to suspect the school's program had problems. But if the UM administration or the NCAA did learn about the league's findings, the response was not apparent.

By then, Bosch had turned selling PEDs to baseball players into such a booming business that rival dealers were cutting into his territory. The previously mentioned UM fraternity brother says that after a few years of buying from Bosch, he and a friend saw an opportunity. After being approached by Bosch's supplier, the frat boy confesses, they decided to cut out the fake doctor and buy peptides straight from his source. They then mislabeled the peptides as HGH and sold the stuff for sizable profit to at least one UM ballplayer and at least five baseball players from Florida International University, the state school ten miles away.

"Bosch kind of pioneered this," says the enterprising frat boy of dealing PEDs to college kids. "He's the one who made it possible."

M arcelo Albir, the rich-kid bar brawler, wasn't drafted after UM. It's unclear what he does for a living. Since his college days, Albir has incorporated several vague companies in Florida and Texas: MAC Investors Inc., Globo Investments LLC, Ecolite Solutions Inc. He remained a regular at Bosch's clinics, however, and is listed nearly a dozen times in portions of his notebooks.

To MLB officials, Albir's role in Biogenesis was clear: He was the man who regularly shepherded PEDs from Bosch to budding superstar Ryan Braun.

Biogenesis founder Anthony Bosch

New York Yankees third baseman Alex Rodriguez

The University of Miami's home field, Alex Rodriguez Park

The tanning salon where Bosch and Jorge Velazquez ran an anti-aging clinic

Biogenesis was housed on the first floor of this Coral Gables office building.

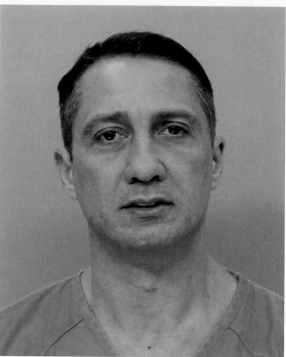

Jorge "Oggi" Velazquez, Bosch's former business partner

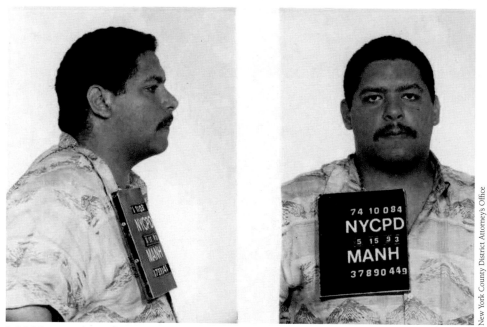

74 10 084
NYCPD
5 15 93
MANH
37890 449

A 1993 mug shot of Yuri Sucart, Rodriguez's cousin

Milwaukee Brewers outfielder Ryan Braun

Outfielder Nelson Cruz, then playing for the Texas Rangers

Outfielder Melky Cabrera, then playing for the San Francisco Giants

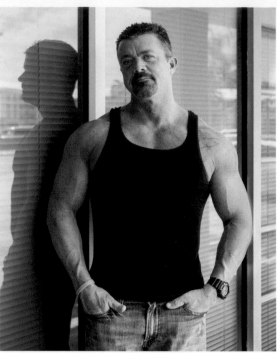

Biogenesis whistle-blower
Porter Fischer

Marta Xochilt Perez

Boca Raton Police Department

Porter Fischer's rental car after the Boca Raton theft of Biogenesis records

Major League Baseball commissioner Allan "Bud" Selig (*left*) and current chief operating officer Rob Manfred

MLB vice president of investigations Dan Mullin

AP Photo/Seth Wenig

Tony Bosch enters MLB headquarters for Alex Rodriguez's arbitration hearing.

Courtesy Joyce Fitzpatrick/Fitzpatrick Communications

On a UM team full of native Floridians, Braun had breezed in from California. He was the son of a tax adjuster father and a mom who worked for Anheuser-Busch as, yes, a brewer. Braun started at UM as a shortstop, a five-tool kid at the position whom UM had missed out on when Alex Rodriguez had bypassed college, but was an outfielder and third baseman by the time he was drafted.

Braun's full scholarship was three-quarters academic and one-quarter athletic. A business major, his grades were perfect. He was Carrillo's roommate throughout college. Also like A-Rod, Braun was fastidious to the point of OCD, keeping his locker and dorm room so *just so* that one *Herald* columnist compared him to Felix Unger, the tidy half of the *Odd Couple*.

He was preternaturally loose under pressure, and his numbers at UM were impressive. In his junior season, he hit nearly .400, swatted eighteen homers, and stole twenty-three bases. When the Brewers took him in the first round, Bud Selig was delighted for his former franchise.

Here was the clean-cut savior of baseball—what Alex Rodriguez was billed as a dozen years earlier—playing for the commissioner's hometown team. In 2007, Braun had a bionic MLB rookie campaign, batting .324 with thirty-four home runs and ninety-seven RBIs.

Braun's father, Joe, was Israeli and had lost much of his family in the Holocaust. So Braun found himself with the nickname "Hebrew Hammer." He had never been an observant Jew or even had a bar mitzvah, and since his mother isn't of the faith he wouldn't be considered Jewish by any strict definition. "But I do consider myself definitely Jewish," Braun said in 2010. "And I'm extremely proud to be a role model for young Jewish kids."

Was this guy for real? Bosch could have told you the answer to that if he was so inclined. Braun later professed—after a twisting saga of denial—that a "nagging injury" drove him to Biogenesis in the "latter part" of the 2011 season, the Brewers superstar's fifth MLB summer. If that's true, it wasn't exactly Tommy John. Braun missed a few games that season—the best of his career—with a strained calf.

It's apparent from the notebooks that Braun and Bosch shared a connection to the player's Miami-based attorney, Chris Lyons. One inscription next to Ryan Braun's name reads "20-30k" and Lyons's name. Bosch provided Braun with a testosterone cream as well as his trademark lozenges.

Bosch, who testified in Rodriguez's later arbitration that he was acquaintances with Lyons, refers at least one other athletic client to the lawyer. Another Lyons client, tennis star Wayne Odesnik, shows up in Bosch's notebooks twenty-six times, at one point next to the dollar amount "500." The South African Odesnik, who lives in Florida, is sort of the A-Rod of the tennis court: He'd already been suspended for two years for attempting to bring HGH into Australia before a tournament, and when the International Tennis Federation halved the punishment to one year for his "substantial assistance," speculation was rampant that he had snitched on other doping players. (Odesnik has denied buying banned substances from Bosch.)

Lyons himself shows up at least six times in Bosch's notebooks, next to the phone number for his Miami law office.

Even as Braun was making illicit purchases from a man running a testosterone clinic on West Dixie Highway, he was on top of the baseball world. Purported nagging injury or not, Braun's numbers were orgasmic in 2011. He batted .332 with 33 homers, 111 RBIs, and 33 stolen bases. The Brewers had the best regular season in the team's forty-five-year history, dating back to before the Bud Selig ownership days.

The Brewers, recognizing that Braun was a once-in-a-franchise talent and personality, had already thrown enough money at him before the season started—$150 million—to keep him in Wisconsin until 2020.

Selig no longer owned the Brewers, of course, but he didn't hide his affinity for the team—or their out-of-nowhere hero. He made it a point to show up periodically at the UM alum's Milwaukee restaurant, Ryan Braun's Graffito, for dinner. As the Brewers reveled in their first division title in twenty-five years, the commissioner was in love. Braun was a Miller Park mensch. His perfectly coiffed hair was dreamy. He was, in a word, perfect.

Starting October 1, 2011, everything got very ugly, very quickly.

*   *   *

In the first game of the National League Division Series against the Arizona Diamondbacks, Braun went three for four with a double and two runs scored, and the Brewers won. As he returned to the clubhouse, Braun was greeted by a representative of Comprehensive Drug Testing. Random piss test. Chaperoned to a side area along with two other players, Braun peed in a cup, which was then recorded and sealed by a thin man with a mustache.

Braun likely wasn't too concerned. As he himself later said, he had been randomly tested three times that year, and also submitted a urine sample when he signed his contract extension. Most important, "Dr." Bosch explained to all of his patients that his testosterone troches were a down-to-the-minute science in order to make sure they wouldn't piss dirty.

The next day, Braun went three for four again with a homer, and the Brewers won. They ultimately dispatched the Diamondbacks, and Braun kept hitting. They were finally outslugged by the St. Louis Cardinals—who went on to win the championship against the Texas Rangers—and on October 16, the Brewers' season ended two games short of the World Series.

Braun and Prince Fielder had pushed the Brewers further in the postseason than the team had gone since 1982—before either of them were born. Braun had hit .405 in the playoffs. The local newspaper dispensed bittersweet plaudits. "But the Brewers were something different, provided something unexpected," a *Milwaukee Journal Sentinel* columnist cooed. "They captured a lot of hearts. For a lot of fans, the next opening day can't come here soon enough."

Three days later, Braun learned that he had pissed positive.

According to later reports, the urine sample had come back with a 20:1 ratio of testosterone to epitestosterone. That was five times the 4:1 marker that flagged a positive test. Braun later said that union reps, informed of the failed test, "told me that the test result was three times higher than any number in the history of drug testing."

As per baseball's Joint Drug Agreement, any test with a ratio of 4:1 or higher causes the sample to be retested, this time with a player's representative present. This more comprehensive test is designed to show whether the high testosterone occurred naturally or was "exogenous"—that is, artificial. Braun's sample came back as exogenous.

At this point, Braun could have canned Anthony Bosch, accepted the fifty-game suspension for a first positive test, sacrificed his golden-boy image, sat out just under a third of the 2012 season, and lost $1.85 million in salary.

Instead, Braun appealed through the union. His tact: viciously attack the urine tester. Pending the appeal, scheduled for early 2012, the positive test was kept confidential.

He hired attorney David Cornwell, a seasoned PED-battle veteran who had shown that he knew how to redirect blame when faced with a player's positive test. When Phillies pitcher J. C. Romero was suspended for fifty games after a failed test, Cornwell sued GNC and four other companies for selling Romero a "tainted" supplement without his knowledge. The case was settled out of court.

Also invited to the war room was Braun's agent, Nez Balelo of Creative Artists Agency, and—according to a later lawsuit and partly confirmed through records collected by the league—a childhood friend who was working on getting a law degree online.

That friend, Ralph Sasson, has claimed that Balelo and Braun asked him to see what dirt he could find on the man who had collected the urine and what arguments he could spin that might help Braun's appeal. Though it sounds absurd that an athlete with a $150 million playing deal might ask his amateur buddy to take a stab at this defense, Sasson produced a signed contract in court. Signed by Balelo, it references "work done" for the agent, his firm, and Braun between November 3, 2011, and February 24, 2012—the latter date being the end of Braun's appeal process. Balelo's attorneys have admitted in court that it is his authentic signature.

Λ record that found its way into the MLB offices backs up Sasson's claim. He says he prepared a brief to help bolster Braun's defense debunking the failed test. In the convoluted process that was Braun's appeal, that brief passed from Balelo to Albir to Bosch, who ultimately handed it over to league officials, according to an MLB source who had seen the brief.

With Sasson on board, Team Braun studied how the outfielder's urine had been collected and shipped to the Montreal lab. They noted the time that the sample was taken, the time on the FedEx slip, and the time that it arrived at the lab. Suddenly, an argument presented itself. It was a loophole, and likely a factually meaningless one, as both the league and doping experts later argued. But it was a loophole large enough for Braun to slip through.

On November 22, 2011—despite presumably crossed fingers in the MLB offices—Braun was awarded the NL MVP award, beating out Matt Kemp and Braun's teammate Prince Fielder. The media still didn't know that Braun was facing an impending suspension. He took a call from the *Journal Sentinel* and said he had been nervously awaiting the award announcement in California. "I was on my balcony, looking at the ocean," said Braun. "It's a beautiful day in Malibu."

Less than three weeks later, ESPN's *Outside the Lines* broke the story, citing anonymous sources, that Braun had been suspended and was appealing. As fans reeled from the news that baseball's newly crowned golden boy had failed a drug test, confusion reigned in the media. Reports differed on whether Braun had tested positive for through-the-roof testosterone levels or a substance that was banned but not a performance enhancer. And Braun's camp began floating their argument, that there had been a breakdown in the "chain-of-custody issues" involving the handling of the urine sample.

"He did not take performance-enhancing drugs," said Cornwell, "and anyone who writes that is wrong."

Braun's hearing began on January 20, 2012. The de facto judge deciding his fate was Shyam Das, a professional arbitrator who had refereed

union battles involving steelworkers, mail handlers, NFL players, and—
since 1999—Major League Baseball players. (The purportedly confidential
appeal process being flaunted in the press acted as a dress rehearsal for Alex
Rodriguez's own bizarre circus two years later.)

In the MLB headquarters on Park Avenue, Cornwell and representatives of the players union laid out their evidence that the sample had been
mishandled by Dino Laurenzi Jr., the Milwaukee-area resident who had
collected it from Braun in the locker room.

Because he'd taken the samples after five P.M. on a Friday, he hadn't
given the urine belonging to Braun and two other players to FedEx on the
same day; Laurenzi instead kept the samples in a Rubbermaid cooler in his
basement. He had then mailed them to Montreal the following Monday.

Braun's camp argued that that procedure violated the Joint Drug
Agreement. The union pact details the handling of urine samples, stating
that "absent unusual circumstances, the specimens should be sent by FedEx
to the laboratory on the same day they are collected. If the specimen is not
immediately prepared for shipment, the collector shall ensure that it is appropriately safeguarded during temporary storage. The collector must keep
the chain of custody intact. The collector must store the samples in a cool
and secure location."

Despite Laurenzi apparently following those instructions, Braun's attorneys argued that the process allowed opportunity for tampering. They
had no evidence that Laurenzi had actually tampered with the sample.
Team Braun pointed out that Laurenzi's son had acted as the official chap-
erone during the sample collection, a fact that the superstar's attorneys used
to suggest that the procedure was a sort of urine-soaked amateur hour.

Laurenzi, who has master's degrees in sports medicine and business
administration, later argued that waiting to FedEx the sample was also
standard procedure set by his employer, Comprehensive Drug Testing,
which was hired by the league. "CDT has instructed collectors since I began
in 2005 that they should safeguard the samples in their homes until FedEx
is able to immediately ship the sample to the laboratory," Laurenzi later said

in a statement, "rather than having the samples sit for one day or more at a local FedEx office."

In a bizarre confluence of scheduling, on the Saturday after the arguments came to a close on Park Avenue, a slicked-back, tuxedo-sporting Braun accepted his MVP award at a midtown Manhattan Hilton less than a mile away. "I've always believed a person's character is revealed through the way they deal with those moments of adversity," Braun ruminated in his acceptance speech.

On February 23, Das issued his ruling: Suspension overturned. It was the first time a player had successfully challenged a drug-related penalty in the history of the sport. Though Das's written decision was confidential, Braun's argument that his sample had been mishandled was clearly what had swayed him. Travis Tygart, head of the US Anti-Doping Agency, called the argument the "technicality of all technicalities." He added: "It's just a sad day for all the clean players and those that abide by the rules within professional baseball."

Again, Braun could have cashed in his chips and felt lucky to escape with his shirt. But instead of graciously handling the overturned suspension, he doubled down.

The next day, Braun stood at a podium in the center of a baseball diamond at the Brewers' spring training complex in Arizona. His was a defiant, angry, and, in hindsight, ludicrous speech. Saying that he had handled the situation "with honor, with integrity, with class, with dignity, and with professionalism because that's who I am," Braun then proceeded to smear with innuendo the as-yet–publicly unnamed urine collector Laurenzi.

"There were a lot of things that we learned about the collector," said Braun, "about the collection process, about the way that the entire thing worked that made us very concerned and very suspicious about what could have actually happened."

Laying the groundwork for leaked accusations to come later, Braun said that if Laurenzi had taken the sample to FedEx immediately, it would not have been in danger of being tampered with due to a "bias . . . based on somebody's race, religion, ethnicity, what team they play for, whatever the case may be."

Saying, "I would bet my life that this substance never entered my body at any point," he then declared that the day's vindication was not just for Ryan Braun, victim. "Today is about everybody who's been wrongly accused, and everybody who's ever had to stand up for what is actually right."

A subterranean smear campaign then spun into action. First, despite arbitration confidentiality rules, an e-mail was sent out from a member of Braun's camp using a transparent pseudonym. "I have reason to know that the circumstances surrounding his testing are very suspicious. You might be interested to know that the person who administered the test, Dino Laurenzi [Jr.], a collection agent for Comprehensive Drug Testing, is an athletic trainer as well as the director of rehabilitation at United Hospital Systems in Kenosha, WI," read the e-mail, which Yahoo! sportswriter Jeff Passan published in its entirety. "This means that Laurenzi would have unfettered access to lab equipment and, if he was so inclined, would provide him the necessary resources and opportunity to tamper with the test."

As Laurenzi's name was leaked to other outlets including the *New York Times* and ESPN, the quiet fifty-one-year-old man received the Yuri Sucart treatment, being thrust from anonymity into the eye of a media storm. He was forced to hire an attorney and issued a statement declaring in part: "I have worked hard my entire life, have performed my job duties with integrity and professionalism, and have done so with respect to this matter and all other collections in which I have participated."

Braun wasn't done. As ESPN and Yahoo! later reported, he called stars around the league—namely Troy Tulowitzki, Joey Votto, and Matt Kemp—as they reported to spring training, and told them that Laurenzi had gone after him because the urine collector was an anti-Semite and a Cubs fan. He also made the same claims to his teammates.

In an interview for this book, Braun's childhood friend Sasson took reluctant credit for those claims. He said that, upon being given Laurenzi's name by Braun soon after the Brewers star learned of the failed test, he found two pieces of information on the urine collector's Facebook page. One: Yes, Laurenzi was a Cubs fan, says Sasson. Two: He was a member of a Seventh-Day Adventist congregation.

Sasson says he told Braun that there had been some history of anti-Semitism in that faith. "I told him to take it with a grain of salt," says Sasson. "But he ran with it."

As Braun not only prepared to play again in 2012 but even reveled in having made a mockery of the drug-testing procedure, baseball's brass was livid. Rob Manfred, then the league's vice president of labor relations, noted that MLB "vehemently disagrees" with Das's decision. The league threatened to appeal to a federal judge but didn't follow through.

The decision had opened up "The Braun Defense." A year earlier, Rockies catcher Eliezer Alfonzo had been suspended for a hundred games after his second failed drug test. Now Alfonso appealed and argued that his sample procedure had the same chain-of-custody issues as the Brewers star's. His suspension was also overturned.

Being an arbitrator is a tightrope position. Both sides can fire you for any reason. And a couple of days after Alfonso successfully appealed his own decision, Selig canned Das despite thirteen years of hearing MLB cases.

Selig knew exactly what that 20:1 testosterone to epitestosterone ratio meant: Braun was guilty of doping, whatever the arbitrator said.

He didn't know where Braun was scoring the PEDs. But he'd spent years assembling a team of ex-cops for just this kind of problem. The Braun debacle taught league officials that they couldn't rely on testing to snare cheats. If players were going to fight dirty, they'd have to react in kind.

CHAPTER ELEVEN

MLB's CIA: Enter the Spies

The dilapidated barn rested in the shadows of the rugged mountains wrinkling the rural countryside west of Valencia, Venezuela's third-largest city. An abandoned farm spread out below the wooden structure with acres of empty, rolling space, making any approach visible for miles.

It was the perfect hideout.

Inside, Wilson Ramos lay silent on a rickety bed, trying to ignore the four men standing guard with assault rifles. A few weeks earlier, the muscular, 220-pound catcher had finished a remarkable first year for the Washington Nationals, swatting fifteen homers to go with a .267 average and solid defense. *Baseball America* had named the twenty-four-year-old to its 2011 All-Rookie Team, noting that "few rookie catchers this century" outhit him. When the Nats missed the playoffs, Ramos had flown back to Valencia, his hometown, to play winter ball for the nearby Tigres de Aragua. He'd landed in an expertly orchestrated trap.

At the center of the web was a twenty-six-year-old spider named Alexander Moreno Bolanos, a guerrilla who'd spent four years training with Colombia's FARC rebels before deserting the revolutionary struggle for more lucrative work. Bolanos had found a construction gig near Valencia as a cover while he assembled more than a dozen cohorts. They started scouting the countryside until they found the farm: remote, protected by peaks that rose to nearly five thousand feet, owned by an elderly couple willing to sell without asking too many questions. In Montalbán, the tiny pueblo below, they bought a small house to use as a headquarters. Bolanos found a cousin of Wilson Ramos's willing to feed him intel on the young catcher's daily movements.

Just after sundown on November 9, 2011, Bolanos struck. Wilson Ramos had wandered into the front yard of his family's home to enjoy the cooler evening air while his mother cooked arepas in the kitchen. Suddenly, an SUV squealed to a halt and two armed men burst out and sprinted into the yard. One grabbed Ramos, put a gun to his temple, and forced him into the car. Before he knew what was happening, Ramos was blinded by a hood, and the car was speeding away.

It was a nearly flawless kidnapping. But Bolanos hadn't counted on Major League Baseball's secret weapon: Joel Rengifo.

The grizzled fifty-five-year-old, nicknamed "La Leyenda"—"The Legend"— by his antidrug colleagues in Caracas, had dealt with thornier plots than this snatch-and-grab. Six years earlier, he'd carried out one of the ballsiest rescues in his nation's history, rescuing pitcher Ugueth Urbina's mom from kidnappers with moves straight out of the Chuck Norris handbook—killing one in a gunfight and another by shooting a propane tank to trigger a massive explosion.

Rengifo returned Urbina's mother unscathed, and MLB was so impressed by the gutsy operation they hired him as a part-time contractor to help Venezuelan players with security. Two years later, a few months after the Mitchell Report, he was hired as the first full-time overseas investigator for MLB's new Department of Investigations.

But now, as he rushed from Caracas to Valencia, Rengifo knew this situation was even more serious than the Urbina case. For the first time, an active major leaguer had been kidnapped.

Whoever took the catcher was a pro, Rengifo knew. After meeting Ramos's distraught parents and assuring them he'd return their son alive, the veteran cop dove into the case. He and his colleagues soon realized the crooks had made a vital error in a separate case.

A few months earlier, Bolanos's gang had snatched a Portuguese man who worked at a local bakery and used cell phones to arrange for the ransom delivery. Police learned through a source that Bolanos hadn't bothered to change his numbers since.

As they worked to triangulate the cell's signal, police found the kidnappers' SUV in the small mountain town of Bejuma. That helped narrow the search. Soon, they homed in on the headquarters in tiny Montalbán. Officers managed to nab one member of the gang from the headquarters and forced him to lead them to the remote barn.

At ten A.M. on Friday, November 11, a team of commandos began making their way over the rugged hills toward the hideout. The terrain was so mountainous the trek took nearly twelve hours, but at nine fifty-eight P.M., the rescuers struck. A fierce gunfight broke out with the kidnappers. Ramos cowered under a bed as bullets popped and wood splintered all around him until—miraculously—he heard police bursting in and calling his name.

The dramatic rescue was without a doubt the biggest public success in the short history of MLB's Department of Investigations.

But it was also light-years from the type of job that Senator George Mitchell had envisioned the unit doing when he'd made its foundation the first recommendation in his seminal 409-page report.

"If you had asked me when [the DOI] was formed, in terms of priorities, if we were concerned about kidnappings, it wouldn't have been high," the department's chief, Dan Mullin, admitted in the wake of the Ramos operation. "It certainly is now."

The story of MLB's Department of Investigations is unique in professional sports. A quasi–police force staffed by ex-cops and federal agents, the unit has millions of dollars at its disposal to carry out open-ended missions— essentially, protecting baseball's best interests—however it sees fit. But finding the definition of "best interests" wasn't easy. Rather than going hard after drug cheats, as Senator Mitchell imagined, it spent years floundering for a mission. Should its detectives go after steroid dealers or gamblers? Should they spearhead international kidnapping rescues or go after prospects lying about their age?

The powerful crew of ex-cops given carte blanche to do Bud Selig's confidential work has also found itself accused of abuses, from interrogating Caribbean prospects to sleeping with a witness. An entire documentary—complete with hidden cameras—was made about one Dominican star's claims that a DOI agent conspired to ruin his draft stock.

In the years before Tony Bosch and Alex Rodriguez made Dan Mullin and his team tabloid fodder in New York, the DOI quietly became the CIA of the sports world: a mysterious, powerful group whose best successes couldn't be broadcast to the public and whose worst excesses threatened to stain the institution they were created to protect.

For all the intrigue, the group traces its history to one of the simplest recommendations made by Mitchell in his December 2011 report. The way the ex-senator saw it, the DOI would have a clear-cut mission. "The commissioner should create a Department of Investigations," the senator wrote, "led by a senior executive who reports directly to the commissioner." Its purpose was to respond "vigorously to all serious allegations of performance-enhancing substance violations."

Throughout the Steroid Era, the closest that baseball had to an internal investigative wing was its security department. Staffed by former police officers, the department had been headed since 1986 by Kevin Hallinan, an ex–NYPD cop trained in counterterrorism.

But Hallinan had made it clear that chasing down steroid rumors was not in his job description, as evidenced by how he reportedly blew off Greg Stejskal's information about Jose Canseco juicing with the help of Curtis Wenzlaff.

The problem wasn't necessarily that Hallinan didn't care about PEDs. As Mitchell realized, his job was to keep ballplayers safe. It didn't make sense to ask the same people protecting players to turn around and mount serious investigations into whether they were cheating. It was like asking a bodyguard to narc on his clients.

If baseball wanted to get serious about steroids, Mitchell believed, it needed to separate its investigations from its security. Then, when the next BALCO erupted, baseball's I-team could aggressively respond instead of watching from the sidelines and hoping local cops or federal agents got the drug dealers.

Selig jumped at the idea. "Senator Mitchell made it very clear to us that we needed an investigative capacity to supplement even the best, even the gold standard of testing programs," Rob Manfred later testified at Alex Rodriguez's arbitration. "We've worked very hard in recent years to develop that capacity."

The plan also offered another way to keep baseball's steroid problem in-house. The last thing the commissioner or the union wanted was Congress to set up an independent drug-testing operation to go after the sport's cheaters. On January 11, 2008, just a month after the Mitchell Report landed, Selig created the Department of Investigations. Baseball doesn't release its internal budgets, but according to one estimate, the group was given an annual budget of $7 million. Within a few years, it employed six investigators, four analysts, three administrators, and an army of part-timers in the Caribbean and Latin America.

Selig knew he needed a powerful personality to lead his new baseball cops. He turned to a brash former NYPD deputy chief named Dan Mullin. A large man with wavy brown hair brushed straight back from a fleshy Irish face, Mullin had spent twenty-three years in in the NYPD, rising from a beat cop to deputy chief of America's largest force. He'd done so with brains, cockiness, and a willingness to get creative to get the bad guys.

Mullin worked his way off the beat and into the Manhattan district attorney's office, where, in the early '90s, he spent three years running that department's detective squad. He distinguished himself with unusual broadsides against the mob, such as planting an undercover cop as an executive in charge of a Manhattan building in order to snare wiseguys running a garbage-hauling racket.

Mullin hand-groomed an officer who he knew had a small-business background to go undercover. "A lot of cops have certain mannerisms and speech patterns, and you know right away that they're cops," Mullin later said. "[He] doesn't act like a cop, doesn't speak like a cop."

The crazy plan was a raging success. The undercover cop spent two and a half years in charge of the building, secretly collecting evidence that later put two garbage-hauling magnates in prison. Just to top it off, he proved so adept at the job that after the trial, he quit the force and was hired on for real as a company vice president in charge of the property.

After leaving the DA's office, Mullin spent several years running precincts around New York. In the late '90s, he was the top cop for the 103rd Precinct, which covered the then-hard-boiled Queens neighborhood of Jamaica. Allegations of rampant brutality by his cops became routine enough that around one hundred residents and leaders called a meeting in June 1999 to confront Mullin and his boss.

Like so many in the NYPD, his defining moment on the force came on September 11, 2001, when he was among the first responders who rushed to the World Trade Center after the first plane hit. Mullin helped shepherd the panicking crowds rushing out of the main concourse to safety. When the South Tower suddenly collapsed just before ten A.M., he was near the corner of Vesey and Church Streets. As a wall of debris and dust rocketed down the block, he rolled under a truck with Ruth Fremson, a *New York Times* photographer.

"I held on to the arm of the man under there with me, not realizing he was a policeman," Fremson later recounted. Mullin later earned a medal for his bravery during the attack.

A year and a half later, he left the force, hired by Selig as senior director of security, the number-two man in the department. After the Mitchell Report, he quickly saw the logic behind creating the DOI. "The security department had some responsibility protecting players at large events and [Mitchell] thought there might have been conflict between trying to protect players, their physical security, and then investigating them," Mullin later said in a court deposition.

For Mullin's deputy, Selig chose George Hanna, an FBI veteran who had once killed a Brooklyn mobster in a bar shootout. In Mullin and Hanna, Selig's new DOI started with two tough-as-nails cops at the top who'd spent decades going after wiseguys and drug runners. To fill out their squad, the men looked for ex-cops who could speak Spanish and understood baseball—a perfect job description for the legions of officers who worked part-time doing security at ballparks around the country.

That's where they found Eduardo Dominguez Jr., a Boston cop who'd spent decades on the drug enforcement beat, and Victor Burgos, a two-decade NYPD vet and Spanish speaker who'd earned distinction leading drug busts on a DEA task force.

Mullin wanted his investigators to hit the ground running. Mitchell had envisioned the team as kind of a "strike force," set up to aggressively respond to steroid rumors, and Selig took the senator's recommendations about how to stir up actionable intel. The commissioner sent an edict to every team spelling out any employee's duty: to immediately contact the DOI whenever they caught wind of drug abuse. An anonymous hotline was also set up for players to narc on teammates.

But Dominguez and Burgos's first big steroid tip didn't come from an anonymous whistle-blower. Far from it. Two months after the formation of the DOI, Jose Canseco published his second book, *Vindicated*, to brag about how the Mitchell Report had verified exactly what he'd warned in his previous bestseller, *Juiced*. Mullin sent his new hires to a Canseco book signing in midtown Manhattan to eat crow and ask if the former Bash Brother would consider coming in for an official sit-down with investigators.

"We asked them, 'Why now? Why not two years ago? Why so long?'" Canseco's attorney, Robert Saunooke, told a reporter. "They said, 'Those are valid questions.'"

Canseco agreed to talk to the investigators, but more important, the episode sent a loud message. Two years earlier, Canseco had been vilified by baseball's establishment. Tony LaRussa spoke for many MLB insiders' feelings on *Juiced* when he called Canseco "envious and jealous" and speculated that "he's hurting for money and he needs to make a score."

Now, Selig's handpicked cops were publicly admitting they'd been wrong to ignore the slugger's warnings. This time around, they'd listen to anyone.

Mitchell had wanted DOI to become a quick-response team to budding steroid scandals. But Mullin's team soon realized that there were numerous threats to the game beyond PEDs that investigators could tackle. But in doing so, DOI's resources and attention were forever being stretched thin in new directions.

Take gambling. Ever since the 1919 Black Sox scandal, game fixing was viewed as baseball's biggest existential threat, a fear reinforced by Pete Rose's lifetime ban for betting on his own teams. Mullin could hardly direct a detail ordered to protect the sport and ignore the threat of Vegas. "We're always worried about the integrity of the game as it relates to the dangers of gambling," Mullin said in a deposition in 2012. "So within our department, we monitor gambling trends."

In that deposition, Mullin revealed that DOI analysts tracked betting blogs and Twitter feeds, and every week cranked out an internal report on arrests linked to baseball betting. They also worked federal sources to get in on cases, like a mob-run bookie ring in New York whose customers, according to a wiretap, included seven major league scouts. In 2010, federal agents clued them in to the case of Charlie Samuels, a fifty-five-year-old clubhouse manager for the New York Mets who was betting more than $30,000 a month in illegal rings. Mullin's team discovered he'd been stealing millions in team memorabilia.

Soon, the DOI was attacking even thornier problems. For decades, teams had lost millions on Latin prospects fudging their ages by wasting huge signing bonuses on players they thought were precocious teenage phenoms who turned out to be middling twenty-year-olds. In one notable 2006 case, the Washington Nationals lavished a $1.4 million signing bonus on a sixteen-year-old Dominican shortstop named Esmailyn Gonzalez, only to learn when he made it to the States that he was actually twenty and named Carlos Alvarez.

Before the Mitchell Report, teams were responsible for doing their own ID checks on prospects. If they screwed up like the Nats, they were probably out of luck.

In July 2009, though, Selig changed everything by giving Mullin's team full responsibility for age and ID investigations—a massive, complex task that came to occupy the bulk of the DOI's work, necessitating dozens of contractors around Latin America.

One of their first cases involved a sixteen-year-old, million-dollar-bonus baby from the Padres named Alvaro Aristy, who investigators soon proved was actually two years older and named Jorge Leandro Guzman. But unlike a real police force, baseball's Department of Investigations was operating without any real checks or balances. And their considerable power and influence sometimes morphed into abuse. Miguel Angel Sano certainly felt he'd been scorched by the unit. In 2009, teams were preparing a bidding war over the hard-hitting, six-foot-three shortstop with power from San Pedro de Macorís. Experts thought the sixteen-year-old kid from the dirt-poor coastal market town could nab at least a $5 million signing bonus.

Instead, a newly hired NYPD veteran named Nelson Tejada landed in the DR to investigate persistent rumors that Sano was too good to be true: too tall, too fast, too developed to be sixteen. Sano, Mullin decided, would be the guinea pig for his new plan to DNA test suspicious recruits. Tejada also started interviewing relatives and neighbors and ordered a full bone scan on the kid.

At the time, Sano was being pursued heavily by a Pittsburgh Pirates scout named Rene Gayo, whom Sano claims offered him a relatively paltry $2 million bonus but promised to get him "amnesty" from Tejada's investigation.

Tejada, meanwhile, personally advised Sano to take Gayo's offer and end the case, the prospect later claimed in a documentary called *Ballplayer: Pelotero*.

"I don't understand why [Tejada] would tell me to sign with the Pirates and they would stop the investigation," Sano later said. "That's why I believe money was exchanged under the table." (MLB denied any wrongdoing in the case. Sano ended up signing with the Twins for $3.15 million, well below his initial estimates. Tejada's tests eventually confirmed that Sano was, in fact, sixteen years old.)

The DOI has faced other accusations back in the States. In 2011, in an incident that has not been reported until now, MLB learned of accusations that Mullin had slept with a DEA employee in California and then used that relationship to get confidential pharmaceutical information about an ongoing steroid case. The commissioner's office was troubled enough that it hired a top New York law firm to investigate; it's not clear what they found (and the DEA agent's attorney declined to discuss the situation), but Mullin was never publicly punished and maintains that he has no knowledge of such an investigation. "It's categorically not true," Mullin says of the accusations. But similar claims arose again in South Florida on an even higher-profile case.

Controversies aside, by 2012 MLB had another serious problem on its hands: The Department of Investigations wasn't doing much steroid busting. Senator Mitchell hadn't asked Selig to set up a DOI to organize mountaintop raids in Venezuela, check DNA samples in the Dominican Republic, and monitor basement Jersey betting rings. They were supposed to be the commissioner's proactive response to PEDs.

Mullin says all those missions weren't necessarily distracting from their anti-steroid mandate. "It's the opposite, because a lot of those other investigations lead to intel about drugs," Mullin says. Many of the men perpetrating ID fraud in the Dominican Republic also sold steroids to prospects, for instance. "It's all related," he says.

But the problem was that for nonanalytic steroid investigations—like any police probe that wasn't based on hard evidence—Selig's cops needed whistle-blowers and solid tips. And that piece of the puzzle was not falling into place.

In the 2012 deposition—one of the rare instances in which the baseball executive divulged information about his department—Mullin admitted that almost no one was using the anonymous tip line they'd set up for players and coaches to report steroid abuse.

In three years, only twenty tips came in, he said, and not all were about PEDs.

The league's drug-testing program, meanwhile, had started strong but had recently showed alarming signs that cheaters were catching up to the PED police. Random testing had begun in 2004 with dopers kept anonymous and sent to counseling. Public punishments started the next year, with the first big leaguer—Tampa Bay's Alex Sanchez—suspended in April 2005. In the three seasons before the Mitchell Report, twenty-three major league players were caught by the tests, including some big names such as Rafael Palmeiro and pitcher Ryan Franklin.

The policy had grown more teeth in 2006, when federal agents raided the home of Arizona Diamondbacks pitcher Jason Grimsley and alleged he'd distributed HGH. Although Grimsley hadn't failed a test, MLB still worked out a deal with the union to suspend him for fifty games, marking the first "nonanalytic" suspension and setting an important precedent that made the DOI's job possible.

After Mitchell's report landed in 2007, the total number of suspensions continued to grow, with sixty-nine suspended in 2008, eighty-three in 2009, eighty-six in 2010, and seventy-three in 2011. But the vast majority were handed down to minor leaguers. Big leaguers were suddenly passing all their tests, with just eleven of those 311 suspensions hitting players on major league rosters. And those eleven "big league" suspensions included only five guys who'd actually been playing at the top level at the time they were caught: Manny Ramirez and J. C. Romero in 2009, Ronny Paulino and Edinson Volquez in 2010, and Mark Rogers in 2011.

Just a decade earlier, Ken Caminiti had estimated half of all big leaguers were doping. Yankees star pitcher David Wells put the number at 25 to 40 percent. Even baseball's own well-publicized, easy-to-avoid testing in 2003 had nabbed almost 10 percent of players at the time. Yet since the Mitchell Report, baseball's testers had caught just five true big leaguers in four seasons of testing.

The numbers suggested that cheaters were getting better at beating the tests; that's exactly why Mitchell had recommended a team of investigators to supplement the imperfect science. Yet the DOI was spending huge chunks of time on ID fraud investigations in the Dominican Republic, largely because of pressure from owners—who, after all, stood to lose millions from those cases. Owners still had little to gain besides their fans' ill will from dopers getting busted, and PED probes were few and far between.

That started to change in 2009, after Manny Ramirez was the first superstar to get nabbed for drug use post Mitchell. That Miami case marked the beginnings of DOI finding its true purpose and signaled a surge in steroid cases for the baseball investigators—though it was four years before another South Florida case gave them their first real victory.

The DOI had sprung into action after Ramirez's failed screening for testosterone, homing in on Dr. Pedro Bosch and his son Tony. That intel gave Mullin's team one of its first meaty PED leads to follow. But with both Bosches and Ramirez uncooperative, the investigation—led by Ed Dominguez and a small team—sputtered out.

And in the unit's next big case, when the Canadian guru Anthony Galea was caught trying to smuggle HGH across the border, the DOI hit legal barriers. The doctor, facing potential criminal charges, wouldn't cooperate with the DOI, and law enforcement proved equally unhelpful. The feds declined to help MLB out, keeping sealed transcripts of interviews with key players such as Alex Rodriguez.

It was frustrating. The I-team finally had steroid leads to chase down, but so far they weren't going anywhere.

When Ryan Braun wriggled out of his positive drug test in 2011, it was an extra slap in the face to the guys trying to bring law and order to the chemically soaked sport.

As baseball headed into the 2012 season, the DOI's antidrug mission was in danger of becoming ineffectual. If the DOI was going to raise its batting average, the detectives needed another scandal—a fat, batting-practice pitch of a case—to swing at.

*   *   *

Melky Cabrera scuffed his neon orange cleats into the Kauffman Stadium dirt and glared out at the pitcher. There was one out in the top of the first inning of the 2012 All-Star Game, and Joe Buck had trouble keeping an incredulous tone out of his voice as he told his national TV audience about Cabrera's season to date.

"This is a guy who's *number one* in the major leagues," Buck intoned, "with a hit total of one nineteen."

Buck's confusion was understandable. The baby-faced Dominican had once been a top Yankees prospect, but he never hit for power in pinstripes. New York gave up on him after he'd notched middling totals of .249 and .274 as a starter, shipping him to Atlanta in 2010. Cabrera was even worse for the Braves. In 147 games at Turner Field, he barely cracked .250 while swatting just four home runs. In the postseason against San Francisco, he went 0-for-8. Local sportswriters thought he looked fat and disinterested. When the Braves cut him loose, one blogger speculated, "He'll be drowning his sorrows in milkshakes."

In 2011, Cabrera found himself in that Midwestern graveyard where so many ex-prospects have watched their final hopes sputter out: the then-perpetually down-and-out Kansas City Royals. But Cabrera—after spending two off-seasons working out with Alex Rodriguez in Miami—suddenly turned his career around. He didn't just relocate his contact swing inside Kauffman, he somehow found his power switch and flipped it hard. By the end of the year, he'd recorded a .305 average, smacked twenty home runs, and logged an incredible 201 hits, putting him on a shortlist with George Brett and a handful of others among Royals to break that barrier.

Suddenly, contenders were looking at the twenty-seven-year-old and wondering: Was 2011 a crazy fluke, or was Melky Cabrera the real deal? The San Francisco Giants had rolled the dice in the off-season, shipping two pitchers to KC for the resurgent outfielder. Cabrera immediately silenced his critics. In May, he'd broken Willie Mays's team record for hits in the month.

In June and July, he'd stung balls all over the park at a record clip—even flashing his newfound power, with eight homers to start the year. The local press gleefully threw nicknames at the new star of McCovey Cove: Here comes the "Melk Man"! Fear the "Melky Way"!

And now here he was, back in Kauffman Stadium for the Midsummer Classic, this time wearing the orange-and-black of the contending Giants. Joe Buck could barely finish counting off Cabrera's extraordinary stat line when he lashed the first pitch he saw from American League starter Justin Verlander—a ninety-eight-mile-per-hour heater—into left center field for a single. "Let's call that one twenty on the year," Buck said. "The guy with electric shoes is *on*."

Was he ever. In the bottom of the fourth, he came up again with two runners on. Cabrera worked the count to 2-2, then ripped a high, inside fastball over the left-field wall for a laser-beam, three-run bomb.

By the end of the game, the National League had creamed the junior circuit 8–0, and Cabrera was trotted out to center field with his crying mom and grandmother. The outfielder grinned as Selig handed him a crystal bat and the keys to a 2013 Chevy Camaro. Melky Cabrera, two years removed from a four-homer, .255 year with the Braves, was the reigning All-Star Game MVP.

(His only real competition on the night was Milwaukee Brewers outfielder Ryan Braun, who'd contributed an RBI double, a triple, and an incredible catch on a Prince Fielder line drive.)

"I didn't come to win an MVP," Cabrera told reporters in halting English. "That's just a surprise. It's a great gift the Lord gave me."

The Lord giveth and the baseball gods taketh away. Cabrera's joy lasted only a few days. Then he learned the news: He'd failed a drug test for synthetic testosterone. He was in line for a fifty-game ban.

Cabrera was frantic. He called the one man he thought could help: Juan Carlos Nunez.

*   *   *

The trio of Dominican Republic–based websites were all plastered with the same bright banner ad, which crisscrossed listings for nutritional supplements, herbal remedies, and protein powders. They were disarmingly basic, showing a jar full of a mysterious substance and a phone number with a DR country code.

Mullin's team had no choice but to follow the ads down the rabbit hole. Melky Cabrera was the first big-name player nabbed by his testers since the Ryan Braun fiasco, and they'd be damned if Cabrera found a way to wriggle out of his suspension too. Losing two high-profile suspensions in less than a year might just be a death knell for baseball's drug police.

Cabrera had filed an appeal to his positive test through the Players Association, seeking cover under a clause in the suspension policy that cut a player slack if he'd unwittingly taken something that caused his testosterone spike. He'd told baseball officials that that's what had happened: He'd ordered a substance advertised on these banners, not knowing what precisely was inside, and had been burned by the medicine.

If the DOI wanted this suspension to stick, they'd have to get to the bottom of the mystery substance.

It wasn't just the Braun fiasco that made Mullin's team so eager. His drug testers believed that Melky's failed test was the clearest sign yet that science was finally catching up to the cheaters.

Testers and cheaters alike knew about the weaknesses of the 4:1 ratio test. By allowing for a natural variation, there's a window for a smart doper like Tony Bosch to make a difference. By giving his clients fast-acting testosterone lozenges and carefully timed creams, his athletes could massage their ratios to stay just below the cutoffs.

"This is the single biggest loophole in Major League Baseball," Victor Conte later said.

But MLB's testing lab in Montreal had quietly started using carbon isotope testing even in cases where athletes had passed their ratio tests. The process is expensive (about $400 a pop), but it finds what ratios miss: traces of the unique isotopes synthetic testosterones leave in the body, even if users keep their ratios below 4:1.

"Athletes who are sophisticated can keep their ratios below four-to-one and still use levels of synthetic testosterone," says Travis Tygart, the director of the US Anti-Doping Agency (USADA). "You need to be able to go directly to that [carbon isotope] test, not rely just on elevated testosterone ratios."

Now, just a few months into the new season, they'd already netted a big fish who may have evaded detection in past seasons. Assuming he hadn't taken it by accident, that is.

Mullin's Spanish-language investigators started probing Cabrera's excuse by calling the number listed on sites. A seller told them they'd have to travel to Santo Domingo to get his product. So DOI investigators made the trip, buying a jar of the mystery medicine and sending it back to the World Anti-Doping Agency's (WADA) Olympic testing lab in California.

Meanwhile, back in New York, analysts took a closer look at the sites themselves. As they called owners and looked at cached pages, they soon noticed a curious pattern. The banner ads all seemed to have appeared out of nowhere—days *after* Cabrera had learned of his positive tests. Finally, the team learned the truth from one of the domains' former owners: They'd sold the entire site days earlier. To a man named Juan Carlos Nunez.

From there, the scheme dreamed up by the former Washington Heights travel agent and ACES "consultant" quickly unraveled. Tests from WADA came back that whatever they'd bought in the DR had tested positive for high levels of testosterone, but Mullin's team believed the truth was murkier than steroid-tainted medicine. When investigators confronted Nunez and Cabrera with the evidence, their elaborate ruse collapsed. The Dominican consultant confessed to his plot: buying three sites for $10,000, planting the fake ad, and even getting a confederate on the ground in Santo Domingo to sell testosterone-infused cream.

On August 15, the Giants outfielder—then leading the league with 159 hits—was suspended for fifty games. He'd miss the rest of the Giants push for a playoff spot and at least the first five games of their postseason if they could make it.

Cabrera didn't mention his website ploy in his contrite statement. "My positive test was the result of my use of a substance I should not have used," Cabrera admitted to reporters, while apologizing to fans and teammates. "I will try to move on with my life."

But five years after the Mitchell Report, the case was the DOI's first real victory in its covert war on steroids. For the first time since the Mitchell Report, a steroid scandal had erupted, a player had tried to deceive them, and they'd ground their way down to the truth.

But questions remained. If Cabrera hadn't accidentally bought tainted drugs from the DR, where *had* his PEDs come from?

Just a week after Cabrera's suspension went public, the question became even more pressing. That's when another starter on a contending team in the Bay Area got the dreaded call from his union reps.

This time, it was Bartolo Colon. Aside from their shared Dominican heritage, Colon and Cabrera could hardly have been more different. Colon had proved his worth in the bigs time and again since coming up in 1997, winning an ALCS game for the Indians, throwing a one-hitter against the Yankees, and even nabbing the American League Cy Young in 2005 while pitching for the Angels. In 2012, he was in the winter of his remarkable career, two years into a surprising comeback after an experimental surgery that implanted stem cells directly into a damaged throwing shoulder. Colon was thirty-nine years old now, chunky and strikingly unathletic, but still pitching well for the surprising Oakland A's. By midsummer, he'd posted a 10-9 record with a 3.43 ERA.

Now, like Cabrera, he was out for fifty games thanks to a testosterone violation. He didn't fight the punishment, apologizing and saying, "I accept responsibility for my actions."

Even without two of their stars, both the A's and the Giants found themselves playing baseball late into October. The Giants could have brought Cabrera back for the NLCS against the Cardinals, his fifty-game penance having been served. But manager Bruce Bochy didn't add the All-Star MVP to his roster. The message seemed clear: We can win without a cheater.

And win they did. Cabrera watched at home as his team came back from a 3–1 series deficit to stun the Cardinals, and then swept the Tigers to take a World Series crown.

The season was over, but Selig's drug police weren't finished yet. On November 7, they announced yet another fifty-game ban, yet again for failing a testosterone test. This time the culprit was a twenty-three-year-old Cuban-born catcher named Yasmani Grandal.

The former UM star had earned a June call-up to the Padres and quickly set an offensive record. In his first major league start on June 30, Grandal homered from both sides of the plate—the first man in the history of the game to record his first two career hits that way. He finished the year strong, batting .297 with eight homers in split action behind the plate, projecting as a middle-of-the-order bat with above-average defensive tools.

But now, his sophomore season would start at home. He'd miss the first fifty games of the year under the ban.

The suspensions, to MLB's testers, were proof that their new policies were working—four legit big league players in one calendar year had been caught doping with synthetic testosterone. That's almost as many as they'd caught in the previous four seasons combined since the Mitchell Report.

But was there a pattern behind the positives? The DOI detectives started to think like epidemiologists, parsing whether this was an outbreak stemming from a single source, or if the failed tests were just a coincidence. In a flash of avian flu or Legionnaires' disease, the CDC starts by looking for commonalities: Did the victims stay in the same place, eat the same food, or share the same flight?

Mullin's team started trying to make the same kinds of connections to find the ties between Braun, Cabrera, Grandal, and Colon. It didn't take long to see that Miami was a nexus point. Braun and Grandal had both starred at the University of Miami, and Cabrera made his off-season home in the Magic City.

The DOI soon began taking a second look at the doctor's son in Miami who had been embroiled in Manny Ramirez's case three years earlier.

"The focus of our interest in Bosch and South Florida picked up in the summer of 2012," Rob Manfred later testified in Alex Rodriguez's arbitration hearing. "We began to realize that there were players who had connections, agents who were connected to those players, trainers who were connected to those players, businesses that were related to Bosch and others that we suspected were involved in the provision of performance-enhancing drugs."

But even with the mounting suspicion, it took a completely unexpected break to unravel Tony Bosch's empire.

CHAPTER TWELVE

The Beginning of the End

Tony Bosch's hand shook as he scrawled a plea into his notebook. His normally steady writing bled straight through onto the next page.

The self-proclaimed doctor was confused and angry. Hadn't he told Melky Cabrera exactly how many testosterone troches he could take without getting caught? Hadn't all of his clients been warned to be more careful after the barely averted piss-test disaster with Braun?

Yet weeks after one of Bosch's greatest triumphs—watching one of his own customers hoist an All-Star MVP trophy on national television—everything was suddenly going to pieces.

Juan Carlos Nunez, the surreptitious ACES employee and Bosch's connection to Melky and other major leaguers, wasn't even returning his calls. Worse, Melky hadn't paid him for his last shipment of "food," the transparent shorthand Bosch used for PEDs in his notes.

There was still hope. Melky's suspension hadn't been made public yet as the Giants star filed an appeal. Bosch was aware of a ballsy scheme Nunez and the outfielder had cooked up to evade punishment.

It seemed like a perfect plan to Bosch. They had bought an unused Dominican website and changed it to make it look like the site was selling tainted nutritional creams. They would then claim that it had sold Melky the substance that caused him to fail a drug test.

Melky's crime, the story would be, was a simple mistake made while web-surfing.

Hell, if Ryan Braun could evade a stone-cold failed test—where his testosterone to epitestosterone was an off-the-charts 20:1 catastrophe—by claiming that his sample was mishandled by an "anti-Semitic" urine tester, anything was possible.

He started the letter snarkily. "Dear Juan," he wrote. "Congrats on the MVP Award! This smells like the 'Braun' advantage."

Bosch referred to the website scheme as a James Bond plot of intrigue, which may have been giving it too much credit. "The 'J. Bond Story' and the food adjustments I made, along with the right representation [and a fall guy], might be able to pull this off! I'm feeling it more and more and so are some industry experts."

Then Bosch started to unload. The slick clinic owner rarely picked a fight. His friends knew he was allergic to confrontation. One acquaintance recalled meeting him at the Ritz-Carlton Key Biscayne for a drink. They'd just sat down when Tony spotted someone coming through the door to whom he owed money. Without a word, he'd set down his drink and quietly slipped out the back.

"He doesn't like arguments," says Roger De Armas, his childhood friend. "He'll walk away and leave rather than continue. Then he'll see you next time and buy you a drink."

This time, Tony Bosch wasn't walking away and he wasn't buying anyone a drink. "I believe that during this self-inflicted fiasco, Mostro has received his salary," Bosch wrote, "and you have been compensated by your employer. However, I have not received payment of any form."

Bosch was used to being on the other end of this letter, the guy perpetually running from debts. "I know this is an alarming issue and detrimental to many careers including my own. However, life goes on, and bills have to be paid," he continued. "I have invested in your players and leveraged my profits in order to accommodate your requests, specifically regarding 'DR' and 'My Son.'"

In Bosch's mind, he had bent over backward to help out Nunez and his clients, particularly Cesar Puello—whom he'd nicknamed "Mi Hijo," or

"My Son"—and fifteen-year-old Ricardo Cespedes, "DR"—Mets prospects who couldn't afford Bosch's major league rate but whom he had added to the Biogenesis roster anyway. Now Nunez was screwing him over. Bosch took a deep breath and put the marker back to the paper.

"This risk has been compounded by Mostro's inconsistent behavior and idle threats, not to mention his lack of irresponsibility [sic] that has led to this 'pressure cooker situation' that we are all experiencing," he dashed off. "Tell your boy to man up and act accordingly."

Nunez had work to do, too. "Furthermore, I would like to send all the food out immediately to you so you may distribute it. And I would like for you to collect payment, set aside your fees, and deposit the remaining balance into my account. This includes Mostro's $9,000 and my $5,000 All-Star bonus that he so vigorously promised."

Nunez and Melky were desperate? Well, so was Bosch! They weren't the only ones sticking their necks out. "I am on the line here! This guy's blunder has me infuriated, along with his stupid 'idle' threat. I am out thousands of dollars because I bought all this month's food. In my helping him, I put all my [doctors] at risk by fabricating patient charts and phony prescriptions. I did it because you promised me compensation and I trust you."

Getting stiffed $14,000 wasn't even the worst of it. The failed test—the "blunder" he was certain was all Melky's fault by not following his instructions on how much testosterone to take and when to take it—was imperiling the most valuable relationship Bosch had ever cultivated.

Melky's failed test could jeopardize Alex Rodriguez's faith in the Biogenesis regimen.

"This also has put my relationship with 'Cacique' at risk at the tune of $12,000 per month," Bosch wrote, using his nickname for the Yankees star. "And I have four years remaining on that deal. And to top it off, I'm upside down on 'DR' and 'My Son'!

"I demand immediate payment," Bosch finished. "Thank you for your immediate attention to this matter."

Everything was close to collapsing, but if Mostro could just hang on—

Bosch's handwritten regimen for Melky Cabrera,
using his nickname "Mostro"

just fight through it the way Braun had—everything might just work out.
Bosch would get paid, his next generation of clients would inch their way
to the bigs, and most important, A-Rod would stay on board. It wasn't impossible.

But in the meantime, Bosch had a cash-flow problem.

Without his big leaguers, Biogenesis just didn't pay the bills. Consider
his July 2012 financial books, the month before the Melky fiasco. Bosch
recorded only his ordinary Miami clients on the official books—and the

picture wasn't pretty. He'd collected $24,355 from 119 active customers, including the Collazo clan and Elie "Booba" Yaffa.

The same group owed $35,180, so his collection services weren't the best. But the real problem was his expenses: Between weekly payments to his ex-wives, staff pay, rent, and mounting costs for his meds (including a nearly $4,000 debt to Oggi), he owed $32,334 for July.

That didn't include off-the-books expenses. Bosch liked to let off steam by popping bottles at South Beach nightclubs, and there is evidence that he enjoyed the harder, more expensive stuff as well. A friend named Robert Davis Miller later cashed in on his purported knowledge of Bosch's love of Miami's most famous imported product.

Ten years younger than Bosch, Miller was the quintessential cocaine buddy. His criminal career had started when he was just fourteen, bouncing in and out of juvenile detention eleven times on charges including criminal mischief and auto theft. Four years later, he was arrested for fighting his football coach at Sunset High and then threatening to "fuck up" the opposing team's coach. After high school, he started breaking into neighborhood houses and strolling out with thousands of dollars in jewelry. In 1995, he was caught with a gun while out on probation and sent to federal prison.

According to a sworn affidavit Miller later provided to Alex Rodriguez, he and Bosch bonded over a love of cocaine. The ex-con claims that he saw Bosch use cocaine "almost daily," and provided photos of the two hanging out with Baggies of white powder on a coffee table. "He had a reputation for heavy partying and drug use," Lorraine Delgadillo, a former Biogenesis nurse, wrote in a similar affidavit about her one-time boss. Bosch later pled the Fifth when A-Rod's attorneys pushed him on the question of his coke addiction.

Now Bosch's wild lifestyle was unraveling. Except for the thousands coming in from big leaguers, he was operating in the red. There was no way around it.

*   *   *

osch had been trying to leverage his off-the-books cash into that chain of clinics he'd always envisioned stretching across South Florida and into the Caribbean. If Tony Bosch believed, at heart, in one thing, it was that he was destined for greatness. No one was more conned by the Bosch sales pitch than Bosch himself.

His notebooks are littered with half-baked ideas of how to transform his moderate success as a local anti-aging snake oil salesman into international fame and fortune. In one note, he imagines writing books and magazines and producing merchandise for the "Hormone Response Diet," or "Hormone Response Nutrition."

Elsewhere, he plots a diet book with an all-too-appropriate name: *Lose Like Hell*.

Bosch's own credentials are constantly inflated in his writings: "Tony Bosch, Molecular Biochemist, Anti-Aging Director," he writes on one page. On another: "Dr. Tony Bosch, Age Management Consultant." Even better: "Tony Bosch, Physician Scientist, Dr./CEO/President," with specialties in "holistic nutrition, biochemical methodologies . . . sports nutrition, amino acid deficiencies, metabolic syndrome, hormone modulation."

The most telling passage on how Bosch saw himself, though, is the full page he devotes to writing out the famous text from Apple's 1997 "Think Different" campaign: "Here's to the crazy ones, the misfits, the rebels, the troublemakers, the round pegs in the square holes . . . the ones who see things differently—they're not fond of rules—you can quote them, disagree with them, glorify or vilify them, but the only thing you can't do is ignore them because they change things . . . they push the human race forward and while some may see them as the crazy ones . . . we see them as genius because the ones who are crazy enough to think they can change the world are the ones who do."

It's a clichéd, overcited quote from a computer corporation, but it's also a perfect distillation of Tony Bosch's mind-set.

Bosch had always put himself in the same category as his cousin Orlando. He'd never countenance what Orlando had done, of course—firing

A handwritten note in Tony Bosch's notebooks

rockets at cargo ships and allegedly blowing up a commercial airliner—but Orlando had also grasped the same thing as Tony: Living outside conventional lines was thrilling, and it was the only way to really make an impact in this world. Tony Bosch knew in his heart that he was not ordinary. (Of course, the scribbled lines are telling in another way, too; Tony felt the passion in them, but he also misattributes the words to Jack Kerouac, apparently never bothering to Google the quote.)

Bosch didn't just see himself as an anti-aging guru; he imagined himself as an iconoclast. What he was doing may have been illegal, but it was also vital, he thought. On the next page, he put his own self-adulating twist on the Apple quote and referred to himself by his initials: "Mainstream is not in their vocabulary. You honor them once a year at Halloween . . . and dress like them, act like them, emulate them. Sometimes they come from afar, and sometimes as close as Queens. Here is to T. B. . . . . It's not only a name, it's an attitude, it's a lifestyle."

Bosch obsessed over his credentials, plotting out how to turn his unrecognized Belize-based degree into a US medical credential, perhaps with a "BS in education" in Florida, he wrote, or with an online degree. And he fretted over the legality of his clinics, dreaming of how to "create a foolproof legal structure" with a "board of directors."

He also scribbled lyrics and inspirational quotes into the margins, and some seem to offer a window into his increasingly stressed worldview. On one page, he penned a Lil Wayne lyric: "Life is a movie I've seen too many times." Another reminds him that "time heals almost everything," and, more important: "Smile, you don't own all the problems in the world."

But he had problems enough. Friends and business partners were noticing the stress.

Jorge Jaen had known Tony Bosch socially for years, running into him at the Ritz or the Ibis Club on Key Biscayne. He'd thought of Bosch as a charming character, a social magnet who always seemed to be at the right parties, always with a different hot chick on his arm.

Jaen had been working with partners to open a cosmetic surgery center, and he knew Bosch was in the medical game, so they went out to lunch one day in early 2011.

"Tony told me he'd be able to bring in all these famous people, these actresses and people from Univision," Jaen says. He and his partners let Bosch in with a small percentage to do marketing for the clinic.

But by the end of the year, it was obvious Bosch was headed off a cliff. "He would show up with his shirt all wrinkled, smelling like alcohol," Jaen recalls. "We had a young lady who wanted to see him about a deal and comes back out and tells me, 'This guy is drunk. His breath smells like vodka.'"

At another meeting where Bosch was supposed to give a presentation, he showed up late and disheveled. "The guy was a disaster. He came in with this file folder with papers sticking out [in] every direction like a mad scientist. We were like, 'What is with this man?'"

Jaen fired Bosch soon afterward.

Roger De Armas also knew his old friend was in trouble. Close since kindergarten, they were more brothers than friends. But ever since Tony

Bosch had left for Belize, he'd been a changed man. The few times Roger reached out, he heard nothing back.

Years went by without seeing Bosch, who no longer showed up to neighborhood barbecues or family gatherings. When Roger did finally catch a glimpse of Tony, his old friend was lying on the sand in South Beach with a beautiful, much younger woman on his arm. De Armas quietly walked away. A few months later, he saw him at a sushi place in Coral Gables, with another gorgeous woman.

De Armas wondered what had happened to the family man he once knew. "I still have a brotherly love for him," De Armas says. "But part of me just wanted to strangle him."

Despite the string of girlfriends, Tony's personal life wasn't faring much better than his business ventures. He'd rebounded quickly in Miami after his 2007 divorce from Aliette, bouncing around the Key Biscayne social scene and eventually dating a teacher named Claudia, a deeply tanned beauty with long, bleached-blond hair who loved the Miami Heat and Coral Gables wine bars.

But that relationship fell apart for good by 2010, when Tony discovered she'd been seeing a former student and karate instructor. "I am not mad or angry," Tony wrote in a masterfully passive-aggressive breakup letter. "I am, however, a little in shock, hurt and my ego is a little bruised." But he wished her well, adding that "God willing, I can find true love like you did."

He asked to stay friends. That didn't work out, either.

In the summer of 2010, Aliette moved back to South Florida from Texas with Tony's two kids, and—though the two didn't get back together— he agreed to let them stay with him in Key Biscayne until they got settled.

On June 7, Aliette called the local cops. Claudia, she said, had been repeatedly harassing their twelve-year-old daughter with "derogatory" texts and phone calls, and she worried for her daughter's safety. The night before, someone—she suspected Claudia—had even bashed in the windshield of her 2008 Cadillac, parked at the nearby Ritz Hotel. (Tony's ex-girlfriend was never charged in either incident.)

Like Henry Hill at the end of *Goodfellas*, Tony was suffering a rightfully paranoid meltdown. The next month, he was leaving his Key Biscayne office when he heard an engine roar behind him. Heart racing, he turned around to see a guy who'd gotten into a fight with him over a girl at a bar. Bosch sprinted back to his office. His phone started ringing. When he picked up, the man hollered, "I'm strapped, and I'm going to kill you." Bosch locked the door and called the cops.

Worse, bringing Aliette back to Miami didn't help Tony's terrible child support record. The lawsuits she'd started in Texas moved to a Miami court in 2009, where she claimed he owed her $23,940 for their two kids' up-bringing. A judge in April 2010 ordered him to pay $1,250 every other month. He ignored the obligation.

Two weeks before Melky's suspension became official—and Tony's business faced the biggest crisis since he'd expanded into the MLB PED arena—Aliette had dragged him back to the civil courthouse downtown. Now he owed her $41,940. On June 25, a judge didn't cut him nearly so much slack—this time, he'd have to pay her $1,200 every single week. If he didn't, a state prosecutor would get involved.

On August 15, Major League Baseball banned Melky Cabrera for fifty games. Turns out Nunez and Melky weren't British spy material after all: Within four days of the announcement of the suspension, the *New York Daily News* had publicly unwound the website plot.

Two days after that, MLB executives for all thirty teams received a memo from then–league executive vice president Rob Manfred. "Please be advised that commissioner Selig has directed that all major league clubs are prohibited from granting Juan Carlos Nunez access to their clubhouses or other nonpublic areas," the memo read. "Nunez is affiliated with ACES Inc. sports agency. Nunez is currently under investigation for misconduct re-lated to our recent matter under the joint drug program.

"In addition, Nunez is not certified as a player agent by the Major League Baseball Players Association," it continued. "Clubs should not conduct contract negotiations with Nunez or otherwise deal with him regarding players on the 40-man roster."

The Levinsons suspended Nunez from employment on August 20, 2012, according to Jay Reisinger, an attorney representing ACES. (Reisinger said he did not know whether the suspension was with pay.) Nunez was fired "shortly thereafter," says the attorney. He says that Juan Carlos's brother Tirzon was also fired. "I believe it was after Juan Carlos," says Reisinger, though he does not provide the termination date of either of the Nunezes.

Nunez had been exiled. Bosch's best avenue to big league clients was persona non grata.

Former steroid dealer Kirk Radomski spent his days on federal probation hectically driving around his hometown Long Island and New York City delivering supplements—legal ones—to bodybuilding stores. For years, he had been saying that investigating only juicing players—and not their union-certified representatives—was a sure way to make sure steroids never go away. "You're not killing the snakehead!" Radomski yells in an interview with one of this book's authors. "It's the fucking agents!"

In the wake of the Melky Cabrera debacle, Radomski started getting phone calls from league investigators. Nunez's role in the website deceit had turned the league's attention toward ACES.

Though Radomski distrusted the league, he was swayed when MLB investigator Tom Reilly—who happened to know the former dealer from their mutual childhoods in the Bronx—convinced him to take a ride to Manhattan to meet with other investigators and league attorneys.

On September 11, 2012, Radomski sat in MLB offices and signed an affidavit detailing his allegations against the Levinsons, who he said he had known for twenty-seven years: their knowledge of his steroid "program"; Sam Levinson's urging that "whatever you're doing for Todd [Hundley], keep it going"; and the cash and check payments for players like Rondell

White, which Radomski picked up during "dozens" of visits to ACES's Brooklyn office.

Radomski, who also provided the two checks for $3,200 each that were made out to him from a joint bank account belonging to Paul Lo Duca and Sam Levinson and ACES Inc., was unloading the evidence that Senator George Mitchell had declined to use in his report. "I previously disclosed to United States government investigators and to former Senator Mitchell that I picked up certain payments for steroids and HGH from the ACES office," Radomski wrote in the affidavit that was obtained by these authors, "but I was not asked to provide details regarding the Levinson knowledge of the drug use of their clients, or their role in my transactions with their players."

But league officials had trouble corroborating the affidavit with testimony from the players involved. Hundley and White refused to talk, according to a league source intimately familiar with the investigation. Though Lo Duca made statements privately that seemed to back up Radomski's account, the league couldn't get him to detail his own sworn affidavit. "My stance on ACES is those guys are bad guys," Lo Duca said in a brief interview for this book. "Baseball knows it, and they haven't done anything about it."

He then added obliquely, before hanging up: "I was a very good hitter and then when I left ACES I fell off—write that!"

Attorney Reisinger says that Lo Duca's vitriol—and, in fact, Radomski's campaign against ACES—was inspired by a dispute over finances. ACES filed a union grievance against Lo Duca in 2009, according to Reisinger, over $50,000 the former catcher owed for a $1 million signing bonus. Soon thereafter, Reisinger says, Lo Duca called the attorney's office, "verbally threatening my assistant," and vowing to write a book claiming that the brothers were linked to steroids. "On behalf of his buddy," Reisinger says of Radomski, "he writes an affidavit that is not true." (On the phone with an author of this book, Lo Duca said he hadn't seen Radomski in years and cursed him out for dredging up old news about his doping.)

Without the assistance of former players like Lo Duca, Major League

Baseball was left with little recourse. Nunez was clearly implicated in Melky Cabrera's doping cover-up, but there was no evidence linking the scheme or the PED use to the brothers behind ACES. Discipline of agents was ultimately the purview of the union, and MLBPA chief Michael Weiner did not hide his esteem for ACES: In 2011, he had named Sam Levinson to the union's Player Agent Advisory Committee. It was a group Weiner said in an e-mail was designed to "improve the quality of player representation, and better assist players in making informed choices regarding their representatives."

Now Weiner "censured" the agents, a mostly symbolic gesture that did not endanger their representation of MLB clients for not properly supervising their employee Nunez. "We conducted a thorough investigation and concluded that none of the ACES principals were involved in the scheme and that there was no knowledge or involvement by Seth and Sam," the union chief said.

ACES' attorney Reisinger says that union investigators reviewed the agency's business records, telephone logs, and e-mails and interviewed "most if not all" of the agency's employees. "The Players Association made a significant investigation," says Reisinger. "The specific finding was that [the Levinsons] had nothing to do with Melky Cabrera."

It was only a matter of months until officials found out that Nunez's role in PED procurement went far beyond just Melky Cabrera.

B osch's big league clients were already on edge following Cabrera's suspension. Bartolo Colon's suspension sealed the deal: Tony Bosch's testosterone troches, his purportedly perfected "pink cream," and his guarantee that he'd mastered the chemical combos to evade baseball's subpar testers were seemingly no good.

Those monthly $12,000 checks from A-Rod might not be flowing in much longer, he feared. Payments from most of his other minor leaguers and pros would also dry up.

That's why Bosch was so receptive when Porter Fischer—that persistent friend of the Carbones, always pestering him for a job in the clinic or a marketing opportunity for Biogenesis—suddenly announced he'd come into some money.

A Jaguar had smacked into him as he biked through Pinecrest, he explained to Bosch, and he had some insurance cash to invest.

In the big picture, the $4,000 that Tony agreed to take from Fischer may not have been much of a life preserver for a guy whose business world and personal life were sinking beneath the waves.

But Bosch had rent to pay just to keep Biogenesis's doors open, another $1,200 due to Aliette Bosch to keep a state prosecutor from filing charges, and a roomful of doctors expecting their usual "fees" for using their licenses. The only way to keep the machine chugging without the high-profit athletes was to at least pay off that immediate debt so that his regular clients could show up for their hCG weight-loss plans or their HGH/testosterone cocktails. In October 2012, that $4,000 was exactly the lifeline Tony Bosch needed to keep any hope alive. So he agreed and brought Porter on board as a staff member.

Tony Bosch had made a lot of mistakes in his life. When he took Porter Fischer's money, Bosch had to know that the earnest, beefy bodybuilder was unlikely to ever see his investment back. As he had with so many before him, from Roger De Armas to Jorge Jaen to Carlos Acevedo, Bosch took the cash and figured he'd mend the relationship with sweet talk or deal with yet another lawsuit down the line.

Bosch had no way to know that screwing Porter Fischer was the worst mistake he'd ever made.

The e-mail landed in a *Miami New Times* reporter's in-box on November 19, 2012.

"I am looking to get in contact with writer Tim Elfrink," wrote Dave C., "for a follow up and some major new developments from some articles he did in 2009 concerning the Manny Ramirez HGH scandal. I really need to speak with Mr. Elfrink, as I need to get my information out there as safely, legally and responsibly as possible."

A similar note went out to ESPN, with a header looking for T. J. Quinn. He never heard back from the Worldwide Leader in Sports. (Fischer even tried a follow-up note but was rebuffed by an ESPN flack, who said the network didn't give out on-air personalities' e-mail addresses. Quinn never saw the e-mail.)

A week later, "Dave C." met Elfrink at a sports bar in South Miami. He was, of course, Porter Fischer.

It was about three weeks after he'd stormed out of the meeting with Tony Bosch over his $4,000 debt, when Tony had looked him in the eye and told him he just wasn't going to get his money back that week.

Fischer's plan for payback had come from the meeting where Bosch had ranted about needing only the boxes of patient files to run his business.

The scene ran through Fischer's head as he fumed over his lost investment. "That's when it hit me: He needs the files. This motherfucker should get hit where it hurts," Fischer said. "I took an empty box I had at home, took a full box at the clinic, and put an empty box back in its place."

Once Tony noticed the files were gone, Fischer figured, he'd have to pay back his loan one way or another.

Porter Fischer's phone rang late on Saturday, January 26, 2013, about two months after his first meeting with Elfrink. He let it ring through, and then it rang again. He glanced around his darkened guesthouse. He'd carefully armed the alarms at the front and back doors. His two pet Rottweilers were chained up outside. His Beretta 3032 Tomcat was loaded and sitting on the kitchen table.

He had good reason to be on edge. Earlier that day, he'd gotten a call from Elfrink. Ever since that first meeting in November, they'd met almost every week at the same sports bar, going through Tony Bosch's handwritten notebooks over Michelob Ultras and talking through everything Fischer knew about Biogenesis.

Elfrink had a conundrum: The more time he spent combing through the records Porter had taken from the clinic—and then copied onto a flash drive and given to the reporter—the less doubt he had that they were legit. But what they suggested was beyond explosive. *Miami New Times*, the sister paper to New York's *Village Voice* and nine other alternative weeklies around the country, had just three staff writers. *New Times* was well known for hard-hitting local investigative stories, but this was a tinderbox on a whole new scale. If Elfrink was going to write a piece accusing some of the richest men in professional baseball of cheating, he'd better be damned sure he knew what he had. He needed to prove the records were real. As the newspaper's full-time attorney gently put it, if the notebooks were faked they'd all be fucked.

Along with his editor and the attorney, he came up with a plan to confirm the validity of Porter's documents. Elfrink would call the scores of ordinary patients listed in Bosch's handwritten notes and typed business records. If enough of them confirmed their own entries were accurate, it would be powerful proof that Bosch's notes about selling banned drugs to A-Rod, Cabrera, Cruz, and the lot were also correct.

That reporting took two months, during which time Bosch closed up Biogenesis—unable to pay the rent thanks to his disappearing MLB clientele—and largely disappeared. While most patients Elfrink called declined to talk, by early January he'd found a half dozen willing to confirm that their own interactions with Biogenesis matched what was listed in Bosch's records. Fischer also set up a meeting with another former employee at the clinic, who asked to stay anonymous but confirmed his story.

Taken as a whole, it was more than enough to convince readers—and, just as important, the *New Times* attorney. The story would run, *New Times* editors decided, on February 6. But first Elfrink needed to give everyone a fair chance to comment. On Friday, January 25, he sent detailed letters to every big leaguer they planned to name in the story as a Biogenesis client.

Multiple teams forwarded the letters to MLB front offices. In his arbitration testimony, Rob Manfred described league counsel Dan Halem and public relations chief Pat Courtney "buzzing into my office . . . because between the two of them they had received a number of virtually—either identical or virtually identical letters that had been sent to individual teams."

No one responded, although Elfrink did get a mysterious call from a Los Angeles area code late that Friday night. The caller, who identified himself only as an associate of Alex Rodriguez's, sounded breathless and slightly panicked. Was *New Times* really going to write all these things about A-Rod? Everything that was in the letter would be in the story, Elfrink confirmed. "But that's really bad!" the man cried. He asked vaguely if there was any way to forestall the piece, promised to call back, and then never did.

The next morning, it became clear that team or league offices had leaked word of the pending firestorm. Both the *New York Daily News* and the South Florida *Sun Sentinel* ran vague stories quoting anonymous sources speculating that baseball officials were investigating a major PED ring centered on Miami, possibility connected to the father-and-son Bosch operation originally linked to Manny Ramirez.

Everyone tied to the clinic now knew the truth: Their secret was about to become very public. Belatedly, Bosch's camp started frantically reaching out to Fischer. Ashley Bosch, Tony's brother, called and offered to personally pay back all of Fischer's money if he'd give Tony his notebooks back. Ricardo Martinez also called to plead his case. "He was like, 'Please, please, please, can you stop the story?'" Fischer says. "I told him, 'Look, I told Tony there would be collateral damage.'"

Then Elfrink called with the news: It was go time. *New Times* editors realized their own story would never hold until February 6—it had to go to press that Monday. Instead of another week to prepare, the story was going to land much sooner. As he sat at home in South Miami after the call, Fischer felt increasingly paranoid.

Other than Elfrink, he'd trusted only one person through the process: Pete Carbone, his buddy from Boca Tanning. Fischer liked Carbone, but he also saw something useful in his tanned, aviator-wearing friend. He seemed like the kind of guy who knew what to do in a crisis. With his tough-guy New York attitude, he wasn't likely to get rattled. Besides, when Fischer confided in him what he was up to, it had won him major street cred with the salon owner, who considered himself something of a scheme connoisseur.

Weeks before, Fischer had given Carbone a flash drive with copies of Tony's notebooks, just in case something bad happened to him before the story could run. He also confided his fears in Pete.

Now, late on the Saturday before the news would go to print, Pete—the unflappable tough guy—was frantically calling Fischer's phone over and over, refusing to leave a message. Finally, Fischer answered.

"Dude, I need to talk to you now. About that *New Times* story. You've got to stop it!" Fischer recalls Pete saying to him. "Fucking Oggi has been calling me all day, texting 'nine one one.' You have got to make sure Oggi's name is not in this. You don't understand how fucking huge this is. This is not pretend, this is not wannabe shit, this is real gangster shit. You are gonna end up dead. He is gonna have you killed."

Fischer panicked. He'd spent weeks running through all the ways exposing Tony Bosch's clinic—and the ballplayers connected—could land him in hot water. He'd imagined theft charges for relieving the clinic of its records. He'd imagined A-Rod coming down on him with big-money lawyers. But now, with Pete's warning in his head, he was suddenly worried that Oggi was a violent mobster who could have him whacked.

His mind reeling, Fischer agreed to have Pete over to his house to talk out the situation. Right away, Fischer unloaded his anxiety.

"I don't need this anymore," Fischer says he told Carbone. He went to a closet and, from a top shelf, pulled down the four handwritten notebooks he'd taken from Tony Bosch.

Fischer recalls: "Pete sat on the couch and blows out his breath. 'Fuck, dude. Do you know what I'm holding? This is huge.'"

Carbone said he had an idea to save Fischer's ass. He'd get the notebooks back to Tony Bosch. *New Times* had agreed to keep Fischer's name out of the story and to protect him as an anonymous source. If he got the originals back in Bosch's hands, who could prove that Porter was even involved in the imminent Biogenesis news leak?

Carbone left with the four notebooks.

The next day, Carbone called and told Fischer to come by Boca Tanning. When he arrived, Carbone grinned and handed him an envelope with $4,000 inside. Fischer asked him if he'd gotten the money from Bosch. Carbone said he'd visited Bosch on Key Biscayne, where the soon-to-be-exposed fake doctor was "freaking out" with Ricky Martinez.

"So you gave him the books?" Fischer asked again.

"Oh no, I told him they were destroyed," said Carbone, still grinning.

"So what did you actually do with them?" demanded Fischer.

"I gave 'em to A-Rod's people," Fischer says Carbone responded.

Fischer's stomach dropped. "Right then and there, a fucking chill went over me. I was like, 'Holy shit, I was fucking played the whole fucking time.'"

Pete Carbone has refused to tell his own side of this story, either to a reporter or in a legal deposition. His brother, Anthony, pleads nearly complete ignorance of all things Biogenesis.

According to MLB's arbitrator, Oggi later told Tony Bosch that Fischer had sold his original notebooks to A-Rod's newly hired celebrity attorney, Roy Black, for $10,000. Fischer vehemently denies that and claims that the Carbone brothers engineered the sale.

It certainly wasn't the first time the tanning salon entrepreneurs saw an opportunity to profit from Tony Bosch's imploding existence.

A little after six P.M. on Monday, January 28, 2014, *New Times* designers sent PDFs of the week's cover to the printing presses. It showed a bucolic small town's ballfield shadowed beneath a barrage of syringes rocketing through the sky like a Soviet missile launch. The headline read: THE STEROID SOURCE.

Inside the paper's midtown Miami offices, Elfrink went through his usual Monday-afternoon routine, trying hard to ignore the pit of anxiety growing in his stomach. He'd spent hours on Sunday frantically rewriting and fact-checking the five-thousand-word story, calling and re-calling sources. Today, he'd gone through every name and piece of evidence in the piece time and again with his editor and the company's lawyer.

Now, it was done. By nine A.M. the next morning, the story would be online.

In Manhattan that night, MLB officials hunkered down to plan their response, and A-Rod hung on the phone with his PR advisors and lawyers. From Detroit to Seattle to off-season haunts like Venezuela and the Dominican Republic, front-office executives and players alike waited uneasily for whatever the paper might print.

CHAPTER THIRTEEN

A New Steroid Era Exposed

J oe Girardi literally felt the decision in his stomach. He'd been planning it since the day before and even dropped hints of his thought process to beat reporters before the game so they wouldn't be caught off guard. The young Yankees manager knew it was the right move, even if he would be excoriated in the press the next day if it didn't work.

That still didn't make the short walk through the dugout, as the packed Bronx house rocked with tension around him, any easier.

How do you tell one of the greatest hitters in the history of the game—and a notoriously sensitive one at that—that you're taking him out for a pinch hitter in the ninth inning in the playoffs?

On October 10, 2012, the Yankees were down to their last two outs, trailing the Baltimore Orioles by one run. The best-of-five American League Division Series was tied at one win apiece, so the outcome of this game was pivotal. It was the sort of hero-making situation for which the Yankees had traded for Rodriguez, and his monster contract, nine seasons earlier—and then given him a $275 million extension four seasons after that.

But Rodriguez's spark was gone in the Bronx. The thirty-seven-year-old Rodriguez had spent a quarter of the 2012 season sidelined with a hand injury. Every year for a half decade, some ailment or another had landed him on the disabled list.

His slugging percentage was the lowest it had been since he was a twenty-year-old kid in Seattle. An A-Rod homer had become the Fabergé egg of baseball: He hit only eighteen in 2012, each one costing the Yankees about $1.6 million.

And after leading the Yanks to a championship in 2009—with Anthony Galea's surreptitious assistance—Rodriguez had spent each postseason since reclaiming his title as October's reigning underperformer.

The night earlier, with two outs in the ninth and the Yankees down by one, Rodriguez had flailed at Baltimore closer Jim Johnson's sinker to end the game. So far in the Series' three games, he had one hit in twelve at-bats with a grimace-inducing seven strikeouts. It had been a Bronx monsoon of boos, with tabloid columnists and sports radio callers urging the Yankees to figure out a way to trade him after the season.

With Johnson again on the mound and slugger Raul Ibanez on the Yankees' bench, Girardi wasn't going to again let Rodriguez play the goat. The manager later described his dugout conversation. "You're scuffling a little bit right now," he told Rodriguez. "Raul's been a good pinch hitter for us and I'm just going to take a shot."

The words likely sounded hollow. Rodriguez had suffered humiliation in the past for his poor postseason performance, when in 2006 then-manager Joe Torre dropped him to eighth in the batting order, a spot usually reserved for scrawny defense specialists. But removing Rodriguez altogether in such a crucial situation was an even greater slight.

Rodriguez took the news from Girardi graciously. It was only later revealed how bitter he was.

Then Girardi made an even more unusual call. On the dugout telephone, he rang the stadium press box. When a pinch hitter comes in, it's customary for the announcer to name both the new batter and who is being replaced. But now, Girardi asked the announcer to say only that Ibanez was batting and not mention that he was hitting for Rodriguez.

The little moment of eggshell walking revealed how familiar the Yankees were with their highest-paid star's fragile ego. It was also the last time any member of the team's management cared about Rodriguez's feelings.

As it turns out, Girardi's lineup move was genius. Ibanez belted a game-tying home run to right field. And in the twelfth inning, as Rodriguez watched from the dugout, Ibanez hit another solo home run to win the game on a walk-off.

After the game, Rodriguez swore that he was not offended by Girardi's decision, and that he felt ready to break out of his slump. "I wish it was me hitting two home runs tonight, but I'm still feeling good," he said. "I was relaxed tonight. I'm ready to break out."

But privately, Rodriguez was certain that his poor play was a result of an undiagnosed injury so painful that he was popping painkillers throughout the playoffs. He complained to Yankees team doctor Christopher Ahmad that he felt pain in the right hip, the same one that had undergone surgery in 2009. At eight forty-five the next morning, Rodriguez underwent an MRI at the New York–Presbyterian Hospital in Manhattan.

The procedure revealed that Rodriguez's left hip was actually more problematic, according to medical records provided to this book's authors by Rodriguez's attorneys. "Partial evaluation of left hip revealing superior labral tear with small paralabral cyst," reads a note written by a radiologist.

Ahmad reviewed the radiologist's findings. If he was concerned by the torn labrum—meaning hip joint cartilage—revealed by the MRI, he still cleared Rodriguez to play that night in the Bronx. Rodriguez later claimed that amounted to medical malpractice.

Rodriguez went hitless and struck out twice in four at-bats. In the bottom of the thirteenth inning with two outs and the Yankees down by one, Rodriguez was once again lifted for a pinch hitter. This time, pinch hitter Eric Chavez lined out, the Yankees' loss sending the series to a decisive Game Five.

Girardi benched Rodriguez altogether in the rubber match. To reporters, the manager blamed Rodriguez's horrid recent batting against righthanders. There was no talk of a possible injury. Ace C. C. Sabathia threw a gem, and the Yankees got the victory that allowed them to squeak on to the American League Championship Series against the Detroit Tigers—no thanks to their highest-paid player.

Rodriguez's struggles only intensified against the Tigers. In the series' first two games, played in New York, he managed one single in seven at-bats and struck out three times. The Bronx fans booed him lustily every time he stepped to the plate. Humiliation was now routine: He was dropped from third to sixth in the lineup and was once again pinch-hit for, again by Eric Chavez.

This time there were no press box phone calls from Girardi to coddle his feelings. The Yankees lost both games. As the team flew to Detroit to try to piece together a comeback, Rodriguez was at his lowest point as a major league ballplayer. He was no longer a valuable asset to the Yankees. Instead, he was just a very expensive liability. He hadn't been so marginalized since he was fourteen years old, pushed off the varsity squad by Brother Herb Baker.

Maybe the Yankees doctor wouldn't do anything for him. But the pseudomedical hustler whom Rodriguez kept on retainer was always on call.

Since that furtive meeting in a Tampa hotel two years earlier, when Yuri Sucart and Oggi Velazquez had introduced him to the PED peddler, Rodriguez and Bosch had grown extremely—and brazenly—close. In Rodriguez, Bosch had found a patient as willing to experiment as the fake doctor was eager to administer bizarre treatments.

According to information provided by a source familiar with his later arbitration testimony, Bosch recounted meeting with Rodriguez more than a dozen times in New York City and Miami. Rodriguez is a real estate connoisseur, and his treatments took Bosch to a procession of the athlete's newly bought or rented homes in New York's Upper East Side, Upper West Side, Greenwich Village, and the ritziest enclave in Miami Beach.

For the New York meetings, Sucart drove Bosch, who often had a hazy idea of where he was. In 2011, according to Bosch's testimony, Bosch met Rodriguez at an apartment overlooking the Hudson River. Sucart told Bosch to remove his shoes, and once inside, he realized why. The entire apartment, including the wood floor and all of the decor, was bright white.

There, Bosch says he met Bruli Medina Reyes, a Dominican trainer hired by Rodriguez. They played pool for hours while waiting for Rodriguez to arrive. When he finally showed up, Bosch set up an IV that infused Rodriguez with human growth hormone and peptides, according to Bosch's later testimony.

These infusions—which have not been reported as part of Rodriguez's regimen until now—were prominent in Bosch's treatment of the superstar. Bosch believed that by administering the drugs with a mixture of dextrose, he could more effectively deliver them than via his more regular doses of creams and troches. The World Anti-Doping Agency has banned the use of all IV infusions by the athletes it governs. MLB has no rules against IVs of substances that aren't banned, of course.

Bosch also testified that he provided a unique service for Rodriguez during some infusions, by attaching an oxygen mask to Rodriguez's face. His theory was that the pure oxygen could help increase the superstar's production of stem cells, which can aid recovery from injuries. Bosch would have preferred a hyperbaric chamber but figured the mask would do the trick.

Bosch mostly administered these infusions himself to Rodriguez, though he said that at one point Sucart borrowed the IV pole and oxygen mask to meet his cousin in Tampa. Bosch also used an IV to draw blood from Rodriguez, which he tended to do before or during spring training to check his hormone levels.

But sometimes Bosch and Rodriguez weren't exactly clinical. Bosch had previously visited Rodriguez at his home on Star Island, a picturesque plot of mansions of the rich and famous off of South Beach. According to Bosch's later testimony, he had infused Rodriguez with peptides and HGH in a media room in Rodriguez's mansion. But on one instance in 2011, Bosch later said, he had been unable to meet Rodriguez at his home. Needing to draw his blood to determine the dosages he was going to give him, they arranged a backup plan. Bosch would meet Rodriguez at LIV, a nightclub at Miami Beach's famous Fontainebleau Hotel, and draw his blood there.

The syringe procedure went down in a bathroom stall, according to Bosch's later testimony. Sucart stood guard. Because the proper blood-packing paraphernalia would have been conspicuous, Bosch said he just put the vial of Rodriguez's blood in his pocket.

Then, instead of going home or to his office, Bosch headed back inside LIV and spent some time dancing. In an almost unbelievable bit of tomfoolery that has not been reported until now, Bosch then realized he had lost the vial. After some frantic searching amid the thumping techno and milling crowds, he found it lying on the nightclub floor. Bosch told this story during his arbitration testimony, according to a source. When an attorney for Rodriguez pointedly asked whether he had used cocaine that night, Bosch denied it.

Rodriguez was on a monthly protocol, according to Bosch, and besides infusions and blood drawings, they used trusted couriers Sucart and Velazquez to exchange drugs and cash. Bosch gave substances—such as the troches Rodriguez was supposed to use right before games or working out, creams, peptides, and HGH—to Sucart, who then relayed them to his younger cousin. It was Sucart who spoke on the phone and texted with Bosch hundreds of times. The cash traveled a chain, with the wad shrinking with every middleman taking a cut: Rodriguez gave Sucart money, who passed it on to Velazquez, who gave it to Bosch, who usually pocketed a grand or so and then provided the remainder to Biogenesis's chief financial officer, Ricardo Martinez. Bosch's total charges to Rodriguez varied, but they usually maxed out at $12,000 per month. You could say Bosch was a fan of the steady pay: He said in one note that he had a four-year "contract" with Rodriguez, coinciding with the superstar's agreement with the Yankees.

But after Sucart started attracting too much attention and then the sycophantic relationship between "Cacique" and his cousin finally fell apart, Rodriguez decided to go without a middleman separating him from Bosch.

The beginning of the end came when Sucart, in a Yankees hoodie, was spotted casually walking around the lobby of the St. Regis Hotel in San

Francisco, where the team was staying during a series against the Oakland Athletics in late May 2011.

The MLB ban on Sucart didn't apply to public areas, of course, and Rodriguez had been paying for his cousin gofer to accompany him on road trips. But now MLB executive Rob Manfred said of Sucart's continuing association with Rodriguez: "We're looking into it." In arbitration testimony, Manfred was more forthcoming. "I spoke to Yankee officials about who had been around and whether the ban had been violated in any way, and, you know, received assurances that the ban was being properly enforced."

The *New York Daily News* ran a poll asking fans whether they were "concerned" that Sucart was traveling on road trips. Fifty-seven percent chose this option: "Yes. This indicates A-Rod's steroid scandal may not be completely behind him."

This is not the sort of spotlight you want on the courier regularly bringing you illicit drugs. And the timing wasn't good for human Whac-A-Mole Sucart. The month earlier, he and his wife, Carmen, had filed for bankruptcy. They owed $1.6 million, most of it a result of property foreclosures, since the Sucarts had bought big right before the Miami housing bubble burst.

The filings reveal a modest, 2004 Toyota Sequoia–driving existence for a superstar ballplayer's embattled right-hand man. One of his biggest expenses was a $600 monthly tuition to Westminster Christian School, where his son was hoping to be like Uncle A-Rod.

"I love him very much," Rodriguez said of Sucart, but then confirmed that he would no longer be taking him on road trips: "I'm handling it."

And on Thanksgiving 2011, he fired the cousin who had been his professional shadow since his days as a rookie in Seattle, and a brother figure since they were scrambling around that little apartment in Washington Heights. A person close to Rodriguez says it wasn't the increased scrutiny that caused the superstar to can Sucart. According to the source, Rodriguez believed Sucart was mismanaging his money. And Sucart's burgeoning role as Bosch's recruiter was threatening Rodriguez. The source says that Sucart was using Rodriguez's name as a lure for other players, including Yankees teammate Francisco Cervelli, unbeknownst to the superstar. "Alex didn't feel like he could trust the guy," the source says of Sucart.

The arbitration transcript obtained by these authors supports the assertion that Sucart was attempting to make a living as a major league handler beyond Rodriguez. In May 2012, according to a letter entered into evidence in the arbitration, an attorney wrote to Major League Baseball "complaining about the ban on Mr. Sucart from major league facilities," Rob Manfred testified. This was the year after Rodriguez fired him.

Manfred says he was "mildly amused" by the letter's tone. He wrote back saying that if Sucart met with league officials, they would "evaluate" the ban. Neither Sucart nor his attorney ever responded.

Throughout that 2012 season, during which Rodriguez had struggled with the hand injury and elusive power, the superstar was now the one constantly texting Bosch and speaking to him on the phone, according to an arbitration document. "Do you think they are going to test?" Bosch asked Rodriguez, on a day in late spring training in which the Yankee tried out the brand-new Miami Marlins park by knocking in three runs. "If by any chance they make you piss, wait the longest you can and don't use the pink until after," Bosch advised a few days later.

As the season started, Bosch wrote treatment notes to himself concerning "Caciques/AROD," next to those about Melky Cabrera and Yasmani Grandal. "He is paid through April 30th. He will owe May 1 $4,000 + new fee + $800 of old exp[enses] + new exp[enses]; I need to see him between April 13-19," Bosch wrote of an upcoming Yankees homestand in New York. "Deliver troches and pink cream + mo[nth] of May has 3 weeks of Sub-Q," he added, using his abbreviation for "subcutaneous," meaning anything shot under the skin—which is how Bosch administered HGH and peptides.

The "new fee" likely referred to Bosch's post-Sucart monthly charge: $12,000.

When Rodriguez asked whether he could still use the "pink"—

meaning Bosch's complex testosterone cream—even if he was required to piss after a game ("11pmish") Bosch assured him: "No worries . . . good to go." Rodriguez then instructed Bosch to "erase all these messages."

But even with Bosch as his full-time PEDs butler, there is evidence that Rodriguez sought out an even more toxic personality for help with his regimen. Victor Conte, the former BALCO chief convicted of steroid peddling, later said that for months in the spring of 2012, he had received phone calls from Bill Romanowksi, the unhinged former NFL player investigated for his former ties to the Bay Area PED clinic.

Since being released from prison, Conte runs a company selling what he says are legal supplements. Now Romanowski explained that he was buddies with Rodriguez, who was seeking "legal" supplements, Conte later claimed. Romanowski wanted Conte to fly to New York or Los Angeles to meet Rodriguez, but the erstwhile steroid dealer declined—and made it clear he wasn't in his former line of business. "I clearly told Romo it was about legal performance enhancement," Conte later said.

But in May 2012, Romanowski and his edge-seeking superstar associate showed up unannounced at his company's Bay Area offices, Conte says. Rodriguez hid in a Cadillac Escalade while Romanowski made sure the parking lot was clear of prying eyes. Rodriguez and Conte spoke for forty-five minutes about supplements; Conte says he told the Yankee to eschew a certain kind of calcium supplement and to use a protein that fixes muscle tears overnight.

After Rodriguez skulked away, Conte says he spoke on the phone with Anthony Bosch about the star client. Bosch's own records corroborate the correspondence between the two PED kingpins: He wrote Conte's name in his books, along with his San Francisco–area code cell phone number.

Rodriguez knew how risky his movements were. "I can't have any trace of Victor Conte," the BALCO chief's daughter, Veronica Conte, says Rodriguez remarked of keeping their association a secret. And after the bizarre consultation, his dealings with Bosch were the same strange cocktail of paranoia and recklessness.

In text messages, Rodriguez and Bosch referred to Conte's plan as the "VC protocol," according to evidence filed in the later arbitration case. It was this protocol that Bosch said he administered in June 2012, when he met Rodriguez at his new home on Bank Street in Greenwich Village, according to a source familiar with his testimony. Rodriguez had multiple little dogs, and in the basement of his town house he had installed a leased toy inspired by Bosch's treatments: a hyperbaric chamber.

"Why don't we do tomorrow night in Atlanta," Rodriguez texted Bosch that same month, according to messages later entered into evidence. Bosch dutifully met Rodriguez at the Loews Hotel on Peachtree Street—room 1528—where the third baseman was staying during a road series against the Braves. "Try to use service elevators," Rodriguez warned him then.

On such clandestine meetings, Bosch sometimes wore a hoodie and sunglasses. "Careful. Tons of eyes," Rodriguez texted. "Don't tell anyone your full name," he told Bosch another time, when the latter dropped a testosterone-laden care package of two "night creams," two "morning creams," and "a few yellows"—meaning Cialis—at Rodriguez's Miami Beach home, according to Bosch's later arbitration testimony.

In September 2012, Rodriguez took a quick trip to Miami, where he met Bosch at a Starbucks. "Go straight to bathroom," Rodriguez texted. In the Starbucks bathroom, Bosch gave him testosterone cream and morning cream, according to his arbitration testimony. Rodriguez gave him cash.

Their interactions were a cocktail of recklessness and exactitude. "Let's go over it again," Bosch texted him at one point.

Rodriguez replied: "Okay, gummy in the a.m., then liquid at 6:30 p.m."

"No mistakes," Bosch cautioned him. In text messages, they used the mantra "zero tolerance." It referred to MLB's drug policy and to their own tolerance for blunders that would get them caught.

When Bosch slipped out of their transparent code for PEDs in one text, Rodriguez scolded him. "Not meds dude," Rodriguez warned. "Food."

*   *   *

Of course, Rodriguez must have been concerned by a rash of failed tests by close major league colleagues. In August 2012, his former teammate and Miami workout partner Melky Cabrera had been suspended for testing positive for unnatural testosterone levels, as had Bartolo Colon. Immediately after the end of the postseason, former UM catcher Yasmani Grandal was suspended for the same reason. Even if Rodriguez didn't know these friends were Bosch clients—which is unlikely—he certainly knew that one of the main ingredients in the Biogenesis regimen was testosterone.

But Bosch was an expert at blaming his own patients when they failed tests. Most baseball players were sloppy, but Rodriguez was a control freak. If he followed Bosch's down-to-the-minute doping instructions, with twenty-four-hour care and advice from the fake doctor in Miami, Rodriguez had no reason to think that he would fail a test. After all, by the dismal beginning of the League Championship Series against the Tigers, Rodriguez had taken nine random drug tests since hiring Bosch. He had pissed clean each time. And in the end, his desire for the explosive feeling of Bosch's synthetic edge conquered any paranoia at getting caught.

When the Yankees landed in Detroit to continue the series, Bosch traveled there as well. Rodriguez didn't play at all on October 16 at Comerica Park, the third game of the Series and the Yankees' third loss.

In his arbitration testimony, according to a source familiar with the proceedings, Bosch described meeting Rodriguez's girlfriend at the back entrance of the Detroit hotel where the third baseman was staying. After a circuitous route to Rodriguez's suite, Bosch encountered a sour superstar eager to play and frustrated that he was being benched.

Bosch designed a two-day protocol for Rodriguez's Detroit trip, he later testified. Concerned that Rodriguez would be urine tested, he kept it simple: just HGH and peptides. Sure enough, on October 17, with that night's game postponed by rain, Rodriguez was subjected to a random drug test. As always, he tested clean.

On October 18, the fourth game of the series, Rodriguez pinch-hit for Ibanez in the sixth inning of a lopsided game. Missing his chance at cosmic payback, Rodriguez failed to get a hit in two at-bats and the Yankees lost by a score of 8–1. The Tigers had completed a four-game sweep to move on to the World Series, ending the most brutal season of Rodriguez's career. Of course, things were about to get a lot uglier.

In November, Rodriguez went for a routine appointment with Dr. Marc Philippon, the Colorado surgeon who performed the 2009 surgery on his right hip. Now Philippon discovered the labral tear on Rodriguez's left hip, which had been evident on medical records from Rodriguez's MRI during the playoffs. He recommended immediate surgery, which would keep Rodriguez sidelined through much of the 2013 season. When team officials broke news of the injury to the press, they also disclosed to reporters that Rodriguez had requested the MRI after Game Three of the Division Series against the Orioles.

"Rodriguez only had an MRI on his right hip, which came out clean," reported a December 2012 ESPN story. But according to his medical records, the radiologist had noted the labral tear in his left hip at the time, even if Rodriguez says Yankees doctor Christopher Ahmad hadn't informed him or the team of the injury.

That the team doctor had allowed him to play despite the radiologist's findings became, to Rodriguez, a sinister development. Then again, all aspects of the superstar's relationship with his employer were about to take a very dark turn.

Near the turn of 2013, Bosch realized that his composition notebooks, which for years he had filled with information about his clients, had gone missing. He told Oggi Velazquez, who was apoplectic but told Bosch he would take care of it.

Velazquez's relationship with Bosch had started as a patient, and then a partner. But it was clear that by now, Velazquez was a mercenary for Team A-Rod. All he wanted to know was what other records Bosch had that incriminated Rodriguez, and he demanded Bosch's computer. Bosch, who soon went into a panicked hiding, refused to give him anything.

When word reached Rodriguez that records exposing his doping had been stolen by some underling named Porter Fischer, who had given them to a newspaper, he began to prepare for a public relations and legal war. Rodriguez believed that both MLB and the Yankees—with nearly $100 million still owed to him—would take this opportunity to try to push him out of the league for good.

He called Roy Black. The Miami attorney was a confidante of Rodriguez's. He had held annual fund-raisers at his home for the superstar's charity, AROD Family Foundation. And Black's business card is the kind you dig out of the Rolodex when your high-profile life is exploding spectacularly.

Black had represented Kelsey Grammer when the *Frasier* star was dogged by a statutory rape accusation, *Girls Gone Wild* tycoon Joe Francis when he was charged with child abuse and prostitution, race-car driver Helio Castroneves when he was accused of tax evasion, and billionaire sex offender Jeffrey Epstein.

If Roy Black was the legal brain, Oggi handled the extralegal matters. He went into full A-Rod goon squad mode. Multiple people—including Pete Carbone and Rob Manfred—claimed that over the hectic upcoming weeks, Velazquez threatened the lives of both Bosch and Fischer.

Rodriguez's first orders of business were clear: Get the notebooks. And get Bosch to sign documentation that he had never provided Rodriguez with PEDs.

Jose "Pepe" Gomez, a Rodriguez confidante since their days as freshmen at Columbus High School, also sprang into action. As evidenced by his association with Sucart and Velazquez, Rodriguez appeared to be a magnet for criminals. Gomez's record includes a crime spree when he attended college in Tallahassee. He was accused of passing bad checks at a Publix supermarket, and in 1997, Gomez sold a half pound of pot to a cop. Officers found a scale, cocaine, and some pills in his home, according to a police report. "I got in on a very bad crowd," Gomez later wrote in an application for a state license. After being sentenced to sixty days in jail and two years home confinement, Gomez moved back to Miami and took some sports marketing classes. "I got married in Jan. 2003 to my high school sweetheart and I view life as a professional perspective," Gomez wrote.

On paper, the former marijuana dealer was the senior vice president of Newport Property Ventures, Rodriguez's real estate company. Rodriguez called him his "business agent." But when your boss is Alex Rodriguez and trouble is in the air, the job can be flexible.

According to a source close to Rodriguez, a hierarchy soon emerged. Gomez was no longer a "street guy," says the source. But Oggi Velazquez was. So when Gomez needed to deal with characters like Jones or the Carbones, Velazquez was assigned the task.

Rodriguez might condo-hunt on Fifth Avenue in Manhattan, but he's still South Floridian to the bone. If MLB and the media wanted to beat him, they'd have to do it on his home turf. His entourage became a machine.

Rodriguez's team, ready to do whatever it took to exonerate him, sprang into action in earnest when the Yankees forwarded him an e-mail on January 25, 2013. It was from a reporter in Florida. "Mr. Rodriguez," the letter began, "*Miami New Times* is preparing a story about a Miami-area anti-aging clinic run by Anthony Bosch called Biogenesis. . . ."

Twelve people got such letters from *Miami New Times* that Friday: Texas slugger Nelson Cruz, Oakland pitcher Bartolo Colon, Toronto outfielder Melky Cabrera, Detroit shortsop Jhonny Peralta, Washington pitcher Gio Gonzalez, San Diego catcher Yasmani Grandal, Seattle catcher Jesus Montero, Pittsburgh outfielder Felix Pie, former UM star Cesar Carrillo, tennis star Wayne Odesnik, UM trainer Jimmy Goins, and Rodriguez.

Of the professional ballplayers, some were kids just trying to get a lasting taste of the major leagues, like Carrillo, who was a minor leaguer in the Detroit Tigers organization. And some were MLB veterans like corpulent Dominican hurler Colon, who at thirty-nine years old in 2012 had banked more than $70 million despite his drug suspension that year.

The letters reached players in Winter League—like Cruz, who was playing for the Gigantes del Cibao in the Dominican Republic—or already in exile from MLB, like Cabrera, who had watched his Giants win a world championship on television after his steroid suspension.

That original list didn't include every name in Bosch's records, only those whom the newspaper had been able to verify without a doubt had gone to Biogenesis. For example, Ryan Braun was not sent a letter, and his name did not appear in the original *New Times* story. It was a testament to Bosch's salesmanship that even a partial exposure of his big league client list was bound to change the landscape of the sport.

The letters were composed in a way that should have indicated that this was not the sort of story that would go away. The reporter, Tim Elfrink, knew on which date Bosch had traveled to Dallas to deliver drugs to Cruz, knew Peralta's $4,000 balance, and knew Cabrera bought drugs including "pink cream" from Bosch on April 4, 2012.

But even as they privately panicked, not one of the ballplayers receiving letters issued a denial, or any sort of response, to *New Times*.

No athlete had as much evidence tying them to Biogenesis as Alex Rodriguez, who appeared in the notebooks at least sixteen times. *New Times* knew that on one visit, he had shelled out $4,000 to Bosch for troches, pink cream, and other substances. Rodriguez's purchases of steroids, testosterone, and growth hormone were meticulously recorded. Sucart was also amply implicated in the records, including paying Bosch $500 for a week's worth of growth hormone.

And when the e-mails to teams resulted in rushed and vague stories appearing in the *New York Daily News* and Florida's *Sun Sentinel* newspaper on January 26, before *New Times* could go to print, the only player named in these information-thin articles was Rodriguez. Multiple outlets had to issue a correction after running a photo of another man whom it identified as Anthony Bosch. It was clear that in the offices of law-enforcement officials, league and team brass, major news sports desks—and, above all, in the homes of Biogenesis-linked players who were petrified about what might be coming—confusion and a sort of flat-footed panic reigned.

It must have frustrated the hell out of Rodriguez. He was always base-ball's steroid scapegoat, the man whose scowling face adorned the covers of bestselling exposés, when he knew he was only one of many superstars using growth hormones and steroids.

On January 27, as everybody in baseball kept an eye trained on Miami, an outwardly casual Ryan Braun was in Wisconsin. He wore a Brewers jersey over jeans and a sweatshirt, played a *Family Feud*–style game with teammates, and signed autographs for fans. He was at the team's fan festi-val, revamping his image after the overturned steroid suspension of the year before.

The shindig was free that year, an overture to loyal fans who had weathered a losing team and a PED scandal in 2012. But Wisconsinites are an obliging sort when somebody deserves forgiveness, and Braun had been exonerated, hadn't he?

"Ryan Braun skipped the Milwaukee Brewers' fan festival last January, remaining mostly quiet while he waited for a decision in his appeal of a 50-game suspension under baseball's drug policy," ran the sweetly redemptive Associated Press story on his appearance. "What a difference a year makes."

If anybody had thought the little alt-weekly in Miami was bluffing with its letters, they learned the truth on January 29, when the *New Times* story was published online. The story went online around nine A.M. By that night, it led every ESPN broadcast and dominated sports talk radio. It bled imme-diately out of the sports world and into the mainstream press, landing on the front page of the next morning's *New York Times* and earning prominent playtime on NPR's *All Things Considered* and CNN's nightly broadcasts.

A mass of sports reporters booked South Beach hotel rooms and direct flights to MIA. It was a Tuesday of incessant cell phone ringing for players, agents, lawyers, team officials, and MLB investigators as other reporters attempted to catch up with the story.

Some players immediately broadcasted emphatic denials. "My son works very, very hard, and he's as clean as apple pie," said Max Gonzalez, the father of Nationals pitcher Gio Gonzalez. Max said his son was implicated by mistake because the elder Gonzalez had received weight-loss treatments from Bosch.

Others issued statements strangled in legalese by expensive attorneys. "We are aware of certain allegations and inferences," said Farrell & Reisinger, the law firm hired by Texas Rangers slugger Nelson Cruz. The firm also represented numerous players implicated in the Mitchell Report and crafted Andy Pettitte's strategy before he testified to Congress in 2008. "To the extent these allegations and inferences refer to Nelson, they are denied."

And still other players simply went deep underground. Though he wasn't usually hard to spot, SEAL Team Six couldn't have found Bartolo Colon at this time.

Rodriguez was once again the sports world's number one paparazzi target, as was his hapless cousin. Reporters dug through property records trying to figure out where Yuri Sucart, named in the *New Times* story, lived now that his home had been foreclosed.

As major outlets continued to dig into the story, A-Rod and Tony Bosch's relationship began to take on a pulp-fiction feel. ESPN's *Outside the Lines* relied on anonymous sources in painting a portrait of a tempestuous Rodriguez texting Bosch from his Miami mansion, ordering the dealer to come inject him. Rodriguez and Bosch's relationship had ended, according to the story, after the fake doctor had clumsily failed to find a vein on the superstar and been booted from the mansion. "Tony said A-Rod was pissed at him," the source told ESPN. "He said he was bleeding everywhere."

Such gory coverage called for drastic measures. Roy Black contracted Michael Sitrick, a crisis management guru who is said to charge $900 an hour. Sitrick's first move was a conventional one.

On Rodriguez's behalf, he denied all, sending out a statement that was contradicted in totality by later statements. "The news report about a purported relationship between Alex Rodriguez and Anthony Bosch [is] not true," read the statement. "He was not Mr. Bosch's patient, he was never treated by him and he was never advised by him. The purported documents referenced in the story—at least as they relate to Alex Rodriguez—are not legitimate."

At Rodriguez's urging—and a $25,000 wire transfer for his legal fees—Bosch issued his own false statement denying their relationship.

Sitrick's second move, at least according to baseball officials, was entirely unconventional.

The Los Angeles–based Sitrick wrote the book on media spin. Well, the full title is *Spin: How to Turn the Power of the Press to Your Advantage*.

In the book, Sitrick, a former reporter himself, detailed the unconventional tactics that had earned him such temporarily toxic big-money clients as Michael Vick and the Catholic Archdiocese of Los Angeles—hiring reporters with whom he previously had professional clashes, doling out exclusive information in order to get stories published that are positive to his clients, and generally treating the press like an unthinkingly hungry animal. "What the successful spin doctor does," Sitrick writes of the press, "is figure out a way to get it to *want* to go where he'd like it to go—or at least get it to lose interest in going where he'd rather it not poke its nose."

Sitrick did exactly that, Major League Baseball officials believe. After Oggi Velazquez got the notebooks, the LA spin doctor on A-Rod's payroll leaked records that turned the sports world's attention all the way from Miami to Milwaukee.

O n February 5, one hellishly long week after the *New Times* story ran, Yahoo! Sports had its own revelations. Reporters Tim Brown and Jeff Passan had obtained several pages of Biogenesis notes from an unnamed source.

"Baseball," read the header for one of the notes, in Bosch's unmistakable script. Under it, were the names of ballplayers. Three of those players—Alex Rodriguez, Melky Cabrera, and Cesar Carrillo—had already been named in the *New Times* story. But former UM star–turned then–Orioles third baseman Danny Valencia had not been named. Nor had New York Yankees catcher Francisco Cervelli. Nor, of course, Ryan Braun.

In fact, the leaker appeared to be primarily focused on exposing Braun. Three records given to Yahoo! named the Brewers superstar. In one of the instances—under the heading "money owed"—Bosch had written "RB 20-30K" next to Braun's name.

The third note was the seething letter Bosch had drafted to ACES employee Juan Carlos Nunez, demanding payment for Cabrera's treatment. Where Bosch had written "This smells like the 'Braun' advantage," referring to Cabrera's recent All-Star Game MVP award, the Brewers' name had been redacted on the *New Times* website. Yahoo! Sports published an untouched version of the letter. Yahoo! also publicized several instances of Chris Lyons, Braun's Miami-based attorney, being listed in the notes.

So visible two weeks earlier, Braun wouldn't be caught near any autograph booths in Wisconsin now. His representatives released a statement that must have stretched even his loyal Milwaukee flock's suspension of disbelief.

"During the course of preparing for my successful appeal last year, my attorneys, who were previously familiar with Tony Bosch, used him as a consultant," the statement read. "More specifically, he answered questions about T/E [testosterone to epitesosterone] ratio and possibilities of tampering with samples. There was a dispute over compensation for Bosch's work, which is why my lawyer and I are listed under 'moneys owed' and not on any other list. I have nothing to hide and have never had any other relationship with Bosch. I will fully cooperate with any inquiry into this matter."

The statement did not explain how Braun's attorneys knew Bosch. It did, however, conveniently answer the question of how Braun could owe the fake doctor so much money if it wasn't for an illicit service: Bosch had greedily asked for $20,000 to $30,000 for a "consultation," but Braun hadn't necessarily paid that.

The ludicrousness of one of the game's highest-paid players seeking out the advice of an uneducated storefront biochemist apparently didn't rattle Braun. He stood by the statement, refusing to answer questions concerning Biogenesis, even as he reported to spring training under a dark steroid cloud for the second season in a row.

In 2012, Dino Laurenzi had been collateral damage when Braun had thrown a Hail Mary that had connected to save his season and reputation. Maybe he could Brett Favre his way out of this jam, too.

From the very beginning, Major League Baseball—an agency that knows a little something about strategic media leaks—suspected that Rodriguez's camp had fed the documents incriminating Braun to Yahoo! Sports.

Sure, it would be a rotten play even by A-Rod panic-mode, blame-your-cousin standards, especially since one of the leaked pages also implicated his Yankees teammate Cervelli.

But it was a public relations chess move, and Rodriguez's fixer Sitrick was a Kasparov of aggressive spin. And the early timing of the leaks left few other suspects. Though Rodriguez's attorneys have maintained that he never attained Bosch's records or copies of the records, multiple sources contradict that.

The only known trove of Bosch's notes circulating in the days following the exposé were the notebooks that Fischer says he gave to Pete Carbone—and that Carbone, according to Fischer, says he gave to Rodriguez's people. Bosch also told MLB officials that he believed, due to information received from Oggi Velazquez, that Rodriguez had attained the notebooks. "Mr. Velazquez had told Mr. Bosch that Mr. Rodriguez had secured those original notebooks," Rob Manfred testified in arbitration, "and, in sum and substance, Velazquez had assured Bosch that those notebooks would not be seen again."

Immediately after the *New Times* story ran, MLB officials certainly didn't have those documents to leak: As was later revealed, Manfred and another baseball executive were in the offices of the alt-weekly newspaper, pleading with its editor to share with them.

Any far-fetched notion that Bosch may have leaked the documents himself were dashed when the fake doctor backed up Braun's excuse in his ill-advised interview with ESPN. "I just answered a few questions from his legal team, not from Braun or any other ballplayer," Bosch said. Even if for whatever reason he was angry at Braun at the time, he wouldn't have risked more trouble for himself by leaking documents only to then downplay their significance.

One of Rodriguez's attorneys, David Cornwell, has denied that the star had anything to do with leaking the documents, calling the accusation just more staccato in "the drumbeat of false allegations."

In later court filings, Sitrick denied ever possessing Bosch's records in language that, as league officials pointed out, does not specifically rule out the possibility that an underling at his firm handled the leak. MLB tried to get Yahoo! Sports to reveal its source, but, unsurprisingly, the journalists refused. The league took such an interest in the origins of the Yahoo! Sports story that they ultimately battled Sitrick in federal court in an attempt to get him to confess. A judge would rule that Sitrick did not have to comply with MLB's arbitration subpoena to turn over documents related to his representation of Rodriguez.

In that suit, an MLB attorney asked Rodriguez's attorneys to have Sitrick sign a sworn affidavit stating that nobody in his crisis management firm ever had any Bosch or Biogenesis records. "The affidavits have been forwarded to [Sitrick] with Mr. Rodriguez's request that they be executed," Rodriguez's attorney Joe Tacopina responded to the request in an e-mail. But Sitrick never signed the affidavits.

Sitrick advises clients to always respond to media allegations, though he did not take his own advice in this case. He ended an e-mail conversation when an author of this book asked him about the Braun leak.

If Rodriguez was behind the leak to Yahoo! Sports, pity Francisco Cervelli, the middling backup catcher caught up in his teammate's elaborate plot.

On February 6, Cervelli—who made around $500,000 in 2013—opted against the high-priced legal firm and instead took a more economic approach to damage control, issuing this statement on Twitter: "Following my foot injury in March 2011, I consulted with a number of experts, including Biogenesis Clinic, for legal ways to aid my rehab and recovery. I purchased supplements that I am certain were not prohibited by Major League Baseball."

The Venezuelan-born catcher fudged that story a week later when interviewed by beat reporters at spring training. "I just went there, talked, and that's it," Cervelli said then. "I walked away without nothing in my hands.

"Well, you know, sometimes, when we got injuries we get a little desperate to come back quick, and we always want a second opinion," Cervelli expounded. "I went there. At that moment I don't know what kind of clinic it was. So like I said, I take my responsibility. Nobody put a gun to my head to go there, so that's it."

Cervelli, who doesn't have a $900-an-hour fixer or a loyal goon squad, had just trampled on his own claim that he had bought legal supplements from Bosch. Dealing with a media catastrophe is a lot more difficult than signaling fastball or curve.

He later admitted that he bought PEDs from Bosch. But on this day, Cervelli chased down the reporters in a hallway and told them that he wanted to stand by his initial Twitter statement after all.

League honchos who had tried only months earlier to get the ACES agency punished over their ties to Juan Carlos Nunez and the Melky Cabrera website mess now had reason for renewed fury.

Of the nineteen players publicly linked to Biogenesis in the aftermath of the *New Times* story, nine—Jhonny Peralta, Melky Cabrera, Gio Gonzalez, Cesar Puello, Antonio Bastardo, Fautino de los Santos, Fernando Martinez, Sergio Escalona, and Jordany Valdespin—were ACES customers at the time.

Four more—Cervelli, Cruz, Jordan Norberto, and Everth Cabrera—had been clients of the Brooklyn agency in the past.

If the high number of ACES clients flocking to Bosch's clinic was a coincidence, it worked against staggering odds. As the website SB Nation pointed out at the time, nearly 70 percent of Bosch's publicized clients had at one point been represented by ACES. But with 107 clients listed in a major league agency database, ACES represented only 5.7 percent of big league ballplayers.

And because the ACES clients who went to Biogenesis came from multiple Latin American countries and many major league organizations, there appeared to be little else linking them besides those two five-foot-eight brothers who had built a publicity-shy baseball empire on Brooklyn's Montague Street.

Scott Boras, the czar of baseball agenthood, made pointed claims concerning Everth Cabrera, who had jumped from ACES to Boras's agency following the 2012 Melky Cabrera debacle. "He places trust in people who represent them," Boras said of Everth. "And that trust was violated by them, recommending that he not only use PEDs but that he continues to use it."

(Gall is a common trait in successful agents. Boras has represented Alex Rodriguez, Barry Bonds, and Manny Ramirez, to name a few known juicers. A holder of a doctorate in industrial pharmacology, Boras claims to have never known any of his players were on drugs.)

Following the Biogenesis revelations, the Levinsons again blamed former rogue consultant Nunez. "Anyone who knows us, knows that it is absolutely ridiculous to think that we would ever condone the use of performance-enhancing drugs," said Seth in a statement. "Our work over the last 25 years demonstrates that ACES is built on a foundation of honesty, integrity, and doing things the right way. Neither Sam nor I, or anyone else at ACES, have ever met or even heard of Anthony Bosch until the recent news stories, nor does anyone have any knowledge of or connection to Biogenesis."

But the defense that Nunez ushered ACES clients to Biogenesis without the Levinsons' knowledge was ridiculed by rivals. "As an agent you have a responsibility to know what your clients are doing," says one MLB-certified agent, echoing a sentiment shared by many in the industry. "It's hard for me to believe that so many of their clients were using PEDs and they didn't catch on that this was happening."

There was blood in the water in Brooklyn, and the sharks were swirling. Competitors claimed to be besieged by calls from ACES clients looking to jump ship from the troubled agency, and two high-profile players did just that. Everth Cabrera and Shane Victorino had left the previous season; Cruz and Peralta left the Levinsons in the Biogenesis aftermath.

MLB once again opened an investigation into ACES, this time for its role in possibly funneling clients to Tony Bosch. When the league filed a lawsuit in late March against five primaries and associates of Biogenesis, including Nunez, the Office of the Commissioner of Baseball was not after Nunez's erstwhile Washington Heights travel agency fortune. The lawsuit, brazen as it was, was simply used to gather information.

The league's main goal was to gain evidence of players—especially Alex Rodriguez—juicing. But a nice side project would be fleshing out the involvement of Nunez and the Levinson brothers, and perhaps finally burying with bad publicity the agency the players union refused to punish.

By the time Biogenesis was exposed, MLBPA chief Michael Weiner had publicly disclosed that he had been diagnosed with an inoperable brain tumor. It ultimately killed him before 2013 was over. But even as his condition worsened, Weiner kept working—and stood by his old friends the Levinsons. For the second time in six months, he used his clout to help ACES, again by scapegoating Nunez.

"From our perspective, there is no evidence Sam and Seth have been involved in anything directly," Weiner said. "Nobody said: 'Sam and Seth set me up. Sam and Seth knew what was going on.'"

"I think Nunez is a snake," Weiner added. "What he did was horrible. . . . He should have the book thrown at him."

Other agents privately howled at the agency dodging another bullet. "A lot of us smaller agents are pretty sure that we wouldn't have gotten the same treatment from the union," says one certified agent, "if we had more than a dozen players where there was pretty clear evidence that we were involved in their doping."

Any implication that Weiner let the Levinsons off the hook due to their friendship is "an absolute insult to the legacy of Michael Weiner," ACES' attorney Jay Reisinger says. "The Levinsons received absolutely no favoritism from Michael Weiner or anybody else."

Though MLB hogged the Dostoevskian drama, it wasn't only elite baseball players who were named in that initial *New Times* story. Pro athletes from other sports, and two civilians with high-profile links to baseball, were also caught up in the Bosch dragnet.

Tennis pro Wayne Odesnik, who was previously suspended in 2010 for doping, e-mailed *New Times* after the story ran, denying ever purchasing growth hormone or any banned substances from anybody, including Bosch. "The copy of the records that were provided do not show any amount paid to Mr. Bosch or to his clinic," Odesnik wrote. (Bosch's records indicate that Odesnik had him on a $500-per-month retainer.)

Boxer Yuriorkis Gamboa called a press conference and then quickly canceled it. Rapper 50 Cent, dabbling as Gamboa's promoter, now had his back, implying that the only reason Elfrink attempted to smear the Cuban boxer was because of their high-profile relationship. "The additional publicity and notoriety that Gamboa has received from being in connection to me—the timing of it makes me feel like that's a part of it," 50 Cent ruminated.

Gamboa eventually claimed that he had no idea Bosch was selling banned substances. Unlike the ballplayers, his sport has no provision for suspending athletes unless they fail a test at a fight.

University of Miami baseball trainer Jimmy Goins was immediately suspended by the school following being named by the *New Times* exposé. He wrote letters to *New Times* and all other outlets that mentioned his involvement with Biogenesis, threatening to file a lawsuit. Soon after the story broke, the *Miami Herald* published a story virtually exonerating Goins of having provided PEDs to UM players, using quotes from a former university ballplayer and anonymous sourcing. "[Former UM pitcher Kyle] Bellamy, who has been in regular contact with Goins, said that he is convinced Goins is no cheater," read the final sentence of the article.

If the *Herald* was attempting to appease Goins, it didn't work. The squat, bald trainer filed a lawsuit against the *Herald*, *Miami New Times*, the *New York Times*, the University of Miami, Porter Fischer, and Anthony and Pedro Bosch. Oddly, he doesn't dispute the facts in the story. Instead, he argues that his involvement with Biogenesis was not newsworthy and that when he bought HGH and other substances he was duped into thinking that Bosch was a doctor. "Anthony Bosch is not a doctor, however, while James Goins was a patient at Biogenesis," reads one filing. "Anthony Bosch held himself out as a doctor, referring to himself as Dr. Bosch and also wearing a lab coat that said Dr. Bosch." A judge later dismissed his claims against the media companies.

A nd then there was the ballad of Yuri Sucart, unemployed steroid mule. Being once again thrust into the spotlight more than a year after being fired by his famous cousin appears to have been too much to bear.

In late February 2013, the bankrupt Sucart listed an authentic 2009 Yankees championship ring on an online auction site. "In 2009, when the New York Yankees won the World Series, Alex Rodriguez requested an additional ring," Sucart explained in an affidavit included in the auction.

"The Yankees authorized an additional ring which Mr. Rodriguez then presented to me."

The ring, a memento from either better times or the year Rodriguez sold him out to the media, got Sucart $50,398.88. "He didn't know that Yuri Sucart was selling one of them," a Rodriguez spokesperson said flatly of the ring, one of several that he had distributed to family members.

That's about when things started to get very strange between Rodriguez and his cousin, who was being constantly hounded by MLB investigators to tell them about Biogenesis. In early spring 2013, as Rodriguez rehabbed from his surgery in a mutual exile from the team, the *New York Daily News* and other outlets reported that Sucart was threatening to sue Rodriguez.

Sucart was said to be seeking $5 million from Rodriguez. "I know there's a lot of friction," Sucart's attorney, John Ruiz, was quoted as saying. "I know that [Sucart's] name got caught in the cross fire of all the allegations involving all the performance-enhancing drugs." (Asked about the never-filed lawsuit today, Ruiz claimed to have been misquoted.)

Their relationship has never been easily parsed. "Now they're not even associated," says Sucart's longtime friend Roger Ball. Still, Sucart apparently lived in his cousin's house, rent-free. Bankruptcy records indicated that Sucart and his family lived in a $399,000 Kendall home owned by Alexander E. Rodriguez.

As the regular season began in April, nearly four months after the letters from *New Times* that had sent MLB executives "buzzing" into Rob Manfred's office, league investigators were still knee-deep in an investigation that they hoped would lead to suspensions stemming from Tony Bosch's clinic.

An ax hung over the nineteen Biogenesis-linked players. For Cesar Carrillo—once a first-round draft pick, now washed-up in the minors at age twenty-eight—a suspension would likely mean the end of his major league dream. For twenty-five-year-old Cuban Yasmani Grandal, such punishment would derail a promising new career. For Ryan Braun, an affirmation of cheating would be a death blow to his formerly good name in Wisconsin, and his mantle as a modern-era Jewish baseball icon.

(In fact, Braun's image was removed from the cover of the children's tome *Jewish Sports Stars*, replaced by the can't-go-wrong Sandy Koufax.)

But nobody spent the following summer fighting as lonely a battle for his career as Rodriguez.

CHAPTER FOURTEEN

Bad Cops

The counterfeiter and the baseball investigator met at a seedy diner.

As he walked into Cosmos, a Pompano Beach dive with greasy omelets and cracked leather tables, Dan Mullin's back pocket bulged with cash. He carried $25,000 in loose stacks of $20 and $100 bills stuffed into an envelope.

In a corner booth, tanning bed repairman and convicted felon Gary Jones grinned and waved.

Mullin eased his large frame across the table. With a nod, he slid across a yellow envelope. Jones felt its weight and glanced at the currency inside.

A few tables over, one of Jones's cronies silently filmed it all on his cell phone. And two booths behind him, a member of Mullin's crew made his own secret recording on an iPad, straining to win this round of Spy vs. Spy by filming around the head of an old lady enjoying an early lunch.

Two months earlier, Mullin had flown to Florida primed for action. At his side were two senior investigators, a pair of hulking retired NYPD vets named Ed Maldonado and Tom Reilly.

It was February 1, 2013, and Mullin's Department of Investigations had finally been called to duty. After years of chasing down identity fraud cases in the Caribbean and monitoring gambling rings in Jersey, the ex-cops, at last, had a legit steroid scandal on their hands in Miami. A decade after BALCO, another performance-enhancing drug ring was exploding.

But in stark contrast to the BALCO fiasco, this time MLB was in the driver's seat. The San Francisco case had started with a federal raid on Victor Conte's lab. Even if MLB had wanted to get involved, its interests would always come second to the criminal probe. In Biogenesis, Mullin had no such obstacles. Bosch's scheme had been upended by a newspaper, not a cadre of federal agents, so whatever baseball's investigators did in South Florida, they didn't have to worry about stepping on the toes of an ongoing investigation.

Mullin's mandate was simple: Get Commissioner Selig the evidence he needed to suspend every player tied to Tony Bosch.

In the days after *New Times* published its story, Selig made it clear that Mullin's job was vital. The legacy-obsessed commissioner would soon announce his retirement. Allowing the Biogenesis-linked players to escape without punishment would be a public debacle nearly to the scale of the Mitchell Report—especially since the two most prominent players implicated in the scandal had already personally embarrassed the commissioner. Selig's hometown superstar, Ryan Braun, had made the league look incompetent when his suspension was overturned in 2012. And Rodriguez—who was once supposed to be the preternaturally talented Latin American ballplayer who would bridge the gap from the Steroid Era to clean baseball—had repeatedly dominated headlines with steroid scandals for which he had gone unpunished.

For Mullin, job number one was getting their hands on Bosch's records. Under the union's contract, players can be suspended for "nonanalytical results"—but only with enough evidence to convince an arbitrator the player had doped.

That evidence was out there. *New Times* had the records. The newspaper's anonymous source had them. And Tony Bosch presumably had loads of them.

MLB started with the newspaper, though they knew it was a long shot.

On February 4, Manfred and MLB's chief spokesman, Pat Courtney, visited the *New Times* office in midtown Miami and made their pitch to the editors in a conference room lined with faded plaques from Florida press awards. The paper had already made history by exposing Tony Bosch's clients, they argued. Why not help ensure those cheaters got punished?

The paper's editor, Chuck Strouse, was receptive. But he ultimately rejected the idea as journalistically unsound. On March 14, he penned a column telling MLB they'd have to find their own evidence. "We would be handing over the product of our reporting to a for-profit group with a seamy past. What if baseball improperly used our work? What if it decided to punish some players and not others?" Strouse wrote. " . . . We would be sending the wrong message to future anonymous sources. . . . Our source for this article fears for his safety. How could we subject him to greater risk by losing control of the information he had provided?"

So the investigators turned their attention to Biogenesis's owner. Tony Bosch proved an elusive target. He'd abandoned his Key Biscayne condo. Neighbors told the ex-cops they hadn't seen him since the *New Times* story had landed. A stakeout at Pedro Bosch's Coral Gables home had also come up empty. If Bosch was hiding out with his parents, he wasn't going outside.

So Maldonado and Reilly approached their South Florida assignment like any criminal probe in New York City. With their chief suspect on the run, they built the case from the outside in, through anyone who'd ever done business with him. In the case of serial entrepreneur Tony Bosch, they had dozens of names to work with. There were so many leads to follow, in fact, that MLB soon hired GSIS, a security firm founded by an ex–Secret Service chief named Mark Sullivan and co-owned by White Sox honcho Jerry Reinsdorf. Sullivan flew in dozens of his own operatives to help Mullin's team.

Within days of the *New Times* story, that army of ex-cops and federal agents began chasing down everyone from Bosch's close friends like Roger De Armas and Hernan Dominguez to short-term colleagues and casual acquaintances like Jorge Jaen. "They'd chase me, they'd follow me outside

[Bosch's] mom's house," Dominguez says. "They were so hungry for information. I had investigators come to my house multiple times because of my connection to Tony. I was watching my rearview mirror every day."

The investigators pulled business records, plunged into property reports, and weren't shy about harassing friends and family. "They showed up at every one of my relatives' homes looking for me," Jaen recalls. "They went to my office. At the end of the day, I had nothing to hide from them so I finally just met with them."

When Jaen sat down with the DOI, they quizzed him about Tony's businesses, his training, his motivations, and whether he'd ever talked to Jaen about selling drugs to big leaguers. "I told them that I wouldn't consider Tony a con artist exactly, but he reminds me of these guys like Bernie Madoff," Jaen says. "Madoff duped a lot of high-level investors and businessmen and Tony duped a lot of smart people in the medical field down here."

Jaen had worked with Tony only for a few months, though, and hadn't seen him since their business venture failed two years earlier. The witnesses who'd actually worked in Biogenesis were proving just as elusive as their former boss. From office manager Ricky Martinez to Tony's previous partner Carlos Acevedo to Oggi Velazquez, everyone had skipped town or dodged the baseball cops.

Although they sometimes seemed to forget it, MLB's investigators weren't real cops anymore. That distinction carried with it both drawbacks and benefits. The drawback, of course, was that they had no subpoena power and couldn't legitimately wield the threat of arrest.

One of the benefits: They could throw around wads of cash to convince witnesses to talk. Bosch's associates who weren't averse to listening to baseball's overtures soon established a market rate: $5,000 would buy investigators a meeting.

Porter Fischer, whose role as *New Times*'s source was still confidential, was among the first to receive a financial overture from the investigators. Fischer had fled town the day the *New Times* story landed, hiding out for more than a week at his uncle's house in Ocala after Carbone's warning that

Oggi was out to kill him. Back in South Miami, Fischer's sister, Suzanne, soon found herself peering out the door to insistent knocking from Maldonado and Reilly.

The two musclebound "goons," Suzanne later told a reporter, hollered: "We'll give you money!" She cowered inside. She thought the enforcers were mobsters, but reporters later found a business card they'd tucked into Porter's door. It belonged to Maldonado and its message was none too subtle: "Please call—we know time is $. Call ASAP."

Fischer had no intention of playing ball with MLB. After he returned home from eight days in exile, he avoided them. And he had good reason to be wary of them—and everyone else, for that matter. In fact, he had evidence that his life was in danger.

However big a story Fischer had figured the leaked documents would be, the response eclipsed it. *New Times*, as promised, had kept Fischer anonymous, but reporters and investigators quickly learned he had a connection to the clinic.

A week and a half after the story landed, Fischer had decided the air had cooled enough to return to the guesthouse in South Miami. Pete's warnings from two weeks earlier still echoed in his head. He had no idea if Oggi or anyone else was really capable of putting a bullet in his head, but he didn't intend to find out. If he stayed below the radar, he figured he could ride this out.

But on February 19, the radar found him. Fischer had been coming back from a workout at the gym when a strange car turned right down his mother's block right in front of him. The one-block side street connects two other rarely trafficked blocks. No one drove that way by accident, and Fischer had memorized his neighbors' cars. The strange vehicle made a U-turn in front of Fischer, who ducked his head, gunned his truck past the Honda, and headed a few blocks east to Pinecrest Gardens, a small botanical sanctuary, where he switched off his engine and waited.

But now, as he headed back out, he saw that the driver of the Honda had been patiently waiting just outside, ready for him to leave.

Adrenaline kicked in. Fischer had no idea who was tailing him. Reporters? MLB goons? Oggi's guys ready with a bullet for his skull? It didn't matter. He was determined to lose them. He ripped through a red light and sped north for the chaotic traffic on US 1.

But as he turned right on the thoroughfare, he looked back again to see the Honda a few cars back. The driver was barking into a handheld radio.

Porter called the only guy who came to mind who might know how to deal with a car chase. "Pete!" he screamed into his cell. "I'm being followed!"

Carbone and Fischer hadn't been on good terms since the story had landed. After he'd told Fischer he'd given the original Bosch notebooks to "A-Rod's people," Fischer had lost any trust in his friend. He'd been banned from Boca Tanning after nearly coming to blows with Carbone in a fiery argument.

But, as Fischer suspected, the tanning guru couldn't resist a high-speed chase. He jumped into a car plastered with an ad for his salon and told Fischer what to do.

Porter listened, and then coasted into a nearby Winn-Dixie parking lot, turning his truck off. The Honda followed, stopping nearby as the driver talked again into the radio. But he hadn't counted on Fischer having backup. Carbone leapt from his car, pounding on the Honda's window, hollering, "Why the fuck are you following us?"

The driver, with a panicked look, peeled out of the lot as Pete ran to Fischer's car. They had to follow them! But why not throw them off the scent? Fischer hopped into Pete's car, while Carbone took his truck.

For fifteen minutes, Carbone, Fischer, the mysterious Honda driver, and an unseen backup team chased one another through the usually staid suburbs of Miami. They dodged the aggressive midafternoon traffic crawling up US 1 alongside the University of Miami's main campus and headed toward the looming financial skyscrapers in Brickell.

But then Carbone found himself boxed in, hemmed into the curb, and finally stopped a few miles north with cars in front and behind him. He called the cops on his cell phone.

An appropriately confused report from the Pinecrest Police Department did at least solve one of the mysteries: The other drivers were named Lewis Perry, Ernesto Sam, and Julio Moreiras. All three worked for Precise Protective Research, a high-end private eye firm owned by Perry, a veteran Drug Enforcement Agency agent who'd spent thirty-five years chasing narco bosses in Latin America.

All they told the police was that they were "working an investigation" when Carbone started following them "in an aggressive manner."

Carbone, for his part, told police the three private dicks had "dragged [him] out" of his car. But the cop was dubious. "Carbone changed his story numerous times," the officer wrote.

Fischer watched it all play out from a parking lot across the street, his eyes bugging as cops interviewed the three men who'd just chased him down US 1. The incident report, which he picked up the next day, didn't clear much up. Precise Protective Research? Who the hell had hired them? MLB? A-Rod?

One thing was certain: The high-speed game of tag made Fischer more certain than ever that the stakes were higher than just a few ballplayers getting PEDs from a shady clinic. His life was in jeopardy. From then on, he'd be doubly careful, he pledged.

When Reilly and Maldonado came calling again on February 28, Fischer opened his door to give them a piece of his mind. They were offering money, but Fischer was sure someone would put a bullet in his head if he took it. "It's not about money," Fischer told them. "Money doesn't fix everything. It's about my safety. . . . You guys can't fucking protect me."

The ex-cops admitted that he "may have to move to a gated community" if he helped them out but said MLB could pay for the ad hoc witness protection. Fischer told them it was a nonstarter. "If anyone finds out I'm talking to you right now, I'm a dead man," he said.

But Fischer also knew he was in over his head, and that MLB was the most powerful player in this budding South Florida cold war. So he made a deal with Maldonado: If they could keep their mouths shut for ten days, he'd at least meet them again. But if his name showed up anywhere in the press, it was over.

Before they left, he handed over a few scanned medical records from the clinic—nothing of real interest, but enough to show them he was who he said he was.

A quiet week and a half later, he texted Maldonado and arranged to meet in a Coconut Creek parking lot. Fischer found both investigators sitting in a Chevy Tahoe and climbed into the backseat. Without a word, Reilly slid back an envelope stuffed with fifty $100 bills.

"I'm thinking, 'Holy shit, this is just like in the movies,'" Fischer says. "Someone is actually handing me a white, unmarked envelope full of cash in the back of an SUV."

He briefly considered handing the cash back, especially when they asked him to sign an itemized receipt. "But then I thought, 'Why not? I don't have anything to hide. Everyone else is making money,'" he says.

They offered a deal: $10,000 for everything Fischer had. He laughed at them. The investigators laughed, too. "'Hey, we had to ask.'" Reilly shrugged, according to Fischer.

The whistle-blower agreed to meet again on March 11, at a quiet park a few blocks from his mom's house. By now, the investigators were increasingly sure that Fischer had been *New Times*'s anonymous source. They were determined to convince him to give up the goods. This time, Mullin himself flew back to Miami.

The big ex-cop sweated next to Fischer as they sat on a park bench and the odd jogger huffed past through the tropical heat. He made a proposal: The whistle-blower could work as a "consultant" for MLB and hand over his documents. They'd pay him $1,000 a week and hire him an attorney. When Fischer again laughed at the offer, Mullin got angry. "This stuff isn't worth a million dollars, you know," he said, according to Fischer.

Fischer made a counteroffer: If MLB would give him enough cash to leave South Florida and open his own tanning salon somewhere, he'd take it. Anything less wouldn't help him stay bronzed and financially comfortable.

Mullin left, furious. A week later, on March 18, Steven Gonzalez, an MLB attorney, texted Fischer with one final bid. "We can compensate you in the amount of $125,000 for all the records and your signature on affidavits saying nothing more than necessary to authenticate the records. Time is short."

Fischer fumed. Hadn't he told them exactly what it would take? Just $125,000 wasn't buying a quality tanning salon anywhere. "No thank you," he texted back. "Not worth it."

That rejection was the final proof Mullin needed. The carrot of cash payouts could get his investigators only so far. They needed a big stick.

B y early March, Dan Mullin and his NYPD vets weren't the only former street cops on Tony Bosch's trail.

Jerome K. Hill was an oddity in Florida's Department of Health, a dull bureaucracy that had been gutted by the state's Tea Party governor.

Before he won the governor's mansion in 2011, Rick Scott was a health-care magnate whose company pleaded guilty to fourteen felonies and paid the largest fine in US history for defrauding Medicare. Safe to say, Scott was no fan of healthcare regulators. One of his first acts as governor was stripping $55.6 million from his state's DOH and laying off 229 employees. His personal appointees to the department were given a clear mandate: Don't mess with doctors. Even fake ones selling illegal drugs for cash.

As a result, Hill's coworkers were mostly pencil pushers happy to spend their days looking for small violations at massage parlors and ignoring the fact that Florida had become America's healthcare fraud capital.

But Hill was different. A stout man with a hearty laugh, he'd spent seven years as a Baltimore city officer walking the beat on North Clinton Street, a drug-torn block of row houses straight out of *The Wire.*

He was the type of cop who didn't hesitate to punch a punk in the mouth, but by January 2008, that aggressive policing style had gotten one too many complaints from North Clinton's residents. So Baltimore PD's Internal Affairs unit set up an "integrity check." Just after sunset one day, an undercover officer huddled on a street corner while dispatch radioed Hill to report the lure as a suspected drug buyer.

Hill strolled up to the undercover cop and walloped him on the jaw.

The assault earned Hill a Metro-front story in the *Baltimore Sun*, a lengthy purgatory in the records department, and by June 2010, a one-way ticket out of Maryland even though criminal charges had been dropped by a local judge.

Hill had to start over. By the end of the year, he'd moved to Miami and taken a $36,000-per-year gig with Florida's DOH, working as an investigator in a small unit that probed complaints about unlicensed activities.

He was a hell of a long way from gritty east-central Baltimore. He spent most days looking into tips about back-alley dentists and nutritionists without licenses. But when he read the *New Times* piece in January about Tony Bosch and his famous clientele, something clicked.

Finally, a chance for some real police work had landed in his lap.

The evidence, from where Jerome Hill sat, couldn't be any clearer. Dan Mullin and his team might be scrambling for documents to prove the very specific charge that Bosch had sold steroids and HGH to MLB stars, but Hill's bailiwick was a whole lot simpler. All he had to do was prove Bosch had pretended to be a doctor. He could charge him with a felony for practicing medicine without a license—a conviction that brings a minimum one year in jail in Florida and a $1,000 fine.

For Hill, Tony Bosch was his ticket back to the game.

Even though he worked for a small-time state agency, Hill quickly nabbed something that Dan Mullin and his team never could get: Porter Fischer's trust.

Hill met Elfrink for breakfast at a midtown Miami diner and explained what he hoped to do; the reporter replied that he couldn't name his confidential source, but he could pass Hill's contact along to the source in case he wanted to get in touch.

Fischer called the DOH investigator, and Hill quickly won over the Biogenesis whistle-blower by understanding something that the ex-cops had never quite grasped. Fischer hadn't taken the documents from Biogenesis because he wanted to ruin Alex Rodriguez or Ryan Braun. He hadn't given the evidence to *New Times* because he had grand schemes to get rich off the scandal. And he couldn't possibly care less about the integrity of professional baseball.

Every single move Fischer made had been driven by one simple goal: burning Tony Bosch. Six months after Bosch had told the muscle-bound marketer to go to hell over his $4,000 debt, Fischer was still layering a revenge cake.

So Hill made Fischer a simple promise: If the tanning salon snitch would turn over the evidence he needed, the former Baltimore cop would do everything in his power to put Tony Bosch behind bars.

Fischer didn't hesitate. He gave Hill a detailed, sworn affidavit about his entire saga with Biogenesis and Tony Bosch, handed over photos of the clinic and prescription receipts, and put Hill in touch with other patients. Hill knew he'd have a better chance of getting a prosecutor to bite with original documents from the clinic. So in late March, he asked Fischer to hand over some of Biogenesis's medical files.

Fischer was wary of giving Hill any documents that MLB was after. Handing them over to the state meant they could someday end up on a public docket in court, which in turn meant Mullin's investigators could get their hands on them for free.

But Fischer saw no reason not to turn over a few boxes of files from Bosch's more ordinary clientele: the real estate agents, lawyers, and teachers who'd been the bulk of the HGH-, hCG-, and testosterone-buying customer base.

The only issue, Fischer told Hill, was that in an overabundance of caution he'd moved most of that paperwork out of South Florida to a storage unit in Ocala. He'd have to grab it and bring it back south.

On March 24, Fischer rented a silver Toyota, drove three hundred miles north to the central Florida town, and loaded the boxes into his trunk.

That evidence never made it to Jerome K. Hill.

*   *   *

Even though it was only March 24, it was a sweltering day in Boca Raton, with temperatures creeping north of ninety. Officer Lazarus Kimsal tooled his lit-up black-and-white Boca Raton Police car into the parking lot of 2521 North Federal Highway.

A pastel stucco–and-brick edifice fronted by a parking lot lined with unhealthy-looking palms, the address is the sort of dull strip mall that defines suburban Florida. The building houses a Starbucks, a FedEx, a cell phone store, and the Boca Tanning Club.

Although the tanning salon seemed to attract uncharacteristic trouble for a country-club town full of snowbirds—the plot-twisting beatdown of night clerk Adam Godley might leap to Kimsal's mind—for the most part this strip mall is home to the vapid petty crimes that dominate suburbia: a shoving match in the cell phone store; a homeless guy trespassing in Starbucks; sunglasses stolen off a table at the corporate coffee shop; a Boca Tanning customer accusing his girlfriend of cheating on him with a guy named Brett, and her attacking him with Mace in response; vandals spray painting on a FedEx truck: "Fuck FedEx, Honk if ur Gay and UPS."

These are not great American crime sagas. "Dog which was tied up to a table took off running and damaged a car," reads one incident report.

Mostly, the house specialty that dominated Kimsal and his colleagues' schedule at this particular strip mall was car break-ins. An unemployed tennis instructor got her BMW's window smashed and her. teal purse yanked from inside the car. The window of a Boca Tanning employee's Honda was pried off to steal her Clinique bag. A muscular man was seen scurrying from an alarm-blaring car carrying a brand-new Apple computer. A brown leather messenger bag containing a laptop was stolen from a van. Car radios and CDs were pilfered from vehicles.

Boca Raton cops responded to most with the enthusiasm you might expect. One case was closed without further investigation because the officer didn't write down the victim's phone number and she wasn't in the phone book. In another theft case, the cops had the license plate number of a suspect seen speeding away but never made an arrest

So when Officer Kimsal responded to a 911 dispatch for an auto burglary outside the tanning club, it probably seemed like another routine day of paperwork.

As he pulled into the lot, the cop observed two vehicles surrounded by a circumference of shattered glass. The vehicles were a silver sedan and a large white box van. The sedan had its trunk flung open. Two burly white men stood at the scene.

One of the men—frantic, veiny, and sweaty—told Kimsal that his car, the silver sedan, had been broken into while he was tanning in the salon. Kimsal looked in the open trunk and saw a lid from a cardboard box, as well as an empty rifle box labeled HAWK 12-GAUGE 981R.

The rifle box had contained a shotgun, which was stolen, said the man, who gave his name as Michael Porter Fischer. And the lid was from cardboard boxes full of confidential files, which he had just picked up from Ocala, Florida. Those files had also been stolen.

The passenger-side window of Fischer's car had been smashed. He told the officer that more files were stolen from the front seat, along with a black leather messenger bag containing an exercise strap, a loaded .32 Beretta, and a smartphone. From the rear seat, the thief had taken a red-striped black gym bag containing $800, gym clothes, and a laptop computer. Another bag, containing clothes and toiletries, was also stolen.

It was quite a haul for a broad-daylight robbery. But the near-tears bodybuilder seemed most upset about the loss of the files.

The van had also been broken into. Its owner said a laptop computer had been stolen. He didn't want to file a report, so Kimsal did not record his name.

There were no surveillance cameras. There were no witnesses.

Detective Terrance Payne was given the case the next day. Through Kimsal, he pieced together a few more details about the break-in. He learned that the stolen documents "contained profiles of professional sports players

tied to a steroid clinic called Biogenesis," and that Fischer was a witness for
the Florida Department of Health.

Detective Payne spoke on the phone to the DOH investigator on that
case. He learned the names of a few of the players involved: Alex Rodriguez,
Yasmani Grandal, and Gio Gonzalez.

A few days passed. Payne researched pawn databases looking for the
.32 Beretta. No leads were developed.

Then he interviewed Fischer and got the whole story, how the bodybuilder had been offered cash payments by baseball officials, chased by
private detectives, and harassed at the tanning salon where MLB investigators thought he worked because he once joked on Facebook that he was a
"professional tanner at Boca Tanning."

Payne began to see a loose plot. Fischer told him about a friend—a big
man named Gary Jones—who had gotten him to stop by the salon with the
records in his car.

He called Jones but didn't leave a voice mail. He submitted some blood
from the car to the crime lab for DNA testing.

A week or so passed.

Then the cop started getting phone calls from a private detective
named Kevin O'Rourke. Hired by Major League Baseball, O'Rourke was
interested in the case. Then Payne read about the break-in in the *New York
Times*. And this guy Fischer was incessant, calling him and threatening to
go to the media about the slow-moving burglary investigation, and about
his suspicion that MLB had orchestrated the crime.

It finally seemed to dawn on Payne that this wasn't just another iPhone
pinched from Starbucks.

On April 5, two weeks after the break-in, he e-mailed the crime lab,
asking them to process the DNA more quickly.

"We are currently working a Burglary to an Auto case that occurred on
03-24-13 where medical files were stolen that may be related to a Florida
Department State of Health investigation into steroid/performance enhancing drugs and their alleged use by several Major League Baseball players,"

Payne typed. "I know your office is busy, but is there any chance of getting the submitted DNA expedited? Any help would be greatly appreciated."

As spring turned to summer and then fall, this was one Boca Raton burglary finally getting traction at the police department, if at a glacial pace. And when the pieces came together, everything eventually pointed to the complicity of Major League Baseball.

As weeks passed and Bosch's inner circle refused to crack, baseball's investigators started using old tricks from their police days to get results. Not all of these were tactics that you'll find in any police academy handbook.

As a roster full of Bosch associates later testified in sworn affidavits, Mullin and his team didn't hesitate to throw their weight around in South Florida. The ex-cops pretended to be active law enforcement; lied to landlords, security guards, and parents; and threatened witnesses with lawsuits, eviction, and criminal charges.

The statements describing these purported abuses were compiled by Alex Rodriguez's attorneys and shared with these authors. The superstar doled out hundreds of thousands of dollars to the witnesses. But they are also sworn affidavits, filed in court under the penalty of perjury. It's clear Mullin's Florida squad—Maldonado; Reilly; two other DOI detectives, Nelson Tejada and Ed Dominguez; local PI Kevin O'Rourke; and more than twenty others from Global Intelligence & Intelligence Strategies were more than willing to do whatever they thought necessary, whether or not it skirted the bounds of legality and ethics.

Marcelo Albir, the former UM baseball pitcher suspected of being Bosch's conduit to ballplaying alumni including Ryan Braun, says O'Rourke and Dominguez showed up at his Coral Gables apartment building. The investigators told security guards there they were cops to get in.

When the pitcher avoided them, they called his father and warned him that they'd facilitate Albir's arrest if he didn't flip. They threatened to punish

Paco Figueroa, an associate of Albir's playing minor league ball, if Albir kept playing hard to get. In March, O'Rourke even talked his way into Albir's apartment by pretending to be a Miami-Dade cop and then told the former pitcher MLB would sue him into destitution if he didn't cooperate with them.

Others echoed Fischer's tale of a good cop/bad cop routine that alternated offers of cash with threats of legal problems. Pete Carbone says he turned down $200,000 and then dealt with regular harassment from the DOI.

Even Oggi signed a sworn statement that MLB's investigators had gotten the landlord of his latest anti-aging clinic to boot him out in retaliation for giving baseball the cold shoulder.

And the team's leader, Dan Mullin—whose previous alleged sexual relationship with a DEA agent had caused MLB to hire a law firm to investigate him—was again accused of using sex to attain information.

Lorraine Delgadillo, a pretty blond registered nurse, spent years working for Tony Bosch, first at BioKem and later at Biogenesis. The forty-six-year-old knew the inside of his operation as well as anyone, so Mullin was thrilled when she agreed to meet in early February.

Mullin and Maldonado visited her at home and interviewed her twice about the clinic. The talks went so well that Mullin nabbed her personal cell phone number. On Valentine's Day she was surprised to find that the divorced burly investigator had mailed her a bouquet of flowers with a handwritten note: "Thanks for all your help."

The two began regularly texting, and the texts—which were shared with the authors of this book—soon became flirtatious. "I'll be in tomorrow, can you get away for a drink or dinner?" he texted in one. In another, he wrote simply: "I really miss that beautiful face."

She asked him for "personal legal advice" concerning her divorce, and Mullin—a licensed attorney in New York State—happily obliged. After an apparent visit from investigators looking into Biogenesis, she texted Mullin: "Well the DEA finally made it out to me."

She sent him photos of her leftovers. He used emoticons.

On his visits to Miami to investigate Bosch over several months, Mullin and Delgadillo went on several dates. They ate sushi together. They went out for dinner and drinks at Town Kitchen & Bar in South Miami. They had breakfast at Big Pink, a South Beach restaurant famous for its pulled-pork omelet. ("Love that place," Mullin waxed over text.)

And they had sex, at least twice.

The implications of their tryst are tricky to untangle. Mullin isn't a police officer anymore, and he wasn't working on a criminal case. Mullin says that investigators quickly realized that Delgadillo wasn't going to be a useful witness because she had no knowledge of Bosch's ties to ballplayers, so he saw no harm in the relationship. "I would never go out with a witness," Mullin says. "It was so clear to me that she had nothing to do with this case."

But Mullin was leading an MLB investigation and collecting evidence in a case with tens of millions of dollars on the line. The experienced cop had to know that a sexual relationship with a potential witness wouldn't look good in court or in the press.

When news about Mullin and Delgadillo's relationship reached the MLB office, league officials weren't happy—but any discipline would come after the Biogenesis investigation was resolved.

"No dinner for us now," Delgadillo lamented over text late one night after learning that MLB knew about their affair. Mullin replied, "Lol of course we can."

"You risk taker u," teased Delgadillo.

"No risk nothing wrong," ruminated Mullin.

When she asked whether he had gotten "slack" about the rumors, Mullin responded with a happy face.

B ut by mid-March, it was clear that the sweet stuff—envelopes of cash and morning-after pulled-pork omelets—wasn't getting the investigators where they needed to be quick enough. Mullin and his bosses were ready to change tactics.

Bad cop was the new name of the game. And a lawsuit in Miami-Dade Civil Court was the blunt weapon Mullin's team needed. MLB's attorneys filed the lawsuit on March 22 with an eccentric legal argument: that Bosch had interfered with baseball's bottom line by knowingly selling banned drugs to its players. Bosch and his colleagues "participated in a scheme to solicit Major League Players to purchase or obtain . . . substances that the defendants knew were prohibited," baseball's attorneys argued, resulting in "intentional and unjustified tortious interference" with the game's contracts.

But it didn't take much imagination to understand why baseball had actually filed it. For one thing, MLB didn't just name Tony Bosch. They also named Bosch's former partner in BioKem, Carlos Acevedo; Albir; underground Dominican agent Juan Carlos Nunez; office manager Ricardo Martinez; and even Tony's brother, Ashley Bosch.

The message was clear: Either hand over evidence as discovery in our lawsuit and tell us everything in a deposition, or nearly everybody you know will shell out tens of thousands fighting us in court. It was MLB's billions against the crumbling finances of Bosch's gang of grifters.

The case also gave Mullin's crew a believable threat. Everyone from ex–UM pitching coach Lazer Collazo to Daniel Carpman, a doctor who once worked with Bosch, was hit with deposition notices. Now, when investigators went to knock on doors they could tell the witnesses the truth: Either talk now, or spend thousands on an attorney and we'll see you under oath in a law office with a court stenographer typing away.

As useful as the lawsuit proved for the DOI, though, it also created a circus of bad publicity for MLB. Legal experts and sports columnists derided Selig for using the courts to get evidence. "MLB had no subpoena power. So it created some," the *Washington Times* opined.

"They just want to put [Bosch] in a squeeze where they can essentially extort him," Richard Johnson, an Ohio sports attorney, told the *Times*.

"You're not allowed to do that. In any sense of the imagination, that's a frivolous lawsuit."

In its eagerness, baseball was bungling the case. One of the codefendants they'd named was Paulo da Silveira, a "chemist" tied to Bosch. The only problem was that da Silveira was actually a thirty-year-old salesman who'd never heard of Biogenesis or Tony Bosch. "Hell no, man," da Silveira's attorney told a reporter who asked if he had any chemistry background. "The kid works in sales." MLB soon admitted it had screwed up and dropped da Silveira.

Albir, for one, attempted to fight back against baseball using its own tactics. His attorney, John C. Lukacs Jr., filed a demand for depositions of MLB's investigators, as well as documents related to the league's probe into Biogenesis.

To not have to deal with that pesky request, MLB simply dismissed Albir from the lawsuit, prompting his lawyer to promise payback. "MLB's investigative tactics are indefensible," he told a reporter. "We will explore every available legal remedy to address these tactics."

The suit didn't do much to dredge up new information through depositions, either. Bosch skipped several appointments with MLB attorneys and Collazo and Yuri Sucart filed an appeal challenging baseball's standing.

And when baseball was finally able to drag someone in for a depo, the league was once again frustrated by the tanning salon tycoon who claimed to have already turned down its $200,000 offer.

Just after eleven A.M. on a Thursday morning, Pete Carbone arrived for his deposition at a law office on the thirty-fifth floor of a downtown Miami high-rise, wearing a hoodie and dark sunglasses. MLB senior counsel Pat Houlihan was at the deposition, revealed in previously unpublished court documents.

It began with Carbone calmly spelling his name. And then, in the two-hour deposition, which more resembled Abbott and Costello's "Who's on First?" routine than any legal proceeding, MLB attorney John Couriel almost got as far as narrowing down in which county Carbone resided.

MLB: Do you live here in Miami-Dade?

Carbone: I'm going to wait until I have my attorney present before I answer any questions.

MLB: Are you represented by counsel?

Carbone: Again, I'm going to have to wait until I have my attorney.

MLB: What's the name of your attorney?

Carbone: That's another question.

MLB: OK, when do you expect your attorney will be present?

Carbone: From what I understand, any questions that—like any statements that begin with "when," "what," "where," "why," I'm not going to answer any of those.

MLB: Have you ever been deposed before?

Carbone: That's actually another one of those words.

MLB: Actually, it started with "have."

Carbone refused to say whether he knew Bosch, Juan Carlos Nunez, or any pro ballplayers. He said he couldn't recall whether he had driven to the law office for the deposition, or how he found the office, or even why he was there. He couldn't say whether that was him in the BMW with Miami Heat plates that MLB investigators had been following all around town.

Eventually, he just started making noises. "I do not feel comfortable answering any questions—da, da, da. I just got to get out of here." Carbone noticed the stenographer hammering away. "How do you type that, 'da, da, da'? What is that? Is there a key for that?"

While Carbone laughed in MLB's face, in the shadows, it appears he was quietly pulling ingenious strings. Along with his brother, Anthony, and tanning bed repairman Gary Jones, Porter Fischer believes Pete put together a plan that would provide both the league and Alex Rodriguez with all the evidence they'd need to bloody each other in newspapers, union hearings, and courtrooms for months to come.

And he'd make some serious cash doing it.

As the time neared one P.M., Carbone stopped responding at all to Couriel's questions. Instead, he toyed with his wardrobe.

"I would like the record to reflect that you have put your sunglasses back on, and then taken them off, and now you have put them back on," the MLB attorney deadpanned.

After a similarly nonverbal response to another query, Couriel remarked: "The deponent has zipped up his hoodie rather than answer my question."

A few days after Porter Fischer rejected MLB's final offer of $125,000, Dan Mullin got a call from a gravelly-voiced character from Boca named "Bobby."

Bobby had an offer of his own. He had a flash drive with all the evidence *New Times* had cited in its story. Would baseball, perhaps, be interested in purchasing it?

Yep, baseball was interested.

Mullin and his bosses didn't know it yet, but Bobby from Boca was Gary Lee Jones. The tanning bed repairman was actually the same swaggering fifty-four-year-old ex-con who'd done two years in the federal pen for counterfeiting more than $40,000 in twenties in the mid-'80s.

The ex-con had analyzed the playing field and saw two suckers ripe for the taking: MLB and A-Rod would both shell out absurd piles of cash to incriminate the other.

When Pete Carbone talked Fischer out of his original, handwritten Biogenesis notebooks in January with his ruse purporting a bloodthirsty Oggi, he went to Rodriguez for the first payday. Carbone had yet more evidence on his hands, though. As he was working with *New Times*, the always paranoid Fischer had entrusted the tanning salon owner with a flash drive copied with the documents, just in case something happened to him before the story could come out. That was not a wise move.

Jones first tried to talk Rodriguez's people into buying the flash drive. But Rodriguez already had the originals by March, MLB officials believe, in which case he likely wouldn't be in the market for more files. So Jones knew what he had to do with the scanned files. That's when he called Mullin as "Bobby from Boca."

Mullin agreed to meet the counterfeiter for the first time at Cosmos, Jones's neighborhood diner.

"A few hundred thousand isn't going to hurt you," Jones reasoned with the senior investigator.

After a short round of negotiations, Mullin handed over $100,000 for the files. As he walked out of Cosmos that day, the investigator knew that after three months of detective work to little avail, his team finally had what MLB needed.

On that tiny flash drive, hundreds of handwritten pages from Tony Bosch were the key to taking down A-Rod, Ryan Braun, and every other Biogenesis client.

Indications suggest that Dan Mullin didn't know the true identity of who he was doing business with. Perhaps it was willful ignorance. For weeks after that first sale, reporters in South Florida—tipped off by MLB investigators—scrambled to figure out who Bobby from Boca was, suggesting that the investigators themselves didn't know that an ex-con was their bag man.

Rob Manfred later told arbitrators that he authorized the deal believing that "Bobby" was working with Porter Fischer because he'd alluded to details of MLB's failed dealings with the whistle-blower that only Fischer would know. "His knowledge of our interactions with Porter Fischer led us to believe that Bobby from Boca and Porter Fischer were actually working together," Manfred testified in the confidential hearing.

But why would Fischer reject $125,000 outright for the records and then promptly sell them for a lower price through a coconspirator who, presumably, would get a cut of the cash?

At the time, Fischer was also eagerly cooperating with Jerome Hill.

That's why, shortly after Jones sold the scanned files to MLB, he rented a car and drove to Ocala for the stored medical records.

During his meeting with Mullin, the lead investigator had mentioned that should Jones get his hands on any original documents from the clinic they could be worth significantly more to the ex-cops than the scanned files. Jones said he'd see what he could do.

Truth was, ever since the *New Times* story had landed in January, Jones had been quietly gaining Fischer's confidence.

Fischer and his previous confidante, Pete Carbone, had their falling-out not long after the story ran. How could Fischer trust him when Carbone had double-crossed him by selling Bosch's original notebooks to A-Rod?

But unlike Carbone, Jones was easy to trust. Differing from most of the tanning salon crew, he was actually older than Fischer and radiated ex-con wisdom. Slowly, Fischer began unloading his troubles on the tanning bed repairman.

"He seemed to be on my side," Fischer says. "I'm starting to freak out about everything . . . and he's not a thirty-three-year-old like Pete. I'd try to talk to this person and that person, but no one has a perspective because the whole situation is so massive."

As Jones said later, he saw Fischer as an easy mark from the get-go. "He was stupid," the ex-con said. "He didn't know how to make money. That was ridiculous going to *New Times*."

So Jones acted like a "complete idiot," he says, lulling Fischer into trusting him completely. He didn't know precisely what to do with that trust until late March, when Fischer mentioned his plan to retrieve the files from Ocala. Then he apparently set the wheels in motion.

According to Fischer, the bait was a new spray-tan solution. And the weapon was a twenty-year-old employee named Reginald St. Fleur at Anthony Carbone's Boca Raton outlet of the Boca Tanning Club. Reginald handed out flyers outside the club. He had a juvenile criminal record—and had once been questioned by cops about a prior theft from a car in the club's parking lot—but no felony convictions as an adult.

On March 24, it all came together.

On Fischer's three-hour drive back from Ocala, Jones called him mid-morning to chat, casually mentioning that he had just installed a new spray-tan solution with "great color" at the Boca Raton salon. Maybe Fischer wanted to pop in on his way home and check it out?

With Fischer locked into a booth for ten minutes, a spout lacquering his body with orange-brown dye, St. Fleur allegedly went to work. First he bashed in the window of Fischer's rented Toyota, police say, and then he popped the trunk and grabbed what he'd come for: the boxes full of Biogenesis's medical files.

But he also had to make the crime look random. So he also took Fischer's laptop and grabbed the shotgun from the trunk. Then, the finishing touch: St. Fleur busted out the window of Jones's van as well, took nothing, and sped away.

It was almost a perfect crime. Fischer—as he gaped at the damage and then spent months agonizing over who had stolen his documents—never seriously suspected Jones, the plainspoken tanning bed repairman whose van had also been bashed in.

But police later alleged that St. Fleur had made a mistake. Just under a handle on Fischer's rented car, beneath the shattered window, a small streak of blood marked the door.

Anthony Carbone says he and his brother had nothing to do with the break-in, and Jones did not respond to messages seeking comment. Whoever was behind the theft, it didn't take Jones and his cohorts long to plot out how to monetize their new haul. Within the week, Mullin and the ex-counterfeiter were sitting yet again in Cosmos. This time, MLB agreed to pay $25,000 for the original documents.

Not a bad payday for a few minutes of highly illegal work at a tanning salon. But Jones had been playing all the angles since the first day he'd gotten involved in this caper, and his instincts said there was more profit to be made from their latest enterprise.

That's why, as Mullin handed over an envelope full of cash and Jones deliberately passed back the box full of stolen paperwork, a cohort sat in a corner, filming every moment. Multiple sources say that filmer was none other than Anthony Carbone, though as in all things connected to the case, Carbone professes his innocence.

MLB took out its own videotaped insurance policy since they still weren't sure who "Bobby" really was. DOI investigator Ed Dominguez sat just a few tables back from the counterfeiter and the baseball honcho, making his own amateur film of the affair. In the video, shared with the authors, a little old lady eating lunch partially blocks the view of the deal at the diner.

Dan Mullin walked out of the Pompano Beach diner for the second time with reams of Tony Bosch's documents. In a shade more than three months in South Florida, the Department of Investigations had collected evidence that Tony Bosch had sold PEDs to scores of baseball players, and they had multiple witnesses to back them up. Bosch himself was still playing hard to get, but thanks to their lawsuit, the pressure was mounting.

But by paying cash to a convicted felon for stolen documents—evidence, in fact, that had been bound for a state investigation—Manfred and Mullin had played extremely dirty to get what their employer needed. That carried implications far more serious than impersonating cops or an investigator's dalliance with a nurse.

But this wasn't even the endgame. Jones and Carbone apparently also knew how valuable that evidence could be to the Yankees superstar with almost $100 million on the line.

CHAPTER FIFTEEN

A Snitch Is Born

Sweat beaded across Tony Bosch's forehead. He gulped overheated, badly ventilated courthouse air. The walls seemed to close in, sucking the oxygen from the room.

A few days earlier, Bosch had filled out a court-mandated financial survey and stared back at the brutal truth: He had just $100 left to his name. He was unemployed, and with his name plastered on ESPN every night, he was unemployable. He was bouncing from one budget hotel to another to stay a step ahead of the MLB and state investigators trailing his every move.

Worst of all, he now believed that his star client wanted him dead.

It was May 30, 2013, and as he awaited yet another child support hearing in a Miami-Dade courthouse, Tony Bosch hit the lowest moment in the epic free fall that started with Porter Fischer walking out with a stack of his records and accelerated to terminal velocity when *New Times* published its story in January.

For weeks, Bosch had done everything possible to protect Alex Rodriguez. A few hours after *New Times* posted its story online, his lawyer met with Rodriguez's celebrity legal team and carefully toed the company line, agreeing to release a statement he knew was nonsense. The terse release insisted that the *New Times* piece was "filled with inaccuracies, innuendo and misstatements of fact" and added that Bosch "vehemently denied" having anything to do with Rodriguez or any other big leaguers.

Even as he helped A-Rod's defense, though, he was already starting to worry whether he could withstand MLB's heat. He'd pushed back against his biggest customer once, insisting on hiring his longtime friends Julio and Susy Ribero-Ayala as his attorneys rather than the corporate big shots A-Rod suggested. But Bosch wasn't exactly declaring his legal independence from Rodriguez: One of the superstar's attorneys arranged to help with the Ayalas' legal fees, and in February 2013, Rodriguez wired $25,000 for that purpose.

How exactly would MLB come down on him? The question tormented Bosch for weeks as he waited for Selig's next move, and on March 22, it came down with authority. MLB sued him, his brother, Ashley, and all of Biogenesis's officers, claiming they'd harmed the sport by selling PEDs, and potentially seeking millions in damages. He knew the lawsuit was meant to bleed him dry, but he still hoped that as long as A-Rod kept the cash coming, he might hold out.

In the meantime, the army of investigators MLB unleashed onto South Florida made life hell for Bosch and just about everyone he'd ever met. Dan Mullin's ex–FBI agents relentlessly stalked his parents and friends. Everyone who'd ever owned a business with him or sued him or played softball with him was barraged with phone calls and unexpected visits.

Process servers armed with deposition orders chased Tony all over Dade County. One spent days staking out his parents' house in Coral Gables. Then, acting on a tip, he took his subpoena to a Coconut Grove hotel, pacing the hallway just outside room 304. Only pure luck had led Bosch to check out earlier. The exasperated server even ordered God knows how many Frappuccinos at the Key Biscayne Starbucks, staking out a corner seat and hoping Bosch might wander in for a coffee.

"He was living life in hiding, and he's a very social person," says his friend Hernan Dominguez, who stayed at his side in the months after the story ran. Bosch was nowhere to be found at the Ibis Lounge in Key Biscayne, Scotty's Landing in Coconut Grove, or any of his other usual watering holes.

For three months, he managed to evade everyone. But, as with A-Rod's financial largesse, he wondered how long his luck could hold out.

In April, Rodriguez tried to send another bundle of cash to Bosch's attorneys—a hazy incident that later became a hotly debated piece of A-Rod's case. This much is clear: On April 8, a lump sum of $49,901.51 arrived with no explanation in Susy Ribero-Ayala's business account. MLB later called the money a "bribe" meant to keep Bosch docile. Rodriguez's camp claims the cash was meant to pay off a debt to Roy Black, his previous attorney, and had simply been wired to the wrong lawyer.

Either way, Bosch didn't take the money; Ribero-Ayala returned it promptly to Rodriguez. If that rejection was meant as a subtle message, Bosch gave A-Rod even more reason to worry two weeks later.

By April 29, he was sick and tired of all the running. So when ESPN reporter Pedro Gomez and a camera crew caught up with him just outside Scotty's Landing, his favorite bayside bar next to Miami's city hall, Bosch didn't scuttle away. For three months, he'd hidden, taking secret meetings with lawyers and watching his name get dragged through the Internet's darkest corners. Like Victor Conte before him, a piece of Tony Bosch had always wanted to come out of the shadows, to write books and show his face as the guy who'd helped A-Rod and Ryan Braun wallop homers and over-come injuries.

He knew, of course, that he couldn't tell Pedro Gomez about all that. But a national audience waited on the other side of that camera, and a fa-mous journalist wanted his opinions about the national pastime. So Bosch stopped and talked. A boat bobbed in the middle distance. Bosch's top three buttons were undone, his hair was slicked back, and aviator sunglasses hid his eyes.

The interview became Bosch's most revealing moment in the heart-palpitating months after the *New Times* story broke. It showed the world a nervy, terrified man trying hard to project machismo and bravado. "I'm a nutritional advisor," Bosch told Gomez in his husky voice tinged with Cuban Spanish.

"What is a nutritional advisor?" Gomez asked.

"I advise on any natural, nutritional properties," Bosch replied, staring nervously at something behind Gomez and waving his hands vaguely in the air.

This was miles from the polished statement A-Rod's attorneys had helped him to craft. This was Bosch laughing nervously, casting skittish glances while halfheartedly denying everything. "There's been a character assassination," he told Gomez, smiling broadly. "I've been accused, tried, and convicted in the media." He was broke, he said. "My business has suffered, I have suffered, my children have suffered. . . . When you get falsely accused, tried, and convicted in the media, that's a losing battle."

When Gomez pressed him on his connections to MLB clients, Bosch offered a contradictory argument. First of all, reports about his relationship to them were all wrong. But Bosch also couldn't talk about them because they were his clients and he had to respect their privacy.

Then came the key question: Had MLB approached him? "I've always been here, Pedro," Bosch said with a wide grin. "They haven't reached out to my attorneys, they haven't reached out to me. I'll cooperate, but there's no one who has reached out to me."

If A-Rod's posse wasn't already spooked about the clinic owner's intentions, they had good reason to be scared after that interview. At MLB headquarters, Rob Manfred took that final quote as a not-so-subtle invitation. He quickly got a message to Bosch's camp: "I let it be known . . . that we sure as heck did want to speak to him if he wanted to speak to us," Manfred later testified in Alex Rodriguez's arbitration hearing.

Within a few days, Julio Ayala called Manfred back to say that, "In fact, Mr. Bosch was interested in cooperating with Major League Baseball," Manfred recounted.

A-Rod's camp, meanwhile, started its own efforts to win back Bosch's loyalty. A few weeks after the ESPN interview, Oggi asked Bosch to meet him in his apartment in Fortune House, a downtown condo development. Jorge Velazquez had always been an important intermediary between Bosch and A-Rod—it was Oggi who'd helped broker their first connection through Yuri Sucart, and it was Oggi who was a conduit to Rodriguez's tight inner circle of old friends like Pepe Gomez. Bosch had no illusions about his former business partner at Boca Body. He knew that Oggi had a violent past and that when he flew off the handle he could be terrifying.

Bosch didn't dare turn him down. So he met Oggi and Andrew O'Connell, the private investigator Rodriguez had hired to poke holes in baseball's investigation. They pushed a sheet of paper his way: an affidavit stating that he'd never sold PEDs to Rodriguez and didn't have any knowledge about the slugger using drugs. Bosch balked. He wanted his attorneys to look it over first, and he protested that A-Rod wasn't doing enough for him. "I lost a $5-million-a-year business," O'Connell claims Bosch said at the meeting. "I don't have $125 million like a ballplayer." Oggi glowered and O'Connell asked what exactly Bosch wanted, but the fake doc was noncommittal and left.

A few days later, Oggi passed along a new offer over ceviche at Aromas del Perú in Coral Gables. "They said, we think you should leave town," Bosch later told *60 Minutes*. "We're going to get you a plane ticket to Colombia and we want you to stay there until this blows over."

They'd pay him $25,000 a month while he was on the lam and another $150,000 when he safely returned. But Bosch was worried. Something didn't smell right. In Miami, he wasn't exactly safe, but at least he was surrounded by friends and family. He knew the territory. What was to stop someone in Colombia from putting a bullet in his head? He turned down this offer, too.

He hadn't betrayed A-Rod yet. But the signs were increasingly ominous for the superstar and his entourage. They may not have known it, but even as Bosch listened to Oggi's offers, his attorney was talking weekly to MLB. Someone decided the clinic owner needed a stronger message. It came via a text sent to his ex-girlfriend from an anonymous number. "Tony won't live to see the end of the year," it warned in Spanish.

MLB investigators later decided that Oggi was probably to blame. Was he acting alone, or did A-Rod authorize the death threat? Bosch, at least, had no doubts. "Nothing happens without Alex's approval," he later said. "I used to be in that inner circle, and nothing happens without him approving it."

Either way, as the 2013 baseball season moved into its second month, Bosch had more to worry about than vague predictions about his mortality. Amid the lawsuits, the procession of process servers chasing him around town, and the prospects of Oggi putting one in his brain, Bosch's court battles with his ex-wife had only gotten worse.

On April 10, he'd been called to court to explain why he couldn't pay the tens of thousands he owed to support his fifteen-year-old daughter and ten-year-old son. He told the judge that he "runs a clinic that does sports nutrition with high-profile clients," but that he "lost a major contract in July 2012 and [his] income was interrupted." He was also "under investigation" over the clinic, he admitted.

Aliette told the judge the other side of the story. Tony Bosch paid up only when he faced jail time. He viewed everything else as "a joke," she testified. The judge ordered Bosch to pay his ex $1,250 in semimonthly installments. If he didn't come up with $5,000 in the next six months, he'd face that jail time Aliette thought was his only motivator.

Now, a month later with zero new payments to his name, he was back in the same sticky, hot courtroom, still stewing over the death threats, the MLB lawsuit, and the question of what to do about Alex Rodriguez.

Bosch risked a glance across to the plaintiff's table, where Aliette sat with her attorneys. She stared balefully ahead, refusing to acknowledge her ex-husband. He now owed her more than $40,000, she claimed. Worse, the Miami-Dade Office of the State Attorney had already lined up to support her. If Bosch didn't make good on his debts soon, a prosecutor was ready to file charges.

It was all too much. Bosch suddenly grabbed his attorney's arm, gasping. He told his lawyer he couldn't breathe before stumbling to his feet and fleeing the courtroom.

He didn't come back.

Four months after *Miami New Times* blew up his business and exposed his professional clients, Tony Bosch was almost literally penniless and on the run every day from creditors, cops, reporters, and athletes and their handlers. And he believed that the one guy who had enough cash and power to help him weather the storm was threatening his life. If he had any friends left, he wasn't sure who they were.

As Tony Bosch walked out of the courtroom into humid downtown Miami, he knew only one thing for sure: He couldn't run much longer.

Jerome Hill had Tony Bosch by the balls. Porter Fischer had given the DOH investigator everything: flash drives with Tony's records, stacks of files, and names and phone numbers for other Biogenesis clients.

Hill also had an advantage over other cops. Unlike DEA agents or local police, Hill didn't have to prove that Tony Bosch had broken drug laws by selling anabolic steroids, synthetic testosterone, or HGH—charges that, even with the voluminous records Fischer had taken from Biogenesis, can be difficult to establish.

Hill felt burning shame at his department's failure to stop Bosch twice before—once in 2009, when Manny Ramirez had sparked a probe, and again in 2011, when an anonymous complaint had opened another case into Bosch's clinic. That probe ended with no action after another investigator had been assured by Bosch's business partner that they were simply running a medical marketing firm; the state employee never bothered to talk to Bosch or any of his clientele. For Hill, it was enough to see Biogenesis's cocky owner behind bars.

If there is such a thing as an open-and-shut case, this was it. Fischer was the perfect whistle-blower. He'd handed over stacks of prescription forms with Bosch's signature on them. Nearly every regular client at Biogenesis could testify to the fact that Bosch had presented himself as a doctor. In fact, for months after the scandal broke, regular Biogenesis customers interviewed about Bosch muttered in shock when they learned from reporters that he wasn't actually a doctor.

"Are you kidding me?" asked Betty Tejada, a longtime friend on Key Biscayne, when told that Bosch had no license. "He was Dr. Bosch. That's how literally everyone knew him."

Hill's work was complicated, of course, when Gary Jones and his cohorts broke into Fischer's car in Boca and stole the boxes of documents the burned investor had planned on handing over to the DOH. The police veteran from the streets of Baltimore was furious. Hill quickly called Boca PD's detectives to tell them in no uncertain terms that important evidence from a state investigation had been stolen in the robbery.

But Hill also knew that between the scanned records Fischer had given him and the interviews he could conduct, he still had plenty of ammunition to go after Tony Bosch.

Once he started calling former clients, Hill found no shortage of witnesses. On April 9, he sat down with Porter Fischer for a lengthy interview. On the record, Fischer retold his whole story, from meeting Bosch at Boca Body to starting on his chemical regimen to becoming an investor and employee at Biogenesis before finally storming out with the records and going to New Times with the story.

"Bosch [was] wearing a white lab coat with 'Dr. Tony Bosch' on the right breast," Fischer told Hill of their first meeting in Boca Body.

Fischer spelled out the full schedule that Bosch had put him on: hCG shots five times a week, synthetic testosterone once a week, and MIC/B$_{12}$ mixes twice a week, all for $375. Later, he switched to HGH and other drugs, "after 'the doctor' said it was OK." (Fischer even gave Hill photos of Tony's emblazoned lab coat and the Belizean MD degree hanging on his wall.)

Later that afternoon, Hill sat down with Alvaro Lopez Tardon's wife, Sharon, who was waiting for her chance to testify against him in the federal case involving the Spanish cocaine ring. She described going to Bosch four years earlier and starting a regimen of HGH and other drugs, which she

later blamed for her husband's anger problems and low libido. She never
doubted Bosch was a real physician, she told Hill.

"I thought Anthony Bosch was a medical doctor," she said in her sworn
affidavit.

Finally, on April 16, Hill interviewed a client identified as JG in her
affidavit. She'd been diagnosed by an endocrinologist with hyperthyroid-
ism and sought Bosch out on her own for treatment options. "Dr. Bosch
introduced himself as a doctor and therefore I did not ask or inquire as to
his credentials because I had no reason to doubt him," she testified. "I have
seen many doctors throughout my adult life and have never questioned
them or [verified] their credentials."

Later that same day, Hill met with Miami-Dade prosecutors at their
headquarters just off the Dolphin Expressway. The case was already coming together. Hill could see the possibilities: Once they had Bosch in their
grasp, the bogus doctor could drop a dime on every pharmacist and doctor
who aided him in building his steroid enterprise. South Florida law enforcement could finally take a unified stand against the thriving doping
industry.

Dade prosecutors, impressed with Hill's work, made a few calls and set
up a follow-up meeting for the next afternoon. At one P.M., they'd meet in
Brickell with a detective from the Florida Department of Law Enforcement
and a representative from Florida attorney general Pam Bondi's office. There,
they could sketch a game plan for taking down Tony Bosch and everyone
who'd helped him.

Hill went to bed happy.

Just three hours before his Brickell meeting the next day, the investigator got a call from his department's Tallahassee chief. She broke the news
quickly: The conference was canceled. Hill was not to meet with prosecutors or anyone else, and he was to close the case against Bosch immediately,
with no further interviews.

The veteran cop was flabbergasted. The biggest case of his career had
landed right in his lap. The skittish whistle-blower who'd rejected every

other authority on Earth had given *him* the keys to take down Tony Bosch. And now his boss was shutting it all down?

"I explained [the prosecutors'] interest in the case, but to no avail," Hill wrote in an e-mail to his supervisor two days later. "In addition, I was given direct orders to finish the case and have it written by this Friday. The report will be sent up without the quality it requires."

On April 23, Bosch's punishment from the State of Florida became official: a $5,000 fine—later reduced to $3,000 upon Bosch's appeal—and a cease and desist letter ordering him to stop impersonating a doctor. Prosecutors would have to decide whether to charge Bosch with a crime.

But the DOH seems to have done everything possible to ensure that Bosch wasn't charged. It was bad enough that they'd ordered Hill to close his case. Then, instead of sending prosecutors the full eighty-six-page report he'd compiled over two months of work, they sent Miami-Dade state attorney Katherine Fernandez Rundle just a cover letter and a one-page summary.

Rundle's office scoffed, replying that "additional investigative steps are required before this office can initiate criminal proceedings," and suggesting, with a touch of tongue-in-cheek, that the DOH should consider obtaining "sworn testimony from a material witness." (Which, of course, Hill had already done thrice over.)

When a television reporter later gave Hill's full report to Miami prosecutors, a baffled spokesman admitted that he found it "very surprising" his staff had never been given the thick file and confirmed that they'd even followed up with a specific request with the DOH for more details.

Even as Tony Bosch played a dangerous game of cat and mouse with MLB and his millionaire clients, he'd yet again walked away from a state investigation with barely a scratch. But why would the DOH pass up a chance to bust a guy who'd already rubbed two previous investigations in their face?

DOH officials refused multiple requests for answers to that question. But a few facts suggest why the case was doomed from the start.

The biggest impediment to Hill's case was Florida's deep-seated reluctance to discourage its booming anti-aging industry. In the previous decade, the Sunshine State had grown into the nation's capital for the legally dubious, hugely profitable market, its 549 clinics surpassing California for the most in the country. Robert Goldman and Ronald Klatz's A4M is now headquartered in a plush, wood-paneled office space near downtown Boca Raton.

A4M's clinics represented an important, money-generating industry for the state—sales of HGH alone had spiked to $1.4 billion a year in 2012 with a large percentage of that increase presumably coming from clinics like Biogenesis. Those profits, in turn, filter from drug companies—with Roche subsidiary Genentech banking $400 million and Pfizer and Eli Lilly taking in $300 million and $200 million, respectively, according to an AP investigation—to doctors writing prescriptions to clinic owners like Bosch.

Going hard after Bosch would send a message industry wide: Florida isn't open for HGH business.

The fact that Hill's bosses decided to derail his Biogenesis probe was hardly unusual. In fact, under the probusiness, antiregulation governor Rick Scott, Florida's healthcare regulators had been castrated and actively discouraged from pursuing criminal cases.

Remarkably, the most powerful man in the state had a background in medical fraud. Scott, a Republican, had taken office in 2011. Previously, he had founded healthcare giant Columbia/HCA, and led the firm as its CEO. But in 1997, the feds built a massive criminal case against the company, alleging it had stolen nearly a billion dollars from Medicare by lying about marketing costs and overstating how much hospital space was being used. In a civil case tied to the probe, Scott appeared in a video deposition where he invoked his Fifth Amendment right not to incriminate himself seventy-five times. The company later pleaded guilty to fourteen felonies and agreed to pay back $600 million. Scott, who was never personally charged, was forced to resign—with a nearly $10-million golden parachute and $350 million in company stock.

Yet Scott weathered the campaign commercials showing him stammering, "I plead the Fifth," over and over, and won the governorship. And when he moved to Tallahassee, he seemed to take out all his rage over that federal case on his own state's Department of Health. In his first year, he helped the Legislature lop $55 million out of the DOH budget, resulting in hundreds of layoffs. The managers he hired all shared his laissez-faire attitude toward regulation and enforcement.

"The people coming in were all political folks and their direction was all coming straight from the governor's office," says Daniel Parker, who spent fourteen years in the DOH's Division of Environmental Health. "What was driving all this was an ideology that wants to get rid of government altogether."

Turnover was endemic. Nearly a dozen top-level administrators resigned in the first months of 2012, including Scott's first choice to run the department and Parker, who fired off an angry department-wide e-mail after stepping down.

One of the hardest-hit departments was Jerome Hill's own division. The Unlicensed Activity Unit—charged with going after bogus practitioners like Tony Bosch—was racked with bad morale and divisive leadership. Former investigators describe a poisonous atmosphere where criminal investigations were heavily discouraged. One investigator says she quit after a boss demanded she do nothing about an illegal dentistry operation she'd discovered. Another, a former cop named Christopher Knox, says he was fired before Hill opened his Biogenesis investigation when he refused to back off from an unlicensed pharmacy. "They actually ordered me not to assist the police in going after someone who was breaking the law," Knox says.

The department's own statistics confirm that its problems are not the imagination of disgruntled investigators. Between 2010 and 2013, the DOH referred 206 cases involving frauds like Tony Bosch to prosecutors. Just twenty-nine of those cases resulted in arrests and just four netted convictions. In other words, fewer than 2 percent of the Tony Bosches slinging drugs under the table ever faced any jail time—even when caught red-handed.

So it's not surprising the DOH failed to present Miami prosecutors with the ammunition they'd need to lock up Tony Bosch for pretending to be a doctor.

It certainly didn't help, of course, that Gary Jones stole a pile of evidence bound for Jerome Hill, or that MLB bought it to use in its case against A-Rod rather than return it to the state trying to lock up Biogenesis's owner.

Then again, MLB had good reason to keep Tony Bosch out of jail.

The meeting that changed the course of baseball history, cemented Bud Selig's last-minute flip-flop from steroid commissioner to bold antidrug reformer, and heralded the possible crashing end to Alex Rodriguez's career took place at a dockside dive bar that serves conch fritters and buckets of Bud Light on plastic patio tables.

Tony Bosch was a wreck. He fidgeted with his beer, eyed the crowd nervously, and stuttered through his answers. Sweat pooled under his arms in the summertime humidity. Across the table, Rob Manfred and Dan Halem, baseball's senior vice president and senior counsel for labor relations, sat and listened calmly as Bosch unburdened himself about the threats on his life and the web of criminals surrounding Biogenesis.

"Bosch's principal concern was for his safety," Manfred later testified during Rodriguez's arbitration. "He felt the situation had escalated in South Florida to the point that he was concerned that harm could come to him."

In the end, after months on the lam, Bosch had called this meeting with MLB's top officials for two simple reasons. The first was that the pressure cooker strategy Dan Mullin's investigative team had created to bully him into submission had worked beautifully; the lawsuit they'd filed to make Bosch's life hell had done just that. He was broke and facing serious jail time over unpaid child support. They'd even dragged his family into it by naming his brother, Ashley, in the suit.

But there was more than just the mounting financial pain. The truth was, Bosch no longer trusted Alex Rodriguez. Even if A-Rod didn't want him hurt, Bosch had come to believe that his life was in serious danger—if not from the Yankee star's entourage, then from one of the entourages connected to the scores of other players to whom he'd provided illegal drugs. It wouldn't take much of a nudge for someone to bash his head in with a pipe or pop a couple rounds into his car.

"How many hangers-on does Alex have that would love to do a solid for Alex?" Hernan Dominguez asks. "And then there's at least fourteen other players out there, all with their own relatives who want to do a solid for them."

Cooperating with MLB went against every fiber in Tony Bosch's being. He'd made a career out of beating its testers, and the thrill of cheating the system almost equaled the pleasure of knowing he was helping superstars with their game. He was loyal to a fault. And he knew the second he flipped, he'd become one of the most famous snitches in history.

"Tony knew he only had two options: to tell the truth, or to keep his mouth shut. For months, he held out because he wanted to see if it would blow over," Dominguez says. "Tony finally realized that you can't go against Major League Baseball and their billions of dollars. . . . They're going to come after you until they get you."

But on the day that he hyperventilated and ran out of his latest family court hearing with Aliette, Bosch knew they'd already gotten to him. He simply couldn't trust A-Rod to keep him safe. That left only one option: MLB. Bosch's attorneys had sent word to Manfred. He'd meet him in person to talk the terms of his surrender.

They met at Scotty's Landing, the same waterfront dive where ESPN had caught up to him a month earlier. Manfred later called the meeting "one of those get-to-know-you, can-I-trust-you meetings." Bosch, Ayala, and another attorney sat across from Manfred and Halem and began sketching out an agreement: MLB would drop Bosch and his brother from its lawsuit and promise not to force any of his family members ("children, parents, siblings, ex-spouses," reads the agreement) to testify. They'd pay for his attorneys and protect Bosch from whatever civil litigation might come his way. And they'd pay up to $2,400 a day on bodyguards to keep him safe for a year. That last piece was vital.

In the extraordinary proffer between a private corporation and an informant under federal and state investigation, MLB also promised to vouch for Bosch to any agency that might threaten him with arrest. "MLB will inform such agencies of the value and importance of Bosch's cooperation in its efforts to achieve the important public policy goal of eradicating [performance-enhancing substances] from professional baseball, and request that such agencies consider his cooperation with baseball," reads the agreement, a copy of which was obtained by these authors.

Bosch had good reason to ask for a good word from the commissioner. As the public learned two months later, a federal grand jury had been convened to probe whether Bosch should face criminal charges for his clinic. A separate Miami-Dade County investigation by prosecutors was launched months after this.

As part of the deal, Bosch was required to turn over all "notes, photographs, journal or diary entries, electronic communications . . . text messages, telephone records . . . audio or visual recordings . . . prescriptions, courses of treatment, receipts or ledgers"—in short, absolutely any shred of evidence that would incriminate "any Player or individual acting on such Player's behalf regarding the prescription, purchase, sale, consumption, administration, or possession of any [performance-enhancing substance]."

Rodriguez later claimed that Bosch's agreement also included millions of dollars, but that's not strictly true. Bosch's attorneys later collected more than $1 million in fees from MLB, according to an estimate by Manfred in Rodriguez's arbitration, but the agreement sketched out over beers at Scotty's included no cash payouts. Manfred was clear that it would hurt his credibility. "Our interest in him was as a witness," Manfred later testified. "Therefore, we could not pay him. That was just off the table from the beginning."

Still, getting the lawsuit off his back and a bodyguard at his side at least helped to keep the sharks at bay. Within a few weeks of Bosch's baseball summit over cheap beers in Coconut Grove, a Miami-Dade prosecutor filed an update to his child support case. That $5,000 overdue bill to Aliette, the cause of so much grief and so many hours in court, had suddenly been paid in full.

On June 3, Bosch signed on the dotted line. Halem signed on behalf of the league. MLB had its witness.

CHAPTER SIXTEEN

Singled Out

By his usual primped standards, Alex Rodriguez was haggard—heavier than usual, with gray stubble flecking his chin and a blue velour warm-up thrown over a V-neck T-shirt. Sitting alone at a folding table, he looked like an insomniac poker player.

Through a career marked by humiliating revelations and media feeding frenzies, Rodriguez's go-to demeanor under fire has been as the wide-eyed innocent. Going into full-bore attack mode didn't fit Rodriguez. That's what he paid men with law degrees to do.

But Rodriguez wanted reporters—several dozen of whom were crowding him in the bowels of a tiny minor league baseball stadium—to know that he was angry. "I will say this," began Rodriguez. "There's more than one party that benefits from me never stepping back on the field. That's not my teammates and not the Yankee fans."

As the newly flush—and newly flipped—Tony Bosch paid off his child support in Miami-Dade County, Alex Rodriguez was on the comeback tour in Trenton, New Jersey.

His hip surgery rehab assignment, baseball's method of easing major leaguers back by having them play in minor league games, had already taken him to Tampa and South Carolina. On the night of August 2, 2013, he was finally back in the tri-state area. Though he had dominated the back covers of New York tabloids for eight months since the Biogenesis story broke, his only communiqués to date had been statements issued by representatives and the odd tweet.

The plan was for Rodriguez to play two games for the Trenton Thunder, the Yankees' double-A team, and then rejoin the Bronx squad. But speculation was rampant that despite A-Rod's best-laid plans, he would never play another game for the Yankees.

Everyone knew that Tony Bosch cooperating with MLB was a game changer. No doping supplier had ever helped MLB get his clients punished. Armed with his evidence, the biggest round of suspensions in sports history would start cascading through MLB ranks. And Bud Selig's leaky office had already clued everyone in to when that punishment would start raining down: on the following Monday, the same day Rodriguez was scheduled to finally suit up for the Yankees.

News articles were even quoting Major League Baseball sources suggesting that Selig might hit Rodriguez with a lifetime ban, making him the Pete Rose of PEDs.

The confluence of imminent return and imminent exile had turned this double-A baseball game into a strange spectacle. The bandbox stadium was at its capacity of nine thousand. Those in attendance didn't know if they might be witnessing the curtain call of the great A-Rod's baseball career, here on the banks of the Delaware River, separating the grittier edges of both New Jersey and Pennsylvania.

Rodriguez's sleeveless minor league jersey looked like a gag gift. He slammed a two-run homer over a left-field fence papered with local advertisements. At another point, when his baby-faced teammates huddled at the pitching mound to strategize, Rodriguez wandered around the infield alone, blowing bubbles. And after the game, he once again made an unconventional setting his location for another PED-related press conference.

The always-needling media wouldn't allow Rodriguez to get in only a vague jab. Who were the parties that benefited from him never again stepping on a baseball field?

Rodriguez went macabre. "I can't tell you that right now," he said, and then swiveled his head and widened his eyes dramatically. "And I hope I never have to."

Despite his showmanship, it wasn't a great secret that Rodriguez believed Major League Baseball and the Yankees were joined in a conspiracy to end his career.

Certainly, the Yankees did have incentive to root for a lengthy suspension—or, more darkly, a prolonged absence due to injury—of their once-prized third baseman.

He couldn't stay healthy, was a lightning rod for bad press, and had lost much of his pop. And he was owed almost nine figures. With Rodriguez injured, the Yankees paid only the small portion of his salary that wasn't covered by insurance. With him banned, the team wouldn't have to pay even that.

Before arriving in Trenton, Rodriguez had spent the year feuding both privately and publicly with the Yankees. His recovery from hip surgery was being overseen by Yankees doctor Bryan Kelly. But Rodriguez was becoming certain that the team—particularly team president Randy Levine—did not want him back, and Kelly's conversations with Levine confirmed the suspicion. "Levine told me the Yankees would rather [you] never step on the baseball field [again]," Kelly told Rodriguez, according to *New York* magazine. (Levine denied that sentiment, telling the magazine he meant: "Alex, this is your health, this is your life, if you choose to get off the field because you don't want to be disabled, we're fine with that.")

On February 28, Rodriguez sent a lengthy e-mail to Levine, telling him that he had heard the Yankees were offering a "bounty" to the team president if Rodriguez didn't return. "Of course I am very concerned about these rumors and about what the team is doing and saying about me," wrote Rodriguez in the e-mail. "People have been telling me that you have an 8% bounty on my contract. . . . I hope this is the start of us clearing the air between us. I don't want us to be enemies."

Rodriguez and Levine were once chummy, according to earlier e-mails, all of them published by *New York* magazine. Their nickname for each other, a reference to Rodriguez's chip on his shoulder, was "Chip." But now, Levine's reply was terse: "First off, neither I nor anyone at Yankees every [sic] met with your cousin. This is being handled by MLB and we r allowing them to do their job. There is no bounty on you. We have no idea who MLB is meeting with or what course their investigation is taking."

But as the summer wore on and Rodriguez grew increasingly frustrated with the slow pace of his return, he was certain that the team was attempting to stall his comeback from injury.

On June 28, Yankees general manager Brian Cashman had discussed Rodriguez's injury on sports talk radio, saying: "He has not been cleared by our doctors to play in rehab games yet."

Alex Rodriguez is no social media maven. Twitter is a medium of public candor, which was never his strong suit. But in an apparent attempt to gain control of his own return timeline, the day after Cashman's interview, Rodriguez fired off the ninth tweet of his life.

Rodriguez's tact: willful obliviousness. He posted a photo of himself talking with Dr. Bryan Kelly, whom the Yankees had assigned to oversee his recovery. "Visit from Dr. Kelly over the weekend," Rodriguez wrote, "who gave me the best news—the green light to play games again!"

An ESPN New York reporter read the tweet to Cashman. "You know what, when the Yankees want to announce something, [we will]," Cashman responded. "Alex should just shut the fuck up. That's it. I'm going to call Alex now."

Rodriguez later explained that his tweet had been written out of "pure excitement." But he did get his way. Within a week, Rodriguez had started his rehab tour on the Yankees' single-A team in South Carolina.

The *New York Daily News* was certain that Rodriguez had, as the paper broadcast on its back cover, an EVIL PLAN. He was attempting to rush his way back to the Yankees only to then declare that he was unable to play because of a serious injury and spend the rest of his career on the disabled list in order to collect his entire contract regardless of the MLB suspension. (The Yankees' insurance provider would pay the bulk of Rodriguez's salary in the event of this sort of injury.) Unfortunately, the purported plan wasn't exactly grounded in league rules, as a suspended player loses his salary regardless of whether he's on the disabled list.

As Rodriguez jousted with the Yankees, Dan Mullin and his crew were encamped in Florida, building what was becoming a strong case against him. When Bosch had agreed to cooperate in early June, he had turned three of his BlackBerry phones over to investigators. The devices contained a trove of communication with Rodriguez.

Bosch and Rodriguez had exchanged more than five hundred BlackBerry messages and 556 text messages, and they'd spoken on the phone fifty-three times in 2012. These included those furtive text haikus between the duo: "Try to use service elevators"; "Careful. Tons of eyes"; "Not meds dude. Food."

Investigators had the doping protocol Bosch said he had devised for Rodriguez, detailing a baseball season regimen of HGH in the morning, testosterone cream in the evening, and Bosch's special troches right before exertion.

Bosch had also provided evidence against his other MLB clients. But as MLB investigators interviewed the two superstars they were targeting most tenaciously, they were met with stony silence.

Ryan Braun met with MLB on June 29 and refused to answer their questions. Thirteen days later, league counsel Dan Halem met with Rodriguez on a Saturday in Tampa, where his rehab tour had taken him to the Yankees' minor league squad in that city, for an "investigatory interview" concerning Rodriguez's purchases of PEDs from Bosch.

As in any judicial setting, baseball's union procedures have legal precedents. When future Hall of Fame pitcher Ferguson Jenkins was busted crossing the Canadian border with a duffel bag containing cocaine, marijuana, and hashish in 1980, a union arbitrator ruled that he could refuse to answer MLB's questions about the incident so as to not incriminate himself, baseball's version of pleading the Fifth.

Besides the issue of his Biogenesis regimen, Halem asked Rodriguez about obstructing the investigation. The league believed that he had purchased the notebooks they sought as evidence, that he had attempted to get Bosch to sign an untruthful affidavit and offered him cash to "vanish" in Colombia, and that he had paid for the PED dealer's legal fees. Now, Rodriguez channeled Jenkins and refused to answer everything MLB threw at him.

Halem called his boss, Rob Manfred, after the interview. Rodriguez later attested in court filings that MLB "offered" him a 162-game ban if he cooperated, but he doesn't seem to have considered accepting it. Asked in arbitration about the investigatory interview, Manfred said that Halem relayed "that he had asked Mr. Rodriguez numerous questions and that Mr. Rodriguez had taken the Fifth Amendment with respect to virtually every question."

Rodriguez was affected enough by the meeting that he didn't show up at the Tampa stadium for that night's game, an infraction for which the Yankees later fined him $150,000. He had reason to be rattled. Immediately after the league was spurned by Rodriguez, Manfred started discussing possible suspension lengths with Selig. They were sure of one thing: The punishment had to be historic. "Commissioner Selig asked me about longer discipline and specifically the issue of a lifetime ban," Manfred testified in Rodriguez's later confidential arbitration hearing. Though Selig's weighing of banning Rodriguez for life has been reported through anonymous sources, Manfred's testimony is the first confirmation that the commissioner considered it.

Manfred studied the precedents. In a 2008 arbitration case involving Detroit Tigers infielder Neifi Perez, arbitrator Shyam Das had found that, as Manfred termed it, "each use of a prohibitive substance was a separate violation of the Joint Drug Agreement." By Manfred's logic, they could prove through Bosch that Rodriguez had used "more than three distinct banned substances." Since 2006, the Joint Drug Agreement dictates that a third banned substance offense will automatically result in a lifetime ban—

a provision that had never been triggered. "I told Commissioner Selig that there was a rationale under the agreement that a lifetime ban could be supported," Manfred later testified. "That you would make the argument that [there] was a first, a second, and a third offense."

But Manfred advised that they go a different route. In 2008, an obscure but potentially powerful clause had been added into the Joint Drug Agreement. Section 7.G.2 is known as the "just cause" amendment. It reads: "A Player may be subjected to disciplinary action for just cause by the Commissioner for any Player violation" of the rules governing banned substances.

Through its vague terming, the section appeared to give the league free rein to decide the length of a suspension—provided they could get an arbitrator to agree in the event of an appeal, of course. The commissioner had never before invoked the rule. If any case was egregious enough to get an arbitrator to approve of an unprecedented method of lengthy punishment, Manfred reasoned, this was it. Alex Rodriguez's career would be the canary in the coal mine.

Again, Manfred returned to the precedents. The baseball player most harshly punished for performance-enhancing drugs under the agreement was Guillermo Mota, the eleven-fingered relief pitcher who had been suspended for a total of 150 games as a result of two positive tests.

To Manfred, the manner in which Rodriguez had doped for at least three years, and then attempted to cover up his actions, far outweighed Mota's crimes. "Given what I've described about the evidence in this case, it was my belief that the conduct here merited a penalty more severe than that one hundred and fifty games," Manfred explained in arbitration. "That what Mr. Rodriguez had done, and what his impact on the integrity of the game on the field had been, merited more than that one hundred and fifty games. The question became: How much more?"

Though Rodriguez was bracing for a campaign against baseball and the Yankees that spanned more than a year, Braun was clearly spooked. He later claimed that he was never presented with MLB's evidence against him. Instead, it was simply a turn of the conscience. "I realized the magnitude of my poor decisions," Braun said. Either way, after pleading the Fifth during his first investigatory interview with MLB, Braun asked for another sit-down.

Ryan Braun—lying, maneuvering, scapegoating Braun—was finally ready to give in and strike a deal. Since October 2011, when Braun had tested positive for extremely high levels of testosterone, he had defiantly fought punishment, resulting in a smeared drug tester, a fired MLB arbitrator, and the absurd-in-hindsight notion that he'd sought out unlicensed Bosch only for his "expert" biochemist opinion.

But there was a basic financial equation behind Braun finally choosing to give up the fight in a timely manner.

Selig was threatening a hundred-game suspension if Braun wasn't ready to plead guilty and make a deal. If he didn't strike a bargain, he'd get fifty games for the "nonanalytical positive" stemming from his role in Biogenesis, and another fifty for lying to investigators and obstructing their probe with his Dino Laurenzi smear campaign the year earlier.

A hundred-game ban would have ended Braun's 2013 season and cost him nearly the first third of 2014. That would have been a monetarily disastrous suspension, and appealing it could make things even worse.

The contract extension Braun signed in April 2011, six months before his failed urine test, ensured that his highest-paid years were in 2014 and beyond. He was earning $8.5 million in 2013, would get a pay jump to $10 million a year in 2014, and would receive gradually more after that until his salary leveled out at $19 million a season.

If Braun appealed the hundred-game suspension, played through the 2013 season, and then lost his appeal, he would forfeit $6.2 million dollars in playing salary in 2014. The deal his attorneys eventually hashed out with MLB cut those financial losses nearly in half.

On July 22, the league announced that Braun had accepted a sixty-five-game suspension. Braun's public links to Biogenesis ended with a punishment that kept him out of the rest of the 2013 regular season. The year was a sixty-one-game, nine-homer blemish on what had appeared the beginnings of a Hall of Fame career. He was the first superstar casualty of Biogenesis.

Braun's nuclear self-destruction of his image as a modern-day clean superstar for the good folks of Wisconsin was officially complete. Selig wouldn't be eating any more lasagna at Braun's Milwaukee Italian restaurant, which was closed by investors who wanted no part of a PED cheat. As if to seal in amber how far Braun had fallen in the eyes of his Midwestern fan base, even a Green Bay Packers icon shook his head at the antics. "It doesn't feel great being lied to like that," said quarterback Aaron Rogers, who was friends with Braun, "and I'm disappointed in the way it all went down." The Brewers' owners ended up giving away more than $3 million in free food and T-shirts to any fans still willing to come watch the team play.

But Braun knew his contract from 2014 onward was safe. Whatever hit he'd taken to his image, he'd lost only a relatively minor $3.25 million in salary for the rest of the season. Braun, who seventeen months earlier had declared, "I would bet my life that this substance never entered my body at any point," now issued a vague quasi-apology.

"I am not perfect," allowed the outfielder, who did not admit to taking any specific drugs. "I realize now that I have made some mistakes. I am willing to accept the consequences of those actions."

That Braun was the first Biogenesis major leaguer to receive a negotiated settlement, despite his tortured previous two years with the league office, wasn't an accident. Baseball's message to the rest of Bosch's clients—those not named Alex Rodriguez, at least—was clear: Accept your punishment and you can move on with your career.

If Rodriguez was intimidated by Braun's suspension, he didn't show it. He was too immersed in his escalating squabble with the Yankees, a back-and-forth saga that had devolved into a sort of high-stakes game of Injury Battleship.

On July 21, Rodriguez was then with the Yankees' Scranton-area triple-A affiliate. That game was supposed to have been Rodriguez's last in his rehab stint, before rejoining the Yankees for a road series against the Rangers. But after showing up at the ballpark, he complained of stiffness in his left quadricep. The Yankees took him out of the lineup and flew him to New York City, where Dr. Chris Ahmad had him undergo another MRI.

Rodriguez, who believed that Ahmad had failed to diagnose his hip injury during his disastrous playoffs the year before, deeply distrusted the team doctor. And when Ahmad now found that Rodriguez had a mild quad strain, once again derailing his comeback, the superstar spun through his Rolodex of dubious acquaintances for his next trick.

On July 23, the day after Braun announced his acceptance of his suspension, a New Jersey doctor named Michael L. Gross was interviewed on Mike Francesa's WFAN sports radio talk show. Dr. Gross, an orthopedist at the Hackensack University Medical Center, said that he had spent twenty minutes looking at Rodriguez's MRI, studying the quadricep muscle that had him sidelined. "To be perfectly honest, I don't see any sort of injury there," Gross told Francesa.

The doctor added that he had asked Rodriguez in a phone call that morning whether he was in any pain. Rodriguez had said no. "If there's no pain, to me as an orthopedist, that means there's no injury," reasoned Gross. "I'm guessing a guy who's been playing ball his entire life knows his body. If he thinks he's fit to play, that's what he said."

As the bizarre radio cameo spurned scrutiny into his relationship with Rodriguez, Dr. Gross later clarified that he never examined or even met Rodriguez, nor received payment for reviewing his MRI. Rodriguez had been pointed his way through a physical therapist both men knew. "I did it because I thought it would be fun," Gross said later.

As was the case with Dr. Galea—and "Dr." Bosch—when it came to medical consultants, Rodriguez knew how to pick 'em. Reporters quickly uncovered after his appearance on WFAN that Dr. Gross had been reprimanded by the state of New Jersey in February 2013 for allowing an unlicensed underling to treat patients at the Active Center for Health and

Wellness, a facility Gross runs in Hackensack. More significant, Gross was also cited for "failing to adequately ensure proper patient treatment involving the prescribing of hormones including steroids," according to an administrative report.

Gross was fined $40,000 by the state. According to its website, the center offers "Anti-Aging and Bio-Identical Hormone Replacement Therapy," the same services Biogenesis publicly touted. In his defense, Dr. Gross said his center didn't generally treat athletes, and it was not anabolic steroids that he was found to have overprescribed. "We were treating people with a medical problem," Gross said—men with low testosterone.

In a statement, the perpetually peeved Cashman said that he heard about Gross's appearance through a text message. He implied that Rodriguez may have violated union rules. "Contrary to the Basic Agreement," said Cashman, "Mr. Rodriguez did not notify us at any time that he was seeking a second opinion from any doctor with regard to his quad strain."

To the Yankees front office, their ten-year star had gone from "Chip" to shut-the-fuck-up Alex to "Mr. Rodriguez."

As Rodriguez traveled to Trenton at the turn of August for the purgatorial game and press conference at Arm & Hammer Park, those who thought he would surely never play for the Yankees again could not have known how stubbornly he was prepared to fight all consequences of his association with Tony Bosch.

Rodriguez was already waging a secret campaign, with attorneys and private detectives skulking around Florida, investigating the MLB investigators, and lining up signatures on sworn affidavits.

In his next, and last, game for the Trenton Thunder that Saturday, Rodriguez walked four times. His belief that the Yankees were conspiring for him to be banned that Monday boiled over into an e-mail he fired off to his former confidante Yankees president Randy Levine.

"Can u please stop!!" Rodriguez wrote on August 3, according to e-mails later published by *New York* magazine. "I want to play baseball and I could make a big difference to the game. Steinbrenner would roll in his grave IF he knew what was happening! Stop, Randy, this isn't going to be good for any of us!! You are a businessman and what you are doing is ruining the business of baseball. If u want to meet in person to discuss it, let's do it!"

Levine didn't respond immediately. Though the Yankees had taken to calling him Mr. Rodriguez, in one formerly paternal figure's eyes he was still Alex.

"Dear Alex," began the letter he received from Bud Selig on that Monday, August 5. It was strangled in references to baseball statute, but skimming the letter delivered the devastating gist. "This letter is to inform you that . . . you are hereby suspended for 211 regular-season games . . . This represents a suspension for the remainder of the 2013 season (including postseason) and the entire 2014 regular-season. Your discipline . . . is based on your intentional, continuous and prolonged use and possession of multiple forms of prohibited Performance Enhancing Substances, including but not limited to Testosterone, Human Growth Hormone, and IGF-1, that you received as a result of your relationship with Anthony Bosch beginning in the 2010 championship season and ending in or about December 2012."

The suspension would start on August 8, the upcoming Thursday. "In the event you commit a subsequent violation of the Program in the future," Selig warned, "you will be suspended permanently from Major League Baseball."

Two hundred and eleven games represented the longest suspension for the use of performance-enhancing substances in baseball history, a willful exclamation mark meant to end that shameful run-on sentence containing Kevin Koch and Kirk Radomski and Mark McGwire and Barry Bonds. In his arbitration testimony, Manfred said that he recommended the suspension length to Selig. Banning Rodriguez through the rest of 2013 and all of 2014, the way he describes it, was almost a charitable decision. "And the reason I stopped at 2014 was that I felt that it provided the player with an opportunity to resume his career at some meaningful point in terms of his age and contract status," said Manfred. "I thought that was a fair balance of penalties, given other penalties that have been imposed under the program."

Rodriguez disagreed. As he himself later pointed out, the suspension kept him out of the game until exactly when Selig planned to ride off into the Wisconsin sunset. It was almost as if Selig's retirement gift to himself was the banishment of his tenure's most troublesome and disappointing star player.

Once Selig levied the bombshell punishment, Levine returned Rodriguez's previous missive.

"I received your e-mail, the contents of which are a complete shock to me," the Yankees president wrote. "As I have repeatedly told you, this is an MLB investigation. We had no role in initiating the investigation or assisting in the direction of the investigation. Despite your continued false accusations (which you know are false) we have acted consistently. My focus and direction, as well as that of the entire Yankees organization, has been, and continues to be, to treat you in the same manner as we do all of our players, to have you healthy and ready to play as soon as possible."

Levine's sign-off to the terse and guarded message: "Good luck."

Rodriguez was already on a plane to Chicago. The Yankees were playing the White Sox that night, and he was starting at third.

Twelve other baseball players received suspension letters from Selig that day. Black Monday landed with a tabloid storm and a *SportsCenter* frenzy. The headline was A-Rod's record suspension, but the context was the completion of the biggest round of suspensions in history: fifteen players in all, suspended from baseball over their ties to Tony Bosch.

Nobody but Rodriguez appealed their punishment. The Biogenesis suspensions were at once sweeping and incomplete.

Suspended for fifty games were a dozen players ranging the gamut of baseball prominence, from top sluggers and .300-batting-average lineup anchors to Dominican scrappers on the fringes of big league ball.

Of those who had been named in the original *New Times* story, Nelson Cruz, Jhonny Peralta, and Jesus Montero received the fifty-game suspensions that barred them through the end of the 2013 regular season. Melky Cabrera, Bartolo Colon, and Yasmani Grandal weren't punished for Biogenesis connections in 2013. They had all served fifty-game suspensions the season earlier, after testing positive for drugs that baseball believed came from Bosch's clinic. Cesar Carrillo, a minor leaguer with no protection from the MLBPA, had been suspended back in March for one hundred games. And then, of course, there was Mr. 211, Alex Rodriguez.

The following players had been suspended for fifty games following outing in Yahoo! or Bosch's revelations to baseball investigators: Everth Cabrera, Francisco Cervelli, Antonio Bastardo, Jordany Valdespin, Fernando Martinez, Cesar Puello, Sergio Escalona, Jordan Norberto, and Fautino de los Santos. Braun, already weeks into his own suspension, also fell into that category.

But several other players exposed in Bosch's notebooks, some of whom were not listed in the *New Times* article and have not been named in connection with Biogenesis until now, had evaded punishment altogether. Their reprieves came, according to MLB sources, because Bosch denied giving them PEDs and there wasn't other evidence to contradict him.

MLB investigators had "cleared" Washington Nationals pitcher Gio Gonzalez and Baltimore Orioles third baseman Danny Valencia, both University of Miami alum. "Their names came up in Biogenesis," MLBPA chief Michael Weiner said of Gonzalez and Valencia. "That's really about all I can say. It was determined that they didn't use performance-enhancing substances, that they didn't possess performance-enhancing substances and that they were—in the end, they weren't disciplined."

Danny Valencia was implicated in the pages of Bosch's records supplied to Yahoo!, with his name listed, with those of Rodriguez, Melky Cabrera, Carrillo, and Cervelli, under the heading "Baseball."

Gonzalez's apparent association with Bosch was more frequently documented. In the portions of Bosch's notebooks possessed by this book's authors, he is named seven times, at one point next to his cell phone number. His father, Max Gonzalez, had claimed that Gio was as "clean as apple pie" and that the family's only association with Bosch was that Max was on a Biogenesis weight-loss program..

Though Gio denied ever meeting or speaking with Bosch, at one point the fake doctor wrote "off visit"—presumably meaning office visit—next to his name. In another, Bosch jotted down Gonzalez's pitching statistics. One note indicates that Bosch planned to order zinc, B_{12}, and Arimidex "for Gio" at a charge of $1,000. None of those drugs are banned by baseball, but in another note Bosch records that he sold "creams" to "Gio/Max." Gio's mother, Yolanda Cid, is also listed six times in the books, at times next to the words *blood* and *delivery*. Bosch said that he'd only sold the pitcher legal supplements, MLB sources say.

Former UM star Gaby Sanchez was never even mentioned publicly by MLB as having ties to Biogenesis. But Bosch's records named Sanchez at least seven times—with one note reading, "$$$$"—and indicate that Bosch at least attempted to meet the ballplayer on multiple instances in a relationship facilitated by former UM coach Lazer Collazo. An MLB source involved in the investigation says the league couldn't prove the meetings took place or that Bosch sold Sanchez anything.

In the clique of former UM players caught up in the Biogenesis dragnet, rumors swirled that Gonzalez, Valencia, and Sanchez had helped their own situations by cooperating with the league's quest to bury their former teammate Braun and UM benefactor Rodriguez. League sources deny that MLB let anybody off the hook in return for cooperation.

The inverse does appear to be true, however. Fellow UM player Cesar Carrillo had refused to cooperate with league investigators. After being hit with the hundred-game suspension, he was released by the Detroit Tigers organization and was next spotted playing independent league ball in Sugar Land, Texas.

Marcelo Albir, the former UM phenom who had already washed out of baseball, also refused to cooperate with MLB's probe. Selig couldn't punish him with a suspension, but he was left tens of thousands of dollars in the hole from trying to fend off MLB litigation.

Other players named in the portions of the notebooks possessed by these authors escaped the league's discipline, according to an MLB source, because Bosch maintained they were clean or provided no evidence to the contrary, or the players weren't under MLB control when they doped or by the time they were caught.

Those players include Dominican outfielder Wilkin Ramirez, who has played parts of three seasons including 2013 for Detroit, Atlanta, and Minnesota, and is currently still in the Twins organization. He is listed at least five times in Bosch's books, next to two charges for $1,000 each and the phrase "delivery and protocol."

Felix Pie has had a six-year big league career, and in 2013 he played for the Pittsburgh Pirates. Bosch indicated that Pie owed him $2,500 on two occasions and even referred to him by his baseball nickname of "Felix the Cat." (As of this writing, Pie is playing baseball in Korea.)

Ronny Paulino, a catcher, has played for four major league teams since 2005, and he spent 2013 in the farm systems for the Baltimore Orioles and Detroit Tigers. His name makes nine appearances in Bosch's notebooks, next to a cell phone number once registered in his name, the phrase *minor leaguer*, and an address in Weston, Florida. Bosch's records indicate that he provided testosterone troches and made deliveries to Paulino—who played for the Mets and the Orioles in 2011 and 2012, respectively—in New York and Baltimore.

Baseball officials apparently determined that Paulino shouldn't face additional punishment for his Biogenesis links, because he had been suspended for fifty games in August 2010 after failing a drug test, presumably while on the Bosch regimen. (Paulino claimed that the positive test was the result of taking a diet pill.) In February 2014, however, Paulino tested positive for exogenous testosterone and was suspended for one hundred games.

At the time of the Biogenesis suspensions, Adrian Nieto was a prospect in the Chicago White Sox organization. Nieto was enrolled at the Fort

Lauderdale–area Plantation High School when he first started seeing Bosch. He is listed at least seventeen times in the Biogenesis records—his customary payment was $500 cash—and Bosch wrote "ballplayer" after his name.

And nineteen days after the suspensions, Ricardo Cespedes signed a $725,000 contract with the New York Mets on his sixteenth birthday. Cespedes was—as revealed by Bosch's letter to Juan Carlos Nunez—an apparent Biogenesis client under the wing of the ACES employee, though MLB could garner no evidence that he received PEDs from Bosch.

If any baseball fan—some mythically naïve kid in America's heartland—still considered the sport's stars to be infallible heroes, that notion must have finally been euthanized after thirteen players accepted their punishment. Players who had adamantly and angrily denied any links to Bosch now accepted their suspension, mostly in silence.

Some tepid, vague apologies were issued via representatives or read aloud to reporters. (Cruz: "I want to apologize . . . for the mistake I made." Peralta: "In spring of 2012, I made a terrible mistake that I deeply regret.") Cervelli, the Yankees catcher who MLB officials believed was outed by his far wealthier teammate, was so disturbed by his suspension that he didn't even show up for the game that night, causing him to be fined by the team.

With the rest of the suspensions issued, Braun issued a one-thousand-word statement in which he finally confessed to the drugs he said Bosch gave him. "During the latter part of the 2011 season, I was dealing with a nagging injury and I turned to products for a short period of time that I shouldn't have used," the statement read. "The products were a cream and a lozenge which I was told could help expedite my rehabilitation."

All eyes were on A-Rod, though one retired major league pitcher was fixated on a lesser, appropriately named former nemesis from their joint tenure in the Philadelphia Phillies bullpen. "Hey, Antonio Bastardo," tweeted Dan Meyer, "remember when we competed for a job in 2011. Thx alot. #ahole."

Bud Selig took a probably premature victory lap. "We continue to attack this issue on every front from science and research, to education and awareness, to fact-finding and investigative skills," the commissioner said in a statement.

In his mind, he had lopped "steroid commissioner" cleanly from among his honorary titles.

Jose Canseco, for one, wasn't buying it. "All of a sudden, Bud Selig, that coward, doesn't want his legacy to be that he was the steroid commissioner," the former slugger said in an interview for this book. "It shows his arrogance. That's like me saying I don't want my legacy to be that I *used* steroids."

But drug-testing experts laud the turnaround, however tardy it may have come. Just a decade earlier, the idea of baseball's commissioner lobbing more than a dozen suspensions at players who hadn't even failed tests—and the union supporting the punishments—would have been a fever dream.

"The light switch went on in terms of the threat these drugs played in the game of baseball," says Travis Tygart, the USADA chief. "After BALCO hit them hard, they made a really smart move in hiring Senator Mitchell and his team . . . and that report laid the groundwork for the response we saw in Biogenesis."

To have Alex Rodriguez return to Major League Baseball on the same day his record suspension was announced created a bizarre spectacle. Sportswriters traveled to Chicago from all over the country. A Boston media outlet live-blogged the otherwise unremarkable August contest.

As word of the suspension broke on every news channel, Rodriguez sat on a couch and watched canned footage of that night's opposition, White Sox pitcher Jose Quintana. Reporters stalked Rodriguez from a distance in the visiting clubhouse at US Cellular Field in Chicago.

As he had already announced, the next day the union would appeal the suspension on his behalf, allowing Rodriguez to play through the rest of the 2013 season.

For every other Biogenesis-linked major leaguer, the suspensions added up to a cost of doing business. All of them would be back in time for the playoffs if their teams made it. New, lucrative contracts would be signed in the off-season. Careers would go on.

Rodriguez peeled himself off the couch and headed to yet another press conference. It was a choked-up, emotionally schizophrenic appearance. At one moment, he lamented the "nightmare" of the last seven months. He complained of undergoing multiple surgeries and being thirty-eight years old. A few seconds later, he was exclaiming with bright eyes that he felt once again like an eighteen-year-old making his debut at Fenway Park in 1994. He thanked his "Dominican people and all the Hispanics all over the world."

Then he remarked: "I'm fighting for my life. I have to defend myself. If I don't defend myself, no one will."

Though Rodriguez and his juicing ilk have often been accused of ruining the sport, nobody can imbue a no-account dog-days-of-summer ballgame with a carnival atmosphere quite like an embattled A-Rod. The Yankees were a mediocre team and the White Sox were worse, but seemingly all of South Side Chicago streamed into the stadium in order to rain boos on Rodriguez's every at-bat. A cadre of Yankee fans—calling themselves "A-Rod Army"—waved signs featuring drawings of syringes and the slogan: "A-Roid's better than no 'roids!"

He singled once in four at-bats. The Yankees lost 8–1 in a game where almost nothing interesting occurred on the field.

At war with Major League Baseball and the Yankees, Rodriguez seemed to be adding enemies to his shit list daily. The players union was next on the docket.

Confined to a wheelchair with a voice made raspy and weak by the brain tumor that was killing him, MLBPA chief Michael Weiner went on Sirius/XM's Mad Dog Sports Radio to talk A-Rod the day after his comeback in Chicago.

Weiner called the 211-game punishment "far too much," but then revealed that he had told Rodriguez to accept a suspension for a lesser amount of games if Selig had offered it. "I don't want to give a number," said Weiner, "but there was a number that I gave A-Rod that we advised him to take. He was never given that number."

Host Chris Russo wondered: Wouldn't that be an admission that Rodriguez took PEDs?

"It's a question of evidence," Weiner responded. "Each player has to make his own decision as to whether he used or not. Based on the evidence that we saw, we made a recommendation. The commissioner's office didn't meet it."

Though Rodriguez refused to answer reporters' questions about Weiner's comments after another game in Chicago, privately he was fuming. Rodriguez's public stance was always that he was completely innocent and undeserving of one day—"one inning," as he liked to say—of suspension. And Don Fehr and Gene Orza would never have spoken of accepting suspensions. During the heyday of the Steroid Era, the former union bosses had been too busy railing against the league and claiming that baseball had no doping problem to worry about. Now, Weiner, who by virtue of his position was responsible for defending Rodriguez in his appeal, appeared to be undermining him.

Rodriguez believed that early on in the Biogenesis aftermath, the union had decided not to charge hard on his behalf, instead saving its fire for other battles with the league.

The thin-skinned Rodriguez has total recall for the times he's been wronged. This was the last straw in his relationship with Weiner, who had irked Rodriguez with his public comments since July. "Our players that deserve suspensions, we will try to cope with their suspensions," Weiner had said during the All-Star Game. Then he had told the *Daily News*: "I can tell you, if we have a case where there really is overwhelming evidence, that a player committed a violation of the program, our fight is going to be that they make a deal."

The day after Weiner's appearance on Mad Dog Sports Radio, Rodriguez had his legal team fire off a letter to the union expressing his "extreme shock and disappointment."

It was the beginning of a terminal rift between Rodriguez and his union. In the good old days, Donald Fehr would have raged against the suspension, thrown the whole drug-testing program into doubt, and made Selig's life a living hell. Rodriguez never seemed to realize that times had changed and as far as Weiner was concerned, the majority of players who were clean wanted the kinds of tests that Fehr had fought against for so long.

The way Rodriguez saw it, the Players Association should have been condemning MLB's strategic media leaks and intimidating legal and extra-legal tactics in Florida. The MLBPA "has made matters worse by failing to protest M.L.B.'s thuggish tactics in its investigation," Rodriguez's attorneys wrote in another letter later that month, "including paying individuals to produce documents and to testify on M.L.B.'s behalf, and bullying and intimidating those individuals who refuse to cooperate with their 'witch hunt' against the players—indeed principally Mr. Rodriguez."

He asked the union not to represent him in his arbitration hearing, a request they rejected. The union then leaked the letter to the *New York Times*, according to Rodriguez, only infuriating him further.

On August 10, Rodriguez was drug tested. He pissed clean.

Six days later, a week and a half into Rodriguez's return to the Yankees, *60 Minutes* aired a story that was bound to make his life in a major league clubhouse yet more awkward. The show, citing "two sources with direct knowledge of the matter," claimed that members of Rodriguez's "inner circle" had leaked the documents implicating Braun to Yahoo! Sports.

Rodriguez attorney David Cornwell denied the allegations and called them "another attempt to harm Alex"—he didn't say by whom—"this time by driving a wedge between Alex and other players in the game."

But Team A-Rod, as has been stated, was the only entity with Bosch records and any conceivable motive to leak them at this time. Though *60*

Minutes did not name who exactly supplied the documents to Yahoo! Sports, baseball officials were already positive (to the point of fighting him in federal court to admit the fact) that Rodriguez's PR guru, Michael Sitrick, was the leaker.

By mid-August, Rodriguez had successfully ostracized his employers, colleagues, professional allies, and family members alike. Confidantes and loved ones who had been with him throughout his life had abandoned him. That uncle, Augusto Bolivar Navarro, who had lived in Washington Heights during Rodriguez's first years and been like a surrogate father, had died in 2005. A-Rod's relationship with formerly inseparable cousin Yuri Sucart had been lost to public betrayal and threats of litigation. Eddie Rodriguez, who had practically raised Alex at a Miami-area Boys & Girls Club, had finally had enough of his former protégé upon hearing about the renewed cheating, according to a mutual acquaintance. Yankees president Randy Levine, from whom Alex Rodriguez had once regularly received paternal e-mails—"U are the man. I told u that for years. U can and will do it," is one such message from 2011—now appeared to Rodriguez as a member of the enemy cabal. Even Don Hooton, who traveled the country speaking with Rodriguez to kids about the dangers of steroids following the first scandal in 2009, had cut ties. "Once the Biogenesis news broke, we basically just hit the pause button," Hooton says in an interview for this book. "The word that I'd use to describe my feelings is *disappointment*."

Like a fat man in a brothel, it appeared that the only friends Rodriguez had left were those whom he paid handsomely. He had replaced Roy Black, the Miami attorney, and Sitrick with another extremely expensive team of specialists. An Atlanta-based sports statute wonk, Cornwell was the seasoned vet at defending athletes in doping cases. He had represented Braun in his successful fight to overturn the 2012 ban. (In the Biogenesis aftermath, Cornwell also defended Cervelli, making the situation trickier if Rodriguez was behind leaking the documents to Yahoo! Sports.)

James McCarroll and Jordan Siev of the high-profile Manhattan law firm Reed Smith were also in Rodriguez's entourage. Ron Berkowitz, who represents Jay Z—a presumably far easier client—handled Rodriguez's publicity.

And Rodriguez's lead private investigator, Andrew O'Connell, was a former Secret Service agent and federal prosecutor. When Dominique Strauss-Kahn was accused of raping a Manhattan hotel maid, the head of the International Monetary Fund hired O'Connell. Through interviews with hotel employees and analysis of phone records, surveillance videos, and key card entries, the bald, pugnacious investigator pieced together a labyrinthine timeline of the day of the alleged attack that cast doubt on the purported victim's story. The charges were ultimately dismissed.

Now O'Connell was in Miami, trying to unravel a case that was just as complicated.

Flanking O'Connell on these Florida fact-finding missions was a former hockey enforcer squeezed into a tailored Italian suit. Attorney Joe Tacopina became the public face of Rodriguez's defense, a deflecting figure whose heady grandiosity made his client appear almost down-to-earth in comparison.

The "most hated lawyer in New York," as Tacopina was dubbed by the *New York Post*, dresses like a playboy and wears his hair slicked straight back. A former hockey player at Skidmore College, he holds the NCAA record for minutes spent in the penalty box for brawling: 412. A Brooklyn kid who worked as a prosecutor in that borough, Tacopina—a Yankees fan—is now part-owner of the Italian soccer team A.S. Roma.

"Mr. Tacopina is to the defense bar what Donald Trump is to real estate," a *New York Times* scribe once wrote. The Maserati-driving Tacopina is proud of his reputation for winning the freedom of some of Gotham's most villainous characters. In his office in a Madison Avenue high-rise, he's framed the cover of the *New York Post* from the day after he gained the acquittal of two NYPD officers charged for their alleged roles in the 1997 sodomy of prisoner Abner Louima. JUSTICE DEFILED, screams the headline. Next to that—and a Yankees-branded bat signed by Alex Rodriguez—is a framed op-ed for the *Daily News* in which Tacopina wrote that a Florida jury was correct to acquit George Zimmerman in the shooting death of Trayvon Martin.

In an interview for this book, Tacopina did not veil his hatred for Bud Selig. "He's the world's biggest hypocrite," Tacopina said. "Here's a guy who's been found guilty of collusion, and he wants to talk about the integrity of the game."

But Tacopina's national television debut performance in defense of Rodriguez did not go well. On August 19, Tacopina was interviewed by Matt Lauer on the *TODAY* show. In a gambit he had tried on shows with lesser audiences, Tacopina lamented that he couldn't talk about Biogenesis, or Rodriguez's drug-testing history, because of the confidentiality agreement between the union and the league. "If the vice president of Major League Baseball would be good enough to waive the confidentiality clause," Tacopina told interviewer Matt Lauer in his tumbling cadence, "I would love nothing more than to talk about Alex's Rodriguez's testing history and various things."

MLB was clearly prepared for Tacopina's bluff. Lauer indicated a document in his hand. "Joe, that office sent us a letter overnight saying they are willing to do exactly that," said Lauer, handing the paper to Tacopina.

The letter stated that with Tacopina's signature, both Rodriguez and league officials would be permitted to fling open Rodriguez's closet full of skeletons: the results of every drug test he'd taken, all prior violations of the drug program, all documents and messages related to Rodriguez's treatment by Bosch, all documents related to Rodriguez's treatment by Anthony Galea and Victor Conte, and all evidence of Rodriguez's obstruction of the MLB investigation.

Unsurprisingly, Tacopina did not sign the letter unleashing the records.

Gaining less ink was the fact that Rodriguez's story had now changed. Immediately after the Biogenesis exposé, Sitrick had released the statement denying any "purported relationship" between Bosch and Rodriguez. It was a lie that became more bold-faced when Bosch showed that Rodriguez had wired him just under $75,000 soon after the *New Times* article. (Roughly $50,000 was returned, as a purported error.)

And now Tacopina told Lauer of Rodriguez and Bosch: "There was a relationship, obviously, but these facts will be answered at an appellate process hearing."

Later, in an appearance on CNN, Tacopina reiterated: "Clearly there was a relationship—a consulting relationship." Even if you believed that Bosch had aided Rodriguez only on nutritional matters, which became Team A-Rod's new story, there was no denying that Rodriguez had initially lied.

A bruising day turned literal as, on the evening after Tacopina's *TODAY* appearance, the Yankees traveled to Fenway Park for their first game against the loathed Red Sox since Rodriguez's return from injury.

The first pitch Rodriguez saw from Red Sox starter Ryan Dempster just missed his knees, sending him skittering out of the batter's box. Three pitches later, Dempster corrected his aim, beaning Rodriguez in the left shoulder. Fenway erupted in roaring approval.

An umpire issued warnings to both teams but didn't eject Dempster, causing Yankees manager Joe Girardi to race out of the dugout cursing, getting tossed from the game himself as a result.

Rodriguez seethed silently as he took first base. It was clear Dempster was expressing the shared opinion of the Red Sox pitching staff: that Rodriguez shouldn't be allowed to play while his appeal was pending. "I've got a problem with it," Boston pitcher John Lackey had told reporters. "You bet I do. How is he still playing?"

In the sixth inning, with the Yankees down 6–3, Rodriguez got what he later called "the ultimate payback" by slamming a pitch from Dempster ten rows deep into Fenway's center-field bleachers. The homer sparked a comeback in a wild game that ended with the Yankees winning by a score of 9–6.

Wearing a business suit in front of his locker after the game, Rodriguez excoriated Dempster in his *Leave It to Beaver*–under-pressure speaking style.

"Whether you like me or hate me, what's wrong is wrong, and that was unprofessional and silly," he declared.

Asked if Dempster should be suspended for beaning him, Rodriguez entered a Catskills comedy routine. "I'm the wrong guy to be asking about suspensions," said a wide-eyed Rodriguez as the crowd of beat reporters burst out laughing. "Holy mackerel!"

So he would never be Derek Jeter. But Rodriguez was making the slightest inroads toward being sympathetic again. Considering he had started his season as the most loathed active athlete in pro sports, there was nowhere to go but up.

B y mid-September, AROD Corporation—the corporate entity that controlled his little empire—was firmly in the clandestine information-gathering business. If MLB was going to unleash an battalion of ex-cops and former FBI agents on Miami to take down Rodriguez, the slugger decided he'd deploy his own squad of underlings to outwit baseball's detectives. Their job was simple: Collect evidence that MLB had screwed up in its unfair crusade to snare A-Rod. That evidence was later shared with these authors.

O'Connell, Oggi Velazquez, and Pepe Gomez, among other Rodriguez associates, had retraced the MLB investigators' warpath through South Florida. In May, Team A-Rod had gotten Pete Carbone to sign a sworn affidavit stating that MLB investigators had harassed him and his tanning salon customers, and that Porter Fischer was "mentally unstable and an abuser of alcohol and drugs."

Now as Rodriguez prepared for his arbitration hearing, they had Albir sign an affidavit declaring that the MLB investigators "repeatedly pressured, harassed and threatened me and my family" and impersonated cops in their attempt to get the former UM player to talk. Collazo signed a document for Team A-Rod in which he said he had been "intimidated" by MLB, which had threatened to involve his family and go to the media.

Robert Davis Miller dished on his old party buddy's alleged prolific cocaine use and provided the photo of Bosch and two baggies of white powder resembling cocaine.

And Lorraine Delgadillo provided an affidavit describing her tryst with Mullin. "After dinner we drove back to my home. There, Investigator Mullin and I had sex," read a couple of lines of her account, which, by the very nature of being an affidavit, is not extremely romantic.

As the MLB investigators had, Rodriguez attained these testimonials by throwing around great gobs of baseball profit. A game's salary to Rodriguez was a life-changing sum to an average person. For Delgadillo's affidavit, the Valentine Mullin had left at her door, and her cell phone containing text messages between them, Team A-Rod gave Delgadillo $105,000.

MLB and Rodriguez played human tug-of-war over a potentially important witness. Since May, Major League Baseball had been collecting the testimony of Bruli Medina Reyes, the Dominican trainer who Rodriguez had met at the 2009 World Baseball Classic. Sucart had arranged for Reyes to train Rodriguez in 2010 and 2011.

MLB investigators first showed up at the door of his home in the DR in the wake of the Biogenesis exposé. They flew him to New York City, where he sat through marathon debriefing sessions at MLB headquarters. They had Reyes sign an affidavit describing Rodriguez's relationship with Bosch, and having personally observed Sucart and Bosch injecting Rodriguez.

Reyes was looking like a star witness, and MLB stalked him across the globe, visiting him in Florida and Canada and bringing him and his family back to New York on baseball's dime in September. That's where he learned that the league intended to have him testify against Rodriguez. Reyes later claimed that MLB investigators threatened to jeopardize his US work visa if he refused.

Pepe Gomez found Reyes in the New York City hotel where MLB had him holed up. He told Reyes that Rodriguez would "take care of him," according to a later arbitration document, arranged for the trainer to be moved with his family to another nearby hotel where MLB wouldn't have control over him, and took over his legal and New York living expenses.

Reyes had switched sides. When he did speak at the arbitration, it was about how MLB made him sign their bogus affidavits. An arbitrator ultimately declared Reyes moot, saying "his demeanor under oath and contradictory declaration rendered all of his testimony suspect and unreliable."

Rodriguez tracked these cold war chess moves while suited up for the Yankees. These were bizarre characters to have dealings with one of the world's wealthiest athletes: a tanning salon owner, a convicted counterfeiter, an ex-con who bragged about cocaine use. But Rodriguez—he of Pepe, Yuri, and Oggi—has never surrounded himself with only the glossy hangers-on that might be in the orbit of somebody like David Beckham.

Besides, Rodriguez was less ballplayer and more litigant as the summer wore on. In forty-four games for the Yankees in 2013, Rodriguez did show some pop. He hit seven home runs, and on September 21 even passed Yankee legend Lou Gehrig for the all-time grand slam record when he hit the twenty-fourth of his career. The Yankees lingered in playoff contention until late in that month but were ultimately shut out of the postseason for only the second time since 1994.

Rodriguez spent the last three days of the 2013 baseball season riding the bench in Houston. His legs were stiff, so he watched from the dugout, surely plotting, as the Yankees played three absolutely unimportant games against the lowly Astros.

On September 30, the day after the season ended, Rodriguez reported to his arbitration hearing while Team A-Rod made its largest, and seemingly most important, purchase in Florida.

Bobby from Boca had, earlier in the summer, reached Rodriguez and offered to sell him stolen Biogenesis records. Rodriguez had turned him down, likely because he already had a set. But now Bobby—real name Gary Lee Jones—had something else to sell.

Jones signed an affidavit in which he detailed Dan Mullin's purchases of two sets of stolen records—the flash drive that he claimed Porter Fischer had given him, and the records that were pilfered from Fischer's rental car—for a total of $150,000 of baseball's money. (In his own account, Rob

Manfred has put the figure at $125,000. Also, Jones did not say how he got possession of the stolen docs, only that he "obtained" them.) He described Mullin pushing him envelopes of cash at Cosmos Diner. "The cash was loose, in fifties and hundreds," Jones added.

Jones described in the affidavit a later meeting with Mullin in which the investigator, apparently without irony, warned him of his legal liability. "They told me that I could be arrested for having been involved with stolen property," wrote Jones.

Then, with Rodriguez at MLB headquarters on the first day of his fight for his baseball future, Jones sold a member of Team A-Rod video of Mullin purchasing one set of the documents. The film had been surreptitiously recorded by Anthony Carbone one booth over, according to multiple sources familiar with the video.

Gary Lee Jones demanded $200,000 for the film. (A source close to Rodriguez denies that they received the full video. The source says Jones was paid only a "deposit" for the film but never produced the entire recording.)

MLB may have bought itself all the evidence it needed to try to boot A-Rod from the game, but the slugger had purchased his own evidence that baseball's investigators had skirted ethics and broken the law to do it.

CHAPTER SEVENTEEN

The "Farce"

Those twelve men who had gathered outside of MLB's Park Avenue head-quarters with signs bearing slogans like BOSCH LIAR! after the last game of the Yankees' season had transformed into a noisy daily horde by mid-October as Rodriguez's arbitration proceeding entered its second week. The hearing upstairs ultimately stretched for eleven calendar weeks, or thirteen actual days of the court-like proceeding.

The number of protesters topped one hundred. They were men and women, young and old, all of them apparently Hispanic, some of them waving Dominican flags. Rodriguez could have slipped in through a side door each morning undetected. But that's not his style.

He developed a daily routine. Around nine A.M., an Escalade zoomed up to the curb and a natty Rodriguez hopped out, his attorneys stiff-arming their way through a crowd of whistling and nonsense-yelling reporters and photographers, as their superstar charged toward the crowded corral of protesters.

He never spoke to the reporters, only cooed sweet nothings to the pro-testers as he signed photos, baseballs, and T-shirts with the text SUPPORT A-ROD arced over his number thirteen.

Then he bounded up the stairs and into the building. He exited again at five, six, or seven P.M., after a day spent listening to Anthony Bosch detail his drug regimen or watching Joe Tacopina spar with Rob Manfred. Rodriguez looked markedly more harried during these exits, rushing straight into the backseat of the waiting Cadillac SUV.

The slogans on the supporters' placards—often written in the same hand—tended to resemble something unloaded directly from Rodriguez's increasingly paranoid brain, referencing disputes that had not yet been made public.

For example, RANDY LEVINE IS THE DEVIL was a popular sign slogan in the protest pit during the arbitration hearing, a reference to the Yankees president, who Rodriguez was certain had betrayed him to MLB. A newsperson asked the protesters carrying the signs if they knew who Randy Levine was, and they confessed they had no idea. BUD SELIG IS A CHILD KILLER, read another sign, a reference to the commissioner being weak on mandating steroid testing for young prospects in the Dominican Republic. TONY BOSCH IS A DRUG DEALER FOR MINORS. The signs were like a daily diary for Rodriguez's most bitter musings.

One of the protesters tweeted: "Getting paid, breakfast and lunch is on the house just to support my favorite player A-Rod hell yeah." (The man later said he was not getting paid after all.) Another protester wrote on Twitter: "I'm Dominican for today lol." At lunchtime, pizza was delivered to the protest pit via a mystery benefactor.

The protesters were led by a squat, dark-browed bald man named Fernando Mateo, the founder of the Manhattan-based charity Hispanics Across America. Years earlier, he had hand-delivered caskets to MLB headquarters in a stunt to urge the league to test Dominican prospects for performance-enhancing drugs. Now, as Rodriguez hustled into the building one morning, Mateo jostled with a stern female security guard in a pantsuit.

She spilled coffee on him. The next morning, Mateo was again outside the building—in a neck brace—vowing to press charges concerning the java assault.

"Their key witness," Mateo then said of Bosch, "is a guy you can't trust. He's a liar! He's a drug dealer! He injected kids with steroids!"

"I have a lot of good Jewish friends who agree with me!" Mateo suddenly declared. Up stepped a man in a yarmulke—who later gave his name as Jona Rechnitz—to announce that he too supported Alex Rodriguez.

Mateo later acknowledged that his non-profit received $100,000 from an anonymous donor with the stipulation that the money be spent on supporting Alex Rodriguez. The superstar's camp denies that he was behind the donation.

In mid-October, Hispanics Across America took out a full-page ad in the *New York Times* with a photo of Bud Selig next to banner reading, WHO IS PUBLIC ENEMY NO. 1 IN BASEBALL?

"We remember Selig sitting in the front rows watching Slamming Sammy Sosa and Mark McGuire hitting crazy home runs while using performance enhancing drugs," read a line of the accompanying open letter signed by Mateo. (The ad cost $106,000, according to the newspaper, although apparently very little was spent on copyediting.)

New York State lawmakers showed up to join the fray: Assemblywoman Gabriela Rosa, Senator Adriano Espaillat, and Senator Ruben Diaz, best known for his virulent opposition to gay marriage.

One early afternoon Diaz, wearing a cowboy hat, led a vigil of about fifty Hispanic ministers outside the Park Avenue building. In the broad daylight as businesspeople hustled around them to lunch appointments, Diaz and the ministers lit candles and prayed quietly for A-Rod's safe return to baseball.

I f the scene downstairs was bizarre, a circus of a different breed was developing on the sixth floor of the building, over green tea muffins, Greek yogurt, and lattes in a conference room in MLB offices.

Though arbitration hearings are required to be kept confidential, a procession of media leaks kept arbitrator Fredric Horowitz constantly agitated, forcing him on a near-daily basis to admonish both MLB lawyers and Rodriguez's legal team to stop gabbing to reporters. Attorneys representing Rodriguez and Bosch nearly came to blows during a bathroom break. Rodriguez was scolded for grimacing and muttering during the proceedings. Tacopina and Manfred got into heated under-oath battles as Rodriguez's attorney accused the baseball executive of helping to shield a man who dealt narcotics to minors, in proceedings detailed for the first time by these authors. And ultimately, the defendant in this de facto prosecution stormed out of the proceeding in a cursing rage.

Ten years before Rodriguez's arbitration, Horowitz, a Berkeley graduate and Santa Monica–based professional arbitrator between union workers and their employers, was hearing cases like that of a $65,000-per-year professor who was fired for letting his students out of class early. He worked his way to bigger-money disputes, like those between Delta Air Lines and its pilots as a strike loomed, and arbitrated National Hockey League union disputes. By 2008, the Los Angeles Dodgers fan had made it to the "Transactions" small print of newspaper sports pages, deciding the salaries of baseball players who hadn't vested enough time in the bigs to be declared free agents.

Being an MLB arbitrator is a well-compensated part-time gig for a specially licensed attorney. Horowitz had taken over as baseball's lead arbitrator, putting him in charge of suspension appeals, in early 2012 after Shyam Das was canned by Selig for overturning Ryan Braun's punishment. Horowitz received $69,141 from the Players Association for his work in 2013, according to publicly released union financials. The league paid him at least $62,000 as well, their share of his pay for arbitrations. The bulk of Horowitz's year of baseball work was the case of Alex Rodriguez.

But Horowitz's first drug suspension appeal hearing showed that he was no pushover for players, even if there was evidence that the athlete had committed the infraction accidentally. In mid-2012, pitcher Guillermo Mota—before Rodriguez, the harshest-punished ballplayer for performance-enhancing drugs—appealed a hundred-game suspension for testing positive for the banned substance Clenbuterol, his second such failed test.

Mota claimed he had accidentally drunk the substance in his kid's cold medicine. Horowitz upheld the hundred-game ban "despite finding Mota's ingestion of a [PED] contained in a cough syrup taken to treat a cold was unintentional," according to an arbitration document made public following Rodriguez's hearing.

The sixty-three-year-old had never arbitrated a hearing like that of Rodriguez's. Then again, nobody had.

Held in a conference room past corporate baseball's strangely decorated hallways featuring thirty life-size figures in MLB uniforms with televisions for heads, the hearing resembled a lax court proceeding.

Technically, Horowitz was only one of a three-person panel deciding Rodriguez's fate. But the other two panel members were partial by design. MLBPA counsel David M. Prouty, who had taken the union's reins during Michael Weiner's illness, represented the Players Association. Rob Manfred, baseball's hard-nosed chief operating officer, represented the league. The rubber vote, and thus the only one that mattered, belonged to panel chair Horowitz.

The proceeding was transcribed, and all testimony was under oath. There were opening statements. Witnesses were called and cross-examined, documents were entered into evidence, and there were closing statements.

Rodriguez had eleven of his attorneys and legal associates in the arbitration room with him. Major League Baseball had a rotating cast of more than a dozen of its own attorneys. Between transcribing and other personnel, according to a source at the hearing, the room was packed with as many as thirty-five individuals.

Despite having enough legal defenders to field a baseball team and keep two on the bench, Rodriguez was technically defended by Prouty, as the representative of the union. This was much to the chagrin of the embattled superstar, who had tried in vain to appoint his own arbitrator. "The MLBPA-appointed arbitrator consistently advised Mr. Rodriguez that he represented the interests of the union as a whole, and not Mr. Rodriguez individually, and had to act accordingly," Team A-Rod complained in a later lawsuit.

Rodriguez argued that Bosch had provided him only with nonbanned nutritional supplements, including amino acids, vitamins, BioEFA, alpha lipoic acid, cider vinegar, ginseng, and fish oil.

The greatest evidence that Rodriguez hadn't used a banned substance in the three years he was purportedly a Bosch client, his side argued in the hearing, was *science* itself. Since 2010, Rodriguez had been tested by MLB for banned drugs twelve times. On none of those instances had he tested positive.

Team A-Rod also railed that he was being unfairly punished in comparison to the suspensions levied against Bosch's other clients—an argument Rodriguez quickly lost. Since the other Biogenesis clients had all negotiated "nonprecedential" settlements with MLB, Horowitz said the length of their suspensions couldn't be considered.

As the opening statements wrapped up, in the afternoon of the first day of the hearing, Anthony Bosch strolled in. With his hair neatly trimmed and stubble scoured from his cheeks, the steroid dealer cleaned up nice. Bosch was the star witness for MLB and ultimately the only witness of much significance to the arbitrator's ruling.

As MLB attorney Howard Ganz asked questions, Bosch told the story of his Belizean education, his pseudomedical work in Texas and Florida, and his aspirations, through Biogenesis, to "build a nutritional consulting practice with an emphasis on clinical nutrition, research, education, and product development." His testimony was his grandiose notebook scrawlings come to life.

Then he told how, through Bosch's clients Oggi Velazquez and then Yuri Sucart, Alex Rodriguez had tried one of his testosterone troches and fallen in love with its "explosive effect."

In explicit detail, Bosch described his three-year dalliance with the Yankees' third baseman, one of meeting in a bathroom at a Miami Starbucks and using a service elevator in an Atlanta hotel room and supplying Rodriguez with HGH and peptides during his dismal Detroit playoff series.

As MLB attorneys painstakingly entered notebook pages, doping protocols, and BlackBerry and text messages into evidence, Bosch verified and explained the materials. He described to Horowitz his and Rodriguez's bumbling virtual spy game of transparent codes and text-messaged questions as to "pink" and piss tests.

As Bosch's testimony wore on, the former hockey brawler Tacopina got agitated. During a bathroom break, according to a person who was at the hearing, Tacopina asked Ganz how much longer Bosch was expected to monopolize the witness stand.

Probably another day and a half, Tacopina was told. "We'll have to recall him in October, then," Tacopina said of Bosch, before taking a jab at the fact that a grand jury in Florida was reportedly investigating Bosch. "That's if he's still at liberty."

"Yeah, well, if he goes down, everyone's going down!" shot back Julio Ayala, Bosch's attorney and longtime friend. They jawed at each other some more, and suddenly Tacopina and Ayala were in each other's faces. "Keep talking, tough guy!" the source says Tacopina yelled. Only senior citizen Ganz saved the conference room full of attorneys from turning into a brawl, jumping between Tacopina and Ayala, with his hair wild and tie askew.

More attorneys restrained the men before any blows were thrown.

Bosch and Rodriguez missed the scuffle because they were—not for the first time, according to Bosch's testimony—in the bathroom together.

Each night, Tony Bosch returned to the New York hotel room where he was holed up for weeks. He was scared to leave and too stressed out to talk to anyone.

When the arbitration began, Bosch was a conflicted mess, says his longtime friend Hernan Dominguez, who traveled to New York to stay with Bosch during parts of the process: "He felt like he was doing something wrong by testifying against this guy."

At first, Bosch felt no anger toward his former client Rodriguez and blamed only Porter Fischer and others for putting him in a situation where he had to snitch. "He has a lot of guilt because he feels he didn't bring this down on himself," says Dominguez. "This was brought on by his disgruntled business partners."

But then it was Rodriguez's turn to cross-examine Bosch. That lasted two full days. Rodriguez's attorneys grilled him about the deal he had struck with MLB, with the league protecting him and his family from civil litigation, vouching for him to criminal prosecutors, and rewarding him with financial remuneration including a $2,400-a-day security retainer.

It was the same argument most any defendant makes in court when confronted by a snitch: suggesting that the witness has enough at stake to fabricate testimony.

Then Team A-Rod attempted to attack Bosch's character. The attorneys asked Bosch about his use of forged prescriptions. They asked him who was his wholesale source for the banned and illegal substances. They tried to snare Bosch into talking about the high school students he supplied, those clients in the notebooks with "HS" written next to their names.

He asked about Bosch's alleged cocaine habit. He wondered whether Bosch had declared all that income he'd received from Rodriguez and other cash clients. Team A-Rod was trying to drive home a point: How could Horowitz trust a man who made his living selling banned and illegal substances?

Bosch's guilt began to fade. Whatever happened, he thought to himself, Alex Rodriguez would still be one of the richest athletes in the world. He'd still have beautiful women throwing themselves at his feet. Bosch was penniless and facing jail time, all for helping him out. And now Rodriguez was sliming his name in attacks that were leaking out to tabloids?

"By the third or the fourth or the fifth day when they'd been treating him so badly, he started to think, 'Why am I taking the hit here?'" Dominguez says. "A-Rod is still going to his mansion. And Tony is left with lawsuits and a criminal grand jury."

He actually started to enjoy himself. Four little words became his best friend: *I plead the Fifth.*

Rodriguez's attorneys were furious. Bosch had readily answered all of Manfred's interrogatories. Now he refused to respond to any questions they posed, hiding behind the Fifth Amendment.

It was clearly a premeditated strategy. Team A-Rod argued that all of Bosch's testimony should be stricken if he pleaded the Fifth to any question. Horowitz rejected that argument.

By October 4, when Bosch's testimony finally ended on the fifth day of arbitration, Rodriguez felt he was being thwarted at every turn. He believed the arbitrator was in MLB's pocket, afraid to receive the same payback termination as Shyam Das.

His vociferous legal team felt confined even by the flimsy gag order, which kept them from openly airing their grievances with the press and Rodriguez's fans. Team A-Rod had so many complaints to share with the world.

That night, Alex Rodriguez filed two lawsuits. The first, in Bronx County, was against Yankees doctor Christopher Ahmad and New York–Presbyterian/Columbia University Medical Center. The ongoing case (as of April 2014) accuses Ahmad of hiding the results of the October 2012 MRI, as Rodriguez struggled in the playoffs, without informing him of the labral tear in his left hip. Ahmad "knowingly cleared [Rodriguez] to resume playing as a third baseman for the New York Yankees during the . . . playoffs, thus allowing [Rodriguez] to further injure himself and the necessity for additional surgeries," according to the legal complaint.

The lawsuit goes to the edge of conspiracy. His e-mails with Randy Levine, and his claim that the Yankees president had said that the team "would rather Alex never step on the baseball field" after the hip injury, leaped over that precipice. Rodriguez is convinced that the Yankees had purposely attempted to injure him.

The second legal action, this one initially filed in a Manhattan courthouse, was against Bud Selig and Major League Baseball. It accused baseball of filing a "sham" lawsuit in Miami-Dade County; attempting to breach his attorney-client privilege by probing whether Michael Sitrick leaked the Braun documents to Yahoo! Sports; leaking negative stories in violation of union rules; and buying, harassing, intimidating, and pressuring its way through Florida in order to bury A-Rod.

This lawsuit was A-Rod's Ginsbergian "Howl," his poetic recitation of the injustices inflicted on him as a result of baseball's malice since the Biogenesis news story broke.

He had been dropped from the Yankees-themed animated film *Henry & Me*, even though "he had already performed his own voice work for his character as the team's hero," the suit lamented. Nike and Toyota had ended sponsorship negotiations. In one claim, Alex Rodriguez made the case that he was a wronged small-business owner, MLB's leaks and premature allegations ruining "his good name and reputation" and interfering with his construction company and Houston-area Mercedes-Benz dealership.

One section of the complaint was titled "The Disastrous Tenure of Commissioner Selig." With admirable narrative tension, Rodriguez's attorneys dug back thirty years, from villain Bud Selig's "scheme to collude" as an owner to his "contentious and damaging failures" as a commissioner, including overseeing the Steroid Era.

"For the third time in his troubled tenure as owner and Commissioner, Selig had to reinvent himself," Rodriguez's attorneys wrote, referring to his post–Mitchell Report malaise. "In early 2013, such an opportunity presented itself in Southern Florida."

Rodriguez later added new exhibits to the suit, including a photo designed to show just how much Selig hated him. Taken at a 2009 All-Star Game event, it showed a smiling Selig posing with a teenager.

The kid's T-shirt read: A-ROID.

I f MLB was cowed by Rodriguez's excoriation of their scorched-earth investigation, its attorneys didn't show it. As the arbitration continued, people across the country with even a tangential relationship to his possible doping started receiving subpoenas in the Alex Rodriguez matter: "You are hereby commanded that all business and excuses be laid aside to appear and attend before the Arbitration Panel, at The Office of the Commissioner of Baseball, 245 Park Avenue . . ."

In particular, MLB attorneys were fixated on confirming the league's belief that Dr. Anthony Galea, who had treated Tiger Woods and Rodriguez at the same time, had given A-Rod performance-enhancing substances.

In mid-October, Rodriguez's fight took a field trip to Buffalo, New York, where Galea had been indicted for bringing HGH over the Canada–US border in 2009. Attorneys for MLB had filed a motion with the federal judge to unseal confidential grand jury testimony in the case, in a brazen attempt to discover whether Rodriguez or any other players had admitted to procuring banned substances from the Canadian doctor.

Attorneys for Galea, Rodriguez, and the federal government argued for a judge to keep the records sealed. Their arguments were closed to the public and supposed to be kept secret. "My understanding is that MLB's attempts to get the grand jury records were in themselves a sealed proceeding," says Galea's Canadian attorney, Brian Greenspan, in an interview for this book. "And yet you know of it, which lets me know that the MLB leaked information about their efforts. The MLB once again is conducting themselves outside the law and has breached the rules of grand jury secrecy. MLB, in its pursuit of Alex Rodriguez, has broken all the rules and its lawyers should be ashamed."

The Buffalo judge rejected MLB's motion and kept the records sealed. But league officials' attempts to lay hands on the grand jury testimony remained dogged and elaborate. In the midst of Rodriguez's arbitration, MLB's attorneys took an avid interest in an obscure small-potatoes lawsuit in suburban New York.

For years, former Toronto Blue Jays and New York Mets slugger Carlos Delgado had been embroiled in a dispute with memorabilia dealer Spencer Lader for $767,500 the player said he was owed from an autograph contract.

Lader, a disbarred attorney, learned that Delgado had been treated by Galea while on the Blue Jays. He argued in court that the contract should be voided if Delgado had used performance-enhancing substances, possibly leading to injury and reducing his memorabilia value. "I would rather spend a million dollars fighting him in court than pay him a dollar," Lader says in an interview.

In court filings, Delgado denied ever using performance-enhancing substances and provided a letter from the MLBPA stating that he had never failed a league drug test. But on October 9, Delgado sat for a deposition in the case, answering questions about his treatment by Dr. Galea. By a Nassau County judge's order, the deposition transcript was sealed.

MLB sent Lader a subpoena for any information and documents he might have gleaned concerning Rodriguez's past use of performance-enhancing substances, a demand made impossible by the Nassau County gag order. The league's interest was not in any potential doping by Delgado, who had retired after the 2009 season. They were hopeful the fellow Galea client might have somehow implicated Rodriguez.

Lader says that during conversations with the league, an MLB senior counsel asked him to subpoena the grand jury testimony from Galea's criminal case in Buffalo. Certain that the federal judge would not loosen the secret records for a civil state matter, and not wanting to spend $20,000 on legal fees involved in the attempt, Lader decided not to pursue that gambit, either.

Rodriguez wanted to complain to Horowitz about efforts by MLB to unseal his grand jury testimony in the federal Galea investigation. It was the league once again acting as if its corporate interests—delving into the drug use of an employee—trumped law-enforcement principles, in this case the secrecy of grand juries.

But the union declined to bring it up during the arbitration. Rodriguez was constantly bickering with the union honchos with whom he was supposed to be allied. He tried to get the Players Association to file a federal lawsuit seeking to end MLB's media leaks about the arbitration. Again, the union demurred, "stating that the proper venue was the ongoing grievance procedure," Rodriguez complained in a later lawsuit, "a procedure that had proven entirely ineffective at halting MLB's media campaign."

As he squabbled with the union, Rodriguez continued to attempt to discredit his accusers and the evidence they brought against him in the arbitration proceedings on Park Avenue.

An expert hired by Team A-Rod tried to cast doubt on the veracity of the Bosch BlackBerry data MLB had introduced, but he had no clear evidence of his own that it had been tampered with. Rodriguez's attorneys decried the lack of specific dates, times, and dosages in some of the records implicating the player. Tacopina and Company argued that without knowing where Bosch purchased the alleged substances, and no samples being introduced into evidence, it was impossible to determine whether the stuff was banned by baseball.

Rodriguez's former chum Randy Levine was grilled on the stand as to the purported Yankees conspiracy to exile the superstar from baseball and the e-mails he sent to Rodriguez in which he referred to PEDs, saying second baseman Robinson Cano needed some "liquid" and some "steroids fast!"

Levine, a burly man with a halo of curly hair, denied a bounty or bonus if Rodriguez was cut from the payroll, denied urging Selig to issue a lengthy suspension, said the Yankees did not speak with Yuri Sucart, and claimed that the e-mails about Cano were a joke. Bruli Medina Reyes, who had initially signed affidavits concerning Rodriguez being injected by Yuri Sucart, now testified for the defense, claiming that the league had threatened to ruin his immigration status.

Yuri Sucart himself refused to testify in the arbitration. Having washed his hands of his little *primo* after being fired and apparently threatening to sue him, Sucart ignored MLB's subpoenas just as adeptly as he had for years ignored reporters' notes and calls seeking comment.

Arbitrator Horowitz seemed unimpressed by the "indiscreet sexual liaison," as he later put it, between Dan Mullin and a former Biogenesis employee—evidence that A-Rod had paid $100,000 to get his hands on.

As the hearing stretched deep into November, Rodriguez's case appeared to have boiled down to the possibly unlawful tactics of MLB investigators and the faulty ethics of making a deal with a witness like Bosch, who had dealt drugs to minors.

On November 17, Rob Manfred took the stand. Balding and intense with a David Letterman–esque gap between his front teeth, Manfred was the heir apparent as commissioner upon Selig's departure following the 2014 season. And for better or worse, he was the scent hound who had nosed through every detail of the convoluted and potentially toxic aftermath to the Biogenesis exposé, and directly authorized baseball's actions. He was also the arbitration panel member representing the league. The transcript of his eight-hour day of testimony was obtained by these authors, a record that revealed much about Rodriguez's past PED use—the exemptions for testosterone and clomiphene citrate in 2007 and 2008 described earlier in this book—and the current scandal rocking the league.

Tacopina jousted with Manfred during his cross-examination of the baseball executive. He pointed out the letters "HS" next to certain names in the notebook pages entered into evidence. "So, of course, you had an indication Mr. Bosch was distributing drugs to minors before you entered into this agreement with him, correct?"

"Honestly, whether or not Mr. Bosch had distributed drugs to minors was not of paramount importance to me," Manfred shot back. "Rarely do you get a witness who is prepared to testify firsthand about his distribution of drugs to professional athletes, who hasn't engaged in other conduct that's illegal."

Tacopina seized on the fact that MLB had agreed to vouch for Bosch's role in advancing "the public policy goals of eradicating" PEDs from baseball. He asked Manfred if he had asked the parents of those kids on Bosch's client lists whether they were OK with MLB defending him to the Department of Justice. (Manfred's answer: "No, I didn't.") Eventually, their back-and-forth reached an acid pitch, which ran over arbitrator Horowitz's ability to interject.

"Were those important public policy goals, were they advanced by agreeing to go to authorities on behalf of Mr. Bosch for distributing narcotics to children?" Tacopina demanded. "Were they advanced?"

Over the objection of the league's own attorney, Manfred emphatically responded: "I believe those goals were advanced by disciplining players who had used performance-enhancing drugs, and thereby set a terrible example for young people who might be tempted to do the same thing, yes, I do believe that."

By November 20, with the arbitration stretching longer than any before it, cold had set in and Rodriguez's rowdy supporters had largely disappeared from Park Avenue. As far as Rodriguez's hopes of overturning the suspension, the writing was on the wall, and it was pessimistic graffiti. His lawyers were already discussing appealing Horowitz's decision to a federal judge.

The wheels fell off the proceedings that day. Rodriguez's attorneys had called Selig as a witness. Rodriguez later said that he planned to take the witness stand himself after Selig's turn.

But Horowitz issued a ruling that Selig would not have to testify in the arbitration and that Manfred could instead answer all questions concerning the decision process behind the 211-game punishment.

"This is ridiculous!" Rodriguez yelled, according to multiple news reports. He then directed his wrath at Manfred. "You're full of shit and you know it. This is fucking bullshit!"

He then stormed out of the proceedings, attorney James McCarroll in tow.

As Rodriguez left the MLB offices, possibly for the last time in his life, Team A-Rod issued a statement. "I am disgusted with this abusive process, designed to ensure that the player fails," read Rodriguez's statement. "I have sat through 10 days of testimony by felons and liars, sitting quietly through every minute, trying to respect the league and the process. This morning, after Bud Selig refused to come in and testify about his rationale for the unprecedented and totally baseless punishment he hit me with, the arbitrator selected by MLB and the Players Association refused to order Selig to come in and face me."

"The absurdity and injustice just became too much," Rodriguez's statement concluded. "I walked out and will not participate any further in this farce."

Since Rodriguez is not known for his spontaneity—or, for that matter, his truthfulness—there could have been legal choreography at work. MLB was certainly going to ask Rodriguez about his history of performance-enhancing drug usage, after all, and his treatment by Anthony Galea. His testimony would be under oath. And his grand jury testimony concerning PED use and Dr. Galea, also under oath, was sitting in a locked file cabinet in Buffalo.

If the two testimonies didn't match, Rodriguez could be accused of perjury, the same felony charge that had troubled Barry Bonds.

After leaving the hearing, Rodriguez's Escalade took him directly to a friendly face in Manhattan's West Village. WFAN radio host Mike Francesa had defended Rodriguez throughout the Biogenesis scandal. The gray-maned "pope" of New York sports coverage on the AM dial, Francesa had the month previous engaged in a shrill on-air screaming match with *Daily News* reporter Michael O'Keeffe, accusing the newspaper of carrying water for Major League Baseball in its feud with Rodriguez. O'Keeffe countered that Francesa was a softball host to the superstar and had given Rodriguez a "big bro hug" in 2010.

Now Rodriguez, wearing a dark suit in Francesa's studio, seemed to have been purified by rage of his usual hokey artificiality. "Today I just lost my mind. I banged a table and kicked a briefcase and slammed out of the room," Rodriguez told Francesa, saying of the arbitration process: "I knew it wasn't fair but what we saw today—it was disgusting."

Referring to Selig as "the man from Milwaukee," Rodriguez seethed: "He doesn't have the courage to come see me and tell me, 'This is why I'm going to destroy your career'?"

To Rodriguez, New York was now "our city." He said of Selig: "I know he doesn't like New York. I love this city. I love being a Yankee. My daughters grew up in New York."

This was a new A-Rod. This was the people's champion, even if he had to write a check for said people to wave signs in his defense. Like a pro wrestler, he challenged Selig: "I thought, rightfully so, this should end with

Selig on Thursday and me on Friday, under oath, put your money where your mouth is. Or we can go to Milwaukee and we can do it there."

Rodriguez asserted that he had never purchased PEDs from Bosch, obstructed the investigation, or bought evidence. He called the arbitration process a "kangaroo court" and said if it were up to him, he'd release the hearing transcripts.

Asked where he thought he'd be on Opening Day next year, Rodriguez joked: "I'll be either at third base, or I'll be sitting with you, Mike."

With Team A-Rod calling no more witnesses, the arbitration hearing was over. Arbitrator Horowitz returned to California to determine his ruling. The baseball world entered a six-week purgatory. To Rodriguez, this whole mess had been a "farce," and declaring just that in front of the arbitrator likely hadn't helped his effort at significantly reducing his penalty. To baseball, it had been a bruising battle. League officials set to planning a public relations–boosting television event so that if they won this thing, they might just convince fans it had been a righteous fight.

Reckoning was the course du jour. While Rodriguez awaiting his, some of the same was about to be served up in a Florida tanning salon parking lot.

J ust under three weeks after the arbitration hearing ended, there was a break in the car burglary that had played a pivotal role in the case against Rodriguez. Though it was too late to help the superstar—and likely wouldn't have moved the arbitrator anyway—the development bolstered the claim that Gary Jones may have played a role in the theft of Biogenesis records from Porter Fischer's car nine months earlier.

It was also further evidence that MLB officials might have known that they had purchased stolen documents.

What had first appeared to be a simple smash-and-grab in a parking lot had turned into the most heavily scrutinized break-in since Watergate.

The detective who caught the case, Terrence Payne, and the department's lone media specialist had been besieged by requests from the *New York Times*, *Washington Post*, ESPN, and the *Miami Herald*. Reporters wanted crime scene photos, witness testimony, rival outlets' requests in order to steal their scoops; and the authors of this book had requested the detective's full e-mail exchanges. *New York* magazine had given the break-in the glossy treatment in a story that included Gary Jones appearing to boast of masterminding the crime. "He didn't know how to make money," Jones said of Fischer's "stupid" handling of the Biogenesis records.

The case had initially been closed without arrest, but—in what had to be a law-enforcement first—it was reopened after a reporter forwarded a copy of Alex Rodriguez's lawsuit that alleged that MLB and Dan Mullin knowingly bought the records stolen from Fischer's car.

On December 10, Detective Payne finally received the results from the DNA test of the blood smear found on Fischer's vehicle. It matched the DNA of twenty-year-old Reginald St. Fleur, who Payne quickly discovered was an employee of Boca Tanning.

Payne found St. Fleur at the tanning salon the next day. The kid claimed he had never touched Fischer's car and wouldn't recognize Fischer if he "walked up that moment."

That's not how Fischer described it. Fischer told Payne that not only did he know Reggie, but they fist-bumped whenever they saw each other. The tanning salon lackey was charged with felony burglary. When he showed up for his arraignment, he was represented by an attorney who had been hired by the Carbones.

In Porter Fischer's mind, it all very neatly confirmed that the Carbones and Jones had put an underling up to the robbery. "I was definitely targeted. I'm positive," Porter Fischer told the *Palm Beach Post* in a story that ran the day after the arrest. "People break into cars to take stereos . . . people don't break in to steal four boxes of files."

Since the break-in and Jones's sales to both Alex Rodriguez and MLB, he and the Carbones have thrown around some entrepreneurial capital. Jones cofounded a new Pompano Beach–based company offering "tanning equipment service, installation [and] sales," according to state records. (Two weeks after its founding, his partner in the company was arrested for allegedly selling cocaine and Xanax.) Pete Carbone had incorporated Total Nutrition Weston, a supplement store in Broward County. His brother, Anthony, was planning a Boca-area cigar bar, according to business records, and had also launched his own line of protein brownies. (Oggi Velazquez hasn't turned his own role in the many handoffs of records into a happy-ever-after. During Rodriguez's hearings, he was arrested twice for domestic violence against his much-younger girlfriend, including allegedly attacking her with a bicycle pump. None of those charges were prosecuted.)

Fischer's comments to the *Palm Beach Post* lit the fuse in the simmering relationship between the former tanning club patron and its owners. Anthony Carbone called an author of this book, offering to share e-mails that disparaged Fischer—but only if the messages would be published in *Newsday* the next morning. (The author declined.) Carbone then sent the author Fischer's online mug shot from his 2007 marijuana arrest in Marion County. "Boca PD is acting on the word of this man," he wrote. He railed on the phone about Fischer's legal trouble with Zig-Zag, an episode he heard about from a reporter. "Let's do a little background on this motherfucker," Carbone demanded. "Whistle-blower? Is that what we're calling thieves these days?"

But Fischer maintains that the only money he ever got out of the whole Biogenesis affair was the $5,000 he took from MLB in exchange for a first meeting. After turning his records over to a federal grand jury and being ordered to stop talking to the press—a tough assignment—he quietly found another marketing job. He's also founded a non-profit called the Porter Project, which he says will educate young athletes about the dangers of PEDs and push state legislators and regulators to keep the Tony Bosches of the world out of business.

Carbone calls allegations that he had anything to do with the break-in, or even filming Jones's sale of the records to Mullin, a "good fairy tale." He repeatedly said that he would tell a New York–based author "everything" if taken out for a steak dinner. He even planned his order—surf and turf—and asked if he could bring friends. But when the author arrived in South Florida ready to take Carbone to the chic steakhouse Prime 112, Carbone stalled for days, said he was in meetings, and never spoke to the author again.

If the theft of the Biogenesis records was not random, it sets up a simple calculus. Dan Mullin, on behalf of MLB and with the approval of at least top baseball executive Manfred, purchased the records from tanning club regular Gary Jones. If Jones was behind the theft of the records, a straight line implicates MLB as buying stolen property that was bound for a state investigation.

According to Detective Payne, league officials did not contact him after purchasing the records. Since the records were being investigated as stolen, league officials were legally obligated to do so, Payne indicated in an e-mail.

Shoes will be dropping all over Florida in the aftermath of Biogenesis. Anthony Bosch's clinic is the target of both a federal and a state grand jury, which means he could face prison time for his former bustling drug empire. The Florida grand jury, according to law-enforcement sources, is focusing on distribution of PEDs to minors. That could be worrisome to Tommy Martinez and any other youth coaches whose names appear in Bosch's records.

Biogenesis laid bare how sophisticated and prevalent doping is among teenage athletes, and resulted in changes to state regulations concerning youth competition. Florida High School Athletic Association director Roger Dearing admits that its rules were "outdated," and language has been added to bar HGH as well as steroids, and to ban coaches who allow it. (There would still be no drug testing for student athletes.)

Even Florida's thriving anti-aging industry might finally be regulated thanks to Bosch's excesses—if change isn't trampled by politics. In response to New Times reporting on Biogenesis, state senator Eleanor Sobel introduced the "Health Care Clinic Act," which would require clinics like Bosch's to be inspected and certified.

And Major League Baseball may still have to answer for its apparently extralegal tactics in Florida. A Boca Raton police spokesperson told an author of this book that Payne is now "investigating whether St. Fleur was acting alone."

But what's a little obstruction of justice when you're trying to clean up baseball?

"You were caught in a vise," intoned Scott Pelley, a journalist who has interviewed multiple sitting American presidents.

"Yes," replied Anthony Bosch, "I was in a dark place. I—"

Bosch appeared to fight off tears, and continued: "I had no idea what I was going to do next."

A later shot showed Bosch on a porch at Scotty's Landing, poking at a propped-up iPad with a drink by his left hand. This was the pensive money shot, designed to show an elusive character now tracked down and recorded in his candid routine. But Anthony Bosch—cheeks and eyes twitching, a goofy smile now forming—couldn't quite pull off candor, and never would be described as pensive.

Of all the strange places his doomed relationship with Alex Rodriguez had taken him, this was perhaps the most unlikely: Anthony Bosch's 60 Minutes moment, eagerly hyped by news outlets around the country and ultimately watched by millions.

Americans had heard a lot about Bosch since the Biogenesis story broke but had seen very little of him: the old mug shot, the sweaty, full-of-lies ambush interview with ESPN's Pedro Gomez, the photo circulated by his publicist of Bosch walking through the MLB offices before testifying against Rodriguez.

This was supposed to be Bosch's true introduction to the nation, and it was fully managed by Major League Baseball. This Sunday prime-time, double-length segment was baseball's uppercut in its one-two knockout of Alex Rodriguez.

The day earlier—January 11, 2014—arbitrator Fredric Horowitz had

finally signed and e-mailed his decision to attorneys representing both Rodriguez and MLB. The confidential thirty-three-page decision was a dry
bombshell. "It is recognized this represents the longest disciplinary suspension imposed on a MLB player to date," Horowitz wrote at one point. "Yet
Rodriguez committed the most egregious violations of the [Joint Drug
Agreement] reported to date . . ."

Horowitz had reduced Rodriguez's suspension to 162 games. This was
vindication for baseball. Rodriguez would still be banned through 2014—
and the rest of Bud Selig's tenure—as baseball had originally sought. It was
still the harshest punishment for performance-enhancing drug use in
American team sports history.

Twisting the knife further was the fact that baseball had originally
attempted to negotiate a 162-game suspension of Rodriguez if he agreed to
confess to his sins, at least according to A-Rod's legal filings. Rodriguez's
millions spent engaging in an unprecedented public fight against punishment, antagonizing the Yankees, the union, and his fellow players, had
bought him only a ticket back to square one.

The key points of Rodriguez's crusade—that Bosch was a criminal not
to be trusted and that MLB used legal intimidation, graft, sex, and media
manipulation to build its case against him—factored little in Horowitz's
decision. Cases were built every day on the word of worse criminals,
Horowitz noted. And "resort to the legal system . . . does not amount to
coercion," he wrote of the Miami-Dade County lawsuit. Rodriguez and his
camp had paid for evidence themselves, Mullin's affair with Lorraine Delgadillo "did not yield any information relevant to the investigation," and
Rodriguez had orchestrated media leaks of his own.

Horowitz boiled down his decision to a skeleton of the reams of evidence both sides had presented him with. By his math, Rodriguez had
committed three violations of the Joint Drug Agreement, one for each of the
2010, 2011, and 2012 seasons in which he had doped through Bosch, as
evidenced by the fake doctor's testimony, notebooks, phone texts, and "rea-
sonable inferences drawn from the entire record of evidence."

As far as obstruction, Horowitz focused only on two allegations: that Rodriguez, after issuing a false denial himself, had "played an active role in inducing Bosch to issue his own public denial" the same day the *Miami New Times* story broke. And that Team A-Rod, in that meeting with Oggi in a downtown Miami condo, had attempted to get Bosch to sign an affidavit stating that he had never plied the superstar with drugs or had any knowledge of Rodriguez using banned substances. "The remaining allegations of obstruction, while troubling," wrote Horowitz, "need not be addressed because they would not affect the ultimate determination regarding the appropriate penalty in this matter."

While MLB issued a statement of understated celebration—"we respect the decision rendered by the Panel and will focus on our continuing efforts on eliminating performance-enhancing substances from our game"— Rodriguez released a statement calling the decision an "injustice."

His own reaction painted himself as a martyr for players' rights, endangered by a decision that led, in his mind, to a dystopia where contracts were voided due to PED violations. "No player should have to go through what I have been dealing with, and I am exhausting all options to ensure not only that I get justice, but that players' contracts and rights are protected through the next round of bargaining, and that the MLB investigation and arbitration process cannot be used against others in the future the way it is currently being used to unjustly punish me," said Rodriguez, suddenly channeling his freedom fighter father.

Though Horowitz's decision dominated sports coverage and ran above the fold on the front page of the *New York Times*—RECORD DOPING PENALTY FOR TOP-PAID YANKEE, read the headline, given side-by-side placement with the obituary of former Israeli prime minister Ariel Sharon—all that sports fans knew about the official case against Rodriguez was from the original *New Times* story exposing the records, and subsequent articles based almost entirely on unnamed baseball sources.

News show *60 Minutes*, then, was baseball's bullhorn to finally air the details of their case against Rodriguez, with the network television debut of their star witness. MLB was barred from releasing Horowitz's report, but nothing stopped their chief witness from spilling his guts on air. Pelley bragged of more than five hundred text messages the CBS show had obtained from Bosch, and read a few of the more damning missives between Bosch and Rodriguez.

Bosch stammered, appeared puffy and somewhat dazed, and even Pelley observed that his subject was a heavy drinker and smoker. But he dished the scatological details, of meeting Rodriguez at a nightclub in the Fontainebleau Hotel to draw blood—he did not mention the vial lost on the dance floor—and injecting the superstar himself.

"Alex is scared of needles," Bosch explained, in a revelation similar to Jose Canseco's claim that he shot up Mark McGwire in a stadium bathroom. For whatever Freudian reason, few images appear to be as titillating to Americans as that of the highly paid athletic superstar partially disrobing in a bathroom stall and getting pricked with a needle at the hands of another man.

Even Bud Selig appeared on the show to condemn Rodriguez: "In my judgment his actions were beyond comprehension."

The segment appeared neatly arranged by MLB to lay out its case against Rodriguez, with little skepticism concerning the motives and methods behind Major League Baseball's trench warfare against A-Rod.

Most notably, Selig wasn't questioned about the allegation that his office bought stolen documents. Manfred, who also appeared, was asked about giving a guy he knew only as "Bobby" $125,00 for the records, but only as it pertained to the documents' authenticity. "We were eyes wide open with respect to the questions that would surround these documents in terms of authenticating them in any legal proceeding, making sure they hadn't been doctored," Manfred said.

If he discussed whether MLB knew the records were stolen when they bought them, that clip didn't make it on-air. The fact that the original documents were supposed to be part of a state probe by the Department of Health—that baseball had thwarted a law-enforcement investigation—was also never mentioned.

The Players Association, despite its own unraveling relationship with Rodriguez, decried the league's cooperation with *60 Minutes*—clearly planned while Horowitz's decision was still pending—as violating the confidentiality of the Joint Drug Agreement. "It could not resist the temptation to publicly pile-on against Alex Rodriguez," read the MLBPA's statement on the commissioner's office's participation, and said the union was "considering all legal options available to remedy any breaches committed by MLB."

Pelley's send-off to the *60 Minutes* segment was a saccharine one. He noted that Selig was to retire at the end of 2014. "Part of his legacy is the establishment of the toughest anti-doping rules in all of American pro sports," said Pelley, without noting the other parts of Selig's legacy, including being lambasted by the US Congress for allowing doping to overtake baseball in the first place.

But the commissioner's commandeered television program—on which Tacopina appeared in Rodriguez's defense—didn't finally blast his nemesis into submission.

Two days after Horowitz inked his decision, Rodriguez filed a lawsuit— his third post-Biogenesis—against both Major League Baseball and the Players Association, seeking to overturn the suspension in federal court. The suit claimed that Horowitz—a "hard-core baseball fan," Rodriguez added suggestively—was in MLB's pocket and that the union had abandoned him in its timid fight against the league. The suit specifically criticized union chief Michael Weiner, who had died less than two months earlier.

And Rodriguez saved a special ire, of course, for Selig, who had refused to testify at his arbitration hearing but appeared on national television, making "a mockery of the arbitration procedure and the confidentiality supposedly attendant to it."

Rodriguez's attempt to overturn the ban in federal court—where judges don't generally like to interfere in private union matters—was a legal long shot. As a consequence, Rodriguez had to file Horowitz's entire decision in court. The document, detailing his alleged drug regimen and incriminating correspondence with Bosch, among other previously confidential information, would have to be made public, US district judge William H. Pauley III ruled. "Given the intense public interest in this matter and Commissioner Selig's disclosures last night on '60 Minutes,'" Pauley remarked, "it's difficult to imagine that any portion of this proceeding should be under seal."

Rodriguez had allowed public access to a document that painted him, quite convincingly, as a prolific liar and cheat. Thanks to the suit, anyone could read thirty pages of testimony about how Bosch had doped up A-Rod for years and peruse detailed breakdowns of his chemical cocktails. But strangely, after that sacrifice of what remained of his public image in order to pursue a slim chance at returning to baseball in 2014, Rodriguez's attitude suddenly appeared to shift from sanguine to apathetic.

A couple of days after filing the lawsuit, he surfaced in Mexico City, at the opening of a new Alex Rodriguez Fitness Center, a gym franchise in which he has a stake. The gym had kept his impending arrival secret, ensuring that only local reporters would show. As he grabbed a microphone and addressed the small crowd in Spanish, Rodriguez had the air of a washed-up lounge singer, exiled from Vegas and plying his trade at a saloon in Topeka instead. "The league could have done me a favor because I've played twenty years without a time-out," Rodriguez ruminated. "I think 2014 will be a year to rest mentally, and physically prepare myself for the future, and begin a new chapter of my life."

Maybe Rodriguez had considered the notion that, after filing a lawsuit against his players union, a forced early retirement might be a rosier prospect than playing major league ball again after all. Prolonged litigation against a multibillion-dollar corporation is one thing. But summers full of fastballs to the ass?

The same day that he made that appearance, a few dozen major leaguers joined a union conference call in which they seethed about Rodriguez suing his colleagues, railed that he should be expelled from the MLBPA, and contemplated revenge in the way only baseball players can, according to an account of the phone call later published by Yahoo! Sports.

Remarked one of those players: "When he gets up to bat, you can hit him and hit him hard."

An MLB source with direct knowledge of Rodriguez's actions in the weeks following that Mexico City appearance clears up the reasoning behind his sudden change of heart. Soon after filing the federal lawsuit, which would bring more animosity, more embarrassing disclosures, more danger of being unable to avoid going under oath and and more legal fees, Rodriguez was feeling uneasy. So as he has always done just before being led off a cliff—though perhaps a little too late this time—Rodriguez reached out to a confidante.

According to the source, he called Jim Sharp, a Washington, DC–based attorney who Rodriguez had replaced with Tacopina back in March.

Sharp advised Rodriguez that he was being milked for more money and was going to lose.

A person close to Rodriguez boils it down to this: He still wants to be loved. And he realized that slamming the brakes on the fight now was the only way to salvage any future in baseball. Rodriguez has no doubt he will be back in 2015, when he will be turning forty years old. He'll play on the Yankees if they don't buy out his contract. He will collect his remaining $61 million, plus home run milestones. (Willie Mays is only six dingers away, at 660.) And after that, Rodriguez still holds out hope that he might get a job broadcasting. Or maybe coaching, like Mark McGwire, who despite steroid notoriety is the hitting coach for the Los Angeles Dodgers. Heck, maybe he'll put together an ownership group and buy his hometown team, the Miami Marlins.

Rodriguez had Jim Sharp call MLB for him and tell league officials that Team A-Rod was throwing in the towel. On February 7, 2014, Rodriguez's attorneys dismissed the claims against Major League Baseball and the Players Association, officially ending his last shot at playing in the upcoming season. Rodriguez did not dismiss the suit against the Yankees' team doctor, Christopher Ahmad.

Just like that, a single player's battle against the league, which had raged louder and longer than any before it and soiled both baseball's top offices and seemingly what was left of Rodriguez's reputation, was over.

Rodriguez, as unpredictable as ever, did not issue a statement.

B osch's *60 Minutes* appearance hadn't served only to fight MLB's public relations war. It was also the world's introduction to Anthony Bosch, celebrity.

Bosch had laid bare his aspiration in his notebooks when he had written his plans to become "CEO / founder / chairman / lead physician / scientist / professor / author," and master of his own fitness and nutrition conglomerate. When he agreed to cooperate with MLB, he had made sure to add a clause that allowed him to detail his doping of players in future book or movie deals.

When Rodriguez's reduced suspension was announced, Bosch's publicist released a statement in which the narcotics-peddling unlicensed medical practitioner was recast as a benevolent guru. "[Bosch] is glad to have the arbitration behind him and believes he can play a valuable role in the future by educating athletes about the dangers of performance-enhancing drugs," read the statement.

Bosch's predecessors in baseball steroid-dealing notoriety managed to turn their name recognition into niche profits. Kirk Radomski's EPSG Labs peddles supplement pills promising "no crash." Victor Conte's SNAC sells a variety of supplements through a website that bills him as "BALCO's Mastermind" and brags: "ESPN ranks Victor Conte the #1 pioneering sports scientist!" (The *ESPN The Magazine* article referenced was facetious.)

And Florida state records reveal that, even as Rodriguez was still fighting for his career on Park Avenue, Bosch was already laying the foundation for his new business empire. On November 18, Bosch's longtime attorney, Julio Ayala, incorporated the Miami-based Biogenesis Supplements Inc.

Sure, like Radomski and Conte, before Bosch can cash in on providing high-profile clients with illegal drugs, he'll first have to deal with the accompanying criminal fallout. But in a strange way, the catastrophe had accomplished exactly what he'd always wanted. He was famous, every bit as well known as his old cousin Orlando, and his crimes weren't half as bad as the Cuban terrorist's. Who's to say he couldn't rehabilitate his image and turn that infamy into profit? "He's going to figure it out," says Hernan Dominguez of his friend Bosch. "He'll make lemonade out of lemons."

Maybe he could turn those pages of handwritten notes about yachts, offshore corporations, and product lines into a reality. Maybe he'll finally get around to quit smoking. (Not being a doctor, though—that dream's probably scrapped for good, at least in the United States.)

More turbulence lies ahead, he knows: a possible prison sentence, civil litigation, and those never-ending child support bills. But perhaps also a tell-all memoir, maybe a film treatment where he's played by a famous movie star, whole new worlds of revenue that he couldn't have predicted in his most fantastical notebook scribblings.

The world, he knows, won't soon forget the name Tony Bosch.

The Cost of War

How much money did Major League Baseball spend to unravel the Biogenesis scandal?

Even under oath, the man who personally directed the response to Tony Bosch's doping ring can't answer that question. "I couldn't give you a good estimate," Rob Manfred admitted when Joe Tacopina grilled him on the stand during Alex Rodriguez's arbitration hearing.

Some of the numbers are easy enough to add up. Gary Jones pocketed at least $125,000 for his copies of Bosch's notebooks and for the files stolen from Porter Fischer's car. Manfred signed off on another $1 million–plus for Bosch's various lawyers, including at least $700,000 to Bosch's old friends Susy and Julio Ayala. Bosch's round-the-clock bodyguards, meanwhile, could have set MLB back to the tune of $2,400 per day for a full calendar year, which adds up to $876,000 to keep their chief witness safe. That's already a couple million bucks.

Then add in the truly escalating costs: the thousands of billable hours for the squadron of lawyers who prepared the arbitration case against A-Rod, the dozens of freelance investigators hired to scour South Florida, and the travel costs for the DOI's own private eyes.

Ten million? Twenty million? Enough to pay the Miami Marlins' starting payroll next year?

"We spent a lot of money on the investigation," Manfred finally allowed when pushed by Tacopina. "It's a substantial expenditure."

*   *   *

The expense of Biogenesis is relevant because it leads to another question: Was it worth it?

Major League Baseball intimidated potential witnesses. Profits that came from fans buying tickets, jerseys, and Cracker Jack—and, of course, tuning in on television—became cash handed over in diners and the backs of SUVs in return for information and stolen records. The league arguably subverted the civil judicial system in order to threaten destitution against those who resisted. Baseball officials struck a deal to vouch for Anthony Bosch, a medical con man under investigation for dealing narcotics to minors because his cooperation helped baseball "achieve the important public policy goal" of eradicating PEDs from the game. It's a goal that seemed to mean little to the "Man from Milwaukee," Bud Selig, in the late 1990s when steroid-jacked home runs were fueling baseball's comeback from labor strife.

All of this to punish fifteen professional baseball players who used banned substances in order to resurrect fading careers, achieve their dreams of a lasting tenure in the big leagues, recovery quickly from injury, and—in the case of one player in particular—hammer his way into the record books as the greatest slugger who ever lived.

More than any of the others, Alex Rodriguez's saga explains, oddly enough, both why the Biogenesis suspensions are important and why they may have little effect. The suspensions mean a lot to the press, to the fans, and to Selig's legacy. They've destroyed players' reputations, in some cases permanently. But, when it comes to what might be most important to a player, his salary, and his future? They often mean very little. Rodriguez's suspension through 2014 will cost him $22,131,147 in salary. Only his tax man knows exactly how much he spent on Joe Tacopina and scads of other attorneys, as well as private investigators and crisis management flaks. Then there were the purchases, such as the six figures he dropped to buy the text messages and Valentine Dan Mullin exchanged with Lorraine Delgadillo, evidence of a love tryst that ended up playing no role in arbitrator Fredric Horowitz's decision.

Nobody sets aflame more than $30 million without feeling the loss. Not even Rodriguez, who flipped his Miami Beach mansion for a $15 million profit in the midst of the investigation. But in the financial equation involving steroids, Rodriguez probably came out ahead.

His record-breaking contracts were a direct result of supreme power numbers in a career in which steroids were an omnipresent crutch. This is particularly true in the case of the contract extension he signed following his 2007 MVP season, when his agent "hijacked" the World Series broadcast with news of his opt-out, and the New York Yankees rewarded him with a new deal worth at least $275 million.

That's a deal only a three-time MVP would receive. And though the sports world didn't know it at the time, at least two of those times were tainted by PEDs. In 2003, he had used a steroid provided by his cousin. In 2007, immediately before receiving the contract extension, he had been permitted by the league to use the "mother of all anabolics," as Manfred put it: testosterone.

The math is straightforward. Rodriguez would have been paid $81 million to play through the remaining three years of his original contract. Instead, the extension locked him in for an additional $194 million. If he can hit six more career home runs following his potential return in 2015, tying Willie Mays at 660 and triggering the first of his $6 million milestone bonuses, that number will be exactly $200 million.

Subtract $35 million for the estimated lost salary and expenses that Rodriguez blew battling his suspension, and the profit from the extension he signed on the strength of steroid-fueled statistics is still $165 million.

Until they build a steroid exhibit in Cooperstown, A-Rod will never be in the Hall of Fame. Surely that hurts a thirty-eight-year-old kid whose love of baseball has never been questioned. But it doesn't take his good friend Warren Buffett to figure that, financially, juicing was likely a good deal for Rodriguez. No MLB suspension will strip him of those massive profits made from steroid-fueled power production.

On a relatively smaller scale, the same equation has proven true for many of the players linked to Biogenesis.

Ryan Braun signed his own five-year, $105 million extension to his existing eight-year, $45 million deal early in April 2011. At the time, he was baseball's squeaky-clean superstar. That was the season in which Braun won an MVP award and also failed a PED test. After the twenty-one-month battle in which he lied, smeared an innocent MLB subcontractor, and exploited a loophole that caused an arbitrator to be fired, Braun's decision to finally accept a sixty-five-game suspension was a financial no-brainer. He lost just over $3 million. But he had signed contracts worth $150 million since college.

Call it the 2 percent steroid tax. Even Mitt Romney can't get that rate.

Melky Cabrera resurrected his career on Bosch's regimen. In 2010, the former top Yankees prospect had been released by the Atlanta Braves. That's when he started working out with Rodriguez in Miami, and soon afterward met Bosch. He was on Major League Baseball's fringe, signing a relatively middling $1.25 million deal with the Kansas City Royals the next season. Then he broke out that season and the next for the Royals and the San Francisco Giants, signing a $6 million deal in 2012 and being named MVP of that season's All-Star Game. His suspension in August of that year cost him $1.85 million in salary. He still made more money that year than he had in any season in his career. (Additionally, despite not playing in the World Series, he still received a $300,000-plus share from the Giants' championship win.) Following the aborted season, he signed a $16 million, two-year deal with the Toronto Blue Jays.

Jhonny Peralta, whose annual pay was $6 million, forfeited $1.6 million due to his suspension in 2013, the only season in his career in which he batted over .300. He returned to play the hero in the postseason, including belting a three-run home run to lead his Detroit Tigers to a pivotal Game Four victory over the Oakland Athletics in the Division Series. At thirty-one years old, he then signed the monster contract of his career, with the St. Louis Cardinals agreeing to pay him $53 million over four years.

It's the biggest contract ever awarded to a player previously punished for PED use, and it sparked immediate backlash among players like relief pitcher David Aardsma, who vented on Twitter. "Nothing pisses me off more than guys that cheat and get raises for doing so," Aardsma wrote.

Bartolo Colon more than tripled his salary post-Biogenesis, signing a $20 million, two-year contract with the New York Mets at age forty following the 2013 season. After a career full of injuries, Nelson Cruz finally stayed healthy for the Texas Rangers in 2012 and 2013 after hooking up with Bosch. He was suspended in the latter year, but then signed an $8 million deal with the Baltimore Orioles for 2014.

The list goes on. For established millionaires like Rodriguez, Braun, Cabrera, Peralta, and Colon, new contracts spawned by improved production through PEDs mean only more zeros in already-burgeoning bank accounts. But for younger players, especially those from Third World countries, that extra edge as MLB scouts study their performance can mean escape from a life in poverty.

Bosch told MLB officials he didn't give PEDs to Ricardo Cespedes, the then–fifteen-year-old Dominican prospect whose name shows up in his notebooks, in particular his angry note to Juan Carlos Nunez. Perhaps Bosch's reticence stems from his not wanting to implicate himself in dealing to a minor. Either way, the $725,000 bonus the Mets gave Cespedes in August 2013, on his sixteenth birthday, was enough to enable the teenager to provide his family with a whole new way of life.

There is one tactic that might derail the financial equation driving players to juice: teams being allowed to cancel lucrative contracts if those players are caught using PEDs. But, as the Yankees are aware in the case of Rodriguez, the league's drug policy with the union bars that. "All authority to discipline Players for violations of the Program shall repose with the Commissioner's Office," reads the agreement. "No Club may take any disciplinary or adverse action against a Player (including, but not limited to, a fine, suspension, or any adverse action pursuant to a Uniform Player's Contract) because of a Player's violation of the Program."

Player contracts sometimes include "morals clauses," allowing teams to void the deals in certain circumstances, but the language is often vague. The union is known to fight any contract broken due to such a clause.

Rodriguez referred to potential changes in the way that the agreement between the league and the union allows teams to handle PED punishment when he said, after his unsuccessful arbitration, that he was fighting so "that players' contracts and rights are protected through the next round of bargaining."

But despite the fact that Biogenesis-linked players have signed big-money contracts after the suspensions, there's no question that the scandal did represent a seismic change in MLB's attitude. For the first time in a history stretching from the Pittsburgh drug trials to Jose Canseco to Mark McGwire, MLB attacked rather than ignored a mass drug ring in its midst. It did so with a mostly unified front. The union didn't balk at the bulk of the suspensions handed down. The owners didn't pressure the commissioner to ignore the problem. The Department of Investigations, created based on explicit recommendations by Senator George Mitchell, got the evidence needed to suspend the players involved. And when one of the targets went ballistic and attacked the system itself, the arbitration process ultimately upheld the commissioner's judgment.

Part of the reason the MLBPA didn't bring a ferocious fight to the league concerning Biogenesis punishment may be because the union was attempting to stem the bleeding of its power. The union showed in its blocking of Alex Rodriguez's 2003 trade to the Red Sox that a reduced contract is the one thing that must never happen.

Players losing seasons or portions of seasons of salary due to negotiated and arbitrated suspensions is one matter. Teams claiming ignorance of players' PED proclivities and then canceling contracts when it's convenient—as in the case with Rodriguez and the Yankees—is quite another.

New MLPBA executive director Tony Clark, who took over for the deceased Michael Weiner in December 2013, has said "we will never end up in a world where player contracts are voided as a result" of PED violations.

*   *   *

I t's hard to avoid cynicism about the Biogenesis affair, with MLB spending millions to force fifteen ballplayers to miss games—just in time for Selig's 2014 retirement tour—while changing nothing about the basic incentives that drove them to dope in the first place.

But for all the flaws and troubling developments surrounding MLB's response to the scandal, its import as a historic turning point is undeniable. League officials are emphatic that they chased down every scrap of evidence surrounding Biogenesis, and punished every player against whom they could build a case that would hold up in arbitration. There were no free passes given out in return for cooperation, officials maintain.

Ninety-two years earlier, Kenesaw Mountain Landis, named as the game's first commissioner partly to deal with the crisis, suspended eight players for their role in the rigged 1919 World Series. The league hadn't completely cleansed itself of association with gamblers—just ask Pete Rose—but the message was decisive. In his response to Biogenesis, Selig was attempting a similar coda to the game's freewheeling love affair with PEDs.

Only seven years before the baseball season that was rocked by Biogenesis, PEDs remained rampant in baseball. On April 18, 2006, PED-specializing IRS agent Jeff Novitzky followed a package of HGH through the mail to the Scottsdale doorstep of Arizona Diamondbacks pitcher Jason Grimsley. The resulting two-hour interview was just a footnote in MLB's struggle with PEDs, but it was also the beginning of the end of a chapter. Grimsley was a client of both Brian McNamee and Kirk Radomski, whose testimonies formed the crux of the Mitchell Report, the damning investigatory document making it impossible for Selig and other league officials to ignore steroids.

Novitzky's affidavit from his interview with Grimsley suggests that while some aspects of PED use in baseball—chief among them, the league's official reaction—have changed, players' dependency on the drugs and ease with which they can be purchased remains a red flag.

Grimsley talked of coffeepots in major league clubhouses being labeled "unleaded" or "leaded," indicating which had been spiked by amphetamines. He said former MLB player David Segui had "told him of a doctor in Florida that he was using at a 'wellness center' to obtain human growth hormone," according to the affidavit. "Segui told Grimsley that he has had blood work done with this doctor."

Grimsley told Novitzky about several players who he knew were using PEDs, and remarked that "boatloads" of major leaguers used the same source.

These days, players appear to have replaced amphetamines—or "greenies"—with legal speed. In 2013, a record 119 players were granted drug exemptions for attention deficit disorder. These exemptions, allowing players to use drugs that are otherwise banned, are of the same sort Rodriguez once received to use testosterone and clomiphene citrate. That number of ADD exemptions shows that just short of 10 percent of all major league players use Adderall, a figure that is more than double the national adult average.

Manfred has already attempted to downplay the surging ADD numbers just as league officials once attempted to downplay baseball's steroid problem, saying that most MLB players are younger than the average American and "there's no question attention is a key part of what these athletes do."

The exposure of Anthony Bosch's client rolls showed that "wellness" or "anti-aging" clinics in Florida certainly remain a draw for baseball players seeking HGH. Since HGH is extremely hard to test for, remaining detectable in the blood for only a matter of hours, and Florida's permissive medical culture and Governor Rick Scott's regulation-averse reign have made it the nation's capital of the booming gray-market anti-aging industry, the state is likely to draw cheating ballplayers for years. And it's not just baseball. Florida produced the second-most current players in the NFL in 2013, behind only California. Baseball was Bosch's specialty, but it seems likely that Florida is home to HGH-providing clinics specializing in football and basketball as well.

But in other regards—and especially in contrast with those other sports—baseball has cracked down emphatically. A guy like Kirk Radomski, providing steroids to "boatloads" of MLB players while working as a Mets clubhouse attendant, would have a hard time existing in today's baseball culture. So would Jose Canseco.

So maybe the clubhouse hotline set up for players to report PED use— called only twenty times, according to Dan Mullin's 2012 deposition— hasn't helped much in nosing out such cheaters and enablers. But during his testimony in Rodriguez's arbitration, Manfred revealed the league's policy to investigate any claims, no matter how dubious, involving PED use by its players. "Certainly since the issuance of the Mitchell Report there has not been a public allegation of player involvement with performance-enhancing drugs that we have not investigated in some way, shape, or form," Manfred said. "It always happens. It is standard operating procedure. Nothing needs to be done to initiate that investigation. It's literally automatic under our procedures."

As an illustration of how willing MLB is to investigate these days, Rob Manfred testified that two marquee stars were being—or had been— investigated solely on the basis of unsubstantiated allegations. In August 2013, St. Louis radio host and former big-leaguer Jack Clark had aired PED allegations against Los Angeles Angels superstar Albert Pujols and Detroit Tigers ace pitcher Justin Verlander. Clark said that a trainer of the slugger had told him Pujols used steroids, but he had less concerning Verlander. Clark pointed out the pitcher's dipping fastball velocity and remarked: "It's just the signs are there."

In his cross-examination of Manfred, Tacopina brought up those allegations, asking the league executive whether he was familiar with "recent reports of one former Major League ballplayer accusing Pujols and Verlander of using PEDs."

When Manfred answered in the affirmative, Tacopina asked: "Have you commenced an investigation on those two players?"

"The allegations about Albert Pujols have been previously investigated," Manfred replied. Pressed for when that investigation occurred, he said: "I can't give you an exact time, Joe, but there has been a prior investigation of these specific allegations, involvement with the particular individual alleged in the story. The Verlander report is new and is in the process. I was not aware of that one previously."

Both Pujols and Verlander have already emphatically denied Clark's allegations. Pujols sued the radio host in October 2013, causing Clark to publicly apologize and retract his claims, saying in a statement: "I have no knowledge whatsoever that Mr. Pujols has ever used illegal or banned PEDs." (Pujols then dropped the suit.) Verlander called Clark's statements "moronic." MLB has taken no action against either player.

M LB's new policy is a 180-degree reversal from the pre-Mitchell days, when the league was not interested in even strong accusations concerning player steroid use. In Canseco's case alone, FBI agent Greg Stejskal had attempted to share evidence about the player's doping with baseball security chief Kevin Hallihan, Canseco had tested positive for steroids in a Miami-Dade County jail in 2003, and a newspaper reporter for the *Washington Post* had written about Canseco's reported steroid use, causing the slugger's dad to challenge the reporter to a fight.

Canseco wasn't ever punished by baseball for steroid use. But if each of those cases happened today, Manfred's office would investigate. And under the existing Joint Drug Agreement, those investigators likely would have gathered enough evidence to suspend him for at least fifty games.

But the most notable change since the pre-Mitchell days is that baseball has developed the most aggressive and expensive drug-testing policy in American pro sports. MLB players are randomly screened not just via epitestosterone-to-testosterone ratios, but with more exacting carbon isotope tests as well. And starting in 2013, the league was the first among American pro sports to test players' blood for HGH.

In its first year, the testing was implemented only during the season—

not the off-season—and detecting HGH is still nearly impossible unless the player used the substance only hours before the test. But ten years earlier, when the players union was still insisting there was no PED problem in baseball at all and only begrudgingly agreeing to "anonymous" testing with no consequences for those who tested positive for banned substances, it would have been difficult to foresee baseball now carrying the drug-testing flag further than the other sports leagues.

As a result of Biogenesis, MLB's standards have now gotten even stronger. Weeks before the 2014 season, the union and owners agreed to a new drug testing program. Penalties have been toughened, with a first positive test now triggering an eighty-game ban, a second a season-long suspension, and a third a lifetime away from baseball. In a direct answer to Jhonny Peralta's 2013 postseason heroics after serving a fifty-game ban, players caught cheating will now also be barred from the full playoffs.

The frequency of tests has also increased, with in-season random urine tests more than doubling. More HGH tests will be done in-season, and DHEA—the mild steroid claimed as a defense by Manny Ramirez and cannily mixed into "pink cream" by Tony Bosch—is now finally illegal in MLB. Every player will also be subject to carbon isotope testing, the method that catches synthetic molecules in the bloodstream, once per season.

The 2014 changes did soften the policy in a few areas; instead of a "zero-tolerance" rule, players will now be able to reduce suspensions by proving to an arbitrator that they took a drug accidentally, as was the case in reliever Guillermo Mota's failed drug test after apparently drinking his kid's cough syrup. And the suspensions for DHEA use are markedly lower, leaving the door open to using the drug as an excuse.

Still, the changes are the clearest sign yet that Clark, who was confirmed as the new union chief during the off-season, has the support of most players in going hard after PEDs. The new rules move MLB even further into the lead among American sports for PED testing.

In his prophetic 1969 *Sports Illustrated* survey of athletic doping, Bil Gilbert wrote that drugs that fundamentally change how players can perform on the field "menace the tradition and structure of sport itself." It's one thing to have bigger, faster, stronger players because nutrition has improved, and longer careers because doctors can repair ligaments and mend tears. It's another to see middling outfielders belting enough homers to be a Hall of Famer in another era. PEDs tear the baseball space-time continuum, the fabric of stories that links father-to-son-to-grandfather at every ballpark.

It's the notion that statistics can no longer compare the performances of generations of ballplayers—unless you believe, based on single-season records, that the three best home run hitters in history all played in the late 1990s, and Babe Ruth is not among them—that makes cheating in that sport so irksome to fans.

But the pro football and basketball seasons, despite being shorter than the baseball schedule, arguably present for those sports' players a greater demand for the effects of PEDs. The eighty-two-game NBA campaign is notoriously arduous and physically exhausting, and players could certainly benefit from substances that boost stamina and recovery. And football is, well, football—a bone-crushing sport where bodies and brains are sacrificed, injuries both severe and lingering are common, and massive bulk rules all. PEDs are a perfect fit.

It's difficult to gauge how big of a problem PEDs are in those leagues, mostly because—especially in the case of basketball—testing and enforcement measures have lagged behind those of baseball. Between 2010 and May 2013, fifty NFL players were suspended for PEDs. In the span of those three years, 339 major league and minor league baseball players were suspended for PEDs. In the NBA, a total of eight players have been suspended since 2000. But there could be an ongoing PED era in football and basketball, and we wouldn't necessarily know it.

As the saga of Dr. Anthony Galea makes clear, there will always be a fine—and moving—line between top physical conditioning and athletic medical care, and banned performance enhancement. After all, NBA superstar Kobe Bryant makes no secret of his periodic trips to Germany to visit a doctor, Peter Wehling, specializing in "biologic medicine." On his friend

Bryant's recommendation, Alex Rodriguez traveled to Germany for the same treatment in December 2011. It's a field—including Galea's trusty platelet-rich plasma (PRP) injections—in which the patient's tissue is manipulated and reintroduced into his body. It's also a science that both athletic and medical regulators appear to regard as murky: PRP treatments were banned by the World Anti-Doping Agency—but currently are allowed pending further findings—and few American doctors will perform biologic medicine because of FDA laws stating that patient's tissue can only be "minimally manipulated" before being reclassified as a drug.

Bryant has the resources to pioneer this medicine's mainstream athletic use by chartering a private jet to Europe for treatments that give him an edge by allowing him, he believes, to recover faster from a troublesome knee. Five to ten years from now, these treatments could be legal and common among athletes. Or they could be considered outright doping.

The same murkiness surrounds HGH, according to one of the sports world's most opinionated figures. Growth hormones have long been banned in all professional sports and are approved for medical use only in rare circumstances, though reports are mixed as to whether they actually unfairly enhance performance, or just speed recovery from injury. Dallas Mavericks owner Mark Cuban has called for more research into the substance's potential role in professional athletics and recovery. "The issue isn't whether I think it should be used," Cuban said in November 2013. "The issue is that it has not been approved for such use. And one of the reasons it hasn't been approved is that there have not been studies done to prove the benefits of prescribing HGH for athletic rehabilitation or any injury rehabilitation that I'm aware of. The product has such a huge . . . stigma that no one wants to be associated with it."

To a longtime ambassador of America's other major sport—football, where players and fans are only now beginning to understand the devastating and lasting physical toll of the game—there's hypocrisy in not allowing players to heal themselves using HGH. "We gotta stay hurt forever?" Mike Ditka, a former player and head coach legendary for his tenure at the helm

of the Chicago Bears, says in an interview for this book. "If it helps you recover from injuries, I have no idea why it would be a bad thing. You're
paying players all this money, wouldn't it help to get them back on the field
where they can earn that money? If I owned a football team, I'd want my
guys to play every week.

"I don't see a damn thing wrong with it," Ditka says of HGH. "I'm
sorry."

To Ditka, it's the same thing—only more effective, less risky, and with
long-term healing benefits   as shooting yourself full of dulling agents to
cope with Sunday violence. He says that as a player, he subsisted on a cocktail of Cortisone and Novocaine.

"I was taking three shots of Cortisone a week for my hips," says Ditka.
"You're supposed to get Cortisone shots at most once every few months.
Back in the '60s, nobody knew what the side effects were."

Former players, from Bosch clients Bernie Kosar and Julio Cortes to
the unnamed retired NFL player listed in Galea's federal indictment, have
discovered HGH's healing effects after a crippling career.

Ditka's open to the substance as well. "I don't think anything can help
you if you've had your hips replaced," he says. "But hell yeah, I'd try it if it'd
help me feel better."

B aseball may be on the forefront, among professional team sports, of the
testing arms race against dopers. But there's still plenty of wiggle room
for innovative cheaters.

Bosch, an unlicensed doctor self-taught in the dark science of athletic
performance enhancing and testing, bragged that beating urine and blood
samples was "almost a cakewalk, actually." His record at backing up that
braggadocio is mixed, considering three of his clients were busted by tests
in 2012. But his star customer, Alex Rodriguez, passed at least a dozen drug
tests while on Bosch's regimen, and baseball's own experts believe that
Bosch helped him do so.

The techniques on display at Biogenesis, in fact, remain at the cutting edge of cheating. In cycling, the Silicon Valley for all doping innovation, Lance Armstrong and his teammates also evaded punishment for years by "microdosing" testosterone and other treatments to stay below the radar of blood and urine tests. In Bosch's case, these were the chewable troches he dispensed to Rodriguez and others.

The science is catching up to that problem. Starting in 2013, MLB became the first league to adopt a "biological passport" program to catch dopers. The idea is simple: Each player establishes a baseline reading for his hormone levels, and the league tests them throughout the season to look for any variation. The program is so tough to fool that when cycling adopted similar protocols in 2008, Lance Armstrong decided to stop cheating, later telling Oprah Winfrey that the test scared him straight "because it really worked."

Even tougher tests are on the horizon; scientists are studying a process that looks at an athlete's RNA and might be able to detect variations caused by chemical enhancement. The tests show great promise in catching the use of HGH. As a *New York Times* writer described the new technology, "Rather than trying to find the drug itself, a new generation of tests would gather evidence from the doper's own body."

Still, it's a sure bet that even now there's another Tony Bosch out there plotting equally ingenious solutions to evade or confuse those new tests, and that more than enough professional athletes will be happy to try his methods.

That's why for all the evolving science, an agency like the DOI will always play a key role in convincing the bulk of professional baseball players that it's not worth the risk to try to beat the system. MLB has now shown that it's willing to spend millions of dollars to gather evidence to punish cheaters. That's a powerful disincentive, even if you're sure you've got the best science in the world in your corner.

But as Bud Selig drowned for months in bad press about his lead investigator's affair with a witness and Alex Rodriguez's accusations concerning a conspiracy between the league's front office and the Yankees to bring him down, the commissioner might have wondered if there was a way to squelch the cold war leaks between opponents in such a doping case.

The US Anti-Doping Agency, which runs drug-testing programs for the Olympics, experienced similar turmoil over the years. During BALCO, the motives of the agency's leaders were assailed, in the same manner that Selig had weathered during his battle against A-Rod. In part because of such blowback, the World Anti-Doping Agency changed its codes in 2009 to kill confidentiality in doping cases. Instead, if an athlete discusses the case to the press, agencies like USADA can respond.

Such transparency in pro baseball might be a hard sell for both sides. Since the advent of testing in the sport, the MLBPA has maintained its greatest concern is confidentiality of its members. And evidence surrounding a player's doping can be just as damaging to the league as the individual. In Rodriguez's case, for example, that he was permitted to use testosterone in 2007—information that would be confidential if not for arbitration transcripts obtained by these authors—is a potentially embarrassing bit of decision making on the independent program administrator's part.

Selig could also consider a more radical step: turning baseball's testing and investigations programs over to an outside agency, as is the case with policing PEDs in the Olympics. Losing control might seem anathema to the commissioner's office and union alike, but Rodriguez's and Braun's strategies—publicly sliming everyone connected to the case—shows the danger of keeping such programs in-house. It's a lot tougher to claim that Bud Selig has a personal agenda to destroy your career when the commissioner doesn't control the anti-doping program.

"This case could be the best single example of why the testing program should be fully independent," Travis Tygart says. "If you're Bud Selig, why would you want to deal with this again? . . . Even though he did the right thing, in this world you're damned if you do and damned if you don't."

In a 2012 deposition, Selig called baseball a "quasi-public institution in which people count on the integrity of the sport." That integrity, he said, "is sacred to the sport and one that you must on a daily, hourly basis protect." As he retires at the end of the 2014 season, the commissioner who wanted to be a history professor must hope that future generations of baseball fans will judge him for the historic crackdown on PEDs in response to Biogenesis—and not the questionable manner in which the suspensions were secured.

And if he doesn't want to be forever known as the commissioner who enabled rampant steroid use, Selig will also have to hope that future fans remember only the increased doping penalties, cutting-edge testing, and dogged investigations that followed the Mitchell Report—and not the way the game was infiltrated by drugs for decades.

The owners of the thirty MLB teams vote on the next commissioner, and there has been no official word on who is in the running to be anointed baseball's next pope. But the logical heir apparent is Manfred, Selig's longtime consigliere, who was named chief operating officer of the league in 2013, during Rodriguez's appeal.

Manfred's appointment would be a fascinating departure, in terms of the battle against PEDs, from the reign of Selig. Manfred, who was hired by MLB in 1998—the same year that Mark McGwire and Sammy Sosa had their home run race, which was later viewed as an embarrassment—was weaned in the fallout from the Steroid Era.

Selig's main defense of his blindness to steroid use during that time is ignorance. When a reporter exposed Mark McGwire's use of the steroid androstenedione, banned in the Olympics but not by baseball, Selig had never heard of the substance, and asked his Milwaukee pharmacist and George Steinbrenner if they had any insight.

But Manfred, as he showed in his testimony in the case against Alex Rodriguez, is familiar with T/E ratio screens, the science surrounding the secretion of doping substances from a player's body, isotope ratio mass spectometry testing, masking agents, and exogenous therapy. He was the point man who organized the controversial investigation into Biogenesis, authorized those cash payments, and argued in Rodriguez's arbitration on behalf of the league.

For the first time, baseball may have a doping specialist as commissioner. And despite Selig's boast in the 2012 deposition—before Biogenesis was exposed—that "we did what we had to do with the help of Senator Mitchell and others and I was very proud of the fact that [the] sport got cleaned up quickly," Manfred appears to understand that battling PEDs is an ongoing saga that will not be won with a single coda.

A small framed photo hangs near a corner of Tacopina's Manhattan office. It shows one of the defense attorney's most famous clients sliding into third base. The photo is penned with the inscription: "Joe T: Love going to war with you. Your friend, Alex Rodriguez."

Rodriguez's war might be over, at least for now. But there will be plenty more wars in baseball's future.

ACKNOWLEDGMENTS

Both authors: We want to start by thanking the duo who made this whole project possible, editor Jill Schwartzman at Dutton and literary agent David R. Patterson at Foundry Media, who suggested that we—a *Miami New Times* managing editor and his former colleague, now at *Newsday*—collaborate to tell a wild story evenly split between South Florida and New York City.

It was a fine idea. Somehow, Jill and David made writing this book not only feasible, but a lot of fun as well. Many thanks to the rest of the Dutton and Penguin Random House team as well: Brian Tart, Ben Sevier, Christine Ball, Amanda Walker, Melanie Koch, Kathy Trager, Andrea Santoro, and Stephanie Hitchcock. And thanks to our film agent, Brandy Rivers, at Gersh Agency and attorney, David Davoli.

Tim Elfrink: Back in South Florida, many sincere thanks go to Chuck Strouse, the editor who brought me to *Miami New Times* six years ago. Chuck fought hard for this story and refused to let me take my foot off the gas pedal. Thanks go to the whole incredible team at *Miami New Times*, whose work turned a year of investigative reporting into reality: Nadine DeMarco, Jose Duran, Miche Ratto, Michael E. Miller, Francisco Alvarado, and resolute attorney Steve Suskin. Just about everyone at the paper and our sister publication in Broward helped me at some time or another and they all have my gratitude. Thanks also to Manuel Roig-Franzia at the *Washington Post* for his invaluable advice.

Several journalists helped add key reporting to this book. I'd like to mention in particular Steve Miller for his work plugging through data from the Florida Department of Health and Michael Rudon, a journalist in Belize City who organized my reporting in that country.

Thanks to my parents, Mary and Ted, my brothers, Pete and Connor, and all my family and friends back in St. Louis, who taught me to love baseball and writing in equal measure.

And lastly, thanks to Adele Coble, who makes it all worthwhile.

Gus Garcia-Roberts: Thanks to my editors at *Newsday* for allowing me to take time off to report this book. In particular, I owe a debt of gratitude to my boss, Director of Investigations Matthew Doig, who has the best story judgment of anybody I've ever known and who immediately recognized the opportunity in this one. Thanks to Will Van Sant, Sandra Peddie, Adam Playford, and Matt Clark, *Newsday* colleagues who were patient with my absence, inspired/tortured me with the incredible work they put together while I was gone, and didn't look at me too funny when I returned with a beard. I appreciated Thomas Maier, longtime *Newsday* reporter and author of several books, allowing me to corral him in the newsroom for impromptu mentoring. And thanks, of course, to Tim, for recruiting me to help tell this incredible story.

Thanks to my family—in particular my mother, Joan; father, Jose; sisters, Chloe and Valentina; brother, Uriel; and aunt Paz—for being equal parts brilliant, noble, creative, hilarious, and steadfast. Thanks for not putting out a missing persons bulletin for me during this process. A special cross-book shout-out goes to Chloe, whose own work of translated Chinese poems should be published right around the same time as this book.

And I truly couldn't have done it without my wife, who kept me in soup and brought me dispatches from the outside world as I camped out and grew haggard in our apartment. Our life together has been a wonderful adventure, Jenny.

NOTES

PROLOGUE

1 **Bosch asked in a gravelly tone:** Porter Fischer, interview by Tim Elfrink, June 2013.

2 **midtown Manhattan's most moneyed blocks**: Observations at scene by Gus Garcia-Roberts, September 30, 2013.

6 **"Please discontinue using the mug shot":** Joyce Fitzpatrick, e-mail to Tim Elfrink, October 1, 2013.

CHAPTER ONE

8 **both the company and the softball team:** Roger De Armas, all quotes in this chapter from interview by Tim Elfrink, September 2013.

9 **he famously punched a police lieutenant:** Guillermo Martinez and Jay Ducassi, "Bosch: Terrorist or Cuban Hero?," *Miami Herald*, April 3, 1983.

10 **the ob-gyn department to general surgery:** All details of Pedro's education come from his medical licensing documents from the Florida Department of Health.

11 **found out he'd been storing bombs there:** Martinez and Ducassi, "Bosch: Terrorist or Cuban Hero?"

12 **claiming his innocence until his death in 2011:** Alfonso Chardy, "Orlando Bosch Dies in Miami at 84," *Miami Herald*, April 27, 2011.

13 **Canseco wrote in his first memoir:** Jose Canseco, *Juiced: Wild Times, Rampant 'Roids, Smash Hits, and How Baseball Got Big* (New York: Harper-Collins, 2005).

14 **"I don't remember this guy being much of a player at all":** Jim Hendry, Mickey Maspons, Nick Martin-Hidalgo, and Jim Bernhardt, interviews by Tim Elfrink and Gus Garcia-Roberts, August to October 2013.

15 **You can't get much more American:** Associated Press, "Burglars Strike Again," January 29, 1998.

15 **shops Armani:** Joan Fleischman, "Alex Rodriguez Comes Up Short in Rip-off, Burglary," *Miami Herald*, January 28, 1998.

15 **travels in a Maybach:** Martin Fennelly, "It's Been Quality A-Rod Time," *Tampa Tribune,* May 7, 2009.

15 **owns a Picasso:** "Q & A ROD: News Sits Down with Yankee Megastar," *New York Daily News,* February 29, 2004.

15 **declares *Wall Street*:** Nate Penn, "MOTY: Alexander the (Expensive, Misunderstood, *but* Undeniably) Great," *GQ,* December 2007.

15 **worked for centavos behind the San Juan:** Ana Lopez, interview by Gus Garcia-Roberts, October 2013.

15 **president who had ruled the island:** "Informaciones del primer número del Periódico Tribuna Libre," accessed November 2013, http://identidadsan juanera.blogspot.com/2010/03/informaciones-del-primer-numero-del.html.

15 **flocked to the apartment to buy them:** All descriptions of Washington Heights apartment and details of family life from Ana Lopez, interview by Gus Garcia-Roberts, October 2013.

16 **Army official who barely knew Alex Rodriguez:** Jack Curry, "Alex and Victor Rodriguez Are Worlds Apart," *New York Times,* September 4, 2007.

16 **"He's been with me since I was born":** Associated Press, "A-Rod OK with MLB Ban on Cousin," June 4, 2011,

16 **getting work at the Ford plant in Edison:** Ana Lopez, interview by Gus Garcia-Roberts, October 2013.

17 **"It was a very close-knit family at that time":** Ibid.

17 **keep the lower classes distracted:** Robert Elias, *The Empire Strikes Out: How Baseball Sold U.S. Foreign Policy and Promoted the American Way Abroad* (New York: The New Press, 2010).

17 **Europe during World War II:** Allen Wells, *Tropical Zion: General Trujillo, FDR, and the Jews of Sosúa* (Durham and London: Duke University Press, 2009).

17 **massacre of more than twenty thousand Haitians:** Palash Ghosh, "Parsley Massacre: The Genocide That Still Haunts Haiti-Dominican Relations," *International Business Times,* October 15, 2012.

17 **"welling hopelessly from our breast: LIBERTY!":** Mendez, "Informaciones del Primer Número del Periódico Tribuna Libre."

18 **began to struggle financially:** Selena Roberts, *A-Rod: The Many Lives of Alex Rodriguez* (New York: HarperCollins, 2009).

18 **Lourdes wanted to stay put:** Bob Finnigan, "Missing Dad," *Seattle Times,* March 22, 1998.

18 **"because he adored those kids":** Ana Lopez, interview by Gus Garcia-Roberts, October 2013.

18 **"My special day":** Finnigan, "Missing Dad."

19 **"Tony always had a love for medicine":** Hernan Dominguez, interview by Tim Elfrink, November 2013.

21 **move to Florida to be the team's ringer:** Peter Slevin, Manny Garcia, and Don Van Natta Jr., "A String of Witnesses, A String of Violence: Buddies Life in the Fast Lane Led to Jail, Drug Trial," *Miami Herald,* July 18, 1993.

21 **"Some of the biggest sponsors back then are in prison now":** Jesus Morales, interview by Tim Elfrink, October 2013.

22 **"He truly loved what he was doing with the team":** Paul Biocic, interview by Tim Elfrink, October 2013.

22 **"Hey, kid, do you want to play?":** Roberts, *A-Rod.*

23 **Alex craved such tough love:** Description of Eddie Rodriguez and coaching style through Tom Bernhardt, interview by Gus Garcia-Roberts, December 2013.

23 **Probing for acceptance and guidance:** Roberts, *A-Rod.*

23 **"so the Boys Club was basically his home":** Tom Bernhardt, interview by Gus Garcia-Roberts, December 2013.

23 **fold-out couch at the Boys & Girls Club:** Eduardo Marcelino Rodriguez v. Lissette Rodriguez, November 4, 1988, Florida, Miami-Dade Marriage Court.

23 **traffic offender out of community service at the club:** Arnold Markowitz, "Traffic offender key to club director's arrest," *Miami Herald*, April 22, 1993.

23 **Danny Tartabull, Rafael Palmeiro, and Jose Canseco:** Jose Canseco, interview by Gus Garcia-Roberts, August 2013.

23 **black shirts and big crucifix necklaces:** Observation of Eddie Rodriguez by Gus Garcia-Roberts, January 2014.

23 **turning against his protégé:** Hernan Dominguez, interview by Tim Elfrink, November 2013.

24 **"The Old Man":** Tom Bernhardt, interview by Gus Garcia-Roberts, December 2013.

24 **and, at times, Yuri Sucart:** Tom Bernhardt, interview by Gus Garcia-Roberts, November 2013.

24 **shifts at a place called El Pollo Supremo:** Julie K. Brown, "Before He Was A-Rod," *Miami Herald*, August 3, 2013.

24 **"And the only answer was sports":** Tom Bernhardt, interview by Gus Garcia-Roberts, December 2013.

25 **"he doesn't even know that today":** Jim Bernhardt, interview by Gus Garcia-Roberts, December 2013.

25 **"This is *the guy*":** Kelvin Cabrera, interview by Gus Garcia-Roberts, November 2013.

25 **"He hadn't filled out yet":** Luis "Wicho" Hernandez, interview by Gus Garcia-Roberts, October 2013.

25 **"behind a palm tree at Columbus":** Classmate of Rodriguez, interview by Gus Garcia-Roberts, October 2013.

25 **the varsity squad in his freshman year:** Butch Staiano, interview by Gus Garcia-Roberts, November 2013.

26 **who idolized Baltimore Orioles shortstop Cal Ripken Jr.:** Roberts, *A-Rod.*

26 **the way he swaggered with bat in hand:** Luis "Wicho" Hernandez, interview by Gus Garcia-Roberts, October 2013.

26 **"Ryan would be the starting shortstop":** Ibid.

26 **"things he probably wishes he wouldn't say":** Tom Bernhardt, interview by Gus Garcia-Roberts, December 2013.

26 **"you'll have an opportunity to get there":** Ibid.

26 **miles north, to Westminster Christian:** Brown, "Before He Was A-Rod."

26 **his tuition through grants:** Ibid.

27 **school with such a small student body:** Kevin Ding, "Playing by the Numbers: Westminster Is the One," *Miami Herald*, April 23, 1996.

27 **"and not A-Rod":** Classmate of Rodriguez, interview by Gus Garcia-Roberts, October 2013.

CHAPTER TWO

28 **Boston had won every single contest:** "1889 Pittsburgh Allehenys," accessed November 2013, http://www.baseball-reference.com/teams/PIT/1889-schedule-scores.shtml.

28 **than any other time in his career:** "Pud Galvin," accessed November 2013, http://www.baseball-reference.com/players/g/galvipu01.shtml.

28 **when he recorded the first-known perfect game:** Charles Hausberg, "Pud Galvin," The SABR Baseball Biography Project, accessed October 2013, http://sabr.org/bioproj/person/38c553ff.

28 **drive and power packed into his stout frame:** No byline, "Steam Engine," *The Atchison Daily Globe*, February 28, 1889.

29 **him picking off three base runners in one inning:** Hausberg, "Pud Galvin."

29 **a wire story out of Indianapolis:** No byline, "Working Wonders: The Success of the Brown-Séquard Injection in Indianapolis," *The Daily Picayune*, August 11, 1889.

30 **under the skin on his stomach:** Roger I. Abrams, *The Dark Side of the Diamond: Gambling, Violence, Drugs and Alcoholism in the National Pastime* (Boston: Rounder Books, 2008). Additionally, Roger Abrams, interview by Tim Elfrink, December 2013.

30 **the Alleghenys to a 9-0 thumping of Boston:** Christopher Klein, "Baseball's First Fountain of Youth," History.com, April 5, 2012, accessed April 2014, http://www.history.com/news/baseballs-first-fountain-of-youth.

31 **"fifty percent psychological and fifty percent physical":** Roger Abrams, interview by Tim Elfrink, December 2013.

31 **pitcher Jim Bouton famously wrote:** Jim Bouton, *Ball Four, Plus Ball Five* (Briarcliff Manor, New York: Stein and Day, 1970), 45.

31 **didn't do much more than get users drunk:** Nicolas Rasmussen, *On Speed: The Many Lives of Amphetamine* (New York: NYU Press, 2009). Additionally, Nicolas Rasmussen, interview by Tim Elfrink, December 2013.

32 **including hallucinations of smoke filling the room:** Rasmussen, *On Speed*.

33 **"like racehorses" with Benzedrine:** Ibid.

33 **where players were force-fed steroids:** T. J. Quinn, "Pumped-up Pioneers: The '63 Chargers," ESPN.com, February 1, 2009, http://sports.espn.go.com/espn/otl/news/story?id=3866837.

33 **doctoral thesis found nearly all football pros:** Rasmussen, *On Speed*. Additionally, Nicolas Rasmussen, interview by Tim Elfrink, December 2013.

33 **"Where's my Dexamyl, Doc?":** Jim Brosnan, *The Long Season* (New York: Dell Publishing Co., 1960).

33 **"dispensed them as much as the players":** Johnny Bench, *Catch You Later: The Autobiography of Johnny Bench* (New York: HarperCollins, 1979), as quoted by Barry Lorge, "The Pressure Is On to Pop," *Washington Post*, May 28, 1979.

33 **"in a bowl, as if they were jelly beans":** Aaron Skirboll, *The Pittsburgh Cocaine Seven: How a Ragtag Group of Fans Took the Fall for Major League Baseball* (Chicago: Chicago Review Press, 2010), 36.

34 **"Some of the guys have to take one":** Bouton, *Ball Four, Plus Ball Five*, 81.

35 **any team in American professional sports:** Stephen Fastenau, "Phils Handed 10,000th Loss," MLB.com, July 15, 2007, http://philadelphia. phillies.mlb.com/news/article.jsp?ymd=20070715&content_id= 2089066&vkey=recap&fext=.jsp&c_id=phi.

35 **Dexarnyl, Eskatrol, Dexedrine, and Preludin at least twenty-three times:** UPI, "Phillies Farm Doctor Accused," November 21, 1980.

35 **"They were made at the request of the ballplayers":** Associated Press, "Charges Dismissed Against Phils Doctor," February 5, 1981.

36 **he wrote that greenies:** Bouton, *Ball Four, Plus Ball Five*.

36 **muscle relaxers all in heavy rotation:** Bil Gilbert, "Problems in a Turned-On World," *Sports Illustrated*, June 23, 1969.

36 **"Unfortunately and regrettably," he told the press:** Associated Press, "Phillies Denounced on Drugs," June 6, 1981.

36 **Mazza's attorney, Emmanuel Dimitriou, was less verbose:** Associated Press, "Charges Dismissed in Phils' Drug Case," February 5, 1981.

36 **speaking about baseball's drug scandals in general:** Dr. Charles Yesalis, interview by Tim Elfrink, January 2014.

37 **Pittsburgh's lime-green mascot:** Skirboll, *The Pittsburgh Cocaine Seven*, 36.

37 **pump him for intel on how many others were hooked:** Ibid.

38 **Keith Hernandez later estimated that 40 percent of big leaguers used coke:** Associated Press, "Hernandez Says 40 Percent of Players Used Cocaine," September 7, 1985.

38 **who represented many of the players involved:** Sam Reich, interview by Tim Elfrink, December 2013.

38 **fuzzy parrot costume for a wire taped to his belly:** Skirboll, *The Pittsburgh Cocaine Seven*, 36.

39 **slides, he told the court, "I'd go in headfirst":** Ibid.

40 **they could order a player tested:** Staff Report, "Baseball Approves Program on Drugs," *New York Times*, June 22, 1984.

40 **"it's a cloud called drugs":** Thomas Boswell, "Ueberroth Pleads for Drug Testing," *Washington Post*, September 25, 1985.

40 **by colluding to underpay players:** Murray Chass, "7 in Baseball Collusion Case Win Free Agency," *New York Times*, January 23, 1988.

40 **doped up with synthetic testosterone:** Shaun Assael, *Steroid Nation: Juiced Home Run Totals, Anti-Aging Miracles, and a Hercules in Every High School: The Secret History of America's True Drug Addiction* (New York: ESPN Books, 2007), 28.

41 **then testing them on his weight-lifting pals:** Justin Peters, "The Man Behind the Juice," *Slate*, February 18, 2005.

41 **"I wish to God now I'd never done it," Ziegler later said:** John D. Fair, "Isometrics or Steroids?: Exploring New Frontiers of Strength in the Early 1960s," *Journal of Sports History* 20, no. 1 (Spring 1993): 3.

41 **attributed in part to his own steroid use, at the age of sixty-three:** Peters, "The Man Behind the Juice."

41 **fining players $50 for not 'roiding with breakfast:** Quinn, "Pumped-up Pioneers."

41 **House recalled his skipper saying:** Tom House and Tim Kurkjian, "The House Experiment," *ESPN The Magazine*, November 8, 2005.

42 **"I pretty much popped everything," he said:** Ron Kroichick, "House a 'Failed Experiment' with Steroids," *San Francisco Chronicle*, May 3, 2005.

42 **"I've tried a lot of other things through the years":** Bouton, *Ball Four, Plus Ball Five*, 81.

42 **father of a Coral Park classmate:** Dale Tafoya, *Bash Brothers: A Legacy Subpoenaed* (Washington, D.C.: Potomac Books Inc., 2008).

43 **"I was kind of sleepwalking through games at that point":** Canseco, *Juiced*, 40.

43 **"I knew he was using some kind of chemicals":** Jose Canseco, interview by Gus Garcia-Roberts, August 2013.

43 **"the needle penetrating your buttock muscle":** Canseco, *Juiced*, 12.

44 **The average salary had almost tripled in five years:** Associated Press, "Average Baseball Salary," undated.

44 **"this unhealthy way players were living":** Jose Canseco, interview by Gus Garcia-Roberts, August 2013.

44 **without any "chemical enhancement":** Ibid.

44 **"The media dubbed us the Bash Brothers":** Ibid.

44 **Rafael Palmeiro, Ivan "Pudge" Rodriguez, and Juan Gonzalez:** Ibid.

45 **"Jose Canseco Milkshake":** Ken Rodriguez and Jorge Ortiz, "Canseco Denies Using Steroids," *Miami Herald,* September 30, 1988.

45 **"You steroid-shooting motherfucker!":** Skirboll, *The Pittsburgh Cocaine Seven*, 234.

45 **"Typhoid Mary" of steroids:** Steve Sailer, "Out of the Park," *The American Conservative*, April 12, 2004.

CHAPTER THREE

46 **The footage is shaky:** Descriptions of this game's footage come from a video shot by former Cardinal Newman players.

46 **Roger Jongewaard wrote of Rodriguez:** All scouting report descriptions are from Jongewaard's scouting report from Rodriguez, released by the Baseball Hall of Fame.

47 **grew up to peddle life insurance:** Joe Capozzi, "Former Cardinal Newman Players Remember the Day They Beat Alex Rodriguez," *Palm Beach Post*, October 28, 2009.

47 **"and I didn't have anything to lose":** Jack Kokinda, interview by Gus Garcia-Roberts, November 2013.

47 **"The best player in the country plays his worst game":** Judy Battista, "Westminster Stunned by Newman," *Miami Herald*, May 12, 1993.

48 **"Alex has a lot of connections":** Rodriguez's high school teammates, interviews by Gus Garcia-Roberts, September to November 2013.

48 **"It's almost like *omerta*":** Wayne Stewart, interview by Gus Garcia-Roberts, January 2014.

48 **a deal in 2006 to write a biography of Rodriguez:** S. L. Price, "The Writer and the Puzzle: Richard Ben Cramer Couldn't Crack A-Rod," *Sports Illustrated*, January 14, 2014.

49 **"Absolutely there was speculation":** Steve Kokinda, interview by Gus Garcia-Roberts, November 2013.

49 **"He was pretty scrawny":** Richard Hofman, interview by Gus Garcia-Roberts, February 2014.

49 **Rodriguez said that he'd like to be a civics teacher:** Finnigan, "Missing Dad."

49 **he had transformed himself in the weight room:** Richard Hofman, interview by the authors, February 2014.

49 **He had packed on twenty-five pounds of muscle:** Tim Wendel, *The New Face of Baseball* (New York: HarperCollins, 2003).

49 **"If you were to sit down in front of a computer":** Ed Giuliotti, "Prospect Perfect: 'Can't Miss' Banner Suits Westminster's Rodriguez Just Fine," *Sun Sentinel*, June 1, 1993.

49 **In his senior year, Rodriguez batted an otherworldly:** Bob Finnigan, "M's Draft Rodriguez—Player of Year Batted .505," *Seattle Times*, June 3, 1993.

49 **almost doubling his sophomore mark of .270:** Barry Horn, "Crowd Pleaser," *Dallas Morning News*, December 17, 2000.

49 **he popped nine homers and stole thirty-five bases in thirty-five tries:** Glenn Sheeley, "Mariners Choose High School SS Alex Rodriguez; Braves Sit Out First Round of Baseball's Amateur Draft," *The Atlanta Journal-Constitution*, June 3, 1993.

49 **able to bench press three hundred pounds:** No byline, "Transcript of Alex Rodriguez's Press Conference," *New York Times*, February 18, 2009.

49–50 **its way to a state berth in 1992:** Roddy Barnes, interview by Gus Garcia-Roberts, November 2013.

50 **"*There's something wrong here*":** Anthony Cancio Bello, interview by Gus Garcia-Roberts, November 2013.

50 **"holding him back was his stature, and he fixed that":** Roddy Barnes, interview by Gus Garcia-Roberts, November 2013.

50 **"because I work for the fire service":** Ibid.

50 **the knowledge of Coach Hofman:** Roberts, *A-Rod.*

51 **"an obscure writer trying to make a name for herself":** Richard Hofman, interview by Gus Garcia-Roberts, February 2014.

51 **Murray Chass calling the book an "abomination":** Murray Chass, "Roberts Whiffs on A-Rod and 'Roids," May 7, 2009, http://www.murray chass.com/?p=700.

51 **students polled knew another kid on steroids:** David Medzerian, "Steroid Scoop Puts Student on Top," *Miami Herald*, March 28, 1987.

51 **Almost immediately, Pelegri:** Mike Phillips, "Final Chance for a Coach," *Miami Herald*, November 28, 1989.

51 **South Florida's Monsignor Edward Pace High:** Monsignor Edward Pace High School website, accessed January 2014, http://www.msgr-pace.com/sports/MeetTheCoaches.php.

51 **attacking one another at meets:** Don Reynolds, interview by Gus Garcia-Roberts, November 2013.

52 **grumbled an Immokalee football coach:** Dan Deluca, "Teams Say State Failed Steroid Test," *The News-Press*, August 12, 2007.

52 **teenagers being coerced to pee in cups:** Don Reynolds, interview by Gus Garcia-Roberts, November 2013.

52 **"daughter a blue chipper in athletics":** William N. Taylor, *Anabolic Steroids and the Athlete* (Jefferson, NC: McFarland, 2002).

53 **"a millionaire by the end of the year":** Rickie Crotts and Jon Dietz, "Legal, Ethical Issues Trap Physicians," *Sarasota Herald-Tribune*, April 15, 1985.

55 **"There was one guy that found it all real funny":** Daniel Persaud, interview by Gus Garcia-Roberts, November 2013.

56 **played financial hardball like a jaded veteran:** Roberts, *A-Rod*.

56 **play for the hometown Florida Marlins:** Victor Lee, "Rodriguez had radical idea so Marlins can draft him," *Palm Beach Post*, May 19, 1993.

56 **future baseball card endorsements:** Roberts, *A-Rod*.

56 **Arriola salvaged a contract:** Ibid.

56 **"He was pretty much a glorified butler. He was a go-to guy":** Wilhelm Ansdale Henricus, interview by Gus Garcia-Roberts, September 2013.

57 **"takes care of things when you don't have time yourself":** Richard Hofman, interview by Gus Garcia-Roberts, February 2014.

57 **"upper-end early yuppie":** Michael Knisley, "All A-Rod, All the Times," *Sporting News*, June 28, 1999.

57 **"Grand Slam for Kids, handle that sort of thing":** Ibid.

57 **enthusiast who he had met at a Miami gym:** Associated Press, "Alex Rodriguez passed out during birth of his first daughter," May 6, 2008.

57 **Sucart's wife and kids:** Wilhelm Ansdale Henricus, interview by Gus Garcia-Roberts, September 2013.

58 **for dinner, drinks, and a cigar:** Ibid.

58 **"agency for professional athlete representation":** Washington State Office of the Secretary of State, Senok Management Group, LLC, corporation filed May 16, 2002.

59 **Canseco says he first started hanging out with Rodriguez:** Jose Canseco, *Vindicated: Big Names, Big Liars, and the Battle to Save Baseball* (New York: Simon & Schuster, 2009).

59 **ramming his wife's BMW with his Porsche:** No byline, "Canseco Rams into Wife's Car," *New York Times*, February 14, 1992.

59 **soon tested positive in jail for steroids:** Diane Marrero, "Canseco Sent Back to Jail for a Month," *Sun Sentinel*, June 24, 2003.

59 **And Canseco claimed to have dated Madonna:** Dave Goldiner, "Jose Canseco Claims Madonna Wanted His Baby, Magazine Sez," *New York Daily News,* July 10, 2008.

59 **Rodriguez reportedly went on to do:** Rebecca Winters Keegan, "A-Rod and Madonna: A Fan's Guide," *Time,* July 8, 2008.

59 **"but he's as milk-and-cookies":** Knisley, "All A-Rod, All the Times."

59 **surrounded by acres of poplar trees:** Jose Canseco, interview by Gus Garcia-Roberts, August 2013.

59 **"Alex didn't believe me":** Ibid.

59 **"A-Rod's 40-40 of Devonshire":** Knisley, "All A-Rod, All the Times."

60 **"That was the most beautiful woman I've ever seen":** Jose Canseco, interview by Gus Garcia-Roberts, August 2013.

60 **"a teenage girl going out to dinner with Madonna":** Jim Street, "Rodriguez Blossoms into Early All-Star," *Seattle Post-Intelligencer,* July 9, 1996.

60 **"Max," who was also a steroids provider:** Canseco, *Vindicated,* location 2093 (Kindle edition).

60 **identified by *Sports Illustrated* as "Max":** Selena Roberts and David Epstein, "Exclusive: The man behind the Max," *Sports Illustrated,* April 18, 2008.

61 **"My life is so clean I don't even take vitamins":** Gus Garcia-Roberts, "Canseco Creams A-Rod," *Miami New Times,* February 26, 2009.

61 **Miami-area Gulliver private school:** Ibid.

61 **Boys & Girls Club mentor, Eddie Rodriguez:** Christian Red, Nathaniel Vinton, Michael O'Keeffe, "Jose Canseco's steroid dealer says he never gave A-Rod drugs," *New York Daily News,* April 18, 2008.

61 **big for small market, mild-mannered Seattle:** Associated Press, "$252,000,000," December 11, 2000.

62 **later revealed by *Sports Illustrated*, failed:** Selena Roberts and David Epstein, "Sources tell SI Alex Rodriguez tested positive for steroids in 2003," *Sports Illustrated,* February 7, 2009.

63 **Primobolan, a steroid, and testosterone:** Ibid.

63 **worst free-agent signings in baseball history:** Page 2 Staff, "Worst Contracts in MLB History," ESPN.com, February 6, 2009, http://sports .espn.go.com/espn/page2/story?page=contracts/090206.

63 **California-based entity that paid Sucart's salary:** Florida Department of State Division of Corporations, Newport Property Ventures, corporation records filed December 30, 2003, Yuri Sucart bankruptcy, case 11-19621-AJC, filed April 10, 2011, Southern District of Florida.

63 **Rodriguez was a budding CEO:** Florida Department of Business and Professional Regulation, Construction Financial Officer license number FRO4147; Rodriguez took a construction financial officer's test in June 2009, during the season.

64 **slugger with a $20 million–plus:** "Manny Ramirez," accessed March 2014, http://www.baseball-reference.com/players/r/ramirma02.shtml.

64 **salary in order to make the deal happen:** Ross Newhan and Jason Reid, "Union's Reservations Block the Blockbuster," *Los Angeles Times,* December 18, 2003.

64 **When Aaron Boone tore a knee ligament:** ESPN.com News Services, "Hurt Playing Hoops, Boone Might Miss Season," ESPN.com, January 28, 2004, http://sports.espn.go.com/mlb/news/story?id=1719255.

64 **trademarked in Seattle in 1996:** United States Patent and Trademark Office, AROD; filed August 8, 1996, serial number 75147052.

64 **Rodriguez became a full-time third baseman:** ESPN.com News Services, "Selig Gives Blessing to Mega-merger," February 17, 2004, http://sports .espn.go.com/mlb/news/story?id=1735937.

65 **rainwear to cloth baby bibs:** United States Patent and Trademark Office, The Curse of the A-Rod; filed October 22, 2004, serial number 78504662.

65 **the youngest ever to that mark:** ESPN.com News Services, "A-Rod Becomes Youngest Player in MLB History to Hit 500 Homers," August 5, 2007, http://sports.espn.go.com/mlb/news/story?id=2961191.

65 **But a transcript obtained:** Grievance number 2013-2 (Alex Rodriguez), Vol. 8, Major League Baseball Arbitration Panel, Chairman Fredric R. Horowitz, October 17, 2013.

66 **On February 16, 2007:** Ibid.

66 **During his testimony:** Ibid.

67 **"do they have a legitimate medicinal purpose?":** Jonathan E. Kaplan, "2007 Brought Spike in Players Taking Stimulants for ADD," *Portland Press Herald*, January 16, 2008.

67 **insulting eighth in the batting order:** John Harper, "Source: By Batting A-Rod 8th in Playoffs, Joe Torre Wrote Him Off," *New York Daily News*, January 26, 2009.

67 **glove to avoid getting tagged out:** No byline, "Rodriguez: A Continual Stir," *New York Times*, January 11, 2014.

67 **"I'll even cheat to win":** Bob Finnigan, "Rodriguez Takes Losing Personally in This Lost Season," *Seattle Times*, September 14, 1998.

67 **harassed by rival fans with cutout masks:** "Sox Fans Can't Mask Hatred for A-Rod," TMZ.com, July 7, 2008, http://www.tmz.com/2008/07/07/ sox-fans-cant-mask-hatred-for-A-Rod.

67 **"Stray-Rod" by the *New York Post*:** "Stray-Rod," cover headline, *New York Post*, May 30, 2007.

67 **"There's big news brewing":** Richard Sandomir, "Rodriguez and Agent Hijack the World Series," *New York Times*, October 30, 2007.

68 **"then we don't want him":** Ed Price, "Hank Steinbrenner Fires Back at A-Rod," *Star-Ledger*, October 29, 2007.

68 **A saga of last-minute resuscitation began:** David Waldstein, "Hitched to an Aging Star: Anatomy of a Deal, and Doubts," *New York Times*, March 30, 2013.

69 **$275 million to stay in pinstripes until 2017:** Jack Curry and Tyler Kepner, "For Rodriguez and Yankees, It's All but Over," *New York Times*, October 29, 2007.

71 **to the good-natured animated ogre:** Roger Ball, interview by Gus Garcia-Roberts, November 2013.

71 **the focus of a three-thousand-word ESPN.com story:** Amy K. Nelson,

"Sucart 'Lives, Breathes to Please Alex,'" ESPN.com, March 2, 2009, http://sports.espn.go.com/mlb/news/story?id=3941742.

71 **filings showing his employment by Rodriguez:** Sucart Navarro v. Holder et al, case number 1:10-cv-20936-JAL, filed March 24, 2010, Southern District of Florida.

71 **Rodriguez paid him $57,499.92 a year:** US Bank v. Yuri Sucart, case number 09-064728-CA-01, filed August 10, 2009, Miami-Dade County Court.

71 **the roughest neighborhoods in the Miami area:** Miami-Dade Property Appraiser, folio numbers 01-3127-008-0022 and 01-3127-008-0022.

CHAPTER FOUR

74 **"Just look at that bomber who is a [Harvard] graduate":** Dr. Murali Rudraraju, interview by Tim Elfrink, January 2013.

74 **"Tony was a great marketer":** Roger De Armas, interview by Tim Elfrink, September 2013.

74 **"They were really aggressive young kids":** Tim Elfrink, "A Miami Clinic Supplies Drugs Sports' Biggest Names," *Miami New Times*, January 31, 2013.

75 **"It was a bad, bad experience":** Ibid.

75 **"Tony likes socializing":** Hernan Dominguez, interview by Tim Elfrink, December 2013.

76 **A landlord sued in 1994:** Erik Calonius v. Anthony Publio Bosch, case number 1994-474-CC-25, Miami-Dade Civil Court, January 20, 1994.

76 **Another man sued over a contract a few years later:** Bruno Rodriguez v. Anthony Publio Bosch, case number 1998-91848-CA-01, Miami-Dade Civil Court, April 21, 1998.

76 **In 1996, Tiki filed the first:** Anthony Bosch v. Tiki Bosch, case number 1992-50645-FC-04, Miami-Dade Civil Court, February 20, 1996.

77 **"He's not here," she told Bosch's old friend:** Roger De Armas, interview by Tim Elfrink, September 2013.

77 **sexually transmit cancer to their lovers:** Tom Farrey, "The Man Who Once Led the Charge Against Steroids Has a New Cause: Human Growth Hormone," *ESPN The Magazine*, July 10, 2012.

78 **clad only in a luridly striped Speedo:** Guinness World Records spokesperson, interview by Tim Elfrink, January 2014.

78 **isolated HGH from a human pituitary:** Vageesh Ayyar, "History of growth hormone therapy," *Indian Journal of Endocrinology and Metabolism* 15, supplement 3 (September 2011): S162–S165.

79 **"This is not a fountain of youth":** Wolfgang Saxon, "Daniel Rudman, 67; Studied Hormones and Aging," *New York Times*, April 20, 1994.

79 **carved years off their sagging pecs:** Farrey, "The Man Who Once Led the Charge Against Steroids Has a New Cause: Human Growth Hormone."

80 **"We cannot recommend it":** Staff Report, "Growth Hormone Fails to Reverse Effects of Aging, Researchers Say," *New York Times*, April 15, 1996.

80 **clinical rotations in Mexico:** Jerry Manier, "The Hope and the Hype," *Chicago Tribune*, April 14, 2002.

81 **"The war on aging has begun!":** Valerie Reitman, "A Rift in Business, Science of Aging," *Los Angeles Times*, January 12, 2004.

81 **the whole nation suffer from:** David B. Caruso and Jeff Donn, "Big Pharma Cashes In on HGH Abuse," Associated Press, December 21, 2012.

81 **"by claiming someone has this deficiency":** Dr. Peter Rost, interview by Tim Elfrink, October 2013.

82 **better-known antidepressants like Zoloft:** Caruso and Donn, "Big Pharma Cashes In on HGH Abuse."

82 **"Adult growth hormone deficiency syndrome is very rare":** Dr. Thomas Perls, interview by the authors, November 2013.

82 *Stopping the Clock*: Manier, "The Hope and the Hype."

82 **tax haven, he told a British reporter:** Tim Hulse, "Prince Lazarus Rules the Waves," *The Independent*, May 31, 1998.

83 **"bring $4,000 to $20,000 in annual gross revenue":** Brian Alexander, "Mainstream Docs Join Anti-Aging Bandwagon," NBC, April 21, 2008.

84 **visit by an author of this book:** Dr. Murali Rudraraju, interview by Tim Elfrink, January 2013.

85 **extended family familiar with his time in El Paso:** A member of Tony Bosch's extended family, interview by Tim Elfrink, January 2014.

86 **she couldn't fly to Miami herself:** In the Matter of the Marriage of Aliette Bosch and Anthony Bosch and in the Interests of Sofia Bosch and Nikolai Bosch, Children, District Court of El Paso County, Texas, 65th Judicial District Court, Honorable Alfredo Chavez.

86 **His records show that he later attended A4M conferences:** Details from Tony Bosch's records obtained by the authors.

89 **vocal critic of Florida's lack of regulation:** Tim Elfrink, "Biogenesis Just Hints at Florida's Anti-Aging Crisis," *Miami New Times*, December 19, 2013.

89 **One was his de facto medical advisor at VIP Med:** Mike Fish and T. J. Quinn, "Anthony Bosch's Tangle of Ties, Titles," ESPN, February 6, 2013.

89 **"He was training to learn how you dosify":** Ibid.

89 **"How do you not overdose somebody?":** Ibid.

89 **Sometimes he'd order concoctions:** Mike Fish and T. J. Quinn, "Records: Fake Scripts Used for PEDs," ESPN.com, April 26, 2013, http://espn.go.com/espn/otl/story/_/id/9215008/forged-prescription-forms-friends-performance-enhancing-drugs-supply-chain-major-league-baseball-players-used-south-florida-clinic.

CHAPTER FIVE

91 **"Listen, you grow up in the Bronx":** Kirk Radomski, interview by Gus Garcia-Roberts, January 2013.

91 **"his only partner in crime was the US Postal Service":** Kirk Radomski, *Bases Loaded* (New York: Hudson Street Press, 2009).

93 **Mandarich admitted that he'd used steroids at MSU:** Associated Press,

"Tony Mandarich Admits to Steroid Use in TV Interview," September 30, 2003.

93 **"that he did these summer camps":** Greg Stejskal, interview by Tim Elfrink, December 2013.

94 **"Millions . . . still look to those people":** Assael, *Steroid Nation*, 28.

95 **"They told us the White House called the FBI":** Greg Stejskal, interview by Tim Elfrink, December 2013.

95 **In Canada, cops seized $20 million in illegal steroids:** Cal Millar, "Top Judge's Son Charged in Massive Steroid Bust," *Toronto Star*, April 12, 1992.

96 **"In terms of steroid knowledge":** Curtis Wenzlaff, e-mail interview by Tim Elfrink, January 2013.

97 **"If Paris Hilton was to take that array":** T. J. Quinn, "Dealer: McGwire Wanted to be 'Bigger,'" ESPN.com, January 24, 2010, http://sports.espn.go.com/mlb/news/story?id=4849158.

97 **He drove a Chevy Caprice:** Howard Bryant, *Juicing the Game: Drugs, Power, and the Fight for the Soul of Major League Baseball* (New York: Viking, 2005), 51.

97–98 **"protect the integrity of the sport":** National Collegiate Athletic Association et al *v.* Christopher J. Christie et al, United States District Court District of New Jersey, Deposition of Bud Selig, November 9, 2012.

98 **Selig's group snatched the franchise:** Bryant, *Juicing the Game*, 51.

98 **While the owners (including Selig):** Associated Press, "Agent: Baseball Owners Agree to Pay $280 Million," November 4, 1990.

99 **"Fay sowed the seeds of his own destruction":** Bryant, *Juicing the Game*, 15.

100 **"It wasn't until 1998 or 1999":** Associated Press, "Selig: New Policy Will Be Effective," February 10, 2005.

100 **franchises were operating in the red:** Bryant, *Juicing the Game*, 56.

100 **"collusion was the turning point":** Selena Roberts, "A $280 Misdeed Still Fuels the Feud," *New York Times*, April 4, 2004.

100 **Vincent had issued a terse two-page memo:** Shaun Assael and Peter Keating, "Who Knew?: MLB Memos, 1991 Memo," *ESPN The Magazine*, November 8, 2005.

101 **venomous letters on his desk:** Bryant, *Juicing the Game*, 50.

102 **hitting the needle back at Scott's condo:** Shaun Assael, "Who Knew?: The Bodybuilder," *ESPN The Magazine*, November 8, 2005.

103 **"He asked what I knew about steroids":** Greg Steskjal, interview by Tim Elfrink, December 2013.

103 **Hallinan later released a statement:** ESPN.com News Services, "Canseco Bragged About 'Helper,'" ESPN.com, February 17, 2005, http://sports.espn.go.com/mlb/news/story?id=1992667.

104 **"It's like the big secret":** Bob Nightengale, "Steroids Become an Issue," *Los Angeles Times*, July 15, 1995.

105 **Musial had leaned over and whispered:** Bryant, *Juicing the Game*, 115.

105 **Attendance in 1995 was down 20 percent:** Associated Press, "1994 Strike Was a Low Point for Baseball," August 10, 2004.

106 **Andro was on the shelves there:** Bryant, *Juicing the Game*, 141.

106 **"I think what Mark McGwire":** Peter Schmuck, "Supplement Talk Going, Going Due to McGwire," *Baltimore Sun*, August 25, 1998.

106 **"no wonder the players loathe the media":** Bryan Curtis, "The Steroid Hunt," *Grantland*, January 8, 2014.

106 **Orza believed steroids:** Mark Fainaru-Wada and Lance Williams, *Game of Shadows* (New York: Gotham Books, 2006), 127.

106 **any move to randomly test players:** Steve Fainaru, "Baseball's Steroid Policy Was Made in Fear," *Washington Post*, December 21, 2003.

106 **steroids were a likely culprit:** Dr. John Cantwell, interview by Tim Elfrink, December 2013.

107 **freak injury came after he'd overused steroids and HGH:** Canseco, *Juiced*, 266.

107 **"I've wondered whether that batter hit":** Bryce Florie and Buster Olney, "I'll Wonder for the Rest of My Life," *ESPN The Magazine*, November 8, 2005.

107 **"I had recently come from the Olympics":** Dr. John Cantwell, interview by Tim Elfrink, December 2013.

107 **more than one in ten minor leaguers failed tests:** Bryant, *Juicing the Game*, 256.

108 **Unlike Sosa and McGwire, Bonds was:** Fainaru-Wada and Williams, *Game of Shadows*, 30.

108 **"If a young player were to ask me":** Tom Verducci, "Totally Juiced," *Sports Illustrated*, June 3, 2003.

109 **ample warning before their tests:** Associated Press, "Barry Bonds Might Have Received Warning of MLB's 2003 Drug Tests," December 14, 2007.

109 **Yet when the results came in:** John Schlegel, "Timeline of 'The List,'" MLB. com, September 30, 2009, http://mlb.mlb.com/news/article.jsp?ymd= 20090730&content_id=6157972&vkey=news_mlb&fext=.jsp&c_id=mlb.

111 **"overwhelming impression that Mr. Canseco is delusional":** Rob Neyer, "Canseco, Steroids, Pitch-Man, All Pumped Up, Nowhere to Go," *New York Observer*, February 21, 2005.

111 **Canadian attorney who would later:** Richard McLaren, interview by Tim Elfrink, November 2013.

113 **Radomski recalls Novitzky saying:** Radomski, *Bases Loaded*.

113 **"I wasn't BALCO":** Ibid.

114 **the senator scoffed:** Ibid.

114 **Radomski led law-enforcement investigators:** Alan Schwarz, "Analysis: The Clemens and McNamee Hearing," *New York Times*, February 13, 2008.

116 **"seemingly clean":** Katie Couric, "A-Rod Denies Doping on *60 Minutes*," *60 Minutes*, December 16, 2007.

116 **Less than a year later:** Associated Press, "A-Rod's Wife Files for Divorce, Alleges Infidelity, 'Other Marital Misconduct,'" July 7, 2008.

CHAPTER SIX

118 **spring training facility in Tampa, Florida:** Don Hooton, interview by Gus Garcia-Roberts, December 2013.

118 **Ten days earlier, *Sports Illustrated*:** Roberts and Epstein, "Sources Tell *SI* Alex Rodriguez Tested Positive for Steroids in 2003."

119 **"and I hope to join Don Hooton":** No byline, "Transcript of Alex Rodriguez's Press Conference," *New York Times*, February 18, 2009.

119 **samples of the 104 players who had tested dirty:** Michael S. Schmidt, "Union Official Says He Did Not Tip Off Rodriguez," *New York Times*, February 9, 2009.

120 **"it was such a loosey-goosey era":** ESPN.com News Services, "Alex Rodriguez Admits, Regrets Use of PEDs," ESPN.com, February 10, 2009, http://sports.espn.go.com/mlb/news/story?id=3894847.

120 **"a lot of ballplayers who played it straight":** Ibid.

121 **"We support Alex":** Ibid.

121 **forgiveness for using growth hormone:** Joe Lapointe, "Pettitte Apologizes to Yankees and His Fans," *New York Times*, February 19, 2008.

121 **no mention of performance enhancers:** David Waldstein, "With a Win, the Ending to Pettitte's Illustrious Career Is Complete," *New York Times*, September 28, 2013.

122 **The name trended on Google:** Google Trends: "Yuri Sucart."

122 **"steroid mule":** Mark Feinsand and Christian Red, "A-Rod's Cousin and Named Steroid Mule, Yuri Sucart, Spotted at Yankees Hotel; MLB Says It's Watching," *New York Daily News*, June 2, 2011.

122 **Rodriguez about the steroids revelation:** Grievance number 2013-2 (Alex Rodriguez) Vol. 8, Major League Baseball Arbitration Panel, Chairman Fredric R. Horowitz, October 17, 2013.

123 **Yuri Sucart's real estate speculation:** Miami-Dade Property Appraiser website, gisweb.miamidade.gov/PropertySearch.

123 **"He practically raised Alex at times":** Roger Ball, interview by Gus Garcia-Roberts, November 2013.

124 **Dr. Anthony Galea's trouble:** USA v. Galea, case number 1:10-cr-00307-RJA-HBS-1, filed October 14, 2010, Honorable Richard J. Arcara, US District Court, Western District of New York.

124 **In 2005, he spent four months:** Associated Press, "NFL Suspended Lewis for Two Games," January 27, 2005.

125 **Anthony Galea, who has arching:** Greg McArthur, "Anthony Galea's Path from Treating Superstars to Pleading Guilty," *Globe and Mail*, July 9, 2011.

126 **"Donna still works as his office manager":** USA v. Galea, case number 1:10-cr-00307-RJA-HBS-1, filed October 14, 2010, Honorable Richard J. Arcara, US District Court, Western District of New York.

126 **"So teenage boys do everything":** Leslie Papp, "Boys' Use of Steroids up Doctor Says," *Toronto Star*, May 6, 1995.

126 **Galea fathered a brood:** USA v. Galea, case number

1:10-cr-00307-RJA-HBS-1, filed October 14, 2010, Honorable Richard J. Arcara, US District Court, Western District of New York.

127 **Galea told an Israeli journalist:** McArthur, "Anthony Galea's Path from Treating Superstars to Pleading Guilty."

127 **Abdul-Karim al-Jabbar recover:** Allan Dunn, interview by Gus Garcia-Roberts, December 2013.

127 **Galea put his own spin on Dunn's methods:** USA v. Galea, case number 1:10-cr-00307-RJA-HBS-1, filed October 14, 2010, Honorable Richard J. Arcara, US District Court, Western District of New York.

127 **made trips to Germany:** Mike Fish, "The Doctor They Call 'Healing Hans,'" ESPN.com, December 15, 2011, http://espn.go.com/espn/otl/story/_/id/7324261/germany-dr-hans-wilhelm-muller-wohlfahrta-great-healer-quack-hyperactive-syringe.

128 **The World Anti-Doping Agency banned:** World Anti-Doping Program Prohibited List, Q & A on 2013 Prohibited List, http://www.wada-ama.org/en/World-Anti-Doping-Program/Sports-and-Anti-Doping-Organizations/International-Standards/Prohibited-List/QA-on-2013-Prohibited-List.

128 **Toronto slugger Carlos Delgado traveled:** Spencer Lader v. Carlos Delgado, case number 021324/2008, Justice Leonard B. Austin, Nassau County Civil Supreme Court, New York State.

128 **They're not best buds by any means:** Hank Haney, interview by Gus Garcia-Roberts, December 2013.

128 **nearly magical healing capabilities:** Randy Starkman, "Canada's Ski Side Is Changing Pace," *Toronto Star*, November 30, 1996.

129 **They had both treated sprinter Donovan Bailey:** Donovan Vincent, "Bailey Takes It Slow on Road to Recovery," *Toronto Star*, December 15, 1998.

129 **Mets speedster Jose Reyes's hamstring:** Former Mets trainer Vern Gambetta, interview by Gus Garcia-Roberts, December 2013.

129 **preferred not to have broadcasted:** Michael O'Keeffe, Teri Thompson, and Nathaniel Vinton, "Buffalo FBI Probing Tiger Woods' Doctor Tony Galea," *New York Daily News*, December 15, 2009.

129 **parachuting out of planes:** Hank Haney, *The Big Miss: My Years Coaching Tiger Woods* (New York: Random House, 2012).

129 **"You're all of a sudden not going to be Tiger Woods anymore":** Hank Haney, interview by Gus Garcia-Roberts, December 2013.

129–30 **"full of guesses":** ESPN.com News Services, "Hank Haney Defends Tiger Book," ESPN.com, March 26, 2012, http://espn.go.com/golf/story/_/id/7738710/hank-haney-tiger-woods-agent-mark-steinberg-trade-barbs-book.

130 **couldn't walk up a hill to greet fans:** Chris Dufresne, "Better Than All the Rest," *Los Angeles Times*, June 17, 2008.

130 **"He wanted somebody progressive":** Hank Haney, interview by Gus Garcia-Roberts, December 2013.

130 **Woods lived in a $2.4 million mansion:** No byline, "Keeping Things Private," *Orlando Sentinel*, December 13, 2009.

130 **On a massage table between:** Hank Haney, interview by Gus Garcia-Roberts, December 2013.

130 **charged $2,000 a session:** Florida Department of Health, Anthony Galea file, case number 2009-24325.

131 **Galea set up his platelet-rich plasma:** Ibid.

132 **"Never performance enhancement":** Brian Greenspan, interview by Gus Garcia-Roberts, January 2013.

132 **"That seems to be a part of Galea's program":** Hank Haney, interview by Gus Garcia-Roberts, December 2013.

132 **a thigh specialist in Vail, Colorado:** Michael S. Schmidt, "Alex Rodriguez Denies Taking Drugs," *New York Times*, April 2, 2010.

132 **"unparalleled in the medical field":** Mike Fish, "Referrals of the Highest Profile," ESPN.com, December 15, 2011, http://m.espn.go.com/wireless/story?storyId=7324265&wjb=&pg=1.

132 **Rodriguez was also quietly treated:** Schmidt, "Alex Rodriguez Denies Taking Drugs."

133 **"a history of complete success":** USA v. Galea, case number 1:10-cr-00307-RJA-HBS-1, filed October 14, 2010, Honorable Richard J. Arcara, US District Court, Western District of New York.

133 **The bridge connects Ontario:** USA v. Catalano, case number 1:10-cr-00142-RJA, filed May 18, 2010, US District Court, Western District of New York.

134 **Washington Redskins football player:** Michael S. Schmidt and Katie Thomas, "Doctor Accused of Doping Is Linked to NFL," *New York Times*, May 18, 2010.

134 **"He's a healer, not a cheater":** Brian Greenspan, interview by Gus Garcia-Roberts, January 2013.

135 **later cracked in court:** USA v. Catalano, case number 1:10-cr-00142-RJA, filed May 18, 2010, US District Court, Western District of New York.

136 **"we love each other":** William C. Rhoden, "Perception's Changed but Rodriguez Hasn't," *New York Times*, November 5, 2009.

136 **then–Mets teammate Carlos Beltran:** Michael S. Schmidt, "Beltran Says He Referred Reyes to Galea for Treatment," *New York Times*, March 2, 2010.

137 **newly heroic third baseman said he had not:** Michael S. Schmidt, "For Rodriguez and Yankees, Another Bout of Disclosure," *New York Times*, March 1, 2010.

137 **the team said in a statement:** Ibid.

137 **days of 2010 spring training:** Michael S. Schmidt and Serge Kovaleski, "Baseball Still Looking at Rodriguez's Care by Indicted Doctor," *New York Times*, June 5, 2011.

137 **HGH to a retired NFL player:** USA v. Galea, case number 1:10-cr-00307-RJA-HBS-1, filed October 14, 2010, Honorable Richard J. Arcara, US District Court, Western District of New York.

138 **Galea's attorneys wrote:** Ibid.

139 **"the sports leagues they played in":** Ibid.

139 **punishable by up to a year in jail:** Florida Department of Health, Anthony Galea file, case number 2009-24325.

141 **"I can assure you if we"**: Brian Greenspan, interview by Gus Garcia-Roberts, January 2013.

141 **"Dr. G, you are the best!"**: Anthony Galea, *The Real Secret to Optimal Health* (Toronto: BurmanBooks, 2013).

CHAPTER SEVEN

142 **"He was devastated"**: Associated Press, "Ramirez Tests Positive, Suspended for 50 Games," uploaded to YouTube, May 8, 2009, http://www.youtube.com/watch?v=rQp-Rs8R7N8.

142 **Fenway's speakers during warm-ups:** Jean Rhodes and Shawn Boburg, *Becoming Manny: Inside the Life of Baseball's Most Enigmatic Slugger* (New York: Scribner, 2009), 2.

143 **he'd grown up poor:** Sara Rimer, "Before Manny Became Manny," *New York Times*, April 25, 2011.

143 **but had also already burned Rodriguez:** Michael S. Schmidt, "Ortiz and Ramirez Are Said to Be on '03 Doping List," *New York Times*, July 30, 2009.

144 **Manny still ended up suspended:** Teri Thompson and Nathaniel Vinton, "Ban of Dodger's Slugger Manny Ramirez Shows Commitment from MLB to Catch Drug Cheats," *New York Daily News*, May 9, 2009.

144 **possibly aided by his son Tony:** Amy K. Nelson and T. J. Quinn, "Miami Doctors Probed in Ramirez Case," ESPN.com, June 25, 2009, http://sports.espn.go.com/mlb/news/story?id=4286540.

144 **"outrageous and slanderous":** T. J. Quinn, "Doctor Says He's Never Prescribed hCG," ESPN.com, July 10, 2009, http://sports.espn.go.com/mlb/news/story?id=4319776.

145 **"Deal with problems: Manny Ramirez":** Tony Bosch's handwritten business records obtained by the authors.

145 **"He was bragging about how he was Manny's boy":** UM fraternity brother, interviews by Gus Garcia-Roberts, November 2013 to January 2014.

145 **Manny for the failed PED test:** In the Matter of Arbitration Between Major League Baseball Players Association and Office of the Commissioner of Baseball, panel decision number 131, grievance number 2013-02 (Alexander Rodriguez), Fredric R. Horowitz, Esq., Panel Chair, December 20, 2013.

145 **advertising for Bosch's services:** Ibid.

146 **"I got really fat":** Porter Fischer, interview by Tim Elfrink, June 2013.

147 **"If you want to know the source":** Tim Elfrink, "MLB Steroid Scandal: How Porter Fischer Exposed the Coral Gables Clinic," *Miami New Times*, June 20, 2013.

148 **they had watched their wealthy father:** Gelband v. Matthews, 00280 TSN 2004, Civil Court of the City of New York, New York County.

148 **"I don't remember him looking":** Former classmate of Anthony Carbone, interview by Gus Garcia-Roberts, January 2014.

148 **"I wanted to be a cop when":** Anthony Carbone, interview by Gus Garcia-Roberts, December 2013.

149 **Jones had first sped into Florida:** USA v. Jones, case number 3:87CR18, Judge Burns, US District Court, District of Connecticut.

151 **The Carbones threatened him:** Beverly West, interview by Gus Garcia-Roberts, December 2013.

152 **tried to pawn the victim's:** Miami-Dade Police Department records, case number 0003169006, June 26, 1991, arrest.

152 **"He is likely bipolar or has some other":** Carlos Alvarez Diez, interview by Gus Garcia-Roberts, January 2014.

152 **ANTI8GE and ANTIAGE:** Coral Gables Police Department, case number 13-007397, October 5, 2013.

153 **"I know Oggi was a partner in Boca Body":** Anthony Carbone, interview by Gus Garcia-Roberts, December 2013.

155 **"Oh my God, you're so skinny!":** Betty Tejada, Tony Lamberto, and Alan Telisman, interviews by the authors, October and November 2013.

158 **He regularly crashed vehicles in an insurance scam:** Miami-Dade Court records. Additionally, Serge Casimir's boss, interview by Tim Elfrink, October 2013.

158 **Far higher up on the criminal food chain:** United States v. Birbragher, Government's Motion for Pre-Trial Detention, United States District Court for the Northern District of Iowa Eastern Division, December 7, 2007.

158 **who spent more than a half-million dollars:** USA v. Birbragher et al, case number 2:07-cr-01023-LRR-1, US District Court, Northern District of Iowa, filed November 6, 2007.

158 **"model citizen":** USA v. Birbragher, case number 1:11-tp-20053-JAL-1, Southern District of Miami, filed April 12, 2011.

158 **under the terms of his probation:** Ibid.

159 **its ritual animal sacrifices:** Michael E. Miller, "Los Miami Gang Nabbed in Huge Drug Bust," *Miami New Times*, August 11, 2011.

159 **"youth, sexual intimacy, digestion":** Investigation summary of Florida Department of Health case number 2013-02216, investigator Jerome K. Hill, April 23, 2013.

162 **Arnold had synthesized it:** Fainaru-Wada and Williams, *Game of Shadows*, 50–53.

164 **"It was unbelievably individualized":** Travis Tygart, interview by Tim Elfrink, February 2014.

165 **Bosch simply wasn't "very sophisticated":** Patrick Arnold, e-mail interview by Tim Elfrink, January 2014.

165 **"This idea of microdosing to give":** Dr. Charles Yesalis, interview by Tim Elfrink, January 2014.

165 **"I had conversations with":** Transcripts obtained by the authors of Grievance number 2013-2 (Alex Rodriguez) Vol. 8, Major League Baseball Arbitration Panel, Chairman Fredric R. Horowitz, October 17, 2013.

CHAPTER EIGHT

167 **came very late on a sweltering night in Tampa:** In the Matter of Arbitration Between Major League Baseball Players Association and Office of the Commissioner of Baseball, panel decision number 131, grievance number 2013-02 (Alexander Rodriguez), Fredric R. Horowitz, Esq., Panel Chair, December 20, 2013.

167 **Instead, Bosch later said:** Scott Pelley, "The Case of Alex Rodriguez," *60 Minutes*, January 12, 2014.

168 **give him an intramuscular injection:** In the Matter of Arbitration Between Major League Baseball Players Association and Office of the Commissioner of Baseball, panel decision number 131, grievance number 2013-02 (Alexander Rodriguez), Fredric R. Horowitz, Esq., Panel Chair, December 20, 2013.

169 **with Miami's area code of 305:** Anthony Bosch's personal records obtained by the authors.

169 **was nearing obesity in his late forties:** In the Matter of Arbitration Between Major League Baseball Players Association and Office of the Commissioner of Baseball, panel decision number 131, grievance number 2013-02 (Alexander Rodriguez), Fredric R. Horowitz, Esq., Panel Chair, December 20, 2013.

169 **newly banned-from-the-MLB cousin:** Yuri Sucart bankruptcy, case 11-19621-AJC, filed April 10, 2011, Southern District of Florida.

171 **The *New York Daily News* called it:** John Harper, "Brian Cashman Says Strategy, Not Thumb Injury, Kept Alex Rodriguez on the Bench During All-Star Game," *New York Daily News*, July 14, 2010.

171 **him to deal to Rodriguez:** Associated Press, "Alex Rodriguez Hits 600th Career Home Run," August 4, 2010.

171 **auctioned for $3 million:** "McGwire's 70th Home Run Ball Sells for $3 Million, Including Commission," CNN, January 13, 1999.

171 **four games in Cleveland, either:** Ian Begley, "A-Rod Still Stuck on Homer No. 599," ESPNNewYork.com, August 3, 2010, http://m.espn.go.com/general/story?storyId=5432846.

171 **went through more than one hundred of them:** Ibid.

172 **starting with Willie Mays at 660:** Associated Press, "Rodriguez Finalizes $275 Million Deal with Yankees," December 13, 2007.

172 **"A-Rod still is a very good":** Andrew Marchand, "Mr. October? Rodriguez Had Better Be," ESPNNewYork.com, August 4, 2010, http://sports.espn.go.com/new-york/mlb/news/story?id=5435643.

172 **They met at a Tampa hotel:** In the Matter of Arbitration Between Major League Baseball Players Association and Office of the Commissioner of Baseball, panel decision number 131, grievance number 2013-02 (Alexander Rodriguez), Fredric R. Horowitz, Esq., Panel Chair, December 20, 2013.

173 **Denzel Washington and Sting:** Owen Moritz, "A-Rod Joins Sting, Denzel Washington, Other Rich and Famous at 15 Central Park West," *New York Daily News*, February 27, 2010.

174 **"That's a chapter of his life I think"**: Tyler Klepner, "Mixed Feelings as Rodriguez Nears 600," *New York Times*, July 21, 2010.

174 **He wanted to be the lone member**: Pelley, "The Case of Alex Rodriguez."

174 **"Being stuck at 599 was really"**: Ben Shpigel, "Yankees Pull Further and Further Away," *New York Times*, August 15, 2010.

176 **address in the DR within seventy-two hours**: Seth Kugel, "Like an Extension Cord That's Really, Really Long," *New York Times*, February 14, 2004.

176 **play for the YSL as a teenager**: Mel Zitter, interview by Gus Garcia-Roberts, December 27, 2013.

177 **Bodega Association of the United States**: Thomas J. Lueck, "Buyers of Ballplayer Phone Cards Say They Were Robbed," *New York Times*, December 8, 2005.

177 **An attorney for the Levinsons**: Jay Reisinger, interview by Gus Garcia-Roberts, April 2014.

177 **"That's a lie"**: Omar Minaya, interview by Gus-Garcia Roberts, April 2014.

178 **an estimated $660 million**: ACES website, accessed March 2014, AcesInc Baseball.com.

178 **The two diminutive**: Athletes Careers' Enhanced v. Jeremy Gilmore; Kings County Civil Court, case number 023456/2009. (According to the process server in the suit, the brothers are five-foot-eight.)

178 **who is older, entered college at age sixteen**: Tiffany Hundley, interview by Gus Garcia-Roberts, January 2014.

178 **became a lawyer in 1985**: New York State Unified Court System, Attorney Detail, registration number 1970722.

178 **"'Get these guys out of here!'"**: Kirk Radomski, interview by Gus Garcia-Roberts, January 2013.

178 **ACES from superagent Scott Boras**: Kirk Radomski, Jeremy Gilmore, and others familiar with ACES, interviews by the authors, October 2013 to January 2014.

178 **"Seth would just talk my ear off"**: Tiffany Hundley, interview by Gus Garcia-Roberts, January 2014.

179 **Radomski says that he visited the Levinsons'**: Kirk Radomski, interview by Gus Garcia-Roberts, January 2013.

179 **Sam Levinson instructed Radomski**: Affidavit of Kirk Radomski obtained by the authors, September 11, 2012.

179 **Stanton has denied that the Levinsons**: Michael S. Schmidt, "Role of Agents Raised in Scandal," *New York Times*, August 24, 2012.

179 **"you got ethics, you got rules. Sam's not"**: Kirk Radomski, interview by Gus Garcia-Roberts, January 2013.

180 **going directly from ACES to Radomski**: Checks, dated 6/26/04 and 8/7/04, obtained by the authors.

180 **In 2012, during Roger Clemens's perjury trial**: USA v. Clemens, United States District Court District of Columbia, trial testimony, May 21, 2012.

181 **Nunez was hired in 2006**: Jay Reisinger, interview by Gus Garcia-Roberts, April 2014.

181 **It appears that Nunez was also a recruiter:** Mel Zitter, interview by Gus Garcia-Roberts, December 27, 2013.

181 **a baseball team executive disputes that:** Baseball executive, interview by Gus Garcia-Roberts, April 2014.

182 **"He wanted to get into a nutritional":** Christian Red, "How Ex-Yankee Melky Cabrera Has Done a Body Good," *New York Daily News*, July 7, 2012.

182 **All three times, he'd pissed clean:** In the Matter of Arbitration Between Major League Baseball Players Association and Office of the Commissioner of Baseball, panel decision number 131, grievance number 2013-02 (Alexander Rodriguez), Fredric R. Horowitz, Esq., Panel Chair, December 20, 2013.

184 **Another Facebook photo shows Paublini:** Cesar Paublini's Facebook photos, accessed March 2014, https://www.facebook.com/cesar.paublini.1?ref=search.

184 **the corporation was nothing more:** RPO LLC, Florida Department of State, Division of Corporations, corporation filed April 11, 2012.

CHAPTER NINE

185 **"He was trying to look more legit":** UM fraternity brother, interview by Gus Garcia-Roberts, October 2013 to January 2014.

186 **"I'm playing racquetball and feeling good":** Julio Cortes, interview by Tim Elfrink, January 2014.

187 **"But a sixteen-year-old kid? That's not right":** A Tony Bosch client, interview by Tim Elfrink, January 2014.

188 **"if everybody's on it, wouldn't that be fair play?":** Pelley, "The Case of Alex Rodriguez."

189 **that the school had no baseball diamond:** Beth Feinstein-Bartl, "Bible School Coach Doing Divinely," *Miami Herald*, July 1, 1993.

189 **"It almost look[ed] like he was cut out of a rock":** Roddy Barnes, interview by Gus Garcia-Roberts, October 2013.

189 **windshields and other dubious methods:** Roddy Barnes and Anthony Cancio Bello, interviews by Gus Garcia-Roberts, October 2013.

189 **Instead she suspected Martinez:** Rana L. Cash, "Florida Bible Shows No Mercy, Has No Excuse," *Miami Herald*, March 26, 1996.

190 **"Only now that I'm thinking back":** Anthony Cancio Bello, interview by Gus Garcia-Roberts, October 2013.

190 **Between the two private schools:** Anthony Uttariello, "Martinez Resigns as Head Coach at Sagemont," BrowardHighSchoolBaseball.com, June 1, 2012, http://www.browardhighschoolbaseball.com/2012/06/martinez-resigns-as-head-coach-at-sagemont/01012298.

191 **Player of the Year in Broward County:** Jame Oyola, "Brandon Sedell Looks to Lead American Heritage Baseball Back Atop Florida," MaxPreps.com, March 7, 2011.

191 **"[He] vehemently denies ever visiting":** Letter from David Kubulian to Tim Elfrink, August 2013.

192 **Radomski did so in the team clubhouse:** George J. Mitchell, "Report to the Commissioner of Baseball of an Independent Investigation into the Illegal Use of Steroids and Other Performance Enhancing Substances by Players in Major League Baseball," December 13, 2007, http://files.mlb.com/mitchrpt .pdf.

192 **exploded one of his testicles, resulting in surgery:** Dick Rockne, "Manzanillo Has Surgery, Goes on Disabled List," *Seattle Times*, April 10, 1997.

192 **Manzanillo is cofounder of Manzy's:** Manzy's Pitching Farm website, accessed March 2014, manzyspitchingfarm.com.

192 **"I have no idea who you're talking about":** Josias Manzanillo, interview by Gus Garcia-Roberts, April 2014.

192 **Chicago Bulls forward Carlos Boozer:** Michelle Kaufman, "Carlos Boozer's No. 1 Choice Is Miami Heat," *Miami Herald*, July 21, 2009.

192 **Hank Kline Boys & Girls Club in Miami:** Boozer's Buddies Inc., Florida Department of State, Division of Corporations, corporation filed June 21, 2010.

193 **Miami Beach's Lincoln Road in October 2013:** CBF Sports Management website, accessed January 2014, cbfcamps.com.

193 **though Fragela's attorney, Richard Barbara:** Richard Barbara, interview by Gus Garcia-Roberts, April 2014.

193–94 **bragged about Manny Ramirez and Melky Cabrera:** UM fraternity brother, interviews by the authors, October 2013 to January 2014.

194 **"We gotta get dinner, you gotta":** Tony Bosch client, interview by Tim Elfrink, November 2013.

194 **"He said [Bosch] was a person who":** Alfonso Otero, interview by Gus Garcia-Roberts, February 2014.

195 **"Shit is fire got purple in it":** Details on Frankie Ratcliff's arrest come from discovery in Miami-Dade State Attorney Katherine Rundle's felony case, F-10-026345, closed November 8, 2010.

195 **Now league investigators followed:** A source with knowledge of the investigation, interview by Tim Elfrink, December 2013.

CHAPTER TEN

198 **taking future pros like Danny Graves:** Judy Battista, "Stellar UM Pitchers Get Perfect Chance to Shine," *Miami Herald*, May 26, 1994.

198 **an uncertified baseball agent in Miami:** Gus Garcia-Roberts, "Cuban Baseball Agents: Risks and Lies," *Miami New Times*, April 19, 2012.

199 **"father figure" to the kid, according:** Kevin Santiago, interview by Gus Garcia-Roberts, February 2014.

199 **Chris Perez threw ninety-mile-per-hour fastballs:** The Baseball Cube website, accessed February 2014, TheBaseballCube.com. Additionally, Greg Cote, "Morris' Finest Season?," *Miami Herald*, June 10, 2004.

200 **"violating team policy," fresh off setting:** Susan Miller Degnan, "Cockroft Finds His Pitching Groove," *Miami Herald*, May 1, 2004.

201 **"It was 'Alex has this car'"**: Steve Tolleson, interview by Gus Garcia-Roberts, January 2014.

201 **Carlos, owns the Miami-based ABCO Products:** ABCO Products Inc., Florida Department of State, Division of Corporations, corporation filed December 18, 1979.

201 **Nicaraguan American Chamber of Commerce:** No byline, "Business Notes," *Miami Herald*, August 22, 1999.

201 **glossies of the string-topped cleaning implement:** Observations from visit to factory by Gus Garcia-Roberts, January 2014.

201 **"them because they would shoot him":** Miami Beach Police Department report filed April 19, 2012, in Miami Beach, Florida.

201 **explained that Albir was a Hurricane:** Associate of the UM team, interview by Tim Elfrink, November 2013.

201 **"university policy" violations:** Jorge Milian, "Two UM Players Suspended," *Palm Beach Post*, January 22, 2005.

202 **"He was sitting in a stall":** Kevin Santiago, interview by Gus Garcia-Roberts, February 2014.

202 **Albir had failed the PED test:** Raudel Alfonso, interview by Gus Garcia-Roberts, February 2014.

202 **"It was a mistake, and Gaby's moved on":** Alfonso Otero, interview by Gus Garcia-Roberts, February 2014.

202 **When MLB investigated the program:** A source with knowledge of the investigation, interview by Tim Elfrink, November 2013.

203 **the Blue Jays and Marlins organizations:** Ryan Patterson, interview by Gus Garcia-Roberts, February 2014.

203 **exactly from whom he purchased them:** Former associate of the team, interview by Gus Garcia-Roberts, January 2013.

204 **an Associated Press article on the statement:** Associated Press, "UM: No Positive Tests," February 7, 2013.

206 **a remarkable third time in one college career:** A source with knowledge of D. J. Schwatscheno, interview by Gus Garcia-Roberts, November 2013.

207 **Like Kosar, he sat on the UM board of trustees:** Associated Press, "A-Rod Named to Miami's Board of Trustees," January 23, 2004.

207 **The pitcher also gummed up:** Two sources familiar with the investigation, interviews by Tim Elfrink, November 2013.

208 **"He's the one who made it possible":** UM fraternity brother, interview by Gus Garcia-Roberts, January 2014.

208 **Globo Investments LLC, Ecolite Solutions Inc.:** MAC Investors Inc. (corporation filed August 2, 2005), Ecolite Solutions Inc. (corporation filed June 21, 2010), Florida Department of State, Division of Corporations; Globo Investments LLC (corporation filed 2007), Texas Secretary of State.

208 **Bosch to budding superstar Ryan Braun:** Tom Haudricourt, "Details on Ryan Braun's Ties to Biogenesis Begin to Emerge," *Milwaukee Journal Sentinel*, July 24, 2013.

209 **Anheuser-Busch as, yes, a brewer:** Ben Bolch, "Braun Is a Premium Brew," *Los Angeles Times*, August 17, 2008.

209　**the tidy half of the *Odd Couple*:** Mike Phillips, "Cleaning Up," *Miami Herald*, April 18, 2003.

209　**"And I'm extremely proud to be a role model":** Bob Nightengale, "Brewers' Ryan Braun Considers Himself Role Model for Jewish Community," *USA Today*, May 24, 2010.

209　**the Brewers superstar's fifth MLB summer:** Braun statement released August 22, 2013.

210　**speculation was rampant that he had:** Ben Shpigel, "A Pariah Returns, to His Peers' Chagrin," *New York Times*, June 27, 2012.

210　**keep him in Wisconsin until 2020:** Joe Lemire, "Five Cuts: Breaking Down Brewers-Braun Contract Extension," *Sports Illustrated*, April 21, 2011.

210　**Ryan Braun's Graffito, for dinner:** Associate of Braun, interview by Gus Garcia-Roberts, December 2013.

211　**sealed by a thin man with a mustache:** ESPN.com News Services, "Collector Says He Acted as Instructed," ESPN.com, February 29, 2012, http://espn.go.com/mlb/story/_/id/7625905.

211　**randomly tested three times that year:** Todd Rosiak, "Transcript of Ryan Braun's Statement," *Milwaukee Journal Sentinel*, February 24, 2012.

211　**they wouldn't piss dirty:** In the Matter of Arbitration Between Major League Baseball Players Association and Office of the Commissioner of Baseball, panel decision number 131, grievance number 2013-02 (Alexander Rodriguez), Fredric R. Horowitz, Esq., Panel Chair, December 20, 2013.

211　**"opening day can't come here soon enough":** Bill Glauber, "Brewers Fans Savor the Season," *Milwaukee Journal Sentinel*, October 16, 2011.

211　**Braun learned that he had pissed positive:** Rosiak, "Transcript of Ryan Braun's Statement."

211　**the urine sample had come back:** T. J. Quinn and Mark Fainaru-Wada, "Braun's defense raises more questions," ESPN.com, February 25, 2012, http://espn.go.com/espn/otl/story/_/page/OTL-Ryan-Braun/ryan-braun -defense-raises-more-questions-doping-experts.

212　**The case was settled out of court:** Christian Red, "J. C. Romero, Former Phillies Reliever Suspended for Performance Enhancing Drugs, Says 'Justice Is Served' after Supplement Is Tainted," *New York Daily News*, January 10, 2012.

212　**spin that might help Braun's appeal:** Sasson lawsuit filed in Milwaukee County court, filed July 2013.

213　**But it was a loophole large enough:** Quinn and Fainaru-Wada, "Braun's Defense Raises More Questions."

213　**"It's a beautiful day in Malibu":** Todd Rosiak, "Braun Named NL MVP," *Milwaukee Journal Sentinel*, November 22, 2011.

213　**Braun had been suspended and was appealing:** Mark Fainaru-Wada and T. J. Quinn, "Ryan Braun Tests Positive for PED," ESPN.com, December 12, 2011, http://espn.go.com/espn/otl/story/_/id/7338271.

213　**"and anyone who writes that is wrong":** Teri Thompson, "Ryan Braun's Initial Test Results Were 'Insanely High,'" *New York Daily News*, December 11, 2011.

213 **The de facto judge deciding his fate:** Shyam Das's résumé available online, accessed March 2014, http://www.nmb.gov/arbitrator-resumes/das-shyam_ res.pdf.

214 **collected it from Braun in the locker room:** Tom Verducci, "Answering Key Questions in Wake of Ryan Braun Suspension," *Sports Illustrated*, July 23, 2013.

214 **He had then mailed them to Montreal:** ESPN.com News Services, "Statement from Dino Laurenzi Jr.," ESPN.com, February 28, 2012, http:// espn.go.com/mlb/story/_/id/7625756.

215 **"rather than having the samples sit":** Ibid.

215 **Braun ruminated in his acceptance speech:** Andrew Keh, "Braun Accepts M.V.P. Amid 'Challenges,' " *New York Times*, January 21, 2012.

215 **"It's just a sad day for all the clean":** ESPN.com News Services, "Ryan Braun Wins Appeal of Suspension," ESPN.com, February 24, 2012, http:// espn.go.com/mlb/story/_/id/7608360.

216 **"Today is about everybody who's been wrongly accused":** Rosiack, "Transcript of Ryan Braun's Statement."

216 **"resources and opportunity to tamper with the test":** Jeff Passan, "Ryan Braun Doped, Lied and Cared Only for Himself," *Yahoo!*, July 23, 2013.

216 **He also made the same claims to his teammates:** Jeff Passan, "Ryan Braun Tried to Discredit Urine Collector by Reaching out to Fellow MLB Players," *Yahoo!*, August 18, 2013.

216 **In an interview for this book, Braun's:** Ralph Sasson, interview by Gus Garcia-Roberts, January 2014.

217 **The league threatened to appeal to a federal judge:** "Ryan Braun Wins Appeal Suspension."

217 **Das despite thirteen years of hearing MLB cases:** Barry Petchesky, "MLB Fires Arbitrator Shyam Das, Days After a Second Player Successful Uses the Ryan Braun Defense," *Deadspin*, May 14, 2012, http://deadspin. com/5910201/mlb-fires-arbitrator-shyam-das-days-after-a-second-player -successfully-uses-the-ryan-braun-defense.

CHAPTER ELEVEN

218 **Inside, Wilson Ramos lay silent:** Juan Forero, "Washington Nationals Catcher Wilson Ramos Says Police, Kidnappers Exchanged Heavy Gunfire in Dramatic Rescue," *Washington Post*, November 12, 2011.

218 **"few rookie catchers this century":** Matt Eddy, "Infield, Pitching Staff Highlight 2011 Rookie Team," *Baseball America*, October 12, 2011.

218 **At the center of the web was a twenty-six-year-old:** Christian Red, "News Travels to the Jungles of Venezuela with the Man Who Pulled Off Daring Rescues of Catcher Wilson Ramos and the Mother of Pitcher Ugueth Urbina," *New York Daily News*, May 6, 2012.

220 **admitted in the wake of the Ramos operation:** Ibid.

222 **Rob Manfred later testified at Alex Rodriguez's arbitration:** Grievance

number 2013-2 (Alex Rodriguez) Vol. 8, Major League Baseball Arbitration Panel, Chairman Fredric R. Horowitz, October 17, 2013.

222 **the group was given an annual budget:** No byline, "2012 Security 500 Leader Profiles," *Security*, November 1, 2012.

222 **army of part-timers in the Caribbean and Latin America:** Christian Red, "Baseball's I-Team Goes Deeper Than PED Probes," *New York Daily News*, May 7, 2012.

222 **"A lot of cops have certain mannerisms":** Elisabeth Bumiller, "Undercover Beat to Executive Suite: Case Over, He Assumes the Life of His Assumed Identity," *New York Times*, November 23, 1997.

223 **After leaving the DA's office:** Christian Red, "MLB's Lead Investigator of Alex Rodriguez Case, Dan Mullin, Says He Was Never the Target of NYPD probe," *New York Daily News*, October 8, 2013.

223 **confront Mullin and his boss:** Martin Mbugua, "Cops Get Rough Time, Top Brass Grilled on Brutality," *New York Daily News*, June 3, 1999.

223 **Fremson later recounted:** Ruth Fremson, "After the Attacks: A Place to Hide," *New York Times*, September 16, 2001.

223 **"The security department had some responsibility":** National Collegiate Athletic Association et al v. Christopher J. Christie et al, United States District Court District of New Jersey, deposition of Dan Mullin, November 19, 2012.

224 **"We asked them, 'Why now? Why not two years ago?'":** Christian Red, "Jose Pumped to Assist MLB, Canseco Booked for Help," *New York Daily News*, April 3, 2008.

224 **LaRussa spoke for many:** ESPN.com News Services, "Canseco: Bush Had to Know About Steroids," February 10, 2005, http://sports.espn.go.com/mlb/news/story?id=1985653.

225 **"We're always worried about the integrity":** National Collegiate Athletic Association et al v. Christopher J. Christie et al, United States District Court District of New Jersey, deposition of Dan Mullin, November 19, 2012.

225 **actually twenty and named Carlos Alvarez:** Ben Badler, "In Latin America, New Fraud Models Emerge to Combat DNA Tests," *Baseball America*, May 1, 2012.

226 **necessitating dozens of contractors:** Ben Badler, "Alvaro Aristy Faked Age, Identity for $1 Million Bonus," *Baseball America*, October 27, 2011.

226 **him "amnesty" from Tejada's investigation:** Jon Paley, interview by Tim Elfrink, December 2013.

226 **"I don't understand why [Tejada]":** Jorge Ortiz, "Documentary Raps MLB's Handling of Dominican Prospects," *USA Today*, July 6, 2012.

227 **it hired a top New York law firm to investigate:** A source with knowledge of the investigation, interview by Tim Elfrink, November 2013.

228 **Just a decade earlier, Ken Caminiti:** Tom Verducci, "Totally Juiced," *Sports Illustrated*, June 3, 2002.

228 **Yankees star pitcher David Wells:** Associated Press, "Boomer Bombshell," February 27, 2003.

230 **"He'll be drowning his sorrows in milkshakes"**: "Goodbye Melky!" *Braves Journal, The House that Mac Built*, October 19, 2010, http://www.bravesjournal.us/?p=6344.

232 **"This is the single biggest loophole"**: Bob Ley, "Victor Conte Believes There Are Major Testing Loopholes," ESPN.com, August 21, 2012, http://espn.go.com/video/clip?id=8289843.

232 **But MLB's testing lab in Montreal had quietly started using**: John Fauber, "All-Star Break: Testosterone Tests MLB Rules," *Milwaukee Journal Sentinel*, July 14, 2013.

233 **"Athletes who are sophisticated can"**: Travis Tygart, interview by Tim Elfrink, February 2014.

233 **Olympic testing lab in California**: Teri Thompson, Michael O'Keeffe, and Nathaniel Vinton, "Melky Cabrera's Phony Website Scam Leads MLB Investigators to the Dominican Republic," *New York Daily News*, August 20, 2012.

236 **"The focus of our interest in Bosch"**: Transcripts obtained by the authors of Grievance number 2013-2 (Alex Rodriguez) Vol. 8, Major League Baseball Arbitration Panel, Chairman Fredric R. Horowitz, October 17, 2013.

CHAPTER TWELVE

238 **"I'm feeling it more and more and so are some industry experts"**: All quotes from Tony Bosch in this section come from Bosch's handwritten notebooks obtained by the authors.

238 **"He doesn't like arguments"**: Roger De Armas, interview by Tim Elfrink, September 2013.

241 **Baggies of white powder on a coffee table**: Description from photo provided to the authors by Alex Rodriguez's attorneys.

244 **"Tony told me he'd be able to bring"**: Jorge Jaen, interview by Tim Elfrink, October 2013.

245 **"I still have a brotherly love for him"**: Roger De Armas, interview by Tim Elfrink, September 2013.

245 **Cadillac, parked at the nearby Ritz hotel**: Key Biscayne Police Department incident report, filed by Officer B. Nusall on July 5, 2010, in Key Biscayne, Florida.

246 **"I'm strapped, and I'm going to kill you"**: Key Biscayne Police Department incident report, filed by Officer Y. Alfonso on August 16, 2010, in Key Biscayne, Florida.

246 **prosecutor would get involved**: From the case Anthony Bosch v. Aliette Bosch, Miami-Dade Civil Court, originally filed April 12, 2007.

247 **"regarding players on the 40-man roster"**: Associated Press, "Melky Cabrera Associate Banned from Ballparks," August 21, 2012.

247 **"It's the fucking agents!"**: Kirk Radomski, interviews by Gus Garcia-Roberts, October 2013 to January 2014.

247 **signed an affidavit**: Affidavit dated September 11, 2012, obtained by Gus Garcia-Roberts.

248 **Hundley and White refused to talk:** MLB source, interview by Tim
     Elfrink, February 2014.

248 **"My stance on ACES":** Paul Lo Duca, interview by Gus Garcia-Roberts,
     January 2014.

248 **Attorney Reisinger says that Lo Duca's vitriol:** Jay Reisinger, interview by
     Gus Garcia-Roberts, April 2014.

249 **In 2011, he had named Sam Levinson:** E-mail from Michael Weiner to
     other MLBPA executives, dated January 20, 2011, obtained by Gus Garcia-
     Roberts.

249 **"We conducted a thorough investigation":** Teri Thompson and Michael
     O'Keeffe, "Sources: MLB Player's Union to Censure Agents Seth and Sam
     Levinson in Wake of Melky Cabrera Cover Up," *New York Daily News*,
     November 6, 2012.

249 **"The Players Association made a significant investigation":** Jay Reisinger,
     interview by Gus Garcia-Roberts, April 2014.

253 **In his arbitration testimony, Rob Manfred described:** Transcripts
     obtained by the authors of Grievance number 2013-2 (Alex Rodriguez)
     Vol. 8, Major League Baseball Arbitration Panel, Chairman Fredric R.
     Horowitz, October 17, 2013.

254 **Fischer recalls Pete saying to him:** Porter Fischer, interview by Tim
     Elfrink, June 2013.

255 **"So you gave him the books?":** Tim Elfrink, "MLB Steroid Scandal: How
     Porter Fischer Exposed the Coral Gables Clinic."

255 **According to MLB's arbitrator:** Grievance number 2013-2 (Alex
     Rodriguez) Vol. 8, Major League Baseball Arbitration Panel, Chairman
     Fredric R. Horowitz, October 17, 2013.

CHAPTER THIRTEEN

257 **Joe Girardi literally felt the decision in his stomach:** Mike Vaccaro,
     "Girardi's 'Gut Move' Pays Off Big for Yankees," *New York Post*, October 11,
     2012.

258 **"You're scuffling a little bit right now":** "Oct. 10 Joe Girardi Postgame
     Interview," MLB.com, October 10, 2012, http://mlb.mlb.com/news/article
     .jsp?ymd=20121010&content_id=39694118.

258 **Then Girardi made an even more unusual call:** Jon Heyman, "Girardi
     Made Special Press-level Call to Spare A-Rod's Feelings," CBSSports.com,
     October 26, 2012, http://www.cbssports.com/mlb/writer/jon-
     heyman/20697847/girardi-made-special-press-level-call-to-shield-A-Rods
     -feelings.

259 **"I was relaxed tonight. I'm ready to break out":** Bill Pennington,
     "Slumping in Middle of Lineup, Rodriguez Is Center of Attention," *New York
     Times*, October 11, 2012.

259 **painful that he was popping painkillers:** Craig Calcaterra, "A-Rod Was on
     Heavy Painkillers, Had to Go to the ER During the Playoffs," *NBC Sports*,
     December 3, 2012.

259 **a note written by a radiologist:** Medical records obtained by the authors.

262 **Then, instead of going home:** A source familiar with Tony Bosch's testimony, interviews by Tim Elfrink and Gus Garcia-Roberts, November 2013 to January 2014.

263 **"We're looking into it":** Feinsand and Red, "A-Rod's Cousin and Named Steroid Mule, Yuri Sucart, Spotted at Yankees Hotel; MLB Says It's Watching."

263 **"Yes. This indicates A-Rod's steroid scandal":** Mark Feinsand, "Yankees' Alex Rodriguez Won't Distance Himself from Yuri Sucart, Even After Steroid Scandal," *New York Daily News*, June 3, 2011.

263 **the Miami housing bubble burst:** Yuri Sucart bankruptcy, case 11-19621-AJC, filed April 10, 2011, Southern District of Florida.

263 **"I love him very much":** Feinsand, "Yankees' Alex Rodriguez Won't Distance Himself from Yuri Sucart, Even After Steroid Scandal."

263 **he fired the cousin who:** Grievance number 2013-2 (Alex Rodriguez) Vol. 8, Major League Baseball Arbitration Panel, Chairman Fredric R. Horowitz, October 17, 2013.

265 **"I clearly told Romo it was about":** Teri Thompson and Michael O'Keeffe, "Alex Rodriguez's Dirty Secret!," *New York Daily News*, August 10, 2013.

265 **"I can't have any trace of Victor Conte":** Terri Thompson and Michael O'Keeffe, "Alex Rodriguez's Dirty Secret," *New York Daily News*, August 11, 2013.

266 **"Try to use service elevators":** Grievance number 2013-2 (Alex Rodriguez) Vol. 8, Major League Baseball Arbitration Panel, Chairman Fredric R. Horowitz, October 17, 2013.

268 **"Rodriguez only had an MRI on his right hip":** Andrew Marchand, "Alex Rodriguez to have hip surgery," ESPNNewYork.com, December 4, 2012.

268 **Velazquez's relationship with Bosch:** Grievance number 2013-2 (Alex Rodriguez) Vol. 8, Major League Baseball Arbitration Panel, Chairman Fredric R. Horowitz, October 17, 2013.

269 **annual fund-raisers at his home:** Jose Lambiet, "Limbaugh's Good Deed Lands Him New Gal Pal," *Palm Beach Post*, January 23, 2008.

269 **billionaire sex offender Jeffrey Epstein:** No byline, "Solange Knowles Hires Famed Attorney in Miami Beach Cop Incident," *CBS Miami*, August 31, 2011.

269 **Velazquez threatened the lives of both Bosch and Fischer:** Rob Manfred made the accusation in Pelley, "The Case of Alex Rodriguez." Porter Fischer made the accusations in interviews with the authors, August 2013 to January 2014.

269 **never provided Rodriguez with PEDs:** Grievance number 2013-2 (Alex Rodriguez) Vol. 8, Major League Baseball Arbitration Panel, Chairman Fredric R. Horowitz, October 17, 2013.

269 **spree when he attended college in Tallahassee:** Tallahassee Police Department reports, arrests June 11, 1995, and December 8, 1995.

269 **"I got married in Jan. 2003":** State of Florida Department of Business and Professional Regulation, master individual application, Jose Gustavo Gomez.

270 **Rodriguez called him his "business agent":** Grievance number 2013-2

(Alex Rodriguez) Vol. 8, Major League Baseball Arbitration Panel, Chairman Fredric R. Horowitz, October 17, 2013.

271 **identified as Anthony Bosch:** Mike Fish and T J Quinn, "MLB Investigating Region in PED War," ESPN.com, January 28, 2013, http://espn .go.com/espn/otl/story/_/id/8884955.

272 **"What a difference a year makes":** Andrew Wagner, "Brewers Optimistic at Winter Fan Festival," Associated Press, January 28, 2013.

272–73 **"My son works very, very hard":** Mike Oz, "Gio Gonzalez—The Player Linked to Biogenesis Who Found Redemption," *Yahoo!*, August 5, 2013.

273 **"To the extent these allegations":** Gerry Fraley, "Pittsburgh Law Firm Denies Allegations Against Rangers' Nelson Cruz," *Dallas Morning News*, January 31, 2013.

273 **"He said he was bleeding everywhere":** T. J. Quinn and Mike Fish, "Sources: Bosch Injected A-Rod," ESPN.com, February 1, 2013, http://espn .go.com/espn/otl/story/_/id/8904501.

273 **who is said to charge $900 an hour:** John Greenwood, "Meet Michael Sitrick: The 'Fixer' You Call When Your Reputation Is on the Line," *Financial Post*, October 19, 2013.

273 **"He was not Mr. Bosch's patient":** Statement e-mailed from Sitrick & Co. to Tim Elfrink, January 29, 2013.

274 **At Rodriguez's urging—and a $25,000:** In the Matter of Arbitration Between Major League Baseball Players Association and Office of the Commissioner of Baseball, panel decision number 131, grievance number 2013-02 (Alexander Rodriguez), Fredric R. Horowitz, Esq., Panel Chair, December 20, 2013.

274 **"is figure out a way to get it to *want*":** Michael Sitrick, *Spin: How to Turn the Power of the Press to Your Advantage* (Washington, D.C.: Regnery Publishing, 1998).

274 **Biogenesis notes obtained from an unnamed source:** Tim Brown and Jeff Passan, "Ryan Braun Listed in Records of Alleged PED Clinic," *Yahoo!*, January 5, 2013.

275 **"with any inquiry into this matter":** ESPN.com News Services, "Ryan Braun responds to report," ESPN.com, February 7, 2013, http://espn.go .com/mlb/story/_/id/8919375.

277 **"I just answered a few questions":** ESPN.com News Services, "Bosch Says PED Reports Inaccurate," ESPN.com, April 30, 2013, http://espn.go.com/ espn/otl/story/_/id/9225734.

277 **"the drumbeat of false allegations":** Cliff Corcoran, "Allegations That A-Rod's Camp Outed Players Puts Union in Tough Spot," *Sports Illustrated*, August 16, 2013.

277 **attempt to get him to confess:** The Office of the Commissioner of Baseball v. Sitrick, 1:13-cv-07990-ER, Honorable Edgardo Ramos, filed November 8, 2013, United States District Court, Southern District of New York.

278 **"I purchased supplements that":** Wallace Matthews, "Francisco Cervelli Denies PED Use," ESPNNewYork.com, February 13, 2013, http://espn.go .com/new-york/mlb/story/_/id/8942985.

278 **"Nobody put a gun to my head to go there":** Ibid.

279 **ACES represented only 5.7 percent of big league ballplayers:** Nathan Aderhold, "Biogenesis: MLB Launching Investigation into ACES Agency," *SB Nation*, August 7, 2013, http://www.sbnation.com/mlb/2013/8/7/4598134/biogenesis-mlb-investigation-aces-agency-peds.

279 **"He places his trust in people":** Bob Nightengale, "Agency's Biogenesis Link Worth Exploring," *USA Today*, August 6, 2013.

280 **"knowledge of or connection to Biogenesis":** Mike Fish and T. J. Quinn, "Sources: Docs Link 5 Players to Clinic," ESPN.com, February 20, 2013, http://espn.go.com/espn/otl/story/_/id/8963926.

280 **"they didn't catch on that this was happening":** Agent, interview by Gus Garcia-Roberts, February 2014.

280 **the Biogenesis aftermath:** Jeff Todd, "Jhonny Peralta Leaves ACES for SFX," MLBTradeRumors.com, September 11, 2013, http://www.mlbtraderumors.com/2013/09/jhonny-peralta-leaves-aces-for-sfx.html.

280 **possibly funneling clients to Tony Bosch:** Craig Calcaterra, "Source: ACES Agency Was Unaware of Players Biogenesis Activities," *NBC Sports*, August 5, 2013.

280 **primaries and associates of Biogenesis:** Office of the Commissioner of Baseball *v.* Biogenesis of America (LLC), 2013-10479-CA-01, Miami-Dade County Civil Court, filed March 22, 2013.

281 **" 'Sam and Seth knew what was going on' ":** Steve Eder, "Between Players and Doping, a Valet Seen as Middleman," *New York Times*, August 7, 2013.

281 **"we were involved in their doping":** Agent, interview by Gus Garcia-Roberts, September 2013.

281 **Any implication that Weiner:** Jay Reisinger, interview by Gus Garcia-Roberts, April 2014.

281 **"The copy of the records":** Tim Elfrink, "Alex Rodriguez, Gio Gonzalez, Wayne Odesnik, Anthony Bosch Deny *Miami New Times* Biogenesis Report," *Miami New Times*, January 30, 2013.

281 **"The additional publicity and notoriety that Gamboa has received":** Mitch Abramson, "Rapper 50 Cent Tries to Explain Away His Boxer's Role in Sports' Latest Drug Scandal," *New York Daily News*, February 26, 2013.

282 **read the final sentence of the article:** Clark Spencer, Susan Miller Degnan, and Barry Jackson, "Ex–Miami Hurricanes Player Says Jimmy Goins Will Be Cleared in PED Scandal," *Miami Herald*, February 1, 2013.

282 **"also wearing a lab coat that said Dr. Bosch":** James Goins *v.* Biogenesis of America (LLC), 2013-20306-CA-01, Miami-Dade County Civil Court, filed June 7, 2013.

283 **"Mr. Rodriguez then presented to me":** Yuri Sucart bankruptcy, case 11-19621-AJC, filed April 10, 2011, Southern District of Florida.

283 **had distributed to family members:** Wallace Matthews, "A-Rod's Cousin Selling '09 Series Ring," ESPN.com, February 25, 2013, http://espn.go.com/new-york/mlb/story/_/id/8980514.

283 **"involving all the performance-enhancing drugs":** Michael O'Keeffe and

Christian Red, "Alex Rodriguez Facing Lawsuit from Cousin Yuri Sucart," *New York Daily News*, March 11, 2013.

284 *Jewish Sports Stars*: David Brown, "Ryan Braun's Image Removed from Cover of 'Jewish Sports Stars' book," *Yahoo!*, September 24, 2013.

CHAPTER FOURTEEN

285 **$20 and $100 bills stuffed into an envelope**: Steve Fishman, "Chasing A-Rod," *New York*, December 1, 2013. Also cited in the arbitration decision of Fredric Horowitz.

287 **"losing control of the information he had provided?"**: Chuck Strouse, "*New Times* Says No to MLB," *Miami New Times*, March 14, 2013.

287 **"They'd chase me, they'd follow me outside"**: Hernan Dominguez, interview by Tim Elfrink, November 2013.

288 **"They showed up at every one of my relatives'"**: Jorge Jaen, interview by Tim Elfrink, October 2013.

289 **The two musclebound "goons"**: T. J. Quinn and Mike Fish, "No Physical Evidence Tied to A-Rod," ESPN.com, April 13, 2013, http://espn.go.com/espn/otl/story/_/id/9165418.

290 **"Pete!" he screamed into his cell**: Unless otherwise noted, all Porter Fischer quotes come from Porter Fischer, interview by Tim Elfrink, June 2013.

291 **chasing narco bosses in Latin America**: Pinecrest Police Department incident report filed by Officer J. Villanueva on February 19, 2013, in Pinecrest, Florida.

292 **"I'm thinking, 'Holy shit, this is just like'"**: Tim Elfrink, "MLB Steroid Scandal: How Porter Fischer Exposed the Coral Gables Clinic," *Miami New Times*, June 20, 2013.

293 **texted Fischer with one final bid**: Texts shared by Porter Fischer with Tim Elfrink, June 2013.

294 **the lure as a suspected drug buyer**: Nick Madigan, "Police Officer Target of Sting, Held in Assault," *Baltimore Sun*, January 26, 2008.

294 **$36,000-per-year gig with Florida's DOH**: Florida Department of Health personnel files for Jerome K. Hill, obtained by the authors.

296 **CDs were pilfered from vehicles**: All descriptions of the crime scene come from Boca Raton Police Department incident report filed by Officer L. Kismal on March 24, 2013, in Boca Raton, Florida.

299 **"Any help would be greatly appreciated"**: E-mails between Boca Raton Police Department detectives obtained by the authors.

300 **baseball the cold shoulder**: Details of MLB investigator harassment come from Alexander Emmanuel Rodriguez v. Major League Baseball, filed in US District Court, Southern District of New York; and via sworn statements from the lawsuit shared with the authors.

300 **"I'll be in tomorrow, can you get away for a drink or dinner?"**: Texts shared with the authors by Alex Rodriguez's legal team.

302 **"substances that the defendants knew were prohibited"**: Office of the

Commissioner of Baseball *v.* Biogenesis of America (LLC), Miami-Dade Civil Court, filed March 22, 2013.

302 **"MLB had no subpoena power"**: Nathan Fenno, "MLB's Biogenesis Squeeze Little More Than Hidden-Ball Trick," *Washington Times*, July 15, 2013.

303 **"Hell no, man," da Silveira's**: Mike Fish and T. J. Quinn, "MLB: Paulo da Silviera Not Involved," ESPN.com, April 5, 2013, http://espn.go.com/espn/otl/story/_/id/9138889.

303 **"MLB's investigative tactics are indefensible"**: Teri Thompson and Michael O'Keeffe, "MLB Dismisses Another Defendant from Lawsuit Filed Against Biogenesis Founder Anthony Bosch and Associates," *New York Daily News*, June 20, 2013.

305 **After a similarly nonverbal response to another query**: Office of the Commissioner of Baseball *v.* Biogenesis of America (LLC), deposition of Peter Carbone, August 30, 2013, Miami-Dade Civil Court.

306 **"A few hundred thousand isn't going to hurt you"**: Steve Fishman, "Chasing A-Rod," *New York*, December 1, 2013.

306 **Manfred testified in the confidential hearing**: From Rob Manfred's testimony in Alex Rodriguez's arbitration case.

307 **"He was stupid," the ex-con said**: Fishman, "Chasing A-Rod."

CHAPTER FIFTEEN

311 **Bosch might wander in for a coffee**: Office of the Commissioner of Baseball *v.* Biogenesis of America (LLC), Miami-Dade Civil Court, filed March 22, 2013, from process server status reports filed in April and May 2013.

311 **"He was living life in hiding"**: Hernan Dominguez, interview by Tim Elfrink, November 2013.

312 **simply been wired to the wrong lawyer**: Steve Fishman, "Did A-Rod Really Try to Pay a $49,901.51 Bribe to Tony Bosch?," *New York*, January 16, 2014.

312 **"I'm a nutritional advisor"**: "Bosch Says PED Reports Inaccurate."

313 **"In fact, Mr. Bosch was interested in cooperating"**: From Rob Manfred's testimony in Alex Rodriguez's arbitration hearing.

314 **"I lost a $5-million-a-year business"**: Fishman, "Chasing A-Rod."

314 **"They said, we think you should leave town"**: Pelley, "The Case of Alex Rodriguez."

314 **"Tony won't live to see the end of the year"**: Ibid.

315 **"Nothing happens without Alex's approval"**: Ibid.

317 **"Are you kidding me?" asked Betty Tejada**: Betty Tejada and Alan Telisman, interviews by Tim Elfrink, October 2013. Additionally, Florida Department of Health Investigator Jerome K. Hill's e-mails obtained by the authors.

320 **$200 million, respectively, according to an AP investigation**: Caruso and Donn, "Big Pharma Cashes In on HGH Abuse."

320 **right to not incriminate himself seventy-five times**: PolitiFact Florida,

"Rick Scott Dodges Answers by Invoking the Fifth Amendment, Democrats Claim in Ad," *Miami Herald*, October 10, 2010.

321 **he helped the Legislature lop $55 million:** Carol Gentry, "Layoffs Hit Some County Health Units Harder Than Others," *Health News Florida*, August 24, 2011.

321 **"The people coming in were all political folks":** Elfrink, "Biogenesis Just Hints at Florida's Anti-Aging Catastrophe."

321 **Nearly a dozen top-level administrators:** Carol Gentry, "Ousted DOH Manager Says 'Ideologues' in Charge," *Health News Florida*, June 18, 2012.

321 **"They actually ordered me not to assist":** Elfrink, "Biogenesis Just Hints at Florida's Anti-Aging Catastrophe."

322 **even when caught red-handed:** Ibid.

323 **"How many hangers-on does Alex have":** Hernan Dominguez, interview by Tim Elfrink, November 2013.

324 **"Our interest in him as a witness":** Transcripts obtained by the authors of Grievance number 2013-2 (Alex Rodriguez) Vol. 8, Major League Baseball Arbitration Panel, Chairman Fredric R. Horowitz, October 17, 2013.

325 **a bodyguard at his side:** In the Matter of Arbitration Between Major League Baseball Players Association and Office of the Commissioner of Baseball, panel decision number 131, grievance number 2013-02 (Alexander Rodriguez), Fredric R. Horowitz, Esq., Panel Chair, December 20, 2013.

CHAPTER SIXTEEN

326 **"There's more than one party that benefits from me":** "Alex Rodriguez completed interview 2013," YouTube.com, accessed March 2014, https://www.youtube.com/watch?v=2RSi0VApbp8.

327 **News articles were even quoting Major League Baseball:** Associated Press, "Source: MLB Prepared to Give Alex Rodriguez Lifetime Ban," July 31, 2013.

327 **The bandbox stadium was at its capacity:** Michael Bamberger, "Alex Rodriguez's Saturday Night in Trenton Felt Like the End is Near," *Sports Illustrated*, August 4, 2013.

328 **With him banned, the team wouldn't have to pay a cent:** Ted Berg, "One Team Still Wants Alex Rodriguez, and He Should Join It," *USA Today*, January 13, 2014.

328 **"Levine told me the Yankees":** Steve Fishman, "The A-Rod Emails," *New York*, December 27, 2013.

329 **"He has not been cleared by our doctors to play in rehab games yet":** Andrew Marchad, "A-Rod Angers GM Brian Cashman," ESPNNewYork.com, January 26, 2013, http://m.espn.go.com/mlb/story?storyId=9422957&wjb=.

329 **an EVIL PLAN:** Bill Madden and Terri Thompson, "Yankees' Alex Rodriguez Planning to Return and Retire," *New York Daily News*, June 26, 2013.

330 **whether he's on the disabled list:** Craig Calcaterra, "*Post, Daily News* Report on an A-Rod Plot to 'Retire' to Avoid Biogenesis Discipline" *NBC Sports*, June 27, 2013.

330 **BlackBerry phones over to investigators:** In the Matter of Arbitration Between Major League Baseball Players Association and Office of the Commissioner of Baseball, panel decision number 131, grievance number 2013-02 (Alexander Rodriguez), Fredric R. Horowitz, Esq., Panel Chair, December 20, 2013.

330 **Ryan Braun met with MLB on June 29:** Adam McCalvy, "Ryan Braun Suspended for Remainder of Season," MLB.com, July 23, 2013, http://mlb.mlb.com/news/article.jsp?c_id=mlb&content_id=54364032&vkey=news_mlb&ymd=20130722.

330 **baseball's version of pleading the Fifth:** In the Matter of Arbitration Between Major League Baseball Players Association and Office of the Commissioner of Baseball, panel decision number 131, grievance number 2013-02 (Alexander Rodriguez), Fredric R. Horowitz, Esq., Panel Chair, December 20, 2013.

331 **162-game ban if he cooperated:** Rodriguez v. Major League Baseball et al, 1:14cv-00244-ER, filed January 13, 2014, Southern District of New York.

331 **Yankees later fined him $150,000:** The Sports Xchange, "Yankees fine Rodriguez $150,000," Yahoo!, August 10, 2013.

331 **"each use of the prohibitive substance was a separate violation":** Transcripts obtained by the authors of Grievance number 2013-2 (Alex Rodriguez) Vol. 8, Major League Baseball Arbitration Panel, Chairman Fredric R. Horowitz, October 17, 2013.

333 **"I realized the magnitude of my poor decisions":** No byline, "Statement from Ryan Braun," MLB.com, August 22, 2013, http://brewers.mlblogs.com/2013/08/22/statement-from-ryan-braun.

333 **Selig was threatening a hundred-game suspension:** Dave Radcliffe, "Ryan Braun Faces a Potential 100-Game Suspension," Yahoo!, June 5, 2013.

334 **"It doesn't feel great being lied to like that":** Will Brinson, "Aaron Rodgers on Ryan Braun: 'It Doesn't Feel Great Being Lied To,'" CBSSports.com, July 26, 2013, http://www.cbssports.com/nfl/eye-on-football/22901615/aaron-rodgers-on-ryan-braun-it-doesnt-feel-great-being-lied-to.

334 **fans still willing to come watch the team play:** Tyler Kepner, "Betrayed by Braun, Brewers Owner Twists in an Ill Wind," New York Times, August 3, 2013.

334 **he'd lost only a relatively minor $3.25 million:** "Ryan Braun," accessed March 2014, http://www.baseball-reference.com/players/b/braunry02.shtml.

334 **"I realize now that I have made some mistakes":** ESPN.com News Services, "Ryan Braun Suspended Rest of Year," ESPN.com, July 23, 2013, http://espn.go.com/mlb/story/_/id/9500252.

335 **Dr. Chris Ahmad had him undergo another MRI:** Peter Botte, Anthony McCarron, Teri Thompson, Bill Madden, and Christian Red, "Yankees Alex Rodriguez Has MRI," New York Daily News, July 21, 2013.

335 **"To be perfectly honest, I don't see":** No byline, "A-Rod's Doctor on WFAN: 'I Didn't See Anything' on MRI," CBS New York, July 24, 2013.

335 **"I did it because I thought it would be fun":** Andrew Marchand, "Doctor

Talks A-Rod Involvement," ESPNNewYork.com, July 25, 2013, http://espn
.go.com/new-york/mlb/story/_/id/9506903.

336 **"failing to adequately ensure proper"**: New Jersey State Board of Medical
Examiners, in the Matter of the License of Michael L. Gross, MD,
25MA05326900, order of reprimand filed January 23, 2013.

336 **$40,000 by the state:** Active Center for Health and Wellness website,
accessed March 2014, www.activecenterforhealthandwellness.com.

336 **"We were treating people with a medical problem"**: Marchand, "Doctor
Talks A-Rod Involvement."

336 **"Mr. Rodriguez did not notify us"**: "A-Rod's Doctor on WFAN: 'I Didn't
See Anything' on MRI."

336 **In his next, and last, game for the Trenton:** Bamberger, "Alex Rodriguez's
Saturday Night in Trenton Felt Like the End Is Near."

336 **according to e-mails later published by New York magazine:** Steve
Fishman, "The A-Rod E-mails," *New York*, December 27, 2013.

337 **"ending in or about December 2012"**: In the Matter of Arbitration Between
Major League Baseball Players Association and Office of the Commissioner
of Baseball, panel decision number 131, grievance number 2013-02
(Alexander Rodriguez), Fredric R. Horowitz, Esq., Panel Chair, December 20,
2013.

339 **Of those who had been named in the original New Times story:** Tim
Brown, "Alex Rodriguez, 12 Other Players Suspended by MLB for Biogenesis
Ties," *Yahoo!*, August 5, 2013.

339 **"in the end, they weren't disciplined"**: James Wagner, "Nationals' Gio
Gonzalez Cleared in Biogenesis Case," *Washington Post*, August 5, 2013.

340 **teammate Braun and UM benefactor Rodriguez:** University of Miami
source, interview by Gus Garcia-Roberts, December 2013.

342 **"I want to apologize . . . for the mistake I made"**: Matthew Fairburn,
"Nelson Cruz Apologizes for Suspension, Could Join Rangers in Playoffs,"
SB Nation, August 30, 2013, http://www.sbnation.com/mlb/2013/8/30/
4677724/nelson-cruz-suspension-rangers-postseason-roster-playoffs.

342 **"In spring of 2012, I made a terrible mistake that I deeply regret"**:
Associated Press, "Tigers' Jhonny Peralta: 'I made a terrible mistake,'"
August 6, 2013.

342 **causing him to be fined by the team:** Wallace Matthews, "A-Rod Faces
Fine of One Day's Pay," ESPNNewYork.com, August 11, 2013, http://espn
.go.com/new-york/mlb/story/_/id/9556796.

342 **"told could help expedite my rehabilitation"**: "Statement from Ryan
Braun."

342 **"Thx alot. #ahole"**: Dan Meyer, Twitter post, August 5, 2013, 12:10 P.M.,
http://www.twitter.com/dmy53.

342 **"We continue to attack this issue"**: No byline, "Commissioner's Statement
on Biogenesis," MLB.com, August 5, 2013, http://mlb.mlb.com/news/article
.jsp?ymd=20130805&content_id=55962046&vkey=news_mlb&c_id=mlb.

343 **"It shows his arrogance"**: Jose Canseco, interview by Gus Garcia-Roberts,
December 2013.

343 **"the response we saw in Biogenesis"**: Travis Tygart, interview by Tim Elfrink, February 2014.

343 **the otherwise unremarkable August contest**: NESN Staff, "Alex Rodriguez Live Blog," NESN, August 5, 2013.

343 **US Cellular Field in Chicago**: David Waldstein, "A Return to the Lineup and a Fight to Stay," *New York Times*, August 6, 2013.

344 **Rodriguez peeled himself off the couch**: D. J. Short, "Alex Rodriguez: 'I'm Fighting for My Life,'" *NBC Sports*, August 5, 2013.

344 **"A-Roid's better than no 'roids!"**: No byline, "Even for Chicago, What a Helluva Night!," *Fox Sports*, August 6, 2013.

345 **"He was never given that number"**: "Michael Weiner Gave Arod a Suspension Number He Should Accept If Offered," YouTube.com, accessed March 2014, http://www.youtube.com/watch?v=LH-lox3QTIs.

345 **one day—"one inning"**: Wallace Matthews, "A-Rod Might Consider Reduced Ban," ESPNNewYork.com, January 9, 2014, http://espn.go.com/new-york/mlb/story/_/id/10270220.

345 **"our fight is going to be that they make a deal"**: Rodriguez v. Major League Baseball et al, 1:14cv-00244-ER, filed January 13, 2014, Southern District of New York.

346 **"extreme shock and disappointment"**: Ibid.

346 **"indeed principally Mr. Rodriguez"**: Steve Eder, "Rodriguez, Citing Missed Opportunities, Rejected the Players Union," *New York Times*, October 5, 2013.

346 **only infuriating him further**: Rodriguez v. Major League Baseball et al, 1:14cv-00244-ER, filed January 13, 2014, Southern District of New York.

346 **On August 10, Rodriguez was drug tested. He pissed clean**: In the Matter of Arbitration Between Major League Baseball Players Association and Office of the Commissioner of Baseball, panel decision number 131, grievance number 2013-02 (Alexander Rodriguez), Fredric R. Horowitz, Esq., Panel Chair, December 20, 2013.

346 **implicating Braun to Yahoo! Sports**: Michael Radutsky, "A-Rod Implicated Fellow Players in Doping Investigation," *CBS News*, August 16, 2013.

347 **making the situation trickier if Rodriguez was behind**: Jarrett Bell, "Sports Attorney to Athletes Who Are in Trouble," *USA Today*, June 25, 2013.

348 **easier client—handled Rodriguez's publicity**: Steve Eder, "In Fight for Legacy, Alex Rodriguez Fields Costy Team of All-Stars," *New York Times*, September 23, 2013.

348 **The "most hated lawyer in New York"**: Brad Hamilton, "The Devil's Advocate," *New York Post*, June 5, 2011.

348 **the penalty box for brawling**: Timothy Dumas, "King of the Courtroom," *Westport*, November 2002.

348 **"Mr. Tacopina is to the defense"**: Lynda Richardson, "When Clients Draw the Spotlight, He Basks," *New York Times*, February 17, 2005.

348 **Gotham's most villainous characters:** No byline, "Joe Tacopina's Most Notable Cases," *ABC News*, undated.

349 **"Here's a guy who's been found":** Joseph Tacopina, interview by Gus Garcia-Roberts, September 2013.

349 **But Tacopina's national television:** "Today," YouTube.com, August 19, 2013, https://www.youtube.com/watch?v=PyjSa0GLTHw.

349 **It was a lie that became:** In the Matter of Arbitration Between Major League Baseball Players Association and Office of the Commissioner of Baseball, panel decision number 131, grievance number 2013-02 (Alexander Rodriguez), Fredric R. Horowitz, Esq., Panel Chair, December 20, 2013.

350 **"Clearly there was a relationship":** Jason Carroll, "Attorney: Alex Rodriguez Had 'Consulting Relationship' with Biogenesis," CNN, August 20, 2013.

350 **The first pitch Rodriguez saw:** "Alex Rodriguez gets hit by pitch from Ryan Dempster," YouTube.com, August 18, 2013, https://www.youtube.com/watch?v=aQVI4RdB4vA.

350 **"You bet I do. How is he still playing?":** Peter Abraham, "John Lackey: Alex Rodriguez Shouldn't Be Playing," *Boston Globe*, August 16, 2013.

351 **"Whether you like me or hate me":** "Alex Rodriguez Pissed Off He Was Hit by Ryan Dempster," YouTube.com, August 18, 2013, https://www.youtube.com/watch?v=47w7SYV5_A8.

351 **"mentally unstable and an abuser of alcohol and drugs":** Pete Carbone affidavit provided to the authors by Rodriguez attorneys.

352 **Team A-Rod gave Delgadillo $105,000:** Tim Polzer, "Report: MLB, Alex Rodriguez Use Extreme Tactics in Arbitration Battle," *Sports Illustrated*, November 4, 2013.

352 **MLB and Rodriguez played human tug-of-war:** In the Matter of Arbitration Between Major League Baseball Players Association and Office of the Commissioner of Baseball, panel decision number 131, grievance number 2013-02 (Alexander Rodriguez), Fredric R. Horowitz, Esq., Panel Chair, December 20, 2013.

352 **New York on baseball's dime in September:** Steve Eder, Serge F. Kovaleski, and Michael S. Schmidt, "In A-Rod Arbitration, Sides Play Hardball," *New York Times*, November 5, 2013.

353 **"his demeanor under oath and contradictory declaration":** In the Matter of Arbitration Between Major League Baseball Players Association and Office of the Commissioner of Baseball, panel decision number 131, grievance number 2013-02 (Alexander Rodriguez), Fredric R. Horowitz, Esq., Panel Chair, December 20, 2013.

353 **two sets of stolen records:** Gary Jones affidavit provided to the authors by Rodriguez attorneys.

354 **Gary Lee Jones demanded $200,000:** Wallace Matthews, "Lawyer: A-Rod Didn't Use PEDs," ESPNNewYork.com, October 23, 2013.

CHAPTER SEVENTEEN

355 **The number of protesters:** Observations by Gus Garcia-Roberts, October 2013.

356 **A newsperson asked the protesters:** Christian Red, Nathaniel Vinton, and Michael O'Keeffe, "Protest Leader Fernando Mateo Says Yankees Star Alex Rodriguez Is Victim of Great Injustice," *New York Daily News*, October 2, 2013.

356 **"Getting paid, breakfast and lunch":** Marc Normandin, "Were A-Rod's Supports Hired to Protest?," *SB Nation*, October 2, 2013, http://www .sbnation.com/mlb/2013/10/2/4794600/alex-rodriguez-supporters -biogenesis-mlb-suspension.

356 **via a mystery benefactor:** Mike Mazzeo, "A-Rod's Park Avenue supporters speak out," ESPNNewYork.com, October 2, 2013, http://espn.go.com/blog/ new-york/yankees/post/_/id/65713.

356 **prospects for performance-enhancing drugs:** Associated Press, "Alex Rodriguez's Hearing to Overturn Suspension Takes Break Until November," October 19, 2013.

357 **spent on supporting Alex Rodriguez:** Eder, Kovaleski, and Schmidt, "In A-Rod Arbitration, Sides Play Hardball."

357 **apparently very little was spent on copyediting:** Jay Schreiber, "Ad Assails M.L.B. in Rodriguez Case," *New York Times*, October 18, 2013.

357 **prayed quietly for A-Rod's safe return to baseball:** Mike Mazzeo, "Ministers Hold Prayer Vigil for A-Rod," ESPNNewYork.com, November 21, 2013, http://espn.go.com/blog/new-york/yankees/post/_/id/67075.

357 **over green tea muffins, Greek yogurt, and lattes:** Source inside arbitration, interview by Gus Garcia-Roberts, February 2014.

357 **legal team to stop gabbing to reporters:** In the Matter of Arbitration Between Major League Baseball Players Association and Office of the Commissioner of Baseball, panel decision number 131, grievance number 2013-02 (Alexander Rodriguez), Fredric R. Horowitz, Esq., Panel Chair, December 20, 2013.

358 **letting his students out of class early:** No byline, "Professor Reinstated at Riverside College," *Inland Valley Daily Bulletin*, December 18, 2013.

358 **National Hockey League union disputes:** From Fredric Horowitz's résumé posted online, http://www.nmb.gov/documents/arbitrator-resumes/ horowitz-fredric_res.pdf.

358 **the Los Angeles Dodgers fan:** Mike Cardillo, "Fredric Horowitz Is the Arbitrator Who Will Decide the Fate of Alex Rodriguez. Here's His Story," *The Big Lead*, August 6, 2013.

358 **Horowitz received $69,141:** US Department of Labor filings, unionreports. gov.

358 **his second such failed test:** In the Matter of Arbitration Between Major League Baseball Players Association and Office of the Commissioner of Baseball, panel decision number 131, grievance number 2013-02 (Alexander Rodriguez), Fredric R. Horowitz, Esq., Panel Chair, December 20, 2013.

359 **belonged to panel chair Horowitz:** Ibid.

359 **Team A-Rod complained in a later lawsuit:** Rodriguez v. Major League Baseball et al, 1.14cv-00244-ER, filed January 13, 2014, Southern District of New York.

359 **cider vinegar, ginseng, and fish oil:** In the Matter of Arbitration Between Major League Baseball Players Association and Office of the Commissioner of Baseball, panel decision number 131, grievance number 2013-02 (Alexander Rodriguez), Fredric R. Horowitz, Esq., Panel Chair, December 20, 2013.

361 **"He has a lot of guilt because he feels":** Hernan Dominguez, interview by Tim Elfrink, November 2013.

362 **hiding behind the Fifth Amendment:** In the Matter of Arbitration Between Major League Baseball Players Association and Office of the Commissioner of Baseball, panel decision number 131, grievance number 2013-02 (Alexander Rodriguez), Fredric R. Horowitz, Esq., Panel Chair, December 20, 2013.

363 **according to the legal complaint:** Alexander Rodriguez v. Christopher S. Ahmad, MD, et al, filed October 4, 2013, Supreme Court of the State of New York, County of Bronx.

363 **through Florida in order to bury A-Rod:** Rodriguez v. Major League Baseball et al, 1:14cv-00244-ER, filed January 13, 2014, Southern District of New York.

364 **"You are hereby commanded that all":** The Office of the Commissioner of Baseball v. Sitrick, 1:13-cv-07990-ER, Honorable Edgardo Ramos, filed November 8, 2013, United States District Court, Southern District of New York.

365 **procuring banned substances from the Canadian doctor:** Mike Fish and Don Van Natta Jr., "Sources: MLB Wants Files Unsealed," ESPN.com, September 25, 2013, http://espn.go.com/espn/otl/story/_/id/9723032.

365 **"has broken all the rules and its lawyers should be ashamed":** Brian Greenspan, interview by Gus Garcia-Roberts, January 2014.

365 **obscure small-potatoes lawsuit:** Spencer Lader v. Carlos Delgado, 021324/2008, Justice Leonard B. Austin, Nassau County Civil Supreme Court, New York State.

365 **"I would rather spend a million dollars":** Spencer Lader, interview by Gus Garcia-Roberts, December 2013.

366 **jury testimony in the federal Galea investigation:** Rodriguez v. Major League Baseball et al, 1:14cv-00244-ER, filed January 13, 2014, Southern District of New York.

366 **"ineffective at halting MLB's media campaign":** Ibid.

367 **claimed that the e-mails about Cano were a joke:** Christian Red and Teri Thompson, "Yankees President Randy Levine Grilled by Alex Rodriguez's Lawyer," New York Daily News, November 19, 2013.

369 **"You're full of shit and you know it":** Joe DeLessio, "A-Rod Storms Out of Appeals Hearing, Rips Bud Selig on WFAN," New York, November 20, 2013.

370 **Rodriguez throughout the Biogenesis scandal:** "Alex Rodriguez Interview

with Mike Francesa," YouTube.com, November 21, 2013, https://www
.youtube.com/watch?v=xkV9CSPSTuw.

372 **ESPN, and the *Miami Herald*:** Boca Raton Police Department obtained by
the authors.

372 **handling of the Biogenesis records:** Fishman, "Chasing A-Rod."

372 **the records stolen from Fischer's car:** Boca Raton Police Department
obtained by the authors.

372 **fist-bumped whenever:** Boca Raton Police report number 2013-004136, in
the arrest of Reginald St. Fleur, prepared by Detective Terrence M. Payne.

372 **"people don't break in to steal four boxes of files":** Sonja Isger, "Biogenesis Scandal Whistleblower Says MLB Drug Data Theft Was Targeted," *Palm
Beach Post*, December 12, 2013.

373 **"tanning equipment service, installation [and] sales":** NB & G Florida
LLC, Florida Secretary of State, Division of Corporations, corporation filed
July 3, 2013.

373 **arrested for allegedly selling cocaine and Xanax:** Palm Beach County
criminal records, 13009981CF10A, arrested July 16, 2013.

373 **a supplement store in Broward County:** Total Nutrition Weston Inc.,
Florida Secretary of State, Division of Corporations, corporation filed
October 25, 2013.

373 **Boca-area cigar bar, according to business records:** Havana Nights Cigar
Bar & Lounge II LLC, Florida Secretary of State, Division of Corporations,
corporation filed July 3, 2013.

373 **launched his own line of protein brownies:** EatMeGuiltFree.com.

373 **attacking her with a bicycle pump:** Coral Gables Police Department,
13-007397, October 5, 2013.

373 **published in *Newsday* the next morning:** Anthony Carbone, interview by
Gus Garcia-Roberts, December 2013.

374 **Payne indicated in an e-mail:** Boca Raton Police Department e-mails
obtained by the authors.

374 **distribution of PEDs to minors:** Law enforcement sources, interviews by
Tim Elfrink, August 2013 to January 2014.

374 **and to ban coaches who allow it:** Roger Dearing, interview by Gus
Garcia-Roberts, October 2013.

374 **Bosch's to be inspected and certified:** Health Care Clinic Act, FL S. SB
746, sponsored by Senator Eleanor Sobel, http://www.flsenate.gov/Session/
Bill/2014/0746.

375 **"investigating whether St. Fleur was acting alone":** E-mail to Gus
Garcia-Roberts from Boca Raton officer Sandra Boonenberg, January 10,
2014.

375 **"You were caught in a vise":** Pelley, "The Case of Alex Rodriguez."

376 **"Yet Rodriguez committed the most":** In the Matter of Arbitration Between
Major League Baseball Players Association and Office of the Commissioner
of Baseball, panel decision number 131, grievance number 2013-02
(Alexander Rodriguez), Fredric R. Horowitz, Esq., Panel Chair, December
20, 2013.

377 **calling the decision an "injustice"**: Reuters, "Factbox: Statements on Rodriguez Suspension," January 11, 2014.

377 RECORD DOPING PENALTY FOR TOP-PAID YANKEE: Steve Eder, "Arbitrator's Ruling Banishes the Yankees' Alex Rodriguez for a Season," *New York Times*, January 11, 2014.

379 **"a mockery of the arbitration procedure"**: Rodriguez v. Major League Baseball et al, 1:14cv-00244-ER, filed January 13, 2014, Southern District of New York.

380 **"it's difficult to imagine that any portion"**: Ibid.

380 **a gym franchise in which he has a stake**: ESPN.com News Services, "A-Rod: 2014 a 'New Chapter of My Life,'" ESPNNewYork.com, January 16, 2014, http://espn.go.com/new-york/mlb/story/_/id/10302554.

381 **phone call later published by Yahoo! Sports**: Jeff Passan and Tim Brown, "Sources: MLB Players Association would expel Alex Rodriguez—if it could," *Yahoo!*, January 21, 2014.

382 **supplement pills promising "no crash"**: EPSG Labs, website, http://www.epsglabs.com.

382 **"the #1 pioneering sports scientist!"**: SNAC Nutrition website, https://www.snac.com.

382 **The *ESPN The Magazine* article referenced was facetious**: Chris Sprow, "The Mag.com Presents: All World Power Rankings," *ESPN The Magazine*, undated.

383 **Miami-based Biogenesis Supplements Inc**: Biogenesis Supplements Inc.; Florida Department of State, Division of Corporations, corporation filed November 18, 2013.

EPILOGUE

384 **"I couldn't give you a good estimate"**: Grievance number 2013-2 (Alex Rodriguez) Vol. 8, Major League Baseball Arbitration Panel, Chairman Fredric R. Horowitz, October 17, 2013.

384 **Gary Jones pocketed at least $125,000**: Ibid.

384 **Bosch's round-the-clock bodyguards**: Agreement between Bosch and MLB obtained by the authors.

384 **"It's a substantial expenditure"**: Grievance number 2013-2 (Alex Rodriguez) Vol. 8, Major League Baseball Arbitration Panel, Chairman Fredric R. Horowitz, October 17, 2013.

385 **Rodriguez's suspension through 2014 will cost him $22,131,147 in salary**: Kevin Davidoff, "A-Rod Suspended for Entire 2014 Season," *New York Post*, January 11, 2014.

386 **flipped his Miami Beach mansion for a $15 million profit**: Miami Dade property records.

386 **"hijacked"**: Sandomir, "Rodriguez and Agent Hijack the World Series."

386 **"mother of all anabolics"** Grievance number 2013-2 (Alex Rodriguez) Vol. 8, Major League Baseball Arbitration Panel, Chairman Fredric R. Horowitz, October 17, 2013.

387 **Ryan Braun signed his own five-year, $105 million extension:** ESPN.com News Services, "Ryan Braun extended through 2020," ESPN.com, April 22, 2011, http://sports.espn.go.com/mlb/news/story?id=6403833.

387 **signing a relatively middling $1.25 million deal:** "Melky Cabrera," accessed March 2014, http://www.baseball-reference.com/players/c/cabreme01.shtml.

387 **he still received a $300,000-plus share:** Al Saracevic, "Rule: Full Playoff Share to Melky Cabrera," *San Francisco Chronicle*, November 3, 2012.

387 **he signed a $16 million, two-year deal:** Associated Press, "Melky Cabrera's Contract Finalized," November 20, 2012.

387 **St. Louis Cardinals agreeing to pay him $53 million over four years:** Paul White, "Jhonny Peralta's Contract with Cardinals Draws Scrutiny," *USA Today*, November 25, 2013.

388 **Bartolo Colon more than tripled his salary:** Marc Carig, "Bartolo Colon, Mets Agree to Two-Year, $20 Million, According to Source," *Newsday*, December 11, 2013.

388 **but then signed an $8 million dollar deal:** Associated Press, "Cruz, Orioles Finalize $8 Million, 1 Year Contract," *Miami Herald*, February 24, 2014.

388 **the $725,000 bonus the Mets gave Cespedes:** Ben Badler, "Mets Sign Dominican Outfielder Ricardo Cespedes," *Baseball America*, August 24, 2013.

388 **"All authority to discipline Players":** Wallace Matthews and Andrew Marchand, "Yankees Eye Voiding A-Rod Contract," ESPNNewYork.com, January 30, 2013, http://espn.go.com/new-york/mlb/story/_/id/8894904.

390 **suspended eight players for their role:** Rob Neyer, "Landis Had Major Impact as First Commish," ESPN.com, January 22, 2004, http://sports.espn.go.com/mlb/columns/story?columnist=neyer_rob&id=1714894.

390 **On April 18, 2006:** Affidavit in support of a search warrant filed by Jeff Novitzky to Honorable Edward C. Voss, United States District Court, District of Arizona, on May 31, 2006.

391 **a record 119 players were granted drug exemptions:** Gabe Lacques, "MLB Exemptions of Adderall Use on the Rise," *USA Today*, December 1, 2013.

391 **"there's no question attention is a key part":** Ibid.

391 **Florida produced the second-most current players:** *Sporting News* staff report, "NFL 2013: Breakdown of total players from each state," *Sporting News NFL*, September 18, 2013.

392 **called only twenty times:** National Collegiate Athletic Association et al v. Christopher J. Christie et al, United States District Court District of New Jersey, deposition of Bud Selig, November 9, 2012.

392 **"Certainly since the issuance of the Mitchell Report":** Grievance number 2013-2 (Alex Rodriguez) Vol. 8, Major League Baseball Arbitration Panel, Chairman Fredric R. Horowitz, October 17, 2013.

392 **"It's just the signs are there":** Mike Oz, "Jack Clark Accuses Albert Pujols and Justin Verlander of PED Use," *Yahoo! Sports*, August 9, 2013.

392 **"The allegations about Albert Pujols":** Grievance number 2013-2 (Alex

Rodriguez) Vol. 8, Major League Baseball Arbitration Panel, Chairman Fredric R. Horowitz, October 17, 2013.

393 **FBI agent Greg Stejskal had attempted:** Greg Stejskal, interview by Tim Elfrink, December 2013.

393 **Canseco had tested positive for steroids:** Diana Marrero, "Canseco Sent Back to Jail for a Month," *Sun Sentinel*, June 24, 2003.

393 **causing the slugger's dad to challenge:** Ken Rodriguez and Jorge Ortiz, "Canseco Denies Using Steroids," *Miami Herald*, September 30, 1988.

393 **baseball has developed the most aggressive:** James Wagner, "MLB Expands Drug-Testing Program, Will Implement in-season HGH testing," *Washington Post*, January 10, 2013.

393 **the league was the first:** Ibid.

394 **In his prophetic 1969 *Sports Illustrated* survey of athletic doping:** Bil Gilbert, "Problems in a Turned On World," *Sports Illustrated*, June 23, 1969.

395 **fifty NFL players were suspended for PEDs:** Mike Sando, "Seahawks' Lead in PED Bans under Carroll," ESPN.com, May 20, 2013, http://espn .go.com/blog/nfcwest/post/_/id/100145.

395 **339 major league and minor league baseball players were suspended:** Violations of Major League Baseball's Joint Drug Prevention and Treatment Program, list dated October 2, 2013, provided to author Gus Garcia-Roberts.

395 **a total of eight players have been suspended:** Henry Abbott, "The Gaps in NBA Drug Testing," ESPN.com, November 11, 2012, http://espn.go.com/ blog/truehoop/post/_/id/51305.

395 **NBA superstar Kobe Bryant makes no secret:** Jonah Lehrer, "Why Did Kobe Go to Germany?," *Grantland*, April 16, 2012.

396 **"minimally manipulated":** Ibid.

396 **Dallas Mavericks owner Mark Cuban has called for more research:** Sam Amick, "Mark Cuban: NBA should discuss allowing HGH use," *USA Today*, November 24, 2013.

396 **"We gotta stay hurt forever?":** Mike Ditka, interview by Gus Garcia-Roberts, February 2013.

397 **"But hell yeah, I'd try it":** Ibid.

397 **"almost a cakewalk, actually":** Pelley, "The Case of Alex Rodriguez."

397 **passed at least a dozen drug tests while on Bosch's regimen:** Ibid.

398 **The program is so tough to fool:** Tom Verducci, "New Testing Protocols Could Change the Game in Fight Against PEDs," *Sports Illustrated*, January 13, 2014.

398 **"Rather than trying to find the drug itself":** Warren Cornwall, "The Secret to a Bulletproof Anti-Doping Test?," *New York Times Magazine*, February 25, 2014.

399 **"quasi-public institution in which people":** National Collegiate Athletic Association et al v. Christopher J. Christie et al, United States District Court District of New Jersey, deposition of Bud Selig, November 9, 2012.

400 **The owners of the thirty MLB teams:** Jayson Stark, "MLB's next commissioner?," ESPN.com, May 8, 2013.

400 **asked his Milwaukee pharmacist and George Steinbrenner:** Assael and Keating, "Who Knew?," *ESPN The Magazine*, November 9, 2005.

400 **is familiar with T/E ratio screens:** Grievance number 2013-2 (Alex Rodriguez) Vol. 8, Major League Baseball Arbitration Panel, Chairman Fredric R. Horowitz, October 17, 2013.

401 **"we did what we had to do":** National Collegiate Athletic Association et al v. Christopher J. Christie et al, United States District Court District of New Jersey, deposition of Bud Selig, November 9, 2012.

401 **"Joe T: Love going to war":** Observation by Gus Garcia-Roberts, February 2014.

INDEX

A 150-YEAR PUBLISHING TRADITION

In 1864, E. P. Dutton & Co. bought the famous Old Corner Bookstore and its publishing division from Ticknor and Fields and began their storied publishing career. Mr. Edward Payson Dutton and his partner, Mr. Lemuel Ide, had started the company in Boston, Massachusetts, as a bookseller in 1852. Dutton expanded to New York City, and in 1869 opened both a bookstore and publishing house at 713 Broadway. In 2014, Dutton celebrates 150 years of publishing excellence. We have redesigned our longtime logotype to reflect the simple design of those earliest published books. For more information on the history of Dutton and its books and authors, please visit www.penguin.com/dutton.